Phantom Menace or Looming Danger?

Phantom Menace or Looming Danger?

A New Framework for Assessing Bioweapons Threats

KATHLEEN M. VOGEL

The Johns Hopkins University Press
Baltimore

Printed in the United States of America on acid-free paper
2 4 6 8 9 7 5 3 1

The Johns Hopkins University Press
2715 North Charles Street
Baltimore, Maryland 21218-4363
www.press.jhu.edu

Library of Congress Cataloging-in-Publication Data

Vogel, Kathleen M., 1970–
Phantom menace or looming danger? : a new framework for assessing bioweapons threats / Kathleen M. Vogel.
p. cm.
Includes bibliographical references and index.
ISBN 978-1-4214-0742-5 (hdbk. : alk. paper) — ISBN 1-4214-0742-6 (hbk. : alk. paper) — ISBN 978-1-4214-0743-2 (pbk. : alk. paper) — ISBN 1-4214-0743-4 (pbk. : alk. paper) — ISBN 978-1-4214-0789-0 (electronic) — ISBN 1-4214-0789-2 (electronic)
1. Biological arms control. 2. Biological weapons—Risk assessment. 3. Biological warfare—Risk assessment. 4. Bioterrorism—Risk assessment. I. Title.
JZ5830.V64 2013
358'.3882—dc23 2012012208

A catalog record for this book is available from the British Library.

Special discounts are available for bulk purchases of this book. For more information, please contact Special Sales at 410-516-6936 or specialsales@press.jhu.edu.

The Johns Hopkins University Press uses environmentally friendly book materials, including recycled text paper that is composed of at least 30 percent post-consumer waste, whenever possible.

CONTENTS

ACKNOWLEDGMENTS

This book could not have been written without the generous feedback and support of several individuals, many giving multiple sets of feedback over several years. Given the need for brevity, I cannot fully elaborate my deep gratitude to everyone who has been involved in this project. Many of you fill both professional and personal roles in my life, and I am thankful for such wonderful people who have given their time and energy to help sharpen this book into its final form.

Cornell University's rich, multidisciplinary intellectual environment has profoundly shaped my thinking on science and security issues and was the unique breeding ground for the arguments and conclusions I have developed in this book. I thank Judith Reppy for her mentorship and friendship over the years. Judith has been a faithful champion of my work since I was a postdoctoral scholar in Cornell's Institute for Peace and Conflict Studies (formerly known as the Peace Studies Program), and I have always valued her close attention to my writing and her detailed feedback on various journal articles and draft chapters. I also acknowledge the wonderful collegiality and support of others at the institute: Matthew Evangelista, Bill Ghiorse, Kurt Gottfried, Peter Katzenstein, Jonathan Kirshner, Sandra Kisner, George Lewis, Elaine Scott, and Zellman Warhaft.

Thanks also to Stephen Hilgartner and Michael Lynch in Cornell's Department of Science and Technology Studies (S&TS). Steve and Mike provided me with key S&TS literature and commentaries that helped me engage deeply at the interface of S&TS and policy; I also appreciate their longstanding support. I am grateful for the broader support of the faculty and affiliates in the S&TS department—Peter Dear, Ron Kline, Christine Leuenberger, Bruce Lewenstein, Rachel Maines, Trevor Pinch, Rachel Prentice, Sara Pritchard, Judith Reppy, Margaret Rossiter, Phoebe Sengers, and Suman Seth—all of whom gave me important feedback during presentations of early versions of this work in the department's Science Studies Research Group (SSRG) and Colloquium.

I thank my Cornell Society for the Humanities / Mellon–funded writing group: Johanna Crane, Durba Ghosh, T. J. Hinrichs, Stacey Langwick, Sherry Martin, Rachel Prentice, Sara Pritchard, Jessica Ratcliff, and Marina Welker. Not only were these women committed to deep engagement with my writing, but they were also marvelous sources of personal support and advice throughout the tenure process (and beyond). Thanks also to Stefan Senders for reading my work at an early stage and for suggesting critical literature.

I am eternally grateful for Lynn Eden's time and close attention to the details and arguments in my book—it profoundly transformed the end product. Sonia Ben Ouagrham-Gormley, Gerald Epstein, Dennis Gormley, and Milton Leitenberg provided important feedback on an early draft of my manuscript. I thank Sonia and Dennis for opening their home in the Shenandoah Valley for a group discussion of my manuscript as well as this group for spending their generous time and attention on my work (even if they didn't always agree with my conclusions). I also value Hugh Gusterson's and Alan Pearson's commentaries on versions of this work. Other scholars who provided important feedback include Theodore Brown, Michele Garfinkel, Jens Kuhn, Andrew Lakoff, and Jonathan Suk. I appreciate the several anonymous reviewers of my manuscript who provided extremely useful commentaries and criticisms.

For wonderful writing space in Washington, D.C., I am thankful for the support of Norman Neureiter and Gerald Epstein at the American Association for the Advancement of Science (AAAS). As directors of the AAAS Center for Science, Technology, and Security Policy, Norm and Jerry provided me with generous office space during many hot and humid D.C. summers while I labored away at various draft chapters. I appreciate Kavita Berger's support and friendship at the AAAS during my summer stays and her organization of the AAAS's biosecurity seminar series, which helped me stay engaged with the bioweapons policy community while in D.C. I also appreciate Cornell's Institute for the Social Sciences (ISS) for including me in its first class of junior faculty fellows. Spending the year in residence at the ISS allowed me to produce the first substantive draft of my book manuscript. I appreciate all of the support of Elizabeth Mannix, Kenneth Roberts, and Anneliese Truame during this time.

I also thank all of the individuals who agreed to be interviewed for this work. Although each person might not agree with the conclusions that I draw from his or her interview, I have greatly valued their time, insights, and comments. I hope that the interviewees will see that I respectfully tried to draw out and document important facts and issues.

I appreciate having had opportunities to present early forms of my work to broader academic and policy audiences at the following: AAAS; George Mason University; the Gordon Research Conferences; the Center for Arms Control and Nonproliferation; the Woodrow Wilson School (Princeton University); the Gerald R. Ford School of Public Policy (University of Michigan); the Economic and Social Research Council–funded Genomics Forum (Edinburgh); the Center for Biosecurity (University of Pittsburgh Medical Center); the Department of Political Science (University of Calgary); the International Studies Association; the Association for Politics and Life Sciences; the American Political Science Association; the Society for the Social Studies of Science; and the Social Science Research Council. In addition, I appreciate the opportunities to present aspects of this work to intelligence practitioners at events sponsored by the Office of the Director of National Intelligence, the Office of Intelligence and Analysis, the U.S. Department of the Treasury, and the U.S. National Intelligence Council as well as during my time as a fellow at the Woodrow Wilson International Center for Scholars.

The final versions of the manuscript for this book were greatly improved by the skilled editorial assistance of Tom Broughton-Willett, Carol Cook, Kathy Goldgeier, Robert Kulik, and Campbell Maloney. I appreciate their careful attention to matters large and small. Thanks also to the three Cornell students who provided excellent help with various background research: Donato Aceto, Bonnie Bolkan, and Thomas Leong.

I am extremely grateful to the late Henry Tom for being an early champion of my book at the Johns Hopkins University Press and serving as my editor in the book's early stages. I have thoroughly enjoyed working with Suzanne Flinchbaugh as my editor during the more rigorous parts of the book publication process. I truly appreciate her unwavering support and enthusiasm for my book. I also value the skilled assistance of Deborah Bors and Martin Schneider, who provided critical editorial support in the final stages of publication.

This book is the culmination of generously funded support by several institutions and foundations. I would like to thank the John D. and Catherine T. MacArthur Foundation for its support of my faculty position at Cornell, which enabled me to conduct this work. Cornell University's Mario Einaudi Center for International Studies, Institute for Social Sciences, and Science and Technology Studies Department provided important and early seed funding for my research. More substantive sources of funding that underpin my research come from the Carnegie Corporation of New York and the Ploughshares Fund. I especially would like to thank Patricia Nicholas at Carnegie and Paul Carroll at Ploughshares for their committed support to my academic and policy scholarship. In addition, the Mellon Humanities Project also contributed funding support for a key chapter to this book. Finally, the groundwork for this book also lies with funding from the National Council for Eurasian and East European Research (NCEEER) and the U.S. Institute of Peace.

The ability to have rest and refreshment in writing this book also comes from wonderful close friends in Ithaca, the D.C. area, and across the United States who would periodically check in to see how I was doing and to encourage me in the writing process or even just to provide me with some opportunities to escape my writing in order to refresh my mind and spirit. Although those individuals are too many to name, please know that I value each and every one of you for your care for me.

Finally, I praise God for his amazing faithfulness to me through good and difficult times along this academic journey.

PART ONE

THE BIOWEAPONS THREAT AND ASSESSMENT PROBLEM

CHAPTER ONE

Bioweapons and National Security

The horrifying terrorist attack on September 11, 2001, and the anthrax attacks that soon followed gave the United States new reason to fear unconventional enemies and unconventional weapons. Along with the use of airplanes as mass casualty weapons, the U.S. government has also worried about the growing potential of attacks involving biological weapons. These fears have prompted extensive research, study, and planning within the U.S. military, intelligence, and policy communities on the following key questions: What biological weapons threats does the United States face? How have the end of the Cold War, the aftermath of September 11, and advances in biotechnology affected these threats? What are the appropriate policy responses? U.S. analysts and policymakers are struggling with these questions as they try to anticipate everything from a rogue state hiding its covert biological weapons program to nonstate actors such as Islamic terrorist groups pursuing bioweapons capabilities to mad scientists and teenage "biological hackers" creating lethal pathogens in garage labs. Although we are now a decade past the September 11 and anthrax attacks, they continue to affect the ongoing U.S. "Global War on Terror" and new policy concerns about future technological threats.

The American focus on the danger of biological weapons emerged as a prominent national security threat in the 1990s when President William J. Clinton took a personal interest in bioweapons policy issues. By the end of his administration, Clinton had increased funding for biodefense preparedness efforts fourfold, to over $400 million per year.[1] Since the September 11 and anthrax attacks in 2001, the U.S. government has spent a total of $62 billion for biological weapons prevention and defense through 2011, and Congress is expected as of this writing to approve another $6 to $7 billion per year in federal funding for these collective biodefense-related activities for the foreseeable future.[2] This funding has enabled U.S. government and nongovernment groups to create new interventions to evaluate and mitigate emerging bioweapons threats. In the early 1990s, for example, the U.S. Central Intelligence Agency (CIA) reorganized its analytic cadre to improve analyses of bioweapons threats. The Defense Intelligence Agency (DIA), the Department of Homeland Security, and the Office of the Director of National Intelligence have created new classified research programs and advisory groups to help predict state and terrorist bioweapons programs. And since the early 2000s, nongovernment researchers have developed sophisticated computer simulations to highlight U.S. vulnerabilities to bioweapons attacks. More recently, several other nongovernmental experts have published reports underscoring ways in which emerging biotechnologies may aid state and terrorist bioweapons efforts.

Nonetheless, there remain persistent shortcomings in U.S. government and nongovernment assessments of biological weapons threats—shortcomings with important national security implications. For instance, during the Cold War, U.S. intelligence and academic analysts failed to determine the extensive scale of the covert Soviet bioweapons program; even now, analysts struggle to understand the scope of this former program. Before the Gulf War in 1991, U.S. intelligence and nongovernmental analysts did not know that Iraq had developed a biological weapons program. After the war, Saddam Hussein ended the program, but U.S. analysts failed to assess this change, even with the benefit of intrusive, on-the-ground inspections in Iraq. As a result of this oversight, virtually all U.S. analysts concluded that Iraq's bioweapons capabilities were continuing to grow, and such mistaken judgments consequently played an important role in U.S. policy justifications for the Iraq War in 2003.

American analysts have also fallen short in assessing the bioweapons efforts of nonstate actors. In the mid-1990s, U.S. analysts initially believed that an obscure Japanese religious group called Aum Shinrikyo had developed a sophisticated bioweapons capability; later evidence indicated that Aum had in fact failed to acquire a virulent pathogen strain. After the U.S. invasion of Afghanistan in 2001, American intelligence analysts were blamed for their faulty assessments of al-Qaeda's bioweapons activities. And, after the 2001 U.S. anthrax attacks, analysts and policymakers were chastised for not having anticipated how bioweapons threats could emerge from scientists working in U.S. biodefense laboratories. Thus, even with new and sustained resources devoted to bioweapons assessments, U.S. analysts and policymakers continue either to underestimate or to overestimate the bioweapons capabilities of state and nonstate actors.

This long track record showing a consistent pattern of error regarding bioweapons threats stems from a striking conformity in judgments about biotechnology and its possible uses. Government and nongovernment analysts assert that the increasing ease, pace, and diffusion of biotechnology is creating a growing, elusive, and more technologically advanced set of bioweapons threats. But this conclusion is misguided, because it fails to incorporate crucial social factors that powerfully shape the development, use, and evaluation of biotechnology for weapons purposes. For instance, existing bioweapons assessments tend to emphasize certain material and information aspects of biotechnology (for instance, availability of dangerous pathogens or toxins, biotech equipment, scientific literature) along with particular assumptions of enemy technological capabilities.[3] Although creating a biological weapon does involve important material components and capabilities, this narrow focus neglects other critical social factors at the individual, organizational, and political levels that can affect efforts to develop biological weapons by state and nonstate actors in unexpected ways. As a result, the United States is plagued by deficient assessments of state and terrorist bioweapons capabilities.

Assessments of the Soviet bioweapons program, for example, typically assumed a homogeneous monolith in the Soviet ability to develop advanced bioweapons technologies. Yet one institute involved in the Soviet bioweapons program had a management style that promoted scientific innovation and the accomplishment of weapons tasks, while another Soviet institute had a management structure that severely stymied weapons work. Owing to these differences, Soviet scientists developed particular kinds of bioweapons know-how unique to specific facilities; this know-how proved difficult to transfer across labs, causing considerable delays and problems. The Soviet economic system of the five-year plan, moreover, instead of stimulating innovation, actually stifled certain kinds of bioweapons work. Therefore, the Soviet bioweapons program was uneven in its technical progress. However, existing assessments that focused on biological material and information alone failed to capture this nuanced understanding of the Soviet bioweapons program.

Similarly, economic sanctions and on-the-ground inspections crippled the Iraqi scientists' ability to maintain scientific work practices for their bioweapons developments. And curiously, Aum Shinrikyo's bioweapons group did not incorporate advanced biotechnologies into its terrorism efforts, even though the group had the resources to do so. By not considering how scientific and technological work is situated within a particular laboratory—and its organizational and political contexts—U.S. analysts and policymakers have failed to grasp the complexity and contingency that profoundly shape (and frustrate) bioweapons development by state and nonstate actors.

The shortcomings of existing bioweapons assessments go beyond merely plugging these omitted pieces of social data into existing models. They include problems emanating from within the social worlds in which U.S. bioweapons analysts do their work: entrenched individual, institutional, and governmental perspectives and work practices also shape bioweapons assessments in detrimental ways. These perspectives and practices are poignantly reflected in the U.S. intelligence failures leading up to the 2003 Iraq War. From the early 1990s to the onset of war in 2003, CIA technical analysts maintained that Iraq possessed a sophisticated bioweapons program. Postwar assessments and on-the-ground investigations demonstrated that these judgments were wrong. Fundamental sources of error in the technical assessments were connected to organizational changes and analytic practices within the CIA's analytic cadre, which privileged certain kinds of abstract technical information and judgments. As a result, the CIA's bioweapons assessments were largely disconnected from social and political considerations "on the ground" in Iraq and the ways these factors might handicap Iraqi bioweapons development. In addition to reflecting on the kinds of information they collect and work with, analysts and policymakers must also become cognizant of how their own organizational contexts and social practices may shape their assessments and constrain analytic outcomes.

At the same time, some of the sources of the CIA's analytic problems are also evident in other bioweapons assessments conducted by separate U.S. government and nongovernment agencies. Moreover, these analytic problems stretch beyond the George W. Bush administration to include the Clinton and Obama administrations as well as nongovernmental analyses conducted across these administrations. The Iraq case is only one example of a larger, national bioweapons assessment problem involving important social factors operating at the micro, meta, and macro levels of U.S. analysis and policymaking that shape how bioweapons threats are envisioned, assessed, and validated.

This volume explicates the embedded technical assumptions and taken-for-granted conventions that have led to the existing conformity and error in U.S. bioweapons assessments and biodefense policymaking since the end of the Cold War. In doing so, it examines the context, processes, and practices of how knowledge about bioweapons threats has been produced by U.S. analysts and policy officials to answer the following questions: What "counts" as information, knowledge, and expertise in U.S. analyses and policymaking? What social, material, and discursive elements and practices underpin the making and ordering of this knowledge? How do these elements and practices privilege particular kinds of analytic and policy priorities at the expense of others? It is clear that U.S. analysts and policymakers explicitly and implicitly construct certain boundaries and rules that govern what "counts" in the inputs and outputs of their bioweapons assessments; as a result, certain kinds of technical information, questions, and expertise become the focal point for analysis and policymaking, while other critical social factors are missed, marginalized, or ignored. Given time, human, and resource constraints, analyses will always have gaps and shortcomings. Prevailing practices, however, miss critical issues and understandings of biosecurity threats that will continue to produce significant flaws in assessments and poor national security policymaking.

For this study, I draw on concepts rooted in the sociology of scientific knowledge to analyze how the judgments produced through U.S. bioweapons assessments are the result of an *assemblage of technological frames*—the dominant conceptions of biology and biotechnology that shape the understanding of bioweapons threats—and *analytic practices*—the mundane, daily work life of analysts—which guides the construction and conduct of bioweapons assessments and the types of work that managers and policymakers support.[4] This assemblage of frames and practices involves material factors (pathogens, equipment, buildings, trailers, scientific texts, databases, intelligence reports) and social factors (who analysts talk to, how they talk to one another, how they spend their research and writing time, how their work is supported by managers and policymakers) that are gathered and operate on the individual, institutional, and national levels. Thus, the production of bioweapons knowledge by U.S. intelligence entities and other government or nongovernment analytic groups should be understood as a manifestation of individual and institutional work practices and norms as well as of the broader political context in which bioweapons policy discussions take place. This assemblage has not only shaped past assessments but also continues to shape the current and prospective judgments that underpin the biodefense programs and policies being developed within the U.S. government.

The term *assemblage* is used here for specific descriptive, analytic, and normative reasons and is intended to emphasize the multiple and interacting discursive, social, and material elements that lead to a particular interpretation of bioweapons threats. By understanding the various elements of the assemblage, one can consider how these elements might be reconsidered, reconstituted, and reassembled to create an alternative and more complete means of producing knowledge about bioweapons threats. This book does just that, presenting a different kind of technological frame and set of analytic practices that could be used for bioweapons assessments rooted in an understanding of the important social dimensions involved in technical work. This new approach challenges U.S. analysts and policymakers to rethink and restructure how they design, conduct, and support analyses on bioweapons threats to mitigate errors and security risks that can result from critical omissions in assessments.

To date, the dominant intellectual streams that have shaped understanding of weapons issues in the policy community come from science, engineering, and political science—the fields that have shaped strategic studies and terrorism studies.[5] Although they provide important tools and techniques for understanding some aspects of bioweapons policy issues, these fields typically do not analyze the processes by which scientific and technological knowledge are constructed. The argument here draws on analytic tools from the field of Science and Technology Studies (S&TS), which focuses attention on the social context and character of scientific and technological knowledge, work, and products. Of particular relevance is the S&TS concept of *co-production,* which examines how scientific (and technical) knowledge and social context are mutually constituted.[6] The co-production idiom is useful because it "stresses the constant intertwining of the cognitive, the material, the social, and the normative" in issues regarding science and technology.[7] It helps illuminate the ways in which social context infuses and gives life to technical objects, expertise, and assessments. By bringing the S&TS field and its tools to bear on policy issues, we stand to gain a range of useful analytic approaches for probing and sorting through the messy, contingent social character of science and technology in weapons development and assessments. Therefore, there is much benefit that can be brought to the S&TS, intelligence, and policy communities by bringing their ideas and problems to bear on one another. This book provides one example of how that can be done.

As an example, U.S. bioweapons analysts and policymakers have produced, and then reinforced, a technological frame and set of analytic practices that emphasize a diffuse, increasing, and technologically advanced set of bioweapons threats to U.S. national security. This analytic and policy focus has prompted the collection and evaluation of technical information, and the use of technical, quantitative methodologies (computational modeling and simulations, laboratory experimentation for assessing bioweapons threats, quantitative risk assessment models). The reliance on technical knowledge to inform bioweapons assessments has produced conclusions focused on narrow technical issues, which are then prioritized in policy forums. This outcome further serves to strengthen and mobilize the existing technological frame and set of analytic practices, all of which continue to rely on material factors, quantitative methodologies, and technical solutions. Yet by omitting social factors, this work provides only a partial understanding of the status of state and terrorist bioweapons programs—one that tends to predict ease of bioweapons development and use.

In contrast, factoring in the social context of scientific work, such as tacit knowledge (know-how), laboratory disciplines, organizational management, institutional norms, and research practices, makes bioweapons development and use much more complex, difficult, and contingent. By way of illustration, Soviet scientists needed to create an entirely new management and organizational structure at a specific bioweapons facility in order to develop their most potent anthrax biological weapon. This new structure for scientific work was paramount for such development; merely drawing on available biological materials, equipment, and scientific protocols was insufficient for achieving success in the creation of this weapon. As a result, the Soviets spent a considerable amount of time, work, and resources on the "social engineering" necessary for this project to materialize, even though the weapon itself was based on an existing technology. In order to mitigate current and future bioweapons threats, we need to invest more resources to investigate and thwart the social engineering of other potential bioweapons proliferators.

More recently, we can see how replicating what seemed to be straightforward, published protocols for synthesizing viruses has also required important social engineering. One well-known case is the artificial synthesis of poliovirus in 2002 by a group of American virologists. When this experiment was published in the open scientific literature, the U.S. policy community used it to illustrate the ease with which terrorists could create a lethal virus from available materials, equipment, and information. But a careful examination of the local and socially embedded laboratory practices that underpinned the experiment points to a different conclusion. The virology researchers who published this experiment relied on vital, yet esoteric, laboratory know-how in key steps of the viral synthesis. Because of its localized social character, the know-how needed to reproduce the experiment has proven very difficult to transfer to other laboratories—even to those laboratories that specialize in viral synthesis.

This finding suggests that terrorists (or other malevolent actors) would face considerable hurdles in trying to use this published scientific method to create a biological weapon. This does not mean that terrorists would never be able to develop such know-how or alternative synthetic methods, merely that there are very specific factors and timescales required to obtain biological know-how that vary according to the biological material, technique, and practice. Existing policy analyses fail to explicate the specific conditions (social and material) required to develop, sustain, and transfer particular kinds of biological and engineering know-how for bioweapons development and use. In contrast to the policy focus on new biotechnologies, there exist much older and less technologically sophisticated means of synthesizing viruses that do not require such stringent and idiosyncratic laboratory know-how. These low-tech methods, however, are absent from existing bioweapons assessments and policy discussions, revealing a consistent analytic bias toward threats involving the use of cutting-edge science and technology.

In addition, this book explains how social factors present in particular organizational work environments powerfully shape bioweapons analyses. The CIA, for example, drew erroneous conclusions about Iraq's bioweapons because it prioritized technical expertise over operational (that is, spycraft) expertise. Ironically, this outcome resulted from organizational changes the CIA instituted in the early 1990s to improve such assessments. Some of the CIA's other institutional practices, such as meeting policy demands for new intelligence information, have discouraged the creation and maintenance of in-depth, multidisciplinary kinds of knowledge within the Agency. Moreover, some aspects of secrecy practices within the CIA (and the larger intelligence community) favored the judgments of the Agency's technical analysts on the Iraqi bioweapons threat, even in the face of competing evidence. These organizational practices reflect often implicit yet deeply ingrained social conventions that underpin the construction of knowledge in institutions; they become so routinized that they fail to be seen as important factors to consider in undertaking weapons assessments.[8] It is clear that to understand the world's emerging bioweapons threats fully, the U.S. intelligence community must examine the pervasive, routine institutional work practices that so often lead to analytic conformity and poor judgments.

One place to start is the U.S. security policy community's approach to weapons analysis. Typically, members of this community tend to view technical knowledge largely as the straightforward collection and accumulation of "facts" that do not take into account the social context of *how* knowledge is produced, either by enemies or analysts. For instance, a prominent security policy expert commented that different bioweapons assessment models require a certain conformity: "Ultimately, descriptions of reality have to describe the same reality. In probability theory we have 'frequentists' and 'Bayesians' who are often at loggerheads on what the appropriate overall frame or model for probability should be. But in the end, are there calculations that the two schools will get different answers for? Ultimately, if they are going to be useful, realistic, and valid, both models have to get you to the same place."[9] This view implicitly correlates weapons assessments with abstract mathematical models. Although most security experts (including this individual) do recognize the importance of human agency in developing biological weapons, the comment reveals an ingrained belief that assessments rely on discrete abstract quantitative data inputs that lead to a neat, uniform answer. In contrast, a social analysis of weapons assessments also considers how analyses are set up, including the social and material factors inherent in their assumptions, boundaries, and practices. As a result, different assessment models can have very different conclusions to inform policy. Understanding this point can help analysts detect taken-for-granted biases within their work.

Certainly weapons assessments are not completely "socially determined," but social factors that have long been marginalized deserve new attention. At present, microlevel analyses (that is, how analysts and scientists do their work) and an explicit reflection on these practices are rarely a part of broader policy discussions on bioweapons assessments. However, these microlevel practices actually have a profound impact on scientific work and assessments as well as on the wider public discourse on bioweapons threats. In addition, one should also broaden the examination of assessments from microlevel practices to macrolevel politics and the intertwining of the two.

In this book, the importance of the social context shaping bioweapons development and assessment is illustrated through three in-depth case studies with ongoing relevance for U.S. intelligence and national security policymaking: the development of the Soviet anthrax biological weapon, assessments of Iraq's purported mobile bioweapons program, and the laboratory practices underpinning two recent synthetic genomics experiments. The Soviet and Iraqi cases show the importance of the different social factors at play in state bioweapons development. The Iraqi case also illustrates how the social context, at the individual and institutional levels, shapes the way CIA analysts conducted their bioweapons assessments. The two synthetic genomics experiments evaluate the social dimensions characterizing new biotechnologies and how these could shape individual or terrorist group bioweapons development efforts.

In using a case study approach, my research employs different sets of ethnographic and empirical materials. A majority of the research for this book consisted of in-depth interviews connected to the case studies; a narrative style, with extended quotations, is often used to communicate this interview material in the text. Ethnography derives its analytic and empirical power from its ability to localize and contextualize in order to reveal the complex interconnections in relationships and processes that yield a rich, in-depth understanding of the "why" and "how" of a particular case. Thus, these cases highlight the important linkage between in-depth qualitative explanation and causation. I have chosen this style of analysis to contrast the more quantitative, thinly descriptive, and model-dependent approaches popular in policy analyses and policy discussions.[10] With this contrast, I demonstrate how existing approaches miss key contextual factors shaping bioweapons threats and how qualitative research methods such as those used in this book can elucidate these important factors. The main goal of this volume is to show the analytic power of a detailed case study approach. Thus, this book is akin to a proof of principle for how new bioweapons assessments could be designed and conducted.

By focusing on the production of science and technological knowledge, this book argues for the importance of pushing analysts and policymakers to reflect on the ways in which questions are asked (not asked), information and expertise are sought (obscured), methodologies are used (ignored), and analyses are set up and conducted (marginalized) in assessing bioweapons threats. There are real stakes in current weapons assessment practices, the understanding of real security threats, and the kinds of policy responses that result. This new and different way of analyzing bioweapons-related technologies and threats would lead policymakers, intelligence analysts, and academic scholars working on security issues to make better-informed decisions about the nation's security.

Key Issues: Expertise, Analytic Practices, Secrecy

To date, the U.S. security policy community has tended to circumscribe expertise in bioweapons assessments as the purview of technically trained biological specialists. Although technical expertise is valuable, many of the critical questions in evaluating bioweapons threats are not "technical" per se. Specifically, assessing bioweapons capability involves important social dimensions such as the development of know-how, work disciplines, interdisciplinary knowledge, and organizational structures. The complexity of these dimensions is not captured by technical, quantitative forms of analysis. And while scientists and other technical experts are aware of the social factors surrounding science and technology, they have not given such factors sustained analytic attention, partly because these scientists and other technical experts do not devote their professional analytic focus and livelihoods to studying and understanding the social dimensions of technical work in great detail. In contrast, other scholars, consisting of a diverse range of anthropologists, sociologists, and historians of science in the S&TS field, have made studying the social context of science and technology their life's work. Just as art historians can bring unique and fruitful reflections on artistic work and trends, S&TS scholars can bring important and complementary sets of expertise to the task of evaluating the development of science and technology within individual, terrorist, and state bioweapons efforts. Likewise, individual and institutional work practices also contribute to the production of current and prospective knowledge about bioweapons threats. Simply increasing the variety of expertise feeding into assessments is not enough; analysts and their superiors must structure and support work practices to identify and use multidisciplinary types of expertise. This shift in work practices means being attuned to how this expertise will be identified, used, and shared in particular institutional settings. This is often difficult because of tensions within the work practices involved in the collection of quantitative versus qualitative material; information-based versus research-based analysis; short-term versus long-term analysis; and the development, ordering, and nurturing of expertise within an organization. Yet the production of knowledge about weapons threats is intimately connected with how analysts are organized and supported in their work.

A related issue is secrecy and its effect on the production of knowledge. Most commentaries have focused on how secrecy hinders information flow in intelligence assessments and results in the omission of critical information. Secrecy, however, can also have a powerful generative effect—it can actively construct its own kind of knowledge. In the CIA's Iraqi bioweapons assessments, for instance, secrecy allowed the circulation of information and imaginaries of the enemy that reified a technologically sophisticated adversary. This secret knowledge and understanding of Iraqi bioweapons capabilities endured even in the light of persistent contradictory evidence on the ground.

Through its use of several in-depth case studies, this book shows the explanatory power and policy benefits that can come from analytic work devoted to illuminating the social processes, practices, and institutions through which weapons knowledge emerges and is developed and sustained, or alternatively, how certain kinds of knowledge are marginalized, ignored, or suppressed. By emphasizing how different sets of information, discourses, frameworks, practices, and values are used in bioweapons analyses, I demonstrate how it is possible to arrive at different descriptions of reality that can profoundly influence how one assesses bioweapons threats. Bringing these social issues to the fore and showing how they are intimately connected to the production of scientific and technological knowledge demonstrates alternatives and specific focal points for policy intervention that can meaningfully improve U.S. bioweapons assessments in ways that should help decision makers design better counterproliferation and counterterrorism policies and programs.

The Plan of the Book

The book is divided into four sections that describe how social factors at the laboratory (micro), organizational (meta), and political (macro) levels shape U.S. bioweapons assessments. The first section illustrates how particular conceptions of technology have shaped U.S. bioweapons assessments and policymaking from the 1990s through 2010. In chapter 2, I describe the dominant conception of biotechnology based on notions of a "biotechnology revolution"—what I call the "biotech revolution frame"—that underlies U.S. bioweapons assessments and policymaking. In examining this frame, I describe its assumptions of biotechnology as well as how it conceptualizes enemy technological capabilities.

In the next section, I use case studies to contrast the dominant biotech revolution frame with an alternative technological frame; this I call the "biosocial frame." This frame incorporates important social and contingent elements that bring biotechnology into its analysis. Using case studies of synthetic genomics (chapter 3) and Soviet bioweapons development (chapter 4), I illustrate the importance of taking into account how technological frames shape bioweapons assessments and the critical role of social factors at work in different laboratory and organizational settings. In chapter 3, I take up the security concerns over the emerging field of synthetic genomics by reexamining the controversies behind the artificial synthesis of poliovirus and a bacteriophage. Although these recent synthetic genomics experiments have been invoked as early harbingers of an increasing bioterrorism threat, I argue that a detailed, microlevel analysis of "what went on in the lab" brings to light social issues that pose serious challenges for terrorists wishing to replicate these experiments. In chapter 4, I discuss the development of bioweapons know-how within a specific Soviet bioweapons facility. This case study reveals how Soviet scientists needed to create new know-how, organizational structures, and norms within the facility to create the Soviet's potent anthrax weapon. In both chapters, I demonstrate how the biosocial frame better accounts for the contingency and complexity present in the development, use, and transfer of bioweapons technologies and how it provides a more fruitful understanding of bioweapons threats from state or nonstate actors.

The third section of the book uses the CIA's Iraqi bioweapons intelligence assessments to demonstrate how social factors are also important to understanding how knowledge-making practices within organizations shape weapons assessments. In these chapters I show how the biotech revolution frame, along with distinct organizational practices and norms, were co-constructed to produce CIA judgments about an Iraqi mobile bioweapons capability. In chapter 5, I examine how CIA analysts and collections specialists were organized to produce knowledge on bioweapons threats, and how this means of organization created disconnects and tensions in the organization of expertise and knowledge within the CIA, hindering a more holistic analytic understanding of Iraqi bioweapons capabilities.

Chapter 6 examines the analytic practice of current intelligence reporting within the CIA. Current intelligence reporting is a type of intelligence writing that emphasizes short pieces of analysis on just-in-time intelligence information. In chapter 6 I explore how the growth and ubiquity of current intelligence reporting, with its reliance on particular analytic practices analogous to journalism, played a fundamental role in the errors constituting the CIA's Iraqi bioweapons assessments. Finally, chapter 7 takes up the question of secrecy and its role in shaping analyst and policymaker understandings about the purported Iraqi bioweapons labs. Here I describe how several secrecy measures, consisting of material objects, social relationships, and work practices, created a particular kind of analytic knowledge about an Iraqi mobile bioweapons capability—that of a covert, technologically advanced enemy. As a result, analysts failed to integrate alternative sources of expertise and to conduct a more holistic interrogation of a purported Iraqi bioweapons capability.

For the final section of the book, I examine alternative models to the production of bioweapons knowledge. In chapter 8, I look at three efforts by the U.S. government since the 1990s to create new knowledge teams for bioweapons assessments: the CIA's Strategic Assessment Group, the Iraq Survey Group, and the Biological Sciences Experts Group. I describe the opportunities and challenges in improving bioweapons assessments based on these models. This chapter ends with my proposal of how to improve U.S. bioweapons assessments and our understanding about biosecurity threats by taking into account the social dimensions of knowledge production as developed in this book. In the conclusion, I reflect on the main lessons to inform U.S. biodefense policymaking.

Government and nongovernment analyses of bioweapons threats provide a vital source of information for U.S. policymakers in national security planning. The prewar intelligence failures leading up to the 2003 Iraq War show the stakes involved when intelligence assessments are incomplete and biased. Through this exploration of the social context of bioweapons assessments, my hope is that this detailed critique of analytic practices opens up new avenues for reform in U.S. government and nongovernment analyses and policymaking on bioweapons threats.

Technological Frames and Narratives in U.S. Bioweapons Assessments and Policymaking

In November 1997, U.S. Defense Secretary William Cohen made a guest appearance on *This Week,* the popular nationally televised Sunday morning news program.[1] In his interview, Cohen emphasized the potential destructive power of small quantities of biological weapons. To illustrate his point, Cohen brought with him a five-pound bag of Domino's brand sugar and picked it up during his interview to show that this amount of anthrax bacteria, if aerially dispersed, could kill at least half the population of Washington, D.C., which at that time was about three hundred thousand people (fig. 2.1).

Six years later, in a 2003 speech to the United Nations, U.S. Secretary of State Colin Powell exhibited a glass vial of white talcum powder to underscore the growing Iraqi biological weapons threat (fig. 2.2). In making his case for the United States to go to war in Iraq, Powell held up the vial and argued that "less than a teaspoon of dry anthrax, a little bit about this amount—this is just about the amount of a teaspoon—less than a teaspoon full of dry anthrax in an envelope shut down the United States Senate in the fall of 2001 . . . forced several hundred people to undergo emergency medical treatment and killed two postal workers."[2]

Skillfully linking the vial of powder, the 2001 U.S. anthrax attacks, and Iraq, Powell then went on to conclude, "Iraq declared 8,500 liters of anthrax, but UNSCOM [the UN weapons inspection team] estimates that Saddam Hussein could have produced 25,000 liters. If concentrated into this dry form, this amount would be enough to fill tens upon tens upon tens of thousands of teaspoons. And Saddam Hussein has not verifiably accounted for even one teaspoonful of this

Fig. 2.1. Secretary of Defense William Cohen in guest appearance on *This Week,* 16 November 1997. © Terry Ashe / American Broadcasting Companies, Inc.

deadly material."[3] Both Cohen's sugar and Powell's talcum powder capture the essence of a consistent frame—one focused on material aspects of biotechnology—that analysts and policymakers have used to think about bioweapons threats since the end of the Cold War. As I will define in more detail below, a frame is an explanatory structure that is used to understand and describe a problem, in this case biological weapons.

Several intelligence and policy studies have highlighted the importance of frames in threat assessments and policymaking, although these communities typically use the terms *mental models, mindsets,* or *groupthink* in their discussions.[4] Drawing on cognitive psychology to explain the influence of mindsets on analysis, Richards Heuer, a former CIA operations officer and intelligence analyst, has long argued that intelligence analysts do not approach their work with a blank slate; rather, "they start with certain assumptions—often about foreign capabilities and intent—that have been developed through education, training, and experience. These assumptions inevitably form a mindset that influences what information the analyst sees and what information is judged reliable and relevant."[5] Heuer emphasizes that perception and interpretation are not merely passive in nature but are active processes by which analysts construct their judgments.[6] He cites the

Fig. 2.2. U.S. Secretary of State Colin Powell speaking to the United Nations, 5 February 2003. Photo by Ray Stubblebine. Photo: Thomson Reuters.

deleterious impact that mindsets have had in known intelligence failures, in which "available information—or the absence of information—was discounted, misinterpreted, ignored, rejected, or overlooked because it failed to fit a prevailing mental model or mindset that influenced the analyst's perception and interpretation of the evidence."[7]

In spite of the extensive literature on the importance of mindsets, or what I call frames, in analysis, the U.S. security establishment has failed to recognize how different frames exist regarding conceptions of science and technology and how they can shape the way analysts select and use data for weapons analyses.[8] Instead, weapons assessments are typically depicted as a rather straightforward collection and evaluation of pieces of data, primarily consisting of the technical characteristics of an enemy's weapons capabilities or of the materials, information, or process in question.[9] What is overlooked, however, is that such an analytic approach itself reflects a particular kind of frame about technology—one that selects and privileges purely technical factors without consideration of the social dimensions that constitute how technologies are designed, developed, and used in a particular state or nonstate context. In contrast, the science and technology studies field has emphasized the need to understand how technological frames are constructed in and by their social milieu.[10] Such considerations can serve to illuminate what is missing in existing bioweapons threat assessments and how policymakers can remedy these shortcomings.

This chapter describes how U.S. analysts and policymakers have constructed and employed a particular technological frame for bioweapons assessment and policymaking since the end of the Cold War. To clarify my use of "technological frame" in this book, I draw on science and technology studies scholar Wiebe Bijker's explanatory structure for technology consisting of "the concepts and techniques employed by a community."[11] Bijker also stresses the problem-solving aspects of technological frames: they structure attention around particular problems as well as the strategies used to solve those problems. I accept this definition and also broaden it: a technological frame consists of the various material, conceptual, methodological, discursive, visual, and social elements that particular actors or groups use to understand, explain, and solve problems related to technology. This definition goes beyond the cognitive focus that intelligence and policy scholars have often used to discuss analytic problems and draws attention to the broader context and set of practices involved in developing and sustaining particular frames in policy and analysis.

Bijker argues that proponents often have invested so much into building up a technological frame that the technology's meaning "becomes fixed—it cannot be changed easily, and it forms part of an enduring network of practices, theories and social institutions."[12] As a result, technological frames should be seen as having both an enabling and a constraining function in allowing certain conceptions to prevail for a given technology. Making technological frames explicit and visible, however, reveals their strengths and weaknesses and makes one aware of how they shape the production of knowledge about weapons threats, opening up the possibility for interventions to address the material, discursive, and social factors that structure deficiencies in particular frames and allowing the consideration of alternative frames in weapons assessments and policymaking.

Cohen's and Powell's props represent American reliance on a particular kind of technological frame in understanding bioweapons threats—what I call the *biotech revolution frame*.[13] The biotech revolution frame is largely based on concepts of technological determinism, which consider technologies primarily in terms of their material elements or end products (blueprints, tools, gadgets, hardware, and so on).[14] With this understanding, technological developments are seen as a set of cumulative technical results, each with its own momentum or trajectory, largely independent and autonomous from social influence or control. Technologically deterministic thinking often incorporates the corollary of a "technological imperative," which assumes that technological developments, once set in motion, are unstoppable, unavoidable, and inevitable. Consequently, technologies are viewed as causing dramatic and direct one-way impacts on society. For example, U.S. bioweapons analysts and policymakers typically emphasize how recent advances in the life sciences will lead to revolutionary changes in the power of biotechnology, its applications, and its potential harms to society.[15]

As MIT historian of technology Merritt Roe Smith has noted, technological determinism has underpinned many popular narratives regarding American technological innovation since the Industrial Revolution.[16] In particular, it has played a powerful role in policy and defense understandings of the development of weapons technologies.[17] Whether we look at media coverage or at "expert" discussions and various academic, government, and nongovernmental reports on bioweapons threats, we see in the biotech revolution frame many facets of technological determinism. This way of thinking about technology, however, has typically failed to acknowledge how critical social dimensions constitute biological practices. Furthermore, this frame privileges a simple, abstracted material conception of biotechnology that fails to capture the more complex and contingent social character of biotechnology and bioweapons threats in the real world.

The Biotech Revolution Frame

As I describe in more detail below, the biotech revolution frame emphasizes: (1) codified knowledge; (2) material end products; (3) the accessibility of biological materials; (4) the economic drivers of technology; (5) the future; (6) the globalization and diffusion of technology; and (7) fixed technological trajectories. These elements can be seen in a variety of government and nongovernment policy reports and presentations as well as in public discussions of biotechnology and bioweapons threats. Most of the core elements of the frame have remained remarkably consistent over the past twenty years; those that have changed largely reflect an intensification and progression of its technologically deterministic aspects.

To begin with, one focus of the biotech revolution frame is codified biological knowledge, such as information found in journal articles, scientific textbooks, websites, databases (for example, genome sequences), or other written sources (fig. 2.3).[18] In February 2001, for example, scientists at the University of Pennsylvania described how they successfully developed a hybrid virus that involved certain components of the HIV and Ebola viruses; this research explored new gene therapy treatments for chronic lung diseases such as cystic fibrosis.[19] One security policy expert, how-

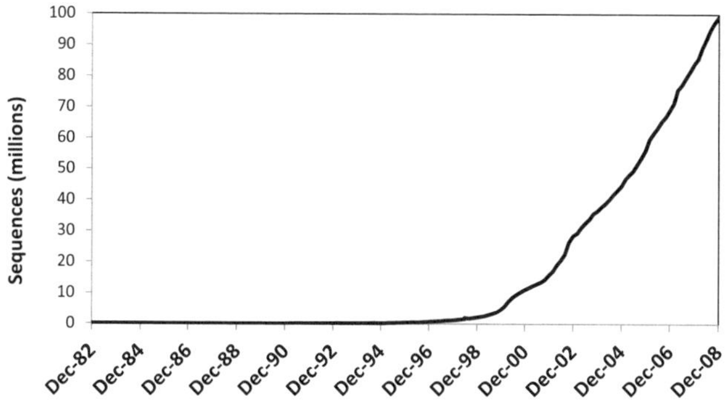

Fig. 2.3. Growth of GenBank. Available at www.ncbi.nlm.nih.gov/genbank/genbankstats.html. As represented in Yu, "Looking Ahead."

ever, noted that the publication of these processes could provide a "roadmap" for how to genetically engineer a novel virus for use as a weapon.[20]

Later that year, a group of British scientists published the full genome of *Yersinia pestis,* the bacterium that causes bubonic and pneumonic plagues, in the prominent scientific journal *Nature.* Some in the policy community questioned whether "releasing genomic information for virulent diseases, such as plague or smallpox, might aid malicious science."[21] Then, in 2002, the U.S. National Academy of Sciences agreed to remove eight hypothetical case studies from one chapter of its study on agricultural bioterrorism because some of the information was thought to pose a security risk.[22] James Petro, a former intelligence and White House official, and David Relman, a Stanford University microbiology professor, have warned that "with publications from nearly 50 years ago, a marginally skilled terrorist could produce a crude agent for use in a limited bioterror attack. However, using more recently published research findings and procedures, casualty rates associated with such an incident would increase dramatically."[23] To make their case, Relman and Petro have displayed photos of scientific documents seized by U.S. forces from an al-Qaeda training facility in Afghanistan (fig. 2.4).

Most policy discussions, however, rarely distinguish between codified knowledge and the know-how required for biological work; even those that do make the distinction assume codified knowledge and know-how to be interchangeable. As an example, a report issued by the Center for Strategic and International Studies states that "know-how that is generated in the course of scientific research is available to anyone participating in that research. If the results of that research are

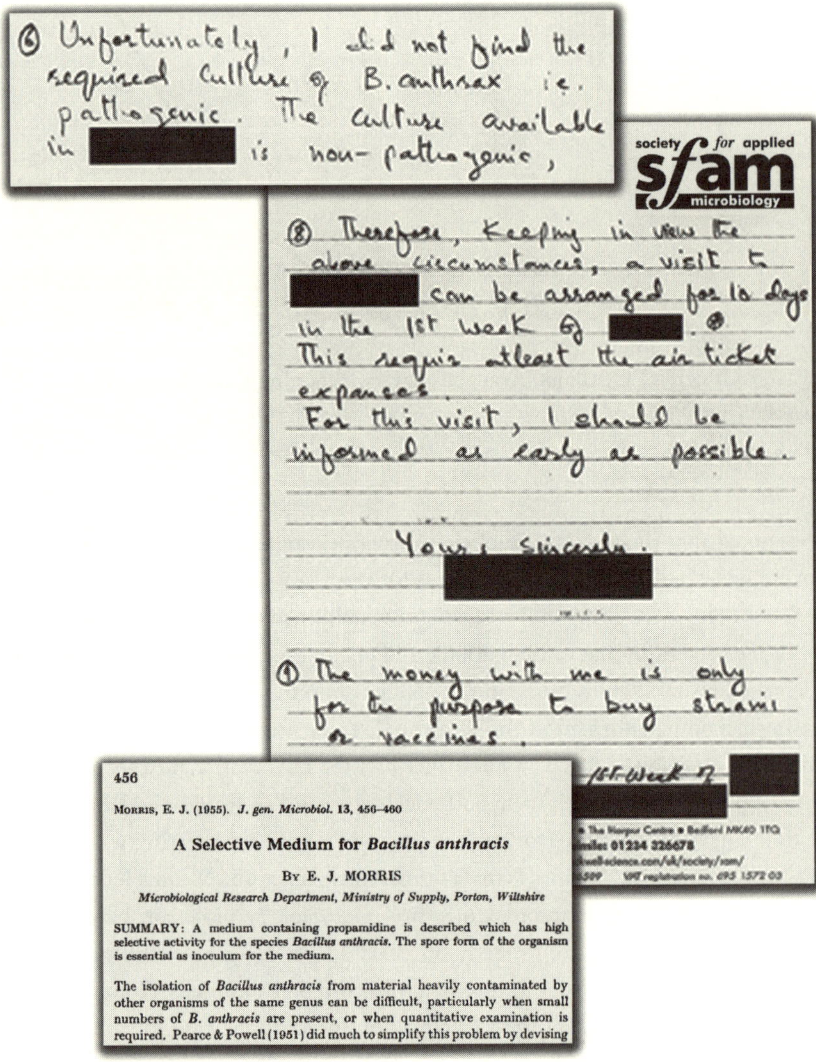

Fig. 2.4. Documents captured at an al-Qaeda training facility. From Petro and Relman, "Understanding Threats to Scientific Openness." Reprinted with permission from AAAS.

published openly, they become available to all—including those who may seek to use those results maliciously."[24] This statement reflects what sociologist of science Harry Collins describes as an algorithmical model of scientific knowledge that presumes that biology and its associated products can be easily transferred or reconstituted by largely impersonal means.[25] This model, however, fails to take into account specific social factors that constitute the know-how behind technical work.

In addition, the biotech revolution frame also emphasizes the material end products of biotechnologies. For example, some policy analysts have invoked the terminology and visual representations of "black-boxing" to argue that advanced biotechnologies are becoming more standardized and less craft-like, and thus more amenable to bioterrorism. The term *black box* refers to a device or piece of hardware that has specified and predictable inputs and outputs, such that the inner workings of the device need not be known for it to be used. As bioweapons policy experts Ali Nouri and Christopher Chyba note, "Advanced biotechnologies, such as DNA synthesis, are becoming increasingly automated and black boxed, providing even novice researchers with powerful tools."[26] Along with this claim, Nouri and Chyba include an illustration of some DNA bases and how they are inputs into a black-boxed piece of biotechnology (not defined or described, although assumed to be a DNA synthesizer). This black box is shown as producing a double-stranded piece of DNA in a straightforward, linear manner (fig. 2.5). Others have emphasized how these biotech black boxes come with easy how-to manuals.

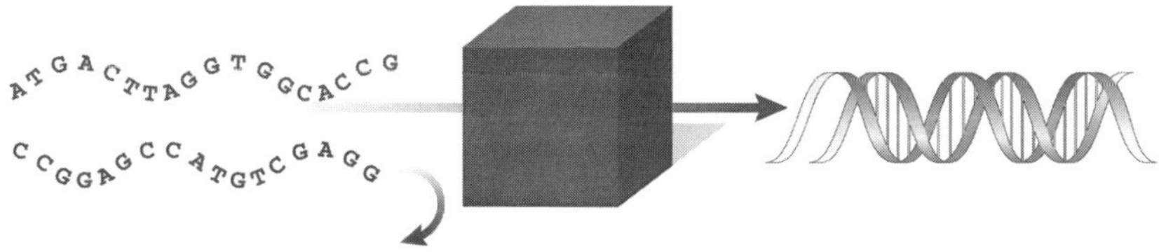

Fig. 2.5. Black-boxing biotechnology. Nouri and Chyba, "Proliferation-Resistant Biotechnology." Reprinted by permission from Macmillan Publishers Ltd: *Nature Biotechnology,* copyright 2009.

For example, Rob Carlson has written, "Commercially available [biotechnology] kits include recipes that allow moving genes between organisms by following simple recipes. The process might be slightly more complicated than baking cookies, but it is for the most part less complicated than making wine or beer."[27]

In a black box, however, the focus is on the end product rather than on, for example, the past troubleshooting efforts and context required to produce the stable end product. The black box focus also fails to acknowledge how the end product and the standardized knowledge it embodies reflect the aggregated and concerted work of particular individuals or collectives of people. In reconsidering figure 2.5, even in "standardized" DNA synthesis equipment, for instance, the chemical reactions involved in the pairing of the DNA bases to produce a double helix are not 100 percent reliable; mispairing of bases, or a failure of some bases to pair, or omission of some bases can occur. These problems can result in a DNA strand with the wrong sequence, which can cause problems for subsequent biological work.[28] As a result, scientists often incorporate several error-screening and correction processes both before and after DNA synthesis, some of which require specialized and laborious kinds of manual work that are not black-boxed.[29] Yet with ubiquitous references in the biotech revolution frame to black boxes, kits, and recipes, the messy and contingent processes by which a biotechnology is developed, stabilized, and used are omitted or marginalized.

Another important material aspect of this biotech revolution frame is the accessibility of biological materials (pathogens, oligonucleotides), biological supplies (reagents, prep kits), infrastructure (DNA synthesizers, laboratory benches), and other tangible items (monetary resources). As a 2005 Institute of Medicine and National Research Council report noted, "The number of agents created by the life sciences revolution (e.g., via recombinant and transgenic technology and even synthetic biology) is increasing practically exponentially. So while there are only half a dozen fissile nuclear materials and dozens of 'dual-use' chemicals that could be diverted for malevolent purposes, the number of potentially harmful biological agents is virtually limitless."[30] Even the ETC Group, a civil-society group critical of biotechnology, has focused on material and informational aspects in its critiques: "Using a laptop computer, published gene sequence information and mail-order synthetic DNA, just about anyone has the potential to construct genes or entire genomes from scratch including those of lethal pathogens."[31] Others have focused on the material cost of producing potent biological weapons, which is described as low as $10 thousand and as high as $10 million, but far below that required for development of a nuclear weapons capability.[32] In 2009, Director of National Intelligence Dennis Blair summarized these material concerns: "We assess the terrorist use of biological agents represents a growing threat as the barriers to obtaining many suitable starter cultures are eroding and open source technical literature and basic laboratory equipment can facilitate production."[33] Policy presentations or articles often highlight this point with pictures of equipment, supplies, and infrastructure that are available commercially (fig. 2.6).[34]

Little attention, however, is given to the social and material conditions required for such biotech equipment to work in different contexts (for instance, an outpost in Afghanistan versus an academic laboratory); nor have there been detailed discussions of its limitations or ability to perform certain biological tasks but not others. As an example, although DNA synthesis equipment might allow one to make short strands of oligonucleotides, constructing an entire pathogenic genome from them requires other techniques, equipment, materials, and complex skills.[35] The focus on equipment, however, marginalizes or ignores these issues.

Another focus of the biotech revolution frame is the economic engine of biotechnology. References to the proliferation of startup biotech companies and the growth of the global pharmaceutical market abound: "Worth approximately U.S. $400 billion, the global pharmaceutical market dominates the life sciences industry and, as such, arguably determines the trajectory of life sciences-related technological development and global spread."[36] Others point to the steady decrease of costs for specific kinds of biological materials (fig. 2.7). As Senator Tom Daschle and biosecurity authority Tom Inglesby have argued, "The cost of human genome sequencing has declined 10,000 fold in the last twenty years. But these advances in science will also lower the cost of creating biological weapons."[37] Emphasizing materials and information, Director of National Intelligence James Clapper testified to Congress that "biological and chemical materials and technologies, almost always dual-use, move easily in our globalized economy, as do the personnel with scientific expertise designing and using them."[38] These claims, however, fail to acknowledge how biotech and pharmaceutical industries have struggled to harness new biotechnology developments for very specific applied purposes even when the necessary resources were readily available.[39]

Temporally, the biotech revolution frame is focused on the future and the possible threats from emerging or cutting-edge technologies. For example, a 2003 unclassified CIA report, "The Darker Bioweapons Future," pointed to the potential development of designer biological weapons, such as stealth viruses, that could lie dormant in a victim until triggered. As the report further noted, such biotechnology developments are likely "to advance very rapidly, causing a diverse and elusive threat spectrum."[40] Echoing this report, a 2005 National Intelligence Council report noted, "Major advances in the biological sciences and information technology

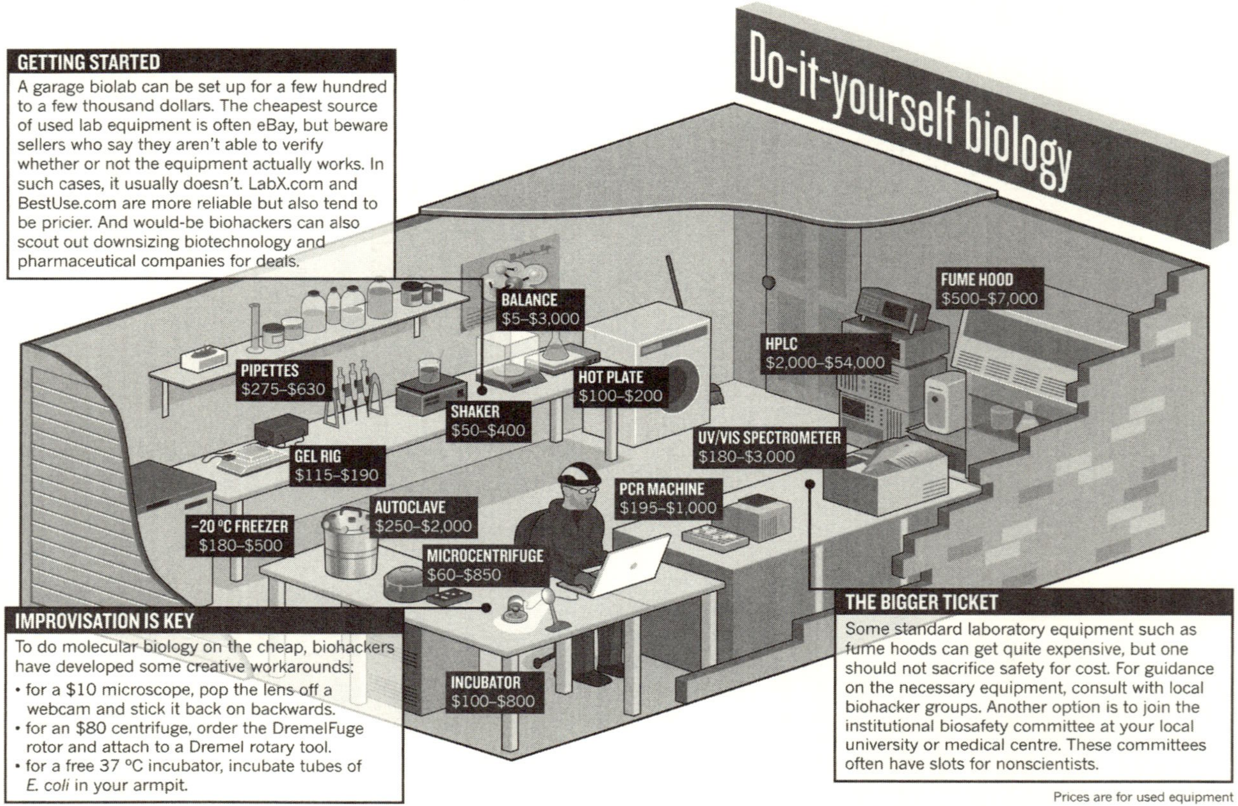

Fig. 2.6. Do-it-yourself biology. From Ledford, "Garage Biotech: Life Hackers." Reprinted by permission from Macmillan Publishers Ltd: *Nature,* copyright 2010.

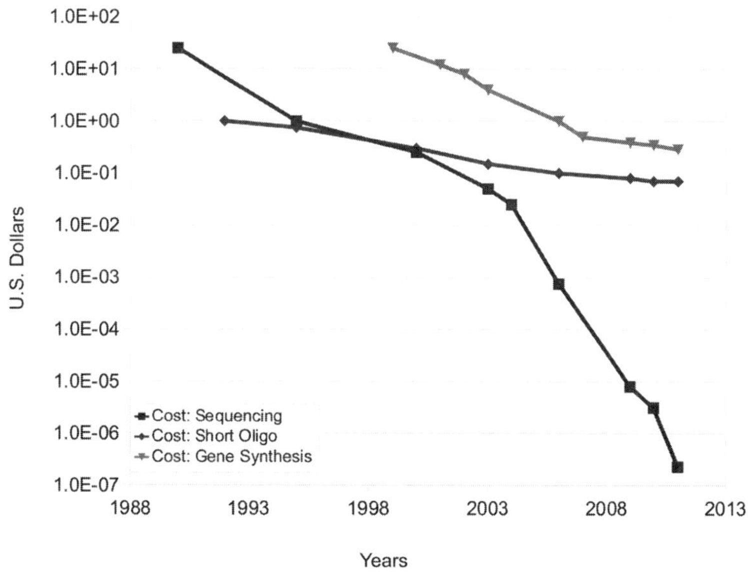

Fig. 2.7. Cost per base of DNA sequencing and synthesis. Reprinted by permission of Robert Carlson, June 2011, www.synthesis.cc.

will accelerate the pace of BW [bioweapons] agent development, increasing the potential for agents that are more difficult to detect or defend against."[41] Summarizing this future-oriented focus, defense and science policy advisor Tara O'Toole, later President Obama's undersecretary for science and technology at the U.S. Department of Homeland Security, plainly stated, "As bioscience and biotechnology advance, the bioterror threat will grow."[42] This future-oriented focus is often depicted in policy presentations with graphics of this growing threat (fig. 2.8).

In this future-oriented frame, the past is typically marginalized. As defense science advisor Roger Brent argues, "The history of the use of biological weapons in war and of the 20th century germ war programs is largely irrelevant to the current strategic situation."[43] Instead, Brent advises more government attention be directed to the current and future biotech revolution because "the revolution in biological capability has also enabled the current grave and increasing threat of biological attack. Over the next two decades, trends now firmly in place mean that the U.S. faces a continually increasing probability of catastrophic strike."[44] New

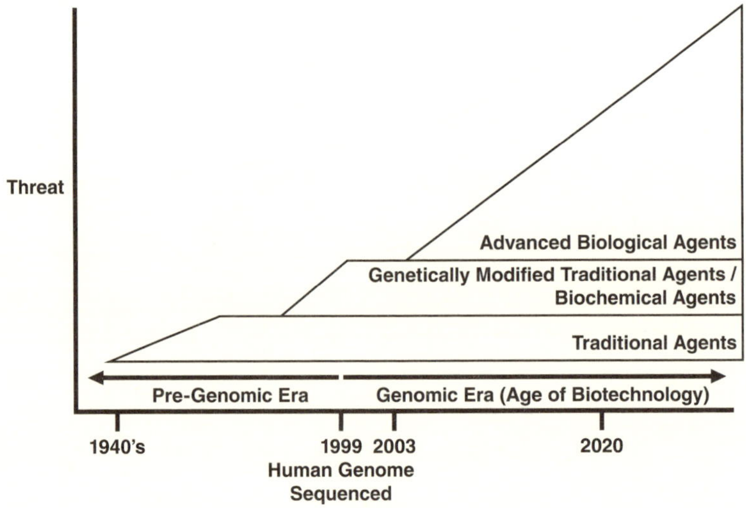

Fig. 2.8. Impact of biotechnology on biological warfare threat. From Petro, Plasse, and McNulty, "Biotechnology." Mary Ann Liebert, Inc., publishers. Reprinted by permission.

biotechnologies are seen as markedly different from historical bioweapons development and use (as figure 2.8 depicts). As a result, this frame ignores how older, cruder biotechnology techniques could be appropriated for bioweapons purposes.

The spatial orientation of the biotech revolution frame is toward the globalized and diffused character of biotechnology. For instance, a 2004 National Research Council report, *Biotechnology Research in an Age of Terrorism,* argued that "it is unrealistic to think that biological technologies and the knowledge base upon which they rest can somehow be isolated within the borders of a few countries."[45] Policy presentations often use maps showing biotech companies located in Iran and other parts of the world to underscore global biotech diffusion (fig. 2.9).[46] But despite this perceived global availability, these representations fail to explain the complicated ways in which individuals, groups, and states take up and use materials and equipment. The biotech revolution frame's emphasis on globalization and diffusion of biological materials and equipment fails to capture nuances of the local context that can create problems for access to the supplies and resources necessary for biotechnology and weapons development.

Based on the seemingly increasing pace and global proliferation of biotechnology, the biotech revolution frame tends to emphasize an increasing threat trajec-

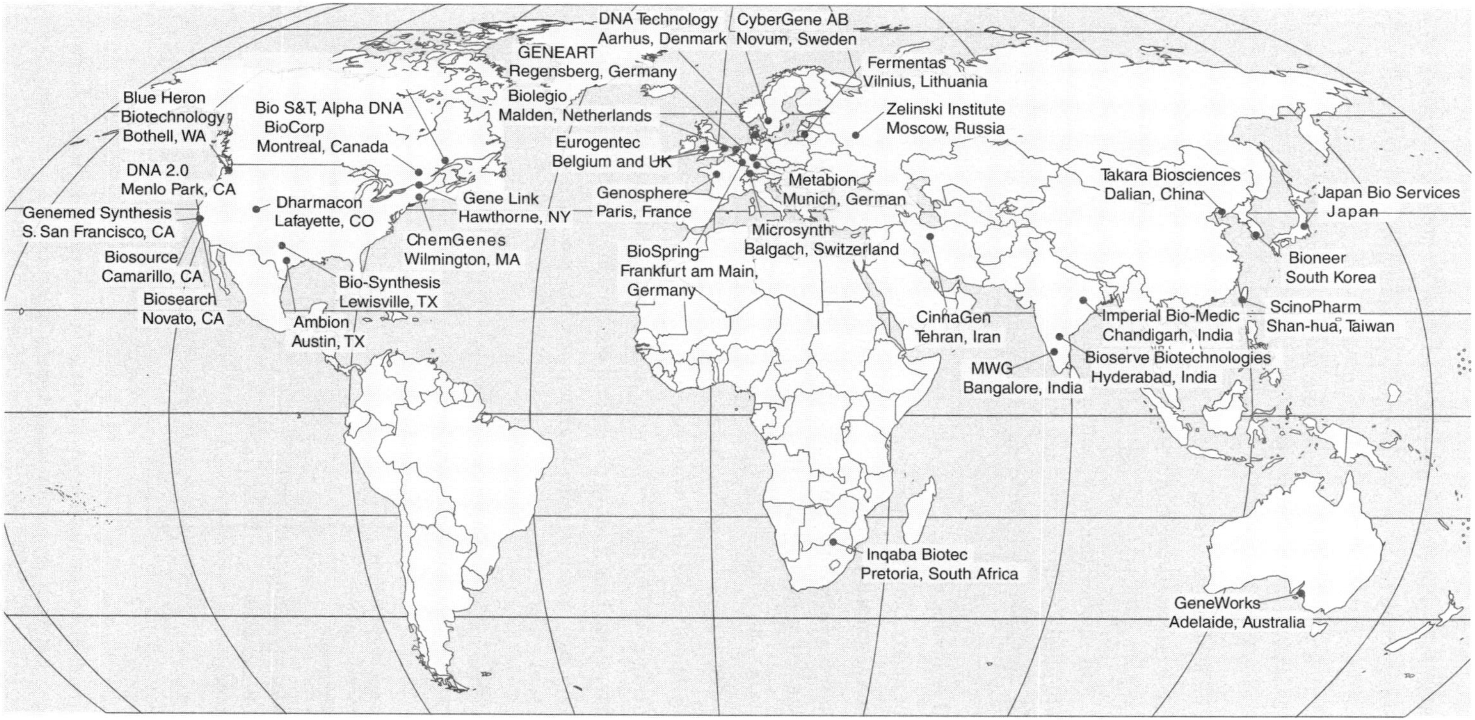

Fig. 2.9. Gene Synthesis Foundries. Synthetic Biology: Globally Distributed Capacity, c. 2007. From Carlson, "Written Comments." Reprinted by permission of Robert Carlson.

tory assumed to be linear or exponential. In a June 2007 high-profile national security policy conference in Washington, one prominent bioterrorism expert highlighted this concern: "In the time required to synthesize strands of DNA, that if you take that as your measure—as a measure of biotechnological power, that power is increasing exponentially at a rate as fast or faster than Moore's law in computing. . . . Also, as with Moore's law, costs are dropping rapidly and barriers to entry, financial and technical barriers, are becoming ever lower. . . . So, advancing, indeed, exponentiating biotechnology brings with it the ability to perform very—potentially, very dangerous manipulations. This power is going to be available to smaller and smaller groups of the technically competent, and perhaps, ultimately, individuals."[47] In his 2005 testimony to the U.S. House of Representatives Committee on Government Reform, bioweapons expert Gerald Epstein used an exponential curve to describe the past, present, and future impact of biological agents and technologies (fig. 2.10). Although the graph depicts a defined trajectory, it offers vague axes and data-point descriptors, and it never explains what constitutes a "typical terrorist," a biological "capability" for terrorism, or "time."

These policy discussions also emphasize the potentially disruptive or unpredictable character of individual biotechnological discoveries that produce the upward threat trajectory. In reflecting on developments in RNA interference and synthetic biology, a 2006 Institute of Medicine and National Research Council report states, "Neither of those developments could have been foretold even a few years back, pointing to the futility of trying to predict with accuracy what will come in the next few years. This leads to the second conclusion, that the task of surveying current technology trends in order to anticipate what new threats may face us down

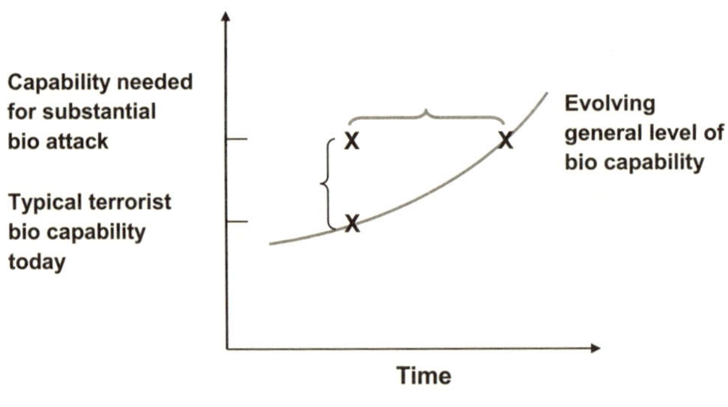

Fig. 2.10. Implications of Technology Advance for Bioterrorism. From Epstein, "Biodefense." Reprinted by permission of Gerald Epstein.

the road will be never ending."[48] Although the technological trajectories are seen as predictable and possessing a powerful momentum—that is, new biotechnologies will emerge and create new and more lethal bioweapons threats—the exact threats themselves are assumed to be unpredictable.

By focusing on abstract biotechnological threats, moreover, the biotech revolution frame fails to address specific social actors. Any elucidation of how those actors develop and use technology is largely absent from discussions, reports, or presentations (figs. 2.1–2.10). Rather, the biological material or biotechnology itself appears to act independently, autonomously, from any individual, group, or state. In the absence of agency, analysts and policymakers assume that biotechnologies become easily standardized, routinized, even automated—with no need for expert, local, or other kinds of specialized knowledge. As microbiologist Mark Wheelis has argued, "A major instrumentation industry has developed to provide the sophisticated technology on which the new biology depends. Instrumentation technology has matured quickly: slow, crude prototypes requiring skilled operators have given way to highly sophisticated equipment that can be operated with minimal technical expertise. . . . This knowledge and related technologies have spread quickly around the globe."[49] In such policy discussions, some people point to a "de-skilling" of biotechnology, arguing that complex skill sets, know-how, and practices will no longer be required to produce novel biological agents or materials.[50] According to this view, such a de-skilling process would lead to a Wikipedia-style radical democratization of biotechnology expertise by giving everyone "the possibility to design and fabricate biological systems without being controlled by any kind of authority."[51] To illustrate this coming trend, some policy discussions and reports have described how high school and college students can now use some of these new tools and techniques to construct novel biological materials (fig. 2.11). Others point to the emergence of independent "do-it-yourself" (DIY) biology groups on the internet for sharing information about biological techniques.[52] More information and more access to information, however, does not necessarily create sophisticated expertise or successful end products in biological work, as the contested, unstable, and sometimes flawed information available on Wikipedia illustrates. But the biotech revolution frame does not address these material and information-sharing limitations.

Thus, we can see that the biotech revolution frame structuring U.S. bioweapons analysis and policymaking focuses on the simple, abstract material and informational aspects of biotechnology, the ease of diffusion of these materials and knowledge, and the steady invocation of future biotech developments and capabilities. Bioweapons threats are presumed to track technological developments

Fig. 2.11. Katherine Aull's closet laboratory in her apartment. From Whalen, "In Attics and Closets." Reprinted by permission of Katherine Aull.

closely, albeit in worrisome, unpredictable ways. Analysts and policymakers have used this frame to interpret bioweapons threats posed by state and nonstate actors. This frame is most aptly summarized in the 2009 "National Strategy for Countering Biological Threats," which emphasized that the biological weapons threat is assumed to be evolving in unpredictable ways and asserted that with advances in biotechnologies continuing to be globally available, barriers of technical expertise and monetary costs will continue to decline, making a potent bioweapons capability available to many U.S. adversaries.[53]

Beyond providing an explanatory structure for biotechnology, the biotech revolution frame also animates a dominant narrative for talking about bioweapons threats in U.S. policy and security circles. Edmund Morgan has written how a narrative, in order to be viable and serve a particular purpose, must bear some resemblance to the real world.[54] By using *narrative* here, I mean to convey the ways in which U.S. analysts and policymakers have described security threats that reflect a particular descriptive telling of reality. Thus, I use *narrative* as analogous to *story,* but my intent is to move beyond an understanding of narratives as pure fiction, solely rhetorical (although they can serve that purpose) or without real-world consequence. Rather, threat narratives are real "things" that are constructed out of assumptions and interpretations of the social and material world.

As I describe below, a dominant bioweapons threat narrative, with specific characters, plot elements, and storylines, has emerged since the early 1990s. The popularity and power of this narrative can be seen in how it is found and used in a wide variety of genres, from bestselling books to newspaper articles, television shows, academic forums, scholarly publications, nongovernmental reports, official government documents, policy briefings, intelligence assessments, congressional testimonials, and presidential speeches. This dominant threat narrative emphasizes the ominous, diffuse, and growing bioweapons concerns emanating from the end of the Cold War.

Technological Threat Narratives and Policy Responses

Technological threat narratives have long been embodied in government decisions for U.S. security policies and programs. In the 1950s and 1960s, for example, U.S. security analysts and policymakers advanced concerns about the "missile and bomber gaps" that reflected fears of Soviet technological advances.[55] These narratives described the Soviets as having ballistic missile and bomber systems superior to those of U.S. military forces. Although they were later shown to be in error—America had always maintained technological superiority in such weapons systems—these narratives provided some analysts and policymakers with ways of describing the enemy and their technological capabilities that would advance and prioritize certain avenues of defense planning and spending. More recently, policy elites within U.S. security circles, from the late 1990s to the early 2000s, invoked the narrative of a "revolution in military affairs," derived from advances in computational and related technologies, to help shape defense planning and spending for U.S. force modernization.[56]

Technological threat narratives on biological weapons are one example among many that the U.S. analytic and policy communities have used to think about and respond to potential security threats. Since the end of the Cold War, the technological threat narratives for biological weapons have drawn on the biotech revolution frame and used a particular literary style. In these narratives, bioweapons interest, development, and transfer by a variety of state and nonstate actors seem to go unchanged by specific issues, contexts, or problems on the ground; the technological threat trajectory is ever on the rise. The power of this frame and its associated narratives lies in their grounding in real-world actors, places, materials, and events over more than twenty years (1991–2011) and continuing to the present day; they are not "merely talk." Moreover, subsequent policy responses based on this frame and these narratives have produced tangible changes in the real world, causing a "looping effect" whereby these policy responses, and the concrete outputs that flow from them, loop back to provide continued support and resources for the biotech revolution frame and its technological threat narratives, which in turn continue to privilege narrow technical analytic and policy priorities for intelligence work and defense planning.[57]

The 1990s Bioweapons Threat Context

In the 1990s, with the striking economic and political changes that followed the demise of the Soviet state, the U.S. government and nongovernment policy community began to focus new, high-level attention on the risks from the growing proliferation of weapons of mass destruction (WMD or WMDs), including nuclear, biological, and chemical weapons and their associated technologies. The vacuum created by the loss of the Soviet Union as the United States' key enemy was soon filled by concerns about a range of newly emerging "rogue states," which included several countries in the Middle East (Iraq, Iran, Syria, Libya, Egypt, Sudan) and Asia (North Korea).[58] Policymakers feared that because of their relatively poor military capabilities, these states would choose to rely on WMDs to challenge the United States and their other enemies.[59] In addition, other countries emerged as possible proliferators during this time, including India, Pakistan, and China, as well as the Soviet successor states that had retained the Soviet weapons and weapons infrastructure (Belarus, Ukraine, Kazakhstan, Uzbekistan). At a 1996 Senate Armed Services Committee hearing, CIA official Gordon Oehler lamented that "the increasingly troubled post–Cold War world has, in a curious way, made us yearn for the dark days of the 1960s and 1970s when we knew the kind of target we were dealing with and the problems we were facing."[60]

With these new proliferation fears, analysts and policy officials began to talk about biological weapons as a potent, yet more accessible type of WMD that could be adopted and used by U.S. adversaries. Starting in the early 1990s, one began to see articulations of the material and economic elements of the biotech revolution emerge within these policy discussions. For instance, several government and non-government reports on biological weapons during the 1990s emphasized the ready availability of bioweapons agents and the means for producing them.[61] In this context, bioweapons production could allegedly be carried out covertly, in small laboratories, as well as be secretly integrated within legitimate biological facilities; policy analysts emphasized the low cost required for production of a small arsenal of deadly biological weapons as compared to that of nuclear weapons.[62] Consequently, analysts and policymakers during this time often called bioweapons the "poor man's atomic weapon."[63] These policy discussions, however, did not address the difficulties and contingencies that had to be overcome before states could develop such capabilities.[64]

The high-level policy concern with bioweapons in the 1990s stemmed from three key revelations of bioweapons activities: (1) the massive, covert, and illicit Soviet program and its potential for proliferation after the breakup of the Soviet Union; (2) Iraq's efforts; and (3) the efforts of the Japanese religious group Aum Shinrikyo. In each of these cases, one also sees elements of the biotech revolution frame embodied in analyses and policy discussions. The technological threat narratives that flow from these cases reflect heightened U.S. policy anxiety about what appears to be a growing set of diffuse, connected, and potentially lethal bioweapons threats in the post–Cold War environment.

The proliferation of bioweapons-related expertise and technologies from the former Soviet biological weapons program became a focal point of intelligence and policy concern. Soviet bioweaponeers themselves revealed the potential magnitude of this threat. In the late 1980s and early 1990s, two Soviet scientists, Vladimir Pasechnik and Kanatjan Alibekov (later known as Ken Alibek), defected to the West and provided detailed information to U.S. and U.K. intelligence about a massive covert Soviet biological weapons program.[65] This secret program had started during the Cold War, after the Soviet Union had signed and ratified the Biological and Toxin Weapons Convention, which prohibited any type of offensive bioweapons activities.[66] Although Western intelligence had long suspected a hidden Soviet biological weapons program, the Pasechnik and Alibek debriefings indicated that the West had significantly underestimated its size and scope.[67] By way of example, the Soviet program had involved more than forty facilities across Russia, Central Asia, and the Caucuses, employing thousands of bioweaponeers who researched, produced, and weaponized a number of biological agents. Without question, the Soviet biological weapons program was the largest and most sophisticated in history.

That U.S. and other western analysts had been unable to detect the entire scope of the Soviet bioweapons program prior to these defections reinforced analytic and policy concerns that the development and production of biological weapons and related activities could be easily hidden. Subsequently, policy discussions also focused on the extensive number of facilities, personnel, and materials involved in the Soviet bioweapons program. For instance, many contemporaneous reports emphasized the large, 20,000-liter fermentors used to make vast quantities of Soviet biological agent, the exotic pathogens the Soviets had prepared for use in sophisticated delivery systems, and the thousands of bioweapons scientists who had worked in the program.[68] Other reports focused on Soviet attempts to apply genetic engineering techniques to make new and more lethal types of bioweapons agents.[69]

These threat narratives, however, rarely mentioned the complexity and contingency embedded in the Soviet program. For example, the narratives paid little to no attention to the specialized skills and know-how developed over the decades by teams of Soviet weapons scientists or the need to assemble these teams with specialized criteria to produce particular kinds of weapons at specific sites. Nor was there any discussion of the technical and managerial difficulties that the Soviets encountered in developing some of their prized weapons, despite ample financial resources; few focused on what Soviet bioweaponeers were *unable* to accomplish.[70] And although the Soviets had implemented an extensive security apparatus to hide bioweapons activities from U.S. and other intelligence agencies, the resulting secrecy practices had a deleterious effect on Soviet bioweapons activities.[71] Rather, drawing on the biotech revolution frame, accounts of the Soviet bioweapons program in the 1990s were largely black-boxed, describing only narrow quantitative and material inputs that characterized the successful end stages of certain portions of Soviet bioweapons activities.[72] U.S. analysts and policymakers then interpreted Soviet advances in bioweapons development as examples of the lethal bioweapons power that a variety of state or nonstate actors in the post–Cold War world could easily develop. These claims, however, did not consider that such bioweapons power required a wide variety of very specific social, political, and material aspects of the Soviet program that cannot easily be abstracted to other contexts.

Subsequently, U.S. government attention focused on the material aspects of technology in bioweapons assessments. In 1999, for example, the CIA launched a highly classified project called Project Clear Vision to try to understand the design and operation of the Soviets' biological munitions in order to predict future biological threats.[73] From earlier investigations of the former Soviet bioweapons test site on Vozrozhdeniye Island, the CIA had acquired small fragments of a Soviet biological munition. With information obtained from Soviet bioweapons defectors and help from a defense contractor, the CIA worked to reverse-engineer the munition. At the end of the project, the CIA was able to construct a similar type of munition. Although it "worked"—that is, the CIA was able to disseminate a biological simulant—it remains unclear whether it accurately resembled the Soviet biological bomb it was supposed to replicate. Furthermore, there is no indication that the CIA-built device corresponded to any real intelligence information on the state bioweapons threats during that time. The munition, however, did illustrate the abstract technological potential of such a weapon—even if the CIA's clandestine efforts failed to find any states or terrorists interested in this potential at the time. Aluminum replicas of the biological munitions were brought to policy briefings about the project; such visuals served as powerful, tangible, material "evidence" of growing advanced bioweapons threats.[74]

In addition to Project Clear Vision, other intelligence assessments focused on other technical aspects of the former Soviet bioweapons establishment. As an illustration, in the 1990s some U.S. government reports showed that Iranian government officials were aggressively recruiting former Soviet biological weapons scientists.[75] Moreover, Iraq attempted to procure large-scale fermentors from the former Soviet bioweapons establishment and had also acquired other types of biological equipment from West European countries.[76] A 1994 intelligence report by the DIA claimed that both Iraq and North Korea had sought Russian smallpox technology.[77] Other worries stemmed from the creation of commercial spin-off companies at former bioweapons facilities across the former Soviet Union as well as the poor export controls in these states. Government and nongovernment experts expressed concern that such conditions might facilitate the transfer of sensitive bioweapons-related expertise, materials, and technologies to U.S. enemies.

Although there is some evidence of tangible physical movements of people and materials from the former Soviet bioweapons program during this period, there is little analytic or policy discussion of how these various elements could be incorporated to develop a *specific* bioweapons capability in another state or terrorist group. Instead, technology transfer in these reports and discussions is typically depicted as the simple physical movement of material or personnel to new locations. As we saw in the graph displayed in figure 2.10, the biotechnology transfer and uptake mechanisms in reports of the time appear largely unaffected by any changes in personnel, locale, or circumstance; they contain no discussion of the complex social and material dimensions needed for such transfers to work in new contexts. Instead, they assume that technology and people can be seamlessly integrated and assembled by U.S. adversaries to produce potent biological weapons capabilities.

With the 1991 Gulf War, Iraq also emerged as a new and dangerous bioweapons threat. Before the war, U.S. intelligence knew little about Iraq's bioweapons efforts, and Iraq repeatedly denied that it had an offensive bioweapons program.[78] After the war, as part of the United Nations cease fire agreement, the UN Special Commission (UNSCOM) was established to verify Iraqi claims about its WMD capabilities.[79] From the outset, UNSCOM was established as a body of technical experts (physicists, chemists, biologists, missile and munition experts, and so on) who would conduct intrusive on-the-ground inspections to search and account for specific physical, technical, and personnel evidence of Iraq's weapons activities.

Between 1994 and 1995, UN weapons inspectors obtained substantial material evidence indicating that Iraq had possessed an offensive bioweapons program prior to the Gulf War. This included information that Iraq had previously imported over forty tons of growth media and other biological materials had gone unexplained and unaccounted for by the Iraqi government. UN inspectors had also noted unsatisfactory explanations from Iraq for the procurement of dual-use equipment and for the suspicious military features of the site surrounding the Al-Hakam single-cell protein facility.[80] When UN officials formally confronted Iraq with this evidence, Iraqi officials ultimately acknowledged that they had produced biological warfare agents before the 1991 Gulf War.[81] With this revelation, policymakers noted that the U.S. intelligence community had underestimated Iraq's past bioweapons efforts.[82] Thus, similar to the failures in detecting the Soviet bioweapons program, U.S. analysts and policymakers interpreted the Iraqi intelligence failure as another indicator of how a potent bioweapons program could be easily hidden over time.

During the 1990s, much of U.S. analytic and policy concerns rested on the full documentation of Iraq's bioweapons-related materials, infrastructure, and expertise, accomplished largely through the technical accounting practices of UN inspections and the limited pieces of intelligence that the United States could acquire. Through this accounting work, U.S. analysts and policymakers did establish that Iraq had possessed a bioweapons program prior to the 1991 Gulf War, and this information also provided UN inspectors with evidence that Iraq had lied in past declarations of its weapons activities. Even with this detailed accounting, however, UN inspectors had difficulty determining the scope of the past Iraqi bioweapons program and its continuation after the war. Historian of technology Theodore Porter has noted that accounting methods, with their quantitative focus, often "leave out much of what is difficult or obscure."[83] For instance, UN accounting practices in Iraq were largely divorced from dedicated studies that considered the complex socioeconomic and political context in which Iraqi weapons activities were taking place, such as the 1991 war; the ongoing, intrusive on-the-ground inspections and surveillance; the continued international bombing campaigns in Iraq that destroyed physical infrastructure; the extensive and lengthy international sanctions; and the political instabilities within the Hussein regime. Such studies would have revealed the massive decays in basic Iraqi infrastructure and the extensive government corruption that had significantly deteriorated Saddam's interest and ability in maintaining his WMD programs. Instead, UN and U.S. analysts continued to rely solely on quantitative accounting methods, with their "trust (or, at times, distrust) in numbers," as the central means to evaluate Saddam's past and present bioweapons programs.[84] But by focusing on the material components alone and assuming a fixed technological and threat trajectory, U.S. and UN analysts judged that Iraqi bioweapons activities were continuing largely unabated.

In the 1990s, the Japanese religious group Aum Shinrikyo catalyzed new concerns about nonstate bioterror threats. Aum was led by a charismatic leader, Shoko Asahara, who had apocalyptic visions: he was interested in launching a series of terrorist attacks in Japan with the aim of overthrowing the Japanese government and starting a worldwide revolution. Unbeknownst to Japanese, U.S., or other intelligence or law enforcement officials, Aum sought to develop WMDs for these terrorist purposes. In 1995, having prepared the chemical warfare agent sarin in its own covert laboratories, Aum members released it in the Tokyo subway system. Although the attack killed thirteen people and injured several hundred more, it failed to ignite the revolution that Aum desired.

The arrest of Aum members and the subsequent police interrogations revealed that in addition to its production of sarin gas, Aum had also dedicated substantial resources to develop biological weapons. It is estimated that Aum devoted up to $10 million for its bioweapons program, which included dedicated biological facilities employing a small group of technical staff with some knowledge of microbiology and molecular biology.[85] To accomplish its goals, Aum had established elaborate front companies and even tried to buy Soviet weapons expertise.[86] Many government and nongovernment reports immediately after the Aum Shinrikyo subway attack emphasized Aum's dabbling with anthrax bacteria as the harbinger of emerging bioweapons threats from nonstate actors.[87] The biotech revolution frame embedded within these reports emphasized Aum's physical and monetary assets, calculated at over $1 billion, and the biological equipment, facilities, and personnel that Aum had dedicated to the effort.

A narrow focus on the availability of material resources, however, fails to capture the contingency that is often involved in bioweapons development by state and nonstate actors. For example, press reports have documented that Aum had purchased a polymerase chain reaction (PCR) machine, used to amplify DNA, during its bioweapons development activities. Although this finding initially raised concerns that Aum had planned to produce dangerous biological agents in its laboratories, investigators later learned that the group had purchased and used this equipment for religious reasons. In 1989, Aum created a new "Initiative of Love" rite using the DNA of the group's leader, Shoko Asahara. In this rite, cult followers who had donated more than one million yen to the group were given liquids to drink that contained Asahara's DNA. In order to generate Asahara's DNA more efficiently, the group had purchased the PCR machine; it was never connected to Aum's bioweapons activities.[88] Thus, the mere acquisition by a malevolent actor of a piece of biological equipment does not necessarily denote a malevolent use.

Subsequent investigations have found that Aum never succeeded in producing a viable bioweapons agent.[89] Despite its efforts to obtain a virulent strain of anthrax bacteria, for example, Aum was able to acquire only a less harmful vaccine strain. Aum also experienced problems handling and producing cultures of the anthrax vaccine strain it had acquired.[90] On top of that, the group seems to have tried to disseminate its anthrax bacterial cultures in several unsuccessful releases across Tokyo. In spite of these technical problems, however, many policy discussions emphasized that the Aum incident fixed the threat trajectory for bioterrorism; it was now no longer "a matter of if, just when."[91] During this time, some terrorism scholars noted that most terrorist groups tend to be technologically conservative and prefer low-tech conventional weapons due to their reliability and ease of use.[92] But policy officials who rely on the biotech revolution frame often discounted that perspective, emphasizing that, due to technological developments, past historical events are poor and unreliable predictors for future bioweapons threats.[93]

Throughout the 1990s, the biotech revolution frame became increasingly embodied in government assessments and studies on bioweapons threats. By way of illustration, a 1997 U.S. Defense Science Board report emphasized the growing threat of biological weapons due to their ease of acquisition; their ability to be produced in inexpensive, small-scale, dual-use facilities; and the difficulty of detecting bioweapons-related activities.[94] Also in 1997, JASON, an elite defense advisory group consisting of leading U.S. scientists, conducted a summer study on bioweapons threats that focused on advances in biotechnology.[95] In addition, as historian of science Susan Wright has noted, a variety of formal and informal science advisors to the government began elevating the technical dimensions of biological weapons as a growing security threat by providing formal and informal briefings and tutorials to government officials along with a variety of public talks (fig. 2.12).[96]

Fig. 2.12. Dr. William Patrick, "International Biological Warfare." During a hearing before the House Select Intelligence Committee, Patrick, former chief of the product division of the former offensive biological weapons program of the United States, demonstrates how biological weapons could be implemented. Photo by Scott J. Ferrell / Congressional Quarterly–Roll Call Group / Getty Images, 3 March 1999.

With this focus on the material aspects of technology, predicting technological trends and thresholds became an important part of U.S. government bioweapons assessments. In the early 1990s, for instance, the CIA created a technical analytic unit called the Nonproliferation Center; in 1997, this unit was given new status and authority to raise the profile and priority of technical bioweapons analysis within the CIA. In 1998, the DIA also created a new science advisory group for the military called BioChem 20/20. Its mission was to "lead and focus the defense intelligence community's assessments of emerging technologies that nation-states or terrorists could use for biological or chemical warfare and to mitigate technological surprise from foreign biological warfare programs."[97] BioChem 20/20 would be responsible for preparing a variety of classified technical intelligence studies for the DIA on biological and chemical weapons issues.

As part of the Clinton administration's new biodefense programs, moreover, the U.S. Department of Defense funded Project Jefferson and Project Bachus to assess emerging bioweapons threats. Project Jefferson was the name of a 1998 contract established under Battelle Memorial Laboratories, with funding from the DIA. The project consisted of a collection of research activities with a technical focus designed to "prevent technological surprise" and to anticipate future bioweapons threats.[98] Although Project Jefferson was an acknowledged "open" project, meaning that its name was not classified, the majority of the work conducted within Jefferson was classified.[99] For example, responding to concerns about genetic engineering and the former Soviet bioweapons program, the $2 million Jefferson project was designed to attempt to reproduce a genetically engineered strain of the anthrax bacteria that had been developed by Russian scientists and published in the open scientific literature.[100]

In 1998, the U.S. Defense Threat Reduction Agency carried out Project Bachus, named after the Roman god of wine. The project was designed to build a covert bioweapons production facility by using commercially available, off-the-shelf materials and to determine if such a facility could be detected through imagery or other intelligence signals and then disabled by military forces. Over an eighteen-month period, U.S. defense employees set up a mock bioweapons facility in Nevada using equipment and supplies purchased domestically and internationally. At the end of the experiment, the facility was able to produce about two pounds of an anthrax bacteria simulant. With its construction, this facility (and the powdered simulant it produced) was touted as demonstrating the accessibility and diffusion of dangerous biological materials and equipment to a variety of state actors, who would not need specialized bioweapons expertise in order to perpetrate harm. In commenting on the project, defense advisor Tara O'Toole said that it "demonstrated quite persuasively that about four people, only one of whom had any biological training at all—and that was not with the U.S. weapons program, that was a degree in biology—could, using materials bought through the Internet, set up shop, undiscovered, and create a *Bacillus anthracis* look-alike."[101]

Although it was not mentioned in O'Toole's remarks or in government briefings, the Bachus project involved substantial specialized expertise. For instance, the defense team selected to carry out the project consisted of seven or eight people, many of whom had postgraduate degrees in the biological sciences or engineering; others had served in special forces and intelligence units.[102] Each team member was selected for his or her specialized skills. Before working on Bachus, the team had also worked together on a similar classified project. Moreover, the team was advised by three highly experienced biological weapons specialists acting as full-time consultants, whose role was to ensure success. For example, each day these advisors reviewed each individual's work for errors. Yet these caveats were not included as part of the technological threat narrative emanating from this project—that this information was not made public is striking.

Technological threat narratives on biological weapons also began to emerge in the public domain. In 1998, journalist and bestselling author Richard Preston published his sci-fi thriller *The Cobra Event*. In his book, Preston told of a mad scientist developing a lethal, genetically engineered virus and secretly releasing it in bioweapons attacks on major U.S. cities. Preston wove together certain technical information of known bioweapons programs (former American, Soviet, Iraqi, and Aum Shinrikyo efforts) as well as imagined ones (a home bioweapons lab, an evil biotechnology company, a mobile bioweapons lab, and a genetically engineered viral weapon).[103] The book exemplified the emerging technological threat narrative based on the biotech revolution frame: a host of state and nonstate actors with easy access to advanced bioweapons capabilities.

The Cobra Event was popular enough that it gained the attention of U.S. policymakers. Upon reading the book, President Clinton called several science and cabinet advisory meetings to discuss the technical threat depicted in the book. Subsequently, Clinton ordered a classified simulation exercise based on the *Cobra Event* scenario to evaluate whether the United States would be able to handle a bioterror event of this type.[104] Yet this simulation, which depicted a genetically engineered viral weapon attack, was something hardly within the technical reach of the Soviet Union—Soviet scientists were never able to make an engineered virus viable outside of very controlled laboratory conditions—and the Soviets' bioweapons program no longer existed. But these caveats were not incorporated as part of the simulation and planning exercise; the technological threat potential from a worst-case scenario remained the emphasis.

This simulation, among other bioweapons-related policy reports, fed into the Clinton administration's support for new resources and authorities for addressing bioweapons threats. In addition, by the end of the Clinton administration, a growing cadre and integrated network of scientific and technical experts were called on to advise the U.S. intelligence and policy communities on bioweapons issues. Moreover, bioweapons assessments conducted during this period increasingly focused on the collection and analysis of data relevant to the biotech revolution frame. Consequently, U.S. government and nongovernment analysts and policy officials largely emphasized the growing number of technologically based bioweapons threats.

The Bioweapons Threat Context during the 2000s

At the beginning of the twenty-first century, four overlapping bioweapons issues emerged that also drew on the biotech revolution frame and existing technological threat narratives, involving: (1) new concerns about Iraq's bioweapons program; (2) the September 11, 2001, attack on the World Trade Center and the subsequent anthrax attacks; (3) revelations in Afghanistan of al-Qaeda's interest in biological weapons; and (4) new biological science experiments published in the open scientific literature. For each of these issues, U.S. analysts and policymakers again emphasized certain material and technological issues in their accounts while marginalizing other relevant contextual matters.

After the halt of UN inspections in the late 1990s, new intelligence emerged about Iraq's suspected bioweapons activities. In November 1999, an Iraqi defector, subsequently codenamed "Curveball," surfaced in Germany and indicated that Iraq had developed a bioweapons capability on mobile trailers. Curveball said that he was a chemical engineer who had developed and worked on these secret trailers; in his reporting, he identified specific sites, designs, and technical processes that he said were associated with the Iraqi mobile bioweapons program. CIA experts and consultants judged the technical and physical details provided by Curveball to be particularly convincing. Such covert mobile bioweapons capability fit with long-held analytic and policy judgments that biological weapons could be easily hidden and that Iraq had continued its bioweapons activities unhindered by UN inspections. By early 2000, CIA intelligence assessments drew heavily on Curveball's evidence, which stated that Iraq possessed an advanced, covert bioweapons program.

When UN inspections in Iraq resumed, UN inspectors returned to their standard accounting practices of documenting Iraq's weapons-related items in order to assess the status of Iraq's weapons activities. This type of accounting-oriented assessment is typified in the UN's March 2003 report *Unresolved Disarmament Issues: Iraq's Proscribed Weapons Programmes,* which provides over one hundred pages of detailed description of Iraq's weapons since the beginning of UN inspections.[105] Although the report does provide some historical background on the development of Iraq's weapons programs, these sections largely reflect a focus on the materials and weapons found in Iraq rather than a more contextual understanding of how these weapons and associated activities were embedded and developed within specific Iraqi social, economic, and political conditions that changed over time. Thus, within their largely quantitative, bioweapons-specific framework, UN inspectors had little ability to assess with any rigor the effects of U.S. bombings, sanctions, and other socioeconomic changes within Saddam's regime that may have affected Iraqi infrastructure, its scientific and technical base, and therefore its bioweapons development. With assumptions of rising technological threat trajectories, the default assumption among UN inspectors, U.S. intelligence analysts, and outside experts was that Iraq's advanced bioweapons program persisted covertly, unabated.

The terrorist attacks on September 11, 2001, and the subsequent anthrax attacks were also interpreted through the biotech revolution frame and the existing technological threat narratives. Within days of the attacks, a variety of government and nongovernment experts stated that a technological threshold had been crossed, indicating that terrorists would seek to develop and use WMDs such as biological weapons in order to further their mass casualty aims. Some terrorism scholars, however, maintained that the September 11 attacks indicated more of an organizational innovation than a technological one. Terrorism expert Bruce Hoffman, for example, emphasized that what was new on September 11 was not the technology but the coordination, synchronization, and complicated logistics and networks used to plan and carry out the attacks—using technologies and tactics that were not new to al-Qaeda.[106] Such arguments, however, were largely ignored among those within the U.S. security policy community dealing with bioweapons issues and adhering to the biotech revolution frame; they interpreted the events of September 11 as evidence of a technological threat based not on the conventional technologies that were actually used but rather on the technological potential of a bioweapons attack by terrorist groups such as al-Qaeda.

The September–November 2001 anthrax attacks, coming so soon after September 11, further strengthened that interpretation. The anthrax attacks involved envelopes containing anthrax bacteria mailed through the U.S. Postal System starting on September 18, 2001, and continuing for several weeks. The letters were sent to U.S. media outlets and to the offices of two U.S. senators. The inhalation of anthrax spores from the envelopes caused five deaths and seventeen injuries; in addition, approximately thirty thousand people in workplaces where the letters were opened were prescribed antibiotics. Scientific analyses determined that the highly virulent Ames strain of the anthrax bacteria was used in the letters. Its quality varied, though; some letters contained small particles of a high-quality, dry powder, whereas other letters contained a coarse, low-grade material.

Soon after the attacks, U.S. policy analysts and officials focused on the technological sophistication of the material in the envelopes. For instance, some in the security policy community were concerned that the use of high-quality, dry, powdered anthrax indicated that certain nonstate actors or individuals possessed the technical competency and resources to make a sophisticated agent. Although some experts emphasized the importance of determining the perpetrator of the attacks before concluding that terrorists had crossed technical thresholds, others insisted that bioweapons-related capabilities were becoming more and more accessible to a wider set of actors and groups.[107]

Interestingly, U.S. government investigations after the anthrax attacks revealed that because of the Clinton administration's biodefense buildup, including Project Jefferson, several U.S. government laboratories had been working for several years with the virulent Ames strain of the anthrax bacteria in high-quality, powdered forms as part of classified biodefense research experiments. In certain cases, investigators found that the anthrax bacteria produced through these biodefense activities had not been properly documented and secured. From this information, U.S. government officials began to amass evidence indicating that instead of a foreign terrorist group, the likely perpetrator of the 2001 anthrax attacks was an employee from a sophisticated U.S. biodefense laboratory; in 2008, the FBI identified a U.S. biodefense scientist as the sole perpetrator.[108] Throughout this multiyear investigation, however, the technological threat narrative about a future bioterrorism attack failed to incorporate the possibility of a domestic threat from an individual working at a specialized U.S. government biodefense laboratory; rather, the narrative continued to focus on the threat posed by the diffusion of biotechnology to other laboratories, in other places, by other kinds of people.

After September 11, the bioweapons threat narrative included a new notion of "reload." Former secretary of the Navy Richard Danzig introduced this concept in his 2003 policy report *Catastrophic Bioterrorism—What Is To Be Done?,* in which he described how terrorists would have difficulty repeating the September 11 attacks very quickly due to their complexity and the resources involved. In contrast, Danzig argued that the anthrax attacks illustrated how biological weapons offered a much more robust "reload" potential for terrorists:

> Making a gram of readily aerosolized anthrax spores in a weaponized 1-to-5-micron range is a technical challenge, but, once production is accomplished, it is a much lesser challenge to make one kilogram. And it is not a significant challenge for a terrorist organization that can make a kilogram to make 10 or 100 kilograms. . . . The ability to reload and repeat an attack obviously amplifies the number of potential victims. An attacker, having disseminated anthrax one evening in Washington, for instance, could do the same thing the next day in Detroit, Chicago, or Los Angeles. . . . In sum, biological weapons readily lend themselves not only to catastrophic effects but also to reload. This is a special

attribute. Even a terrorist detonation of a nuclear weapon, catastrophic as it would be, is not likely to be repeated quickly.[109]

Danzig's reload metaphor captures and extends several elements of the technological threat narrative, in which developing a potent bioweapons capability is black-boxed and simply equated to bullets in a gun. This metaphor, however, fails to consider the social and organizational dimensions evident in past state bioweapons programs that can stymie bioweapons efforts, even with the necessary materials and resources in place. In spite of these caveats, however, the reload concept has been incorporated and cited in several bioweapons-related policy reports that draw on these technological threat narratives.[110]

On the heels of the anthrax attacks and the U.S. invasion of Afghanistan in late 2001, U.S. government forces captured a laboratory site consisting of a few pieces of equipment known to be used by al-Qaeda operatives. Although crude and not yet operational, the laboratory findings suggested that al-Qaeda had acquired an avirulent strain of anthrax bacteria, limited biotech equipment, and some scientific articles. U.S. officials determined that one Ph.D.-level microbiologist from Pakistan was in charge of planning the design and work of the laboratory; he had also visited biotechnology companies and conferences. Subsequent open-source publications by intelligence officials and prominent scientists called attention to these findings as evidence of a growing bioweapons threat by al-Qaeda and other terrorist groups.[111]

Yet declassified U.S. government reports about this Afghani makeshift laboratory have indicated that al-Qaeda was unable to obtain a pathogenic culture of the anthrax bacteria, and there was no evidence of any technical work done at this site, suggesting that al-Qaeda's 2001 bioweapons capabilities never went beyond the trivial.[112] In 2001, moreover, U.S. forces captured a Malaysian biological technician who was seeking to acquire bioweapons materials and equipment for al-Qaeda. Subsequent interrogations revealed that he had failed to procure a virulent strain of anthrax bacteria. This suggested that, at least in terms of agent acquisition, al-Qaeda had faced the same hurdles as the failed attempts by Aum Shinrikyo to develop biological weapons.[113] Additional comparisons of Aum and al-Qaeda's bioweapons capabilities have indicated that Aum's four-year bioweapons effort, although a total failure, was substantially more developed than al-Qaeda's efforts as of 2001.[114]

However, these shortcomings in al-Qaeda's alleged bioweapons activities were not discussed in a high-level U.S. government report issued in 2005 by the Commission on the Intelligence Capabilities of the United States Regarding Weapons of Mass Destruction (also known as the WMD Commission). Instead, the report emphasized that, in spite of the crude laboratory setup, al-Qaeda appeared to have achieved more progress before the 2001 invasion of Afghanistan than had previously been assessed by U.S. intelligence. The report concluded that the U.S. intelligence community had once again underestimated another diffuse, nonstate bioweapons threat.[115] In a separate chapter, this same 2005 commission report emphasized the growing risks of bioterrorism from advances in biotechnology.

In the early 2000s, the U.S. security community extended its concerns to new biological science developments in the open scientific literature and their possibilities for bioterrorism. Some of the key experimental controversies involved the insertion of a synthetic gene into the mousepox virus (2001), the synthesis of smallpox proteins (2002), and the artificial synthesis of the poliovirus from commercially available DNA (2002).[116] Following the publication of the poliovirus experiment, other evidence was invoked as signs of the new and dangerous future from the rapid technological developments in the emerging field of synthetic biology; these included additional artificial genome syntheses by the J. Craig Venter Institute and the work of U.S. government and academic scientists.[117]

This focus on new scientific experiments in the open scientific literature prompted an increasing policy focus on new developments in biology and biotechnology largely disconnected from specific state or nonstate actors. In reports and discussions about synthetic genomic experiments, the only malevolent actor mentioned is a generic class of individuals called "biohackers." As bioweapons policy expert Jonathan Tucker pointed out, a biohacker is "an individual who does not necessarily have malicious intent but seeks to create bioengineered organisms out of curiosity or to demonstrate his technical prowess—a common motivation of many designers of computer viruses. The reagents and tools used in synthetic biology will eventually be converted into commercial kits, making it easier for biohackers to acquire them. Moreover, as synthetic-biology training becomes increasingly available to students at the college and possibly even high-school levels, a 'hacker culture' may emerge, increasing the risk of reckless or malevolent experimentation."[118] This evil biohacker is depicted as easily and secretly brewing up dangerous, genetically engineered pathogens in his or her basement or garage laboratory; in many ways, this image harkens back to the mad scientist scenario depicted in *The Cobra Event*. This new concept of biohacker, however, fits seamlessly into the biotech revolution frame, which abstracts technological capability.

In these policy discussions, new biological developments are assumed to follow an existing technological trend irrespective of the local context in which the scientific work is conducted or the specifics of how this new technology might (or might not) be appropriated for harm. With the 2001 mousepox experiment, more particularly, most of the policy focus was on how the insertion of a particular gene into the mousepox virus created the potential for more advanced bioweapons. What was often not mentioned was that when the mutated mousepox virus was injected into the mice, its lethality was so great that it rapidly killed its host, preventing the host from transmitting the virus to other animals—even animals living within the same cage. Therefore, ironically, the extreme lethality of the virus actually made it a poor candidate for a bioweapons agent. However, the technological threat narrative circulating within the U.S. security community failed to incorporate this aspect into its discussion of the mousepox experiment.

As in the 1990s, new institutional resources, infrastructures, and studies have been sponsored post–September 11 on the intersection of biotechnology and bioterrorism.[119] Initiated under the Clinton administration, Project Jefferson's "technical paradigm" was continued and expanded through the George W. Bush administration. In his July 2002 *National Strategy for Homeland Security,* President Bush proposed the establishment of a new National Biological Weapons Analysis Center in the newly formed Department of Homeland Security.[120] Unlike Project Jefferson, whose work was spread among a number of defense contractors, this new facility would serve as the flagship for a national focus on technical bioweapons assessments. This center, ultimately called the National Biodefense Analysis and Countermeasures Center (NBACC), involved the creation of a new multi-million dollar, high-containment, biodefense research initiative. For the NBACC, a new $141-million, 160,000-square-foot building with high-level biological containment facilities was completed in March 2009 at Fort Detrick, Maryland.[121] In addition, other important off-site components of the NBACC are housed at Lawrence Livermore National Laboratory in Livermore, California; the Plum Island Animal Disease Center in Orient, New York; the new National Bio and Agro-Defense Facility in Manhattan, Kansas; and the related university-based Homeland Security Centers of Excellence.[122]

An early stated vision of the NBACC is to be "the operationally focused, technical biological defense analysis center for homeland security . . . across the spectrum of activity from technical threat and risk assessment, through prevention of technological surprise, to authoritative attribution."[123] In their work, researchers at the NBACC and its associated facilities will develop and apply different computational models, simulations, and laboratory experiments to evaluate U.S. vulnerabilities to different biological agents and other "material threats."[124] These collective technical studies will be used to rank a variety of biological agents and related advances in biotechnology, according to their risk potential as biological weapons. These technical calculations, however, are largely separated from analyses of particular adversaries; for example, no adversary is depicted in the risk assessments of the biological agents. J. Patrick Fitch, the laboratory director of the NBACC, explains that "scientific and technical knowledge determine which threats are realistic."[125] In a 2009 biosecurity conference speech, former secretary Danzig emphasized this scientific abstraction regarding future bioweapons threats: "I regard the risk [of bioweapons] as inherent in the proliferation of the technology. . . . I think that this risk will be around a long time . . . ten years from now it's still going to be here, and in fact ten years from now, whatever happens to al-Qaeda, it will be greater because of the proliferation of the technologies and the development of those technologies."[126] Although one might consider these claims odd, the move away from a consideration of specific, real-world enemies to abstract technical considerations in evaluating bioweapons threats is entirely consonant with the logics structuring the biotech revolution frame and its associated technological narratives.

Building on the early work embodied in the NBACC concept, the Bush administration in April 2004 issued "Homeland Security Presidential Directive 10 (HSPD-10): Biodefense for the 21st Century," which emphasized the importance of increasing "science-based threat assessments" on bioweapons issues.[127] HSPD-10 had an explicit emphasis on assessing futuristic, technologically oriented bioweapons threats. An unclassified summary of the directive stated that the U.S. government is "continuing to develop more forward-looking analyses . . . to understand new scientific trends that may be exploited by our adversaries to develop biological weapons and to help position intelligence collectors ahead of the problem."[128] Under HSPD-10, the Department of Homeland Security was responsible for conducting a national risk assessment of new biological threats every two years, involving traditional biological agent threats (anthrax, smallpox) as well as "enhanced" biological agents (agents selected or modified to increase virulence and stability or circumvent countermeasures), "emerging" agents (newly emerging diseases such as highly pathogenic avian influenza), and "advanced" agents (non-naturally occurring, engineered agents; novel delivery systems).[129] Furthermore, in building on the Clinton administration's *Cobra Event* simulation, since 2000 a set of U.S. government agencies and private entities has used different types of technological simulations for bioterrorism threat assessment and planning (table 2.1).

One simulation that garnered much policy attention was the 2005 Atlantic Storm exercise, in which terrorists in a fictional al-Qaeda splinter group acquired smallpox seed cultures from a biological weapons facility in the former Soviet Union. With the help of a former Soviet weapons scientist as advisor and working in an Austrian brewery, the group developed a high-quality, dry-powder smallpox

TABLE 2.1
Simulation exercises

Date	Name	Main organizer	Nature of attack
May 2000	Top Off I	FEMA and U.S. Department of Justice	Aerosolized plague bacteria
July 2000	Unnamed	U.S. Department of Justice and U.S. Defense Threat Reduction Agency	Aerosolized pneumonic plague bacteria
June 2001	Dark Winter	Johns Hopkins Center for Biosecurity, the Center for Strategic and International Studies, ANSER Homeland Security Institute, and National Memorial Institute for the Prevention of Terrorism (MIPT), Oklahoma	Aerosolized smallpox
April 2001	Sooner Spring	National Memorial Institute for the Prevention of Terrorism (MIPT), Oklahoma	Smallpox virus
May 2003	Top Off II	U.S. Department of Homeland Security and U.S. Department of State	Aerosolized plague bacteria
January 2005	Atlantic Storm	University of Pittsburgh Medical Center, Center for Biosecurity*	Aerosolized dry powder smallpox virus
April 2005	Top Off III	U.S. Department of Homeland Security	Aerosolized pneumonic plague bacteria

Source: Leitenberg, *Assessing the Biological Weapons and Bioterrorism Threats.*
*Formerly known as the Johns Hopkins Center for Biosecurity.

weapon. The agent was then disseminated by terrorists in Europe and the United States, using commercially available spray dispensers. As the exercise progressed, detailed graphics illustrated the rising number of people infected; CNN-like newsflashes were shown to the participants to illustrate new, late-breaking outbreaks of the disease. By the end of the exercise, more than six hundred thousand people were infected with smallpox, with a quarter of those infected projected to die from the disease. Commenting on this outcome, defense advisor O'Toole remarked, "This is not science fiction; the Age of Bioterror is now."[130]

Although such simulations illustrated what might occur in a bioweapons attack, many of the parameters used in them emphasized only certain technological aspects and assumptions. More specifically, the smallpox exercises assumed very high person-to-person transmission rates; yet previous scientific studies have noted that smallpox transmission rates vary widely, depending on a variety of contextual factors.[131] J. Michael Lane, former director of the Centers for Disease Control and Prevention's smallpox eradication program, has noted, "People get desperately sick before they are able to transmit the virus. They're knocked off their feet with high fevers and severe muscle pains before they're contagious."[132] As a result, Lane argues that each patient generally transmits the disease to just one or two other people. The Atlantic Storm exercise also featured a dry-powder form of the smallpox virus—which neither the advanced U.S. nor Soviet bioweapons programs were able to produce. Finally, at their most fundamental levels, the simulations do not specify how terrorists would obtain the pathogen and cultivate or process it for release, nor do they outline the complicated logistics and planning required to conduct such an attack. Rather, the simulations describe bioweapons development and deployment as occurring in a *deus ex machina* fashion.

These simulations emphasized the potential of a mass-casualty bioweapons attack and the vulnerability of the United States to such attacks.[133] The vividness and potential of these exercises are conveyed through the participation of former U.S. and European government officials, visuals of scab-laden smallpox victims, maps and charts, late-breaking newsflashes of the growing number of bioweapons cases, and images or horrific descriptions of public violence and chaos in the wake of the outbreak. However, the simulations' designers failed to specify the actual mechanisms of bioweapons development. One author of the Atlantic Storm exercise has explained that it was not designed to take into account the complex and contingent aspects of biotechnology connected to bioweapons development and dissemination; rather, "The *Atlantic Storm* exercise was designed to provoke imagination and to prompt action by making the reality of a deliberately caused epidemic more vivid."[134] The simulations, through their material and visual qualities, have served to strengthen the biotech revolution frame and its associated technological threat narratives and technological policy responses.

These simulations have parallels with what historian of technology Sharon Ghamari-Tabrizi has described as the models and simulations that nuclear strategist Herman Kahn and his band of defense futurologists at the RAND Corporation used during the Cold War to understand how nuclear wars might be fought. Kahn and his colleagues employed analytic techniques such as systems analysis, Monte Carlo models, operations research, war-game simulations, and role-playing scenarios to create technological narratives about future nuclear war. Because nuclear war had never been fought, Kahn and his cohort argued for the need to conduct extravagant nuclear threat scenarios and simulations in order to flesh out "interesting possibilities." As Kahn argued, "The scenarios are not designed to describe 'most probable' or necessarily 'fairly likely' courses of events, although each is intended to be 'not impossible.' "[135] Ghamari-Tabrizi argues that, in this way, simulations, instead of being seen as rational, scientific planning tools (as they are often portrayed), should be viewed as a kind of aesthetic used to evoke powerful visual and sensory feelings from the telling of a particular kind of narrative about future security threats.[136] Similarly, one can see how analysts and officials have used simulations to also help animate an ominous biotechnological threat narrative.

Conclusion

In his analysis of narratives, literary philosopher M. M. Bakhtin described how all stories involve a particular "chronotope," a plot element that reflects "the intrinsic connectedness of temporal and spatial relationships."[137] To illustrate this concept, Bakhtin outlined a type of chronotope found in the romances of ancient Greece: A boy and girl of *marriageable age* meet *unexpectedly*; where they come from is *unknown* and *mysterious*. When they meet, a *sudden* and *instantaneous* passion flares up between them; however, they *cannot marry right away. Unexpectedly,* they are confronted with *obstacles* that *retard* and *delay* their union. The lovers are *parted,* and they go on extended *journeys* to *exotic countries* to try to find one another. In their travels, they encounter capture by *pirate ships* and *shipwrecks,* serve time in *prisons,* and suffer other maladies in *distant locales* before they once again find one another. The romance ends happily with the lovers, *no less fresh, young, and good-looking* and their love *absolutely unchanged,* united in marriage.[138] The emphasized words above illustrate the standard representations of time and space—the chronotope—that characterize this type of ancient Greek romance. The chronotope is what structures and advances the plot of the story.

The biotech revolution frame also forms a type of chronotope in technological narratives about bioweapons threats. For example, the dominant narrative has emphasized the *portability* and *accessibility* of bioweapons-related material, personnel, and equipment; it suggests that bioweapons technology is *easily transportable* and can be developed *in a variety of different contexts by diverse individuals, groups, and states.* It portrays potent bioweapons programs as being *easily hidden* in *small spaces* as well as *within larger, legitimate biological facilities* at a number of *varied locations.*

Bioweapons threats can *arise suddenly* and *unexpectedly*. Like the lovers in Bakhtin's Greek romances, bioweapons interest, development, and transfer by a variety of state and nonstate actors seems to go *unchanged* by specific issues or problems on the ground; the technological threat trajectory is always on the rise.

Peter Brooks writes that the power of narrative resides in its potential for summary and retransmission.[139] In looking at biothreat narratives reflected in various analytic and policy reports over the past twenty years, the central chronotope has remained largely consistent. Since the 1990s, the "enemy" in this narrative has shifted from specific actors in the real world (Iraq, Aum Shinrikyo, al-Qaeda) to a more generic set of possible malefactors that do not necessarily reside in the real world (biohackers, biological Unabombers) and potential enemies no longer tied to a specific person, group, or state but increasingly embodied in the technology itself (mutated mousepox viruses, synthetic genomes). Over time, biotechnologies have emerged as a central figure or protagonist in the narrative—actors difficult to see but always assumed to be present and on the move. With this technological narrative, predicting technological trends and thresholds has become the focal point of concern in analysis and policymaking. The recent emphasis in U.S. government policy on "science-based threat assessments" is a logical evolution of bioweapons threat assessment activities based on a biotech revolution frame, its chronotope, and its technological threat narrative.

Important visual and material elements are deployed, along with the discourse of the narrative. For example, visuals of common household items such as bags of sugar, a garden sprayer, and a vial of talcum powder have been used to illustrate the ease of developing and using biological weapons and their mass casualty potential. Bioweapons simulations and graphics of assumed biotechnology diffusion and trajectories have been used both to imagine and to assert the existence of threats stemming from advanced biotechnologies. Other material elements that have embodied and co-constructed the narrative include reports and books (government and nongovernment publications and briefings on advanced bioweapons threats, *The Cobra Event*) and bioweapons hardware (munitions, mock bioweapons facilities).

While this popular narrative "front-stages" certain material, visual, and discursive points, it also "back-stages" others.[140] More to the point, the difficulty, complexity, and capriciousness of working with bioweapons agents are excluded from this narrative. Historical and contextual understandings of past state-level and terrorist bioweapons programs are also marginalized. These front-staging and back-staging processes are also reflected in the visual and material elements chosen for public display and their description in the display. Therefore, although this narrative is grounded in real geopolitical events and material issues spanning nearly two decades, it also reflects particular interpretations and articulations of reality. The construction of this narrative is useful not only in the policy attention that it garners but also in the kinds of analytic focal points it emphasizes. By emphasizing imaginative simulations, for example, it does little analytic work to contextualize more rigorously how particular actors and contexts can shape bioweapons developments and activities.

The narrative's power in shaping analytic and policy attention is rooted in its construction and use in the unclassified and classified worlds through a variety of academic, media, public, and policy settings. Questions, discussions, and assessments about bioweapons threats in U.S. analytic and policy circles tend to concentrate on the technical and material characteristics comprising biotechnology or on the biological agent, process, or equipment in question, with set assumptions about technological trajectories and security impacts on society. The biotech revolution frame provides a rational, ordered way of explaining how biotechnology relates to bioweapons threats. At the same time, however, this frame leaves out important social dimensions that can modulate these technologies and their threats in critical ways and that are evident in historical examples of bioweapons programs and in contemporary examinations of biological work. Thus, this reliance on the biotech revolution frame for understanding bioweapons threats and animating threat narratives "will make perfect sense on its own terms, except for an inchoate sense that certain general classes of difficulties never seem to go away."[141]

In contrast to the technological determinism that structures this frame and narrative, the field of science and technology studies has illustrated, over the past thirty years, the importance of understanding the social context of scientific and technological work and its resulting products—of grasping that technologies and technological change are "social through-and-through."[142] As a result, technologies should be understood as intimately constructed within a particular social context. With this understanding, they can be defined not only as materials, hardware, or widgets but also as the knowledge, skills, practices, and tools involved in making or doing things. This more complex understanding suggests a very different frame for thinking about biology and biotechnology than that captured in the popular biotech revolution frame and its dominant narratives. As we will see in the following section, an alternative frame that moves away from the conceptual apparatus of technological determinism toward a more socially grounded explanation of biological work is a better tool for understanding biotechnology and its associated bioweapons threats.

PART TWO

SCIENCE IN A SOCIAL CONTEXT

OVERVIEW
The Biosocial Frame

> The major issue and problem was coordinating all of the seemingly unrelated entities and pieces of equipment to work as a relatively well-oiled machine.
>
> *Kanatjan Alibekov (Ken Alibek), bioweapons scientist*

> We use the same procedure always. What on paper is the same procedure, exactly the same procedure, and many times, most of the time it doesn't work and we just don't know why.
>
> *Aniko Paul, polio virologist*

> Technology is not about universality . . . it is about functioning in concrete, complex situations.
>
> *Brian Wynne, sociologist of technology*

Alibekov, Paul, and Wynne reveal a very different picture of biotechnology than that represented by the biotech revolution frame. Their perspectives form the foundation of an alternative technological frame for understanding biology and biotechnology—I call it the *biosocial frame*.[1] This frame is based on qualitative and quantitative empirical studies of scientific work and makes use of a detailed understanding of the skills, disciplines, organization, management, and other localized social practices that constitute the biological sciences and biotechnology. In doing so, the biosocial frame explores the more historically contingent and socially constructed character of biological work and products and the multiple, negotiated ways they might be developed and used. The explanatory power of this frame lies in its ability to describe the many historical state and nonstate bioweapons efforts and the particular ways these programs have developed or have failed to develop; it also provides a more robust and holistic way of understanding the bioweapons threats stemming from new biological experiments and biotechnologies.

Science in a Social Context

The biosocial frame offers a new lens through which to view technical work based on concepts within the sociology of science and technology, such as co-production, which examines how technical knowledge, work, and products are mutually constituted with a given social context. For scientific knowledge and technological artifacts to be successful, they must be made to fit their context, or else their context must be made to fit them. The process of adjusting pieces of science and technology and their contexts to each other is one of mutual production of the natural, the scientific, and the social. Under this view, science and technology are socially shaped, rather than an autonomously developing force with its own momentum. Therefore, scientific and technological trajectories are not assumed to be predictable or linear but rather multidirectional, depending on the context. Instead of focusing only on the purely material or technical, the biosocial frame pays close attention to the communities of scientific and technical practitioners involved in technical work. This approach involves studying laboratory experimental practices and related knowledge-generating activities, as well as larger laboratory organizational contexts, to understand how the construction of data, scientific work, and technologies is shaped by the skills, cultures, and routines within particular technical settings.

Features of the Biosocial Frame

With this perspective, the biosocial frame emphasizes: (1) the important role of know-how and other uncodified knowledge; (2) the local and contingent character of biological development and use; (3) the importance of understanding past biological work and end products; and (4) the multiple, negotiated biotechnological trajectories that are possible. In each of these areas, we can see important social aspects of biotechnology that challenge the reductionist focus of the biotech revolution frame. Analysts using the biosocial frame strive to unpack the know-how, laboratory practices, and local context that underpin science and technology. In assessments and public discussions about bioweapons threats derived from advances in biotechnology, an analyst using the biosocial frame would emphasize the need to contextualize how the technical work was actually carried out and to talk about the difficulties and failures in biological research that are part and parcel of the scientific enterprise. These insights would illustrate how social components can modulate the technological dimensions of bioweapons threats in powerful ways.

The Importance of Uncodified Knowledge

To begin with, an analyst using the biosocial frame, in addition to explicating the local and contingent character of biological development and use, focuses on the important role of uncodified knowledge. Through extensive ethnographic laboratory studies, scholars in the field of science and technology studies have described how the way science is done—its troublesome, contingent, and messy means of production—often differs from the clean and orderly public representations of scientific work codified in scientific publications and other written accounts.[2] As sociologist of science Karen Knorr-Cetina writes: "In the laboratory, scientific reasoning displays its concerns in savage purity. But in their papers, the savage reasoners of the laboratory seem to change their faith. . . . The scientific paper hides more than it tells on its tame and civilised surface. For one thing, it deliberately forgets much of what happened in the laboratory, although it purports to present a 'report' of that research."[3]

The Local, Contingent Character of Biological Development and Use

Various science studies scholars have described how science writing employs specific communication techniques and ways of representing data in order to remove aspects of contingency and agency from formal scientific publications.[4] For instance, sociologist of science Michael Lynch points out that although authors are listed on published scientific papers, specific individuals are not discussed in connection with the work, and laboratory procedures and results are described without reference to the person(s) who actually did the experiments. Lynch further notes how the use of the passive voice in publications contributes to the sense that the person conducting the experiment is either absent or irrelevant. In this manner, as Lynch writes, the work almost appears to be accomplished through autonomous means.[5] Much technical work, however, relies on particular types of local laboratory knowledge and specialized expertise that go undocumented in most scientific communications. By taking this point into account, the biosocial frame stresses the importance of examining the individuals involved in biological work and the way they are brought together and arranged to carry out specific tasks—even when those factors are not characterized in standard written accounts of the work.

Moreover, others in S&TS have shown how the standard abbreviated format for presenting scientific papers often means that only partial details of scientific work are presented; discussions of the difficulties, circuitous research paths, and experimental failures are often omitted. Thus, processes and results in scientific publications are selectively depicted in a sequential manner that seems to suggest that each part of the experiment naturally, easily, and directly follows from another, instead of representing the more convoluted and protracted way that experiments are normally designed and made to work.[6] Scientists often characterize the management of local problems as "not really science"; as a result, these details, seen as unimportant aspects of scientific work, are excluded from scientific papers.[7] Often, however, these mundane aspects of scientific work are critical to a successful result or end product. Thus, the writing conventions in science mask the important social work involved in the development of science and technology.

The process of constructing an orderly scientific account for scientific publications makes it very difficult to detect the various contingencies that were part and parcel of the final result or product.[8] S&TS scholar Bruno Latour explains that part of the obfuscation of messiness in research reports relates to the objectives of formal scientific communications. The aim of scientific papers is not to reproduce reports on the minutiae of what actually happened in the laboratory but to act on the literature and advance arguments on particular scientific hypotheses. Susan Leigh Star explains that in this way, published scientific results should really be understood as partial or schematic maps of the work actually done in the laboratory, rather than specific how-to guides or detailed "roadmaps."[9] With this in mind, an analyst using the biosocial frame, with its focus on the social and technical, strives to unpack the details of how the biological work was done and what difficulties, failures, and alternative paths were required to produce the end product or result.

Science studies scholars also focus on the important tacit dimensions of scientific practice that cannot be articulated in scientific communications. Karin Knorr-Cetina writes, "For every bit of published 'method' there seems to be a bit of unpublished know-how which not only reconstructs the recipe sequence of steps in the paper into that of feasible doings within the situational logic of laboratory action, but also provides routines for diagnosing and coping with many unspecified problems."[10] Any experimental scientist will acknowledge that the materials and methods sections of a paper rarely tell you all you need to know about the experiment. H. M. Collins writes that this missing knowledge involves, in part, various types of tacit knowledge related to various visual, sensory, and other unarticulated components and skills that are part and parcel of doing scientific work.[11] Collins argues that this type of know-how can only be transmitted either by watching how a particular procedure is done in an apprenticeship fashion or through a painstaking trial-and-error process of individual discovery. Furthermore, Lynch and others submit that, for particular step-by-step scientific methods sections to work, the authors of these sections assume an already competent practitioner who possesses the relevant know-how and the knowledgeable ability to troubleshoot and adapt the method to local circumstances.[12] Lynch, however, finds that for some scientific tasks, even highly skilled practitioners are not able to carry out a task without prior training in the specific lab that wrote the published technique.[13] This indicates an enduring role for local knowledge and specialized expertise in biological work, even with technological advances; an analyst using the biosocial frame seeks to elucidate the presence of these forms of knowledge in understanding bioweapons threats from life science publications.

On top of that, in contrast to the biotech revolution frame, which focuses on black-boxing technology, the biosocial frame brings important social dimensions to the conversation of how technologies are made to work. More specifically, Lynch has noted the technical difficulties that remain even when certain specialized molecular biology techniques are black-boxed into popular commercially available polymerase chain reaction (PCR) kits developed to streamline the amplification of DNA.[14] Lynch finds that these PCR kits failed to work in certain situations, necessitating specialized tacit knowledge or use of an alternative method in order to make the biological ingredients from scratch. This need for new troubleshooting and problem-solving, however, is not captured in the concepts and visual representations of black-boxed biotechnology. But these elements may be critical for getting a piece of technology to work. Although PCR kits are often referred to in bioweapons-related policy discussions to illustrate the ease with which biotechnological knowledge is becoming codified and standardized, Lynch's analysis reveals a more complex reality in practice. Analysts using the biosocial frame explore the various kinds and types of tacit knowledge that were involved in the development and use of a particular biological process, technique, product, or weapon—even those that seem, at first glance, to be standardized.

Along with these considerations of tacit knowledge, science studies scholars argue that we should take into account the locally situated and managed social factors involved in scientific work and its products. As S&TS scholar Brian Wynne argues: "Technology is not about universality . . . it is about functioning in concrete, complex situations. One key task of [technical] experts is to contextualize general ideas into working solutions in this or that situation. . . . The technology should embody some general principles (it should not work only by chance), because otherwise there is no reproducibility, or transportability to other contexts; but all concrete implementation of theoretical ideas or prototype technologies involves ad hoc adaptation to meet specific local factors."[15] This contextualization may involve only parts of the technology, but these parts may be critical to the functioning of the whole. In exploring the role of tacit knowledge in biological work, an analyst drawing on the biosocial frame asks what local circumstances and context contributed to the development of this biological knowledge.

As discussed above, the text in a scientific paper is framed to establish boundaries, by which certain kinds of technical issues and complications, as well as the dynamic and unwritten processes of research—such as acquisition of skill and judgment, craft activities, and troubleshooting strategies—are omitted from the discussion.[16] It is often difficult to judge, from reading or relying on the scientific paper alone, what pertinent information has been omitted; scientists themselves can often lose sight of how the contingencies are managed and represented in scientific communications.[17] By way of illustration, science studies scholar David Gooding explains how scientists can overlook the importance of their own scientific practices: "For experiments and instruments that work: they work in a particular world that has been ordered and prepared in ways that retrospective accounts hide from view. . . . As procedures and pathways are mastered, so the skills that enable them drop out of the account. They lose visibility as they are worked into the repertoire of the shared, taken-for-granted practices of a particular community."[18] Michael Lynch writes that noting the discrepancies between "real" lab work and written texts is not to fault the researchers for their insufficient detail but to remind us that it is important to interrogate the contextual features of successful laboratory work and how such work was designed and produced.[19] Analysts employing the biosocial frame seek to weigh the various contingencies that constitute a published scientific paper and to consider how these factors contribute to the successful outcome of the biological work. In taking into account the limitations of relying on codified knowledge and the importance of know-how, the biosocial frame illustrates the problems in obtaining accurate bioweapons assessments solely from reading a published scientific text or from focusing on material aspects of biotechnology.

In addition to the importance of know-how and the local, contingent character of biological work, the biosocial frame also emphasizes the need to think about other social dimensions that can shape biotechnology and how these can lead to multiple, negotiated bioscience and biotechnological trajectories. As an example, recent qualitative studies find that although biotechnology has had a profound effect on drug discovery and other types of basic biological research, the utility of discoveries diminishes as one moves down the development chain to more applied purposes. This diminishment is due to significant bottlenecks that have been found to emerge in the pharmaceutical and biotechnology industries along the biotech development path, which include both technical (for instance, the complexity of biological systems) and socio-organizational components that can constrain and structure the adoption of a new technology, often taking several decades to resolve. Interestingly, the ease of solving many of these bottlenecks has been largely unaffected by advances in biotechnology.[20] This is not to deny that certain biotechnology developments have yielded (and will continue to yield) successful applications, but one must also consider that advances in biotechnology introduce new aspects of complexity (involving important social components) that are not always easily resolved.

For instance, one biotech industry executive has emphasized the socio-organizational problems that can emerge over the course of the development process. One such problem is the sheer availability of information involved in developing a new biotechnology. In contrast to the biotech revolution frame's lauding of information availability and diffusion, this executive discusses the organizational problems that large quantities of information can pose: "One of the biggest enemies sometimes is just the sheer magnitude of these [biotech] projects. There's so much information. Sometimes the right answer or the solution to the problem is right under your nose but you can't see it because, you know, especially in year eight of a ten-year program, by then you're surrounded by mountains of data, and it isn't clear which piece to look at. It gets to be quite a problem."[21] Although specific organizational and management structures have been established to handle the information overload, this executive notes that even these structures do not remove all the challenges associated with managing and using such high volumes of information across the lifespan of a biotechnology project.

At the same time, financial or other organizational instabilities in the biotech industry, company, or project can lead to the loss of important, skilled workers who have been involved in developing a new biotechnology. The biotechnology executive adds: "Another huge problem that we sometimes have when the business environment gets a little unfriendly is you either have layoffs or you have hiring freezes and you know you have all these administrative interferences. You know you've got attrition of people and you can't place them and there can be significant knowledge lost in those kinds of environments. . . . Any kind of disruption is bad, and prolonged disruptions take their toll for sure. If you're lucky, you get to grab some of the original people . . . [but] the more time that intervenes, the less of your original team you get to pick. . . . Time and forgetfulness, you know, can really get in the way."[22] This executive emphasizes the importance of the long-term maintenance of trained personnel and the accumulated knowledge resident in those personnel for a biotechnology development. He also points to human nature as another social factor that can affect biotechnology development and the ability to bring a biotechnology innovation to market, noting, "You get the occasional person [scientist] who's just got some strange idea in their head and they sabotage the project. . . . I've seen one scientist sabotage the work of another scientist for who knows what reason. All the human failings that you know you imagine in the world creep into the lab and have some level of presence."[23]

These social dynamics, however, are not considered in the biotech revolution frame's technological assumptions and trajectories. There often is no mention of how lone biohackers, al-Qaeda terrorists, or rogue states would be affected by these kinds of work issues in their applications of new biotechnology advances for biological weapons. If these socio-organizational obstacles are mentioned at all, adherents of the biotech revolution frame assume that they can be easily overcome through money, dedication, and coercion. But the historical record clearly shows that socio-organizational challenges have negatively impacted past bioweapons development—and the remedies to fix these problems did not lie in money or inherent dedication to the project.[24] Analysts using the biosocial frame examine these socio-organizational issues to expose the potential hidden costs underlying the development of advanced biotechnologies for weapons or terrorist purposes.

The Acknowledgment and Understanding of Past Work

In addition, the biosocial frame challenges the biotech revolution frame's reliance on "revolutionary" assumptions in explaining technological development. Studies of contemporary biotech industries indicate that many significant biotechnology developments have emerged from incremental, evolutionary advances in science and technology, as opposed to unpredictable, disruptive changes. As one former biotech industry executive explains:

> What made Genentech great was not that you know they made quantum leaps every day, but there were a lot of little incremental improvements that we made, like cobbling a bunch of stuff together. So, for example, we had protein sequencing machines that were ten times more sensitive than what was commonly available off the shelf, because we had guys who knew the 20 or 30 things that these machines did and they took the machine apart and optimized each of 20 little steps and added one or two percent to each one. But, when you put it all back together again, it now worked ten times better than anybody else's machine. And we had a lot of ability to refine things and then put things together, sort of an integrative approach to things.[25]

Consistent with this executive's personal reflection, recent empirical studies of the biotech industry suggest that as biotechnology moves from the scientific bench to a more applied setting, it follows a well-established historical pattern of slow and incremental change and diffusion, consistent with other major technologies.[26] In explaining this pattern, biotechnology expert Paul Nightingale argues that the production of new technology, instead of simply resulting from a passive linear outflow of science, requires the active *construction* of predictability in how people, technology, resources, and infrastructure are brought together for a particular applied purpose.[27] Nightingale argues that this construction involves a dedicated attention and commitment to addressing the varied sociotechnical complexities and contingencies that arise at the micro and macro levels in biotechnology development.

These studies suggest that the popular biotech revolution frame for thinking about biotechnology is an incomplete basis for policymaking, because it overestimates the scale, scope, and speed of changes in biotechnologies and their possible applications while underestimating their difficult, costly, and time-consuming nature. The focus on high technology can also underestimate certain threats that can come from older evolutionary technologies and techniques. Thus, instead of depicting bioweapons threat trajectories disconnected from the past, analysts working with the biosocial frame explore the technological continuities that still exist. This approach analyzes more basic or standardized biotechnologies and how they could be adopted, integrated, and used, rather than focusing exclusively on new and advanced biotechnological threats.

In addition, the biosocial frame considers the user and examines how terrorists or states choose and use technologies for weapons purposes. Sociologists of science Trevor Pinch and Wiebe Bijker have noted that technologies (and the materials associated with the construction of these technologies) have interpretive flexibility, meaning that different social groups can bring different meanings and decisions to their design, construction, and use.[28] A narrow focus on the availability of a particular material or technology fails to capture the contingency that can be involved in its development and application. As stated in chapter 2, we know that the Japanese terrorist group Aum Shinrikyo purchased a PCR machine, but instead of utilizing it for bioterrorism purposes, the group used the machine to amplify DNA for religious activities. Thus, a piece of biotechnology can be chosen for particular uses; the biosocial frame explores the interpretive flexibility of a given technological object among its different users.

Table O.1 provides a succinct reference point for comparing and contrasting the biotech revolution and biosocial frames. While the biotech revolution frame

TABLE O.1
Two different biotechnological framings

Biotech revolution frame	Biosocial frame
Focus on material aspects of biotechnology	Focus on sociotechnical aspects of biotechnology
• Materials, equipment	• Materials and equipment with emphasis on use in communities of scientific and technological practice
• Physical infrastructure	• Socio-organizational infrastructure
• Codified knowledge	• Tacit knowledge
• Simplicity	• Complexity
• Successful end products	• Problems, troubleshooting, and failures on the way to the end product
Temporal and spatial orientation	Temporal and spatial orientation
• Future-looking	• Future not privileged
• Assumes ease of diffusion, routinization	• Assumes challenges in diffusion, routinization
• Assumes increasing pace of growth and diffusion of biotechnology	• Assumes bottlenecks can affect pace of growth and diffusion of biotechnology
• Globalization	• Local specificity
Linear, exponential technological and bioweapons threat trajectories	Varying technological and bioweapons threat trajectories
Increasing pace and momentum	Varying pace and momentum
Technological imperatives	Interpretive flexibility
Assumes potentially disruptive character of biotechnology increases the bioweapons threat	Assumes potentially disruptive character of biotechnologies is modulated by the sociotechnical elements listed above; does not necessarily increase the bioweapons threat

has a material focus, an analyst using the biosocial frame gives more attention to the social component of biotechnology and examines how it is co-constructed with the technical. Through this lens, we can see how the sociotechnical context of biotechnology development infuses and shapes the ways in which materials and infrastructure are used and how experiments and technological developments are structured and carried out. This approach looks at more qualitative aspects of biotechnology, such as development of laboratory skills and disciplines; constitution and maintenance of communities of scientific practice; organizational structures and institutions; contingency and complexity of laboratory work; and local contextual features. This approach is complementary to that of biotechnology scholars Caitriona McLeish and Paul Nightingale, who argue that technology should be understood as stemming from physical artifacts embedded in wider sociotechnical regimes and socially distributed bodies of knowledge.[29]

Multiple Biotechnological Trajectories

The biosocial frame makes certain assumptions and conceptualizations that differ from those of the biotech revolution frame. In its temporal orientation, the biosocial frame does not privilege a future orientation but grounds itself in understanding past and present scientific practices and biotechnological developments. In doing so, it does not assume that developments in biotechnology will inevitably follow a globalized and diffused pattern but recognizes that local and social components shape (and frustrate) standardization, routinization, and diffusion of biotechnologies. And, in allowing for social factors to help shape biotechnology, this approach anticipates varying technology and threat trajectories across dual-use biotechnologies. Finally, this frame considers that, although certain biotechnologies can emerge unexpectedly, their applicability to terrorism is modulated by the overarching social dimension of biotechnology.

The biosocial frame shows how using the tools of the science and technology studies discipline can help analysts better understand and illuminate the social context surrounding bioweapons threats. Although existing U.S. government threat assessments do utilize specific intelligence information regarding particular adversaries and their intentions, motivations, and capabilities, they fail to capture adequately the sociotechnical interaction described here. My interviews with high-level U.S. government officials and examination of reports suggest that current analyses focus primarily on specific agents and other technological end products.[30] A biosocial frame would better elucidate why known bioterrorists such as Aum Shinrikyo and al-Qaeda were unable to create a workable biological weapon, even though they had the relevant expertise, resources, time, and infrastructure at their disposal. A biosocial frame also helps elucidate how and why different state bioweapons programs (for example, the Soviet Union and Iraq) progressed as they did; it also helps explain the social dimensions in the replication and diffusion of new biotechnologies. As I illustrate in the next two chapters, a more nuanced understanding of the social dimensions of these varied weapons development efforts and new biological developments could help reveal the sociotechnical bottlenecks that remain for current and future bioweapons threats.

Chapters 3 and 4 present in-depth case studies that use the biosocial frame to examine and evaluate bioweapons threats. Chapter 3 examines the case of synthetic genomics by looking at two controversial biological experiments that generated security concerns among U.S. analysts and policymakers. The biosocial frame makes clear the importance of considering know-how and laboratory culture in evaluating bioterrorism threats from biological work. In looking at state-level bioweapons threats, chapter 4 describes the important socio-organizational factors comprising the development of the Soviets' anthrax biological weapon and illustrates how the biosocial frame brings to the fore new ways to evaluate proliferation concerns that persist from the former Soviet bioweapons program.

Synthetic Genomics, the Biotech Revolution, and Bioterrorism

> The scientific paper hides more than it tells on its tame and civilised surface.
>
> *Karin Knorr-Cetina,* The Manufacture of Knowledge

Following the September 11 attacks and the growing concern over the bioterrorism threats posed by dual-use biotechnology, several governmental and nongovernmental communities have begun to focus on the emerging scientific field of synthetic genomics.[1] Synthetic genomics focuses on the development of biological techniques and approaches to synthesize artificially biological components and/or organisms. Although scientists have been able to synthesize small pieces of DNA chemically since the early 1970s, advances in molecular biology, computational biology, chemistry, and engineering have enabled the synthesis of larger and more complex biological materials (genes, genomes, viruses, and so on) from chemicals and other materials without the need for original "natural" components. Scientists are interested in using these artificial genomes for basic research and applied purposes. For example, some scientists are exploring whether some of these new artificially constructed microbes could be used to produce alternative fuels or more efficient processes for pharmaceutical developments.[2]

Security concerns about the field of synthetic genomics arose after the publication of a 2002 *Science* article that described how virologist Eckard Wimmer and members of his research group artificially synthesized poliovirus.[3] The original idea for this synthesis project was based on Wimmer's longstanding intellectual interest in whether viruses could be considered "living" species, as they require a host for survival. Thus, basic research questions drove the concept of this experimental work. Yet, after its publication in the open scientific literature, the U.S. policy community raised concerns about whether terrorists might pick up the experimental details and use them to create a virus for a bioweapons attack. With these concerns, Florida Congressman David Weldon proposed House Resolution 514, which denounced the poliovirus researchers and the publisher of *Science,* citing risks to U.S. national security because such an experiment was "a blueprint that could conceivably enable terrorists to inexpensively create human pathogens for release on the people of the United States."[4]

In December 2003, a mere eighteen months after publication of the poliovirus experiment, researchers from the J. Craig Venter Institute published an alternative method for artificially synthesizing another genome, that of the φX174 bacteriophage.[5] In contrast to Wimmer's group, which took three years to produce its synthetic poliovirus, the Venter method appeared to be a faster and simpler way to produce an infectious genome because it took only two weeks and dispensed with the need for several laborious and time-consuming cloning and sequencing steps across the experiment. At the time of the φX174 (also known as "phiX") bacteriophage publication, policymakers raised similar concerns about the presumed adaptability of the Venter protocol to synthesize larger genomes. A front-page article in the *Washington Post* in July 2006, titled "Custom-Built Pathogens Raise Bioterror Fears," emphasized the ease with which terrorists or criminals could take commercially available materials and apply these new synthetic genomics techniques to reconstitute dangerous pathogens or to create novel ones.[6]

Over the past eight years, both the Venter and Wimmer experiments have been invoked as early harbingers of the new and dangerous future involving synthetic genomics for bioterrorism. In policy discussions, attention has focused on the ubiquity of commercial DNA and gene synthesis materials and technologies and the stepwise process for genome construction, the need to screen for dangerous applications of these materials, and the future security risks from these materials and technologies.[7] As described in chapter 2, these concerns reflect the biotech revolution frame, which focuses on material and other tangible aspects of biotechnology that can travel and be used easily. This frame also assumes a linear or exponential trajectory of these technological advances and their resulting security threats.

The biotech revolution frame, however, provides an incomplete basis for evaluating the security threats posed by synthetic genomics. To demonstrate this frame's limitations, set against the strength of the biosocial frame, this chapter revisits the controversial poliovirus and phiX experiments. Through interviews with the scientists involved in the experiments, I will show how a detailed, microlevel analysis of "what went on in the lab" illuminates important sociotechnical factors that challenge the biotech revolution assumptions and technological frame underpinning the public and policy understandings of synthetic genomics experiments. This chapter will show that experimental success in the poliovirus and phiX synthetic protocols rested not simply on buying commercial DNA and following the published protocol. Instead, experimental success in both experiments also involved mastering seemingly mundane yet tacit biological techniques and laboratory disciplines as well as incorporating specific types of expert knowledge to achieve narrowly defined scientific goals. Thus, rather than being revolutionary, both experiments followed much more contingent and evolutionary processes that involve the important social components accounted for in the biosocial frame.

With these findings, however, I am not arguing that the specific conclusions from these two experiments should be assumed to apply to all types of gene synthesis work. Rather, the aim of this chapter is to argue for the need to examine, at a micro level, the social context and relationships that comprise scientific and technological work and the complex practices and timescales that contextualize the replication and transfer of these techniques, even in cases where the science or technology in question seems (or is claimed) to be easily standardized, accessible, and transferable. As sociologists of science Nigel Gilbert and Michael Mulkay have long noted, the public and private discourses on science are very different; only the private discourse reflects the varied, contingent, and messy character that constitutes the social character of scientific work.[8] As a result, scientific publications, presentations, and other formal, codified scientific knowledge involve much that is not articulated. Therefore, understanding the private, micro-level practices that underpin scientific and technological work is critical to evaluating the nontrivial social aspects that can shape the development and transfer of new biotechnologies for terrorism. This chapter closes with suggestions for an alternative approach to evaluating the bioweapons threat from synthetic genomics that takes into account the social context of scientific work; this approach could also be used to improve bioweapons assessments from other types of dual-use or emerging technologies.

The 2002 Poliovirus Synthesis: A Brief Experimental Overview

To understand the scientific background of the work, we begin with some key aspects of the poliovirus synthesis experiment. The poliovirus is a small (~7,500 nucleotides long) ribonucleic acid (RNA) virus. RNA viruses have ribonucleic acid in their genome, in contrast to deoxyribonucleic acid (DNA) viruses—like the smallpox virus—which contain DNA in their genome. Poliovirus is one of the best-characterized viruses, since its X-ray crystal structure and RNA sequence have been known for more than twenty years, and the chemical composition of the virus

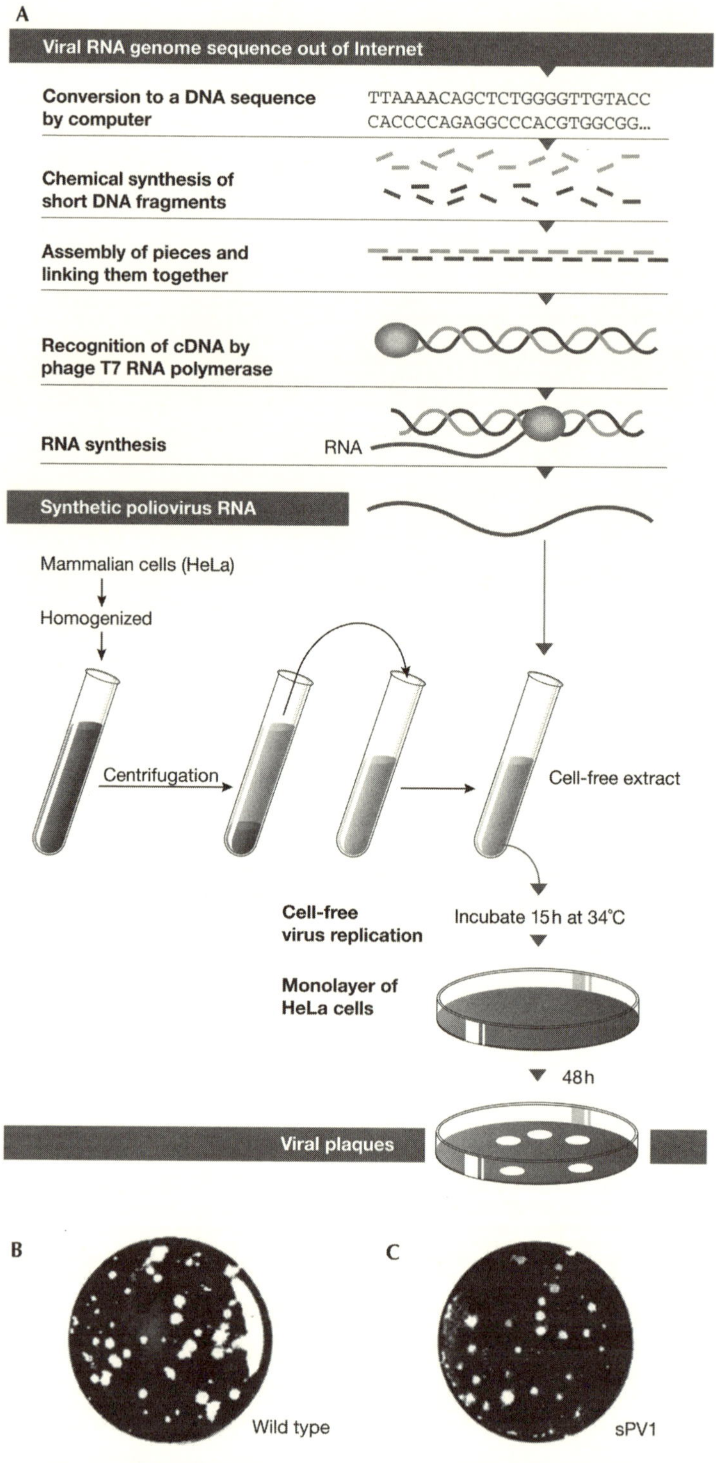

Fig. 3.1. Artificial synthesis of the poliovirus. From Wimmer, "Test-Tube Synthesis." Reprinted by permission from Macmillan Publishers Ltd: EMBO Reports, copyright 2006.

has been known for fifteen years.[9] Interestingly, the same research group that conducted the controversial 2002 experiment had already artificially synthesized poliovirus eleven years earlier. In 1991, Professor Eckard Wimmer and his colleagues from the State University of New York at Stony Brook became the first to synthesize the poliovirus outside a host, using RNA obtained from the natural, wild-type virus (from their own poliovirus collection) and mixing it with HeLa cell–free cytoplasmic extracts.[10] HeLa cell–free cytoplasmic extract is derived from HeLa cells, which are a type of human cancer cell. The extracts of HeLa cells contain the cytoplasm, cellular proteins, organelles (for instance, ribosomes), and important chemicals; however, the nuclei, mitochondria, and some other cellular organelles have been removed. For the controversial 2002 *Science* paper, Wimmer's lab took the 1991 experiment protocol one step further and did not use any natural virus or natural viral components.

Instead, the 2002 synthesis protocol began with the researchers obtaining the published poliovirus RNA genome sequence information from an Internet database (fig. 3.1).[11] Because RNA is too chemically unstable to synthesize directly, the researchers used a computer program to convert the polio RNA sequence data to its complementary DNA sequence data (allowing them to reverse-engineer the poliovirus genome from this more stable DNA sequence). With the computer-generated DNA sequence information, the researchers then ordered small pieces of DNA representative of this sequence from a commercial DNA synthesis company.

Using common molecular biology techniques, they stitched these small DNA pieces together to create a long DNA strand. Then they added a particular enzyme to the DNA, which would catalyze RNA synthesis (that is, transcription). This reaction produced the full-length "synthetic" RNA of the poliovirus. To create the fully intact virus, the researchers put the synthetic RNA into the same type of mammalian HeLa cell–free cytoplasmic extract used in their 1991 synthesis experiment. This extract provided specific nutrients and catalyzed the formation of additional proteins for translation (viral replication), encapsidation (the process by which a virus's nucleic acid is enclosed in a protein shell, called a capsid), and final assembly of the completed virus. The result was an intact, infectious poliovirus.

The Devil in the Details: Extract-Making and Contingency in Viral Synthesis

Conceptually, the artificial synthesis experiment was developed by Eckard Wimmer, the principal investigator on the project, and Aniko Paul, an associate professor of research, both of whom had worked on the 1991 poliovirus synthesis experiment.

Soon after receiving the grant to help fund the project, the Wimmer lab added a new postdoc, Jeronimo Cello. Cello was an immunologist by training, so he provided expertise in working with transgenic mice, which would be helpful with poliovirus experiments involving animal models. Cello, however, did not have experience with certain molecular biology techniques used in the Wimmer lab. Therefore, at the outset, Cello worked for about a month with Paul to learn molecular biology techniques such as growing bacteria, cloning, sequencing, using restriction enzymes, and preparing HeLa cells. After this initial training period, Cello and Paul spent approximately six months working out the optimal and most efficient way to carry out the artificial synthesis, which involved a consideration of various design strategies for merging the small pieces of commercial DNA, for selection of appropriate enzymes, and for other experimental factors.

As the bottom of figure 3.1 illustrates, moreover, the experiment involved the preparation and use of the HeLa cell–free cytoplasmic extracts. There are several published protocols for the preparation of these extracts, some dating back more than twenty years.[12] The Wimmer lab followed an extract protocol modified by a previous postdoc who had been involved in the Wimmer lab's 1991 synthesis experiment.[13] To summarize their extract procedure briefly, they grew HeLa cells in cell culture, a complex process by which cells are grown in specially designed containers under controlled conditions. Next, they removed the HeLa cells from the cell culture, put them on ice, and then broke them with a Dounce homogenizer—a tool used to break the cells mechanically. Following this step, the researchers removed nuclei and other cellular components in the HeLa cells by centrifugation. Then they dialyzed the resulting liquid, which was the HeLa cell–free cytoplasmic extract, recentrifuged it, and stored it in a low-temperature freezer until needed for the experiment.

Although seemingly straightforward on paper, making good HeLa cell–free extracts to support the replication and encapsidation and assembly steps of the artificial synthesis was one of the most difficult parts of the 2002 poliovirus experiment.[14] As Aniko Paul explains:

> What makes it difficult is that [extracts are] highly irreproducible. . . . You can take HeLa cells and make them today and they will work fine . . . and you can take HeLa cells tomorrow and I would say that the likelihood that they don't work is more likely than the likelihood that they do work. . . . Translations [protein synthesis] always work with these extracts, but you don't always get virus and we don't really understand why. . . . We have tried a variety of different things to try and figure it out. It must have something obviously to do with the

> HeLa cells. In my personal opinion, it is not the [viral] replication, but it is the [viral] encapsidation. . . . Maybe it requires something that is possibly lost during making the [HeLa cell–free] extract. . . . It is not only a problem for us, it is a problem for anybody who works with the system. . . . If you've got one [extract] that doesn't work, it will never work.[15]

In spite of the apparent difficulty of this technique, the materials and methods section of the 2002 *Science* paper gives no indication of this contingency: "Transcript RNA derived from sPVM cDNA and virion RNA derived from wt PV1(M) were purified by phenol-chloroform extraction and ethanol precipitation, translated in the presence of [35S] Translabel (ICN Biochemicals) and processed at 34C in HeLa cell free extracts for 15 hours, as described previously (S6)."[16] The S6 footnote refers to the Paul-Wimmer lab's 1991 published synthesis paper, which describes the extract prep in detailed, step-by-step instructions, including warnings about the need to control in a specific way the pH and concentrations of the viral RNA and magnesium.[17] In the text of the paper, however, the authors concede that they had noted considerable variation in translation, the ability of the RNA to make protein, and virus formation when using different cell extracts. They cannot fully explain these variations but speculate that "it is possible that limiting factors for translation or for viral replication (or both) in the extract may vary in their abundance and activity, dependent on extract preparation."[18]

To understand some of the potential variations in HeLa cell–free extract preparation, I asked Paul for additional details and clarification on the procedure. She explained that although the lab has previously attempted various control experiments using different materials and conditions involved in the extract preparation, the researchers still do not understand the exact cause of variability: "We tried a variety of methods way back when we first published in 1991. We kind of feel that it has something to do with the state of the cell, but we don't understand what is the variability. . . . You can make an extract one day and it works, and then the next day, the same cell and the same reagent, and the same everything, will not work."[19]

In fact, Paul estimated that only about one in four batches of extract made in the lab turns out to be good.[20] Although it takes only about a day to make the extracts, it takes about a week of experimental work to determine whether the extract is able to make the virus. If it is not, Paul says, the whole process must be repeated: "All you can do is make a new one. . . . We use the same procedure always. What's on paper is the same procedure, exactly the same procedure, and many times, most of the time, it doesn't work and we just don't know why."[21] Paul adds it is hard to judge how long it will take to make a good extract—several months of work, if not years, if the underlying, unknown problem persists. It is important to note that Paul is an experienced poliovirus researcher who has worked in the Wimmer lab for more than twenty years and carried out important parts of the lab's first successful artificial poliovirus synthesis experiment in 1991, which pioneered the use of HeLa cell–free extracts for natural viral synthesis.

Other polio virologists also cite the contingency of working with HeLa cell–free extracts. One polio virologist who developed one of the first HeLa cell–free extract protocols for poliovirus work agrees that "there is more variability in the end product [HeLa cell–free extract] than I know how to explain from the paper protocol."[22] This polio virologist said that her lab can go for two years making good extract, and then for some reason, one day the viral RNA from their extract preps doesn't work. When new students join her lab, she walks them through the protocol and tells them to try it out several times, but then says to them, "When you have bowed three times to the East or West before putting it in the centrifuge . . . and done your penance before God, She will allow you to make a good extract."[23] Although there are several detailed methods papers and protocols available that describe this procedure in stepwise fashion and various labs have attempted to do various control experiments, making the HeLa cell–free cytoplasmic extracts remains a contingent process.

Contingencies and Laboratory Know-How in Artificial Poliovirus Synthesis

To understand the laboratory techniques involved in the Wimmer synthesis experiment, I interviewed three other polio virologists: Ellie Ehrenfeld, J. Bert Flanegan, and David Barton. Ehrenfeld is head of the Picornavirus Replication Section, Laboratory of Infectious Diseases at the U.S. National Institutes of Health. Flanegan is chairman of the Department of Biochemistry and Molecular Biology at the University of Florida at Gainesville. Barton is an associate professor in the Department of Molecular Biology at the University of Colorado at Denver and received training as a postdoctoral fellow in Flanegan's lab. Ehrenfeld has collaborated with both the Wimmer and Flanegan labs on poliovirus experiments; Barton and Flanegan are considered competitors of the Wimmer lab. Using experimental techniques, equipment, and materials very similar to those in the Wimmer lab, these scientists specialize in studying the various stages of the poliovirus life cycle.

Paul and the other polio virologists interviewed hypothesize that most problems with the poliovirus synthesis experiment involve various factors that affect: (1) the "state" of the HeLa cells during their growth and subsequent preparation into extracts; and (2) the preparation of the RNA used in the synthesis reactions. These investigators have developed particular types of laboratory know-how and disciplines to try to manage these contingencies. For example, all four polio virologists interviewed described the importance of "loving the cells" and keeping them "happy" during their growth phase to yield good extract. The scientists use these phrases as euphemisms for ensuring that the HeLa cells have adequate nutrients and appropriate growth conditions. All of these labs have developed laboratory-specific protocols for how they grow their HeLa cells.

Paul speculates that the problems associated with the growth phase of the cells may originate with specific sera used to grow the HeLa cells, as well as the cell passaging (how cells are transferred to a new vessel during their growth).[24] Fetal bovine serum is used to grow the HeLa cells for poliovirus synthesis.[25] Paul says, however, that she has found variability among the bovine sera sourced from different companies: "That is part of the problem. In the past we used to have one company that supplied us, and we knew exactly how much to add. And now the companies are continuously being bought up and changed."[26] These external commercial changes affect work in the lab, Paul says, because "we make an extract and use it for a year, and then a year later we try to go back and now the company is out of business, the company has a different batch, or a different method of making the serum, so that contributes to the state of the cells."[27] She suspects that variation in serum preparation across different companies affects the composition of various factors (minerals, nutrients, and so on) within the cytoplasm of the cells that are important for making good extracts. Interestingly, Ehrenfeld says that her lab has noticed changes in the quality of the serum with the change in the seasons. She speculates that the cows from which the bovine fetal serum is harvested may be eating different foods during the different seasons, which can alter the content of various nutrients, hormones, and chemicals within the serum and thus affect HeLa cell growth.[28]

Paul said the frequency of cell passaging during the growth phase is another likely contributing factor in keeping the HeLa cells "happy." The Wimmer lab has developed particular procedures they believe are necessary to produce good extracts. Those procedures include storing the cells in liquid nitrogen and using the freshest cells available—ones the lab thaws and then grows to the needed concentration. "If they are passaged for a week or two, which normally you can easily do, the extracts will definitely not work," Paul says.[29] Because of the need for keen attention to the passaging process, Flanegan maintains that keeping the cells "happy" is more reliably done within individual labs, rather than farming out HeLa cell growth to commercial labs or centralized tissue culture facilities.[30] Barton also emphasizes this point, explaining that such facilities may have frequent staff turnovers that can affect not only the types of reagents purchased but also the method of cell preparation, which can affect the state of the HeLa cells.[31]

With respect to the subsequent extract preparation after the HeLa cell growth phase, Paul mentioned several other potential problems: (1) the use of a Dounce homogenizer; (2) the presence of nucleases (enzymes that degrade proteins); and (3) variations in water composition. The Dounce homogenizer used for the experiment is a specialized glass tube with a pestle that fits into it (fig. 3.2). For the homogenizing technique, the HeLa cells are placed into the glass tube and the pestle is moved up and down to break the HeLa cells open gently and release the cytoplasmic extract—a process Paul describes as an art, in which the cells must be broken up just enough, but not too much.[32] "This douncing is the tricky part of the whole thing," Paul said.[33]

Burt Flanegan further elaborates on the "art" of using the Dounce:

> When you pull on a piston part of the Dounce homogenizer, that creates a vacuum, and the cells explode because they swell. . . . If you pull really slow on that you don't create much of a vacuum and so you don't break the cells very efficiently . . . [but] you can actually pull on the piston part so hard that you can actually break the bottom out of the Dounce out. I have had students who have started in the lab and if they are real gentle in terms of just barely pulling back on it, well they don't break the cells, so they have had trouble making a working extract. If the cells are still intact, then you either didn't do enough strokes or you didn't pull hard enough, or a combination of those two things. There is definitely some technique in that, in terms of learning how many strokes do you do and how hard do you pull. . . . But that *is* something that is harder to read from the text of a paper and really appreciate.[34]

If the HeLa cells are broken up too much with the pestle, important cellular components, such as ribosomes and other membranes that are needed for translation and viral synthesis, may be destroyed. On the other hand, if the cells are not broken up enough, the ribosomes may not be released from the cell and may be eliminated when the cells are subsequently centrifuged. David Barton says the process becomes intuitive: "All of this should feel the right way and look the right way. . . . There are any number of physical, visual, and sensory cues like that that you can pay attention to as you work through things, everything from looking at your bottles and making sure there is no contamination from your media and water solutions, salts coming out of solution, and anything else that doesn't look right."[35] Ellie Ehrenfeld says the Dounce may even respond differently to different

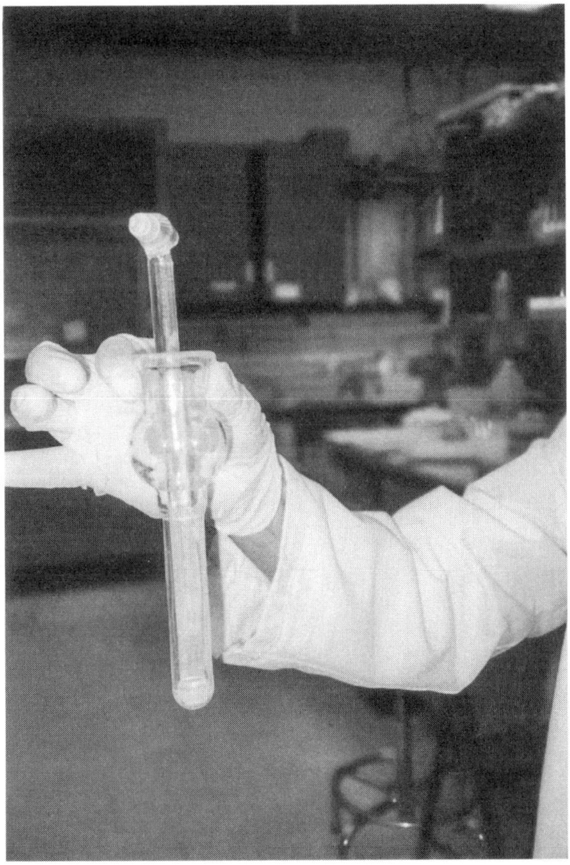

Fig. 3.2. Dounce homogenizer used in Wimmer lab. Kathleen Vogel.

people's touch: "Do big strong men only have to dounce ten times versus me who has to dounce fifteen times? Maybe."[36]

Although a Dounce homogenizer is a standard tool for cell culture work, Ehrenfeld said every lab has its own Dounce, which may be purchased or machined from different suppliers; these Dounces also come in different degrees of tightness between the mortar and pestle components. Due to variations in these Dounces, the exact number of strokes it takes to break a given number of cells needs to be empirically determined in each lab, through a trial-and-error process. Because of this, both Ehrenfeld and Flanegan said that they are very particular about the homogenizers they use and always use the same Dounce, if possible.[37] Moreover, time is of the essence. Ehrenfeld does not recommend being too cautious by slowly douncing and frequently checking the cells under the microscope when making real extract, because that requires removing the HeLa cells from an ice bath, which can cause the cells or other important cellular proteins to heat up and degrade. Ehrenfeld said it is preferable to make the extract quickly and keep it cold, which involves learning how to "sense" the appropriate number of dounces for a particular cell type.[38]

In addition to the state of the cells, Paul mentioned additional factors in the preparation of extracts that might affect viral synthesis: the presence of nucleases and variability in water used in the reagents. A nuclease, which is an enzyme, is added to the extract after the dounce step in order to degrade endogenous HeLa cell RNAs. This step is important because after douncing, HeLa cell RNAs are present in the extract. If these HeLa cell RNAs are not destroyed, they will be mixed with the viral RNA during the translation reaction, and it will be impossible to differentiate the polio-specific protein. Therefore, the nuclease is added to the extract (before addition of viral RNA) to degrade all of the HeLa cell RNAs. As with the fetal bovine sera, however, changes in commercial suppliers can also affect the quality of the nuclease used.

In using this nuclease, care must be taken even after the HeLa cell RNAs are degraded. The nuclease must be deactivated in the extracts or it will degrade the viral RNA that is subsequently added. Since this nuclease is an enzyme that requires metal binding for catalytic activity, typically a metal-binding agent is added to the extract after the HeLa RNAs are degraded. This agent binds the metals away from the nuclease, thereby inhibiting the nuclease's ability to break down viral RNA. If not enough binding agent is used, the enzyme will still be active and degrade the viral RNA when it is added. Since making the virus requires a sequential stepwise process from translation through final virus assembly, if viral RNA degradation occurs at any stage in that process, no RNA or virus will be produced. Thus, even with a standard reagent, such as the nuclease that must be added in the experiment, care must be taken in when, how, and how much of the reagent is used at various stages.

As for the possible variability in water composition and its effect on extracts, Paul describes the case of a Belgian graduate student who successfully made extracts with somebody in the Wimmer lab but could never make them when he returned home to Belgium—which led to speculation that the water might be different.[39] Ehrenfeld explains that water variability can be a factor, since its pH and mineral content vary across laboratories, even with those that use water filtration and distillation.[40] This variability could then affect the quality of reagents or solutions used in the experiment, which in turn could affect the growth of the HeLa cells or their subsequent processing. More specifically, Ehrenfeld described a five-month period in which her lab was unable to make good extracts for translation experiments. First, she assigned a technician to carry out a variety of control experiments consisting of different RNAs, reagents, and extracts, none of which provided a consistent answer to the problem. She then decided to seek outside help and sent one of her postdocs to Burt Flanegan's lab to compare that lab's RNA samples, solutions, and extracts. As a result, Ehrenfeld threw out all her lab's extracts and solutions and remade them using a different water source, which appeared to solve the problem.[41]

In addition to the extract preparation, the scientists mentioned other potentially important sources of error affecting the translation, replication, and viral synthesis steps: (1) RNA quality; and (2) salt concentrations. Paul, Ehrenfeld, and Flanegan all mentioned that quality of RNA is extremely important for making good translations, because RNA is inherently unstable and can easily degrade in the presence of nucleases, warm temperatures, or variations in pH.[42] For example, Flanegan described how a worker in his lab must take great care to avoid getting contaminants into his or her RNA samples:

> Most molecular biology labs are used to just working with DNA. And, you have to be quite a bit more aggressive about protecting the RNA samples themselves against ribonuclease [enzyme]. . . . For example, just on the tip of your finger . . . you would have enough ribonuclease to degrade all the RNA in your sample. . . . You have to learn how to work with it . . . obviously if the RNA is degraded or not prepared properly and then you add that to an extract, well you are not going to see much virus produced . . . and so that is another mistake that I'm sure that a lot of labs are making is that their RNA samples are not what they should be. . . . So they may have a decent extract, but if the RNA isn't good, they are not going to see much happen in terms of replication.[43]

Flanegan further explains how even if RNA is produced, there still could be problems if the subsequent processing is not carried out correctly: "It [RNA] may look okay on a gel [electrophoresis], but it may not be folded correctly. That is another very, very important part of the protocol. If you don't have a good preparation of RNA, if it's not purified from the salts present in the T7 transcription reaction [the process of creating a complementary RNA copy of a sequence of DNA] . . . you are not going to see much happen. You have to pay attention to detail. And you have to do that properly, you can't just skip that or do it a different way and assume that you will get the same result."[44]

Ehrenfeld and Barton discussed the importance of the salt concentrations present during the translation and viral synthesis steps. Barton believes that the concentration of magnesium salt is critical for these steps. He cites the Wimmer lab's 1991 *Science* paper, which documented the sensitivity of poliovirus RNA translation to variations in magnesium salt concentration. Barton explains that it can be difficult, however, to control completely the concentration of the magnesium salts in extracts, since some of the magnesium is endogenous, coming from the HeLa cells themselves. With the endogenous magnesium, there can be variations in its concentration, depending on how "happy" the HeLa cells were during their growth phase. On top of that, the addition of nucleotides as part of the experiment can also affect the concentration of magnesium. Nucleotides, which can be added either endogenously or exogenously, bind magnesium, thereby removing the metal from the solution. If too many nucleotides are present in the extract solution, too much magnesium becomes bound, which in turn can inhibit translation.[45] Interestingly, Paul describes how her lab has managed to control the problem of variability in salt concentrations by incorporating a dialysis step as part of the extract preparation.[46] Both Barton and Paul emphasize the interconnected and sensitive nature of the HeLa cell growth with quantities of nucleotides and magnesium within the cells and extract solution and how these factors affect viral synthesis.

Managing the Contingencies: The Importance of Laboratory Disciplines

Historian of science Hannah Landecker has argued that examining laboratory practices reveals both "the material thing and the field of knowledge produced by work with that thing."[47] As described above, all the scientists interviewed acknowledged a variety of contingencies and particular laboratory practices that can influence the preparation of a good HeLa cell–free extract. In addition, they also describe certain laboratory disciplines that have been inculcated within their labs, which play an important role in managing the contingencies in order to make HeLa cell–free extracts on a more reliable basis. These disciplines include: (1) maintaining "sameness" in the lab; (2) continual preparation of extract; and (3) diligence and attention to detail, and they appear to be developed through intentional and sustained pedagogical practices within these particular laboratories as well as through a self-selection process by individual researchers.

In my interviews, the virologists often referred to the importance of maintaining "sameness" in their labs, which is reflected in the materials, equipment, and protocols used as well as the staff employed.[48] More specifically, the virologists all mentioned that they have a couple of Dounces and always use the same ones. Burt Flanegan also described how his lab uses the "same" serum for all its extract work. When I asked how this was possible, since the serum is a commercial product, he explained how he maintains consistency in his extract preparations: "We test it [serum] to see how well our cells grow when we add that serum to our medium. If our cells grow well in that batch, then we buy a whole bunch of that serum from that manufacturer. We buy two years' worth of serum and freeze it away. We spend a lot of money, since that costs a lot, but then you don't have to buy any for a year or something and you know it's good."[49]

This need to maintain sameness extends to Wimmer's and Flanegan's views on lab personnel. Professor Wimmer has employed the same technician in his lab for more than fifteen years. Significantly, for the 2002 poliovirus synthesis experiment, the technician, and not the postdoc listed on the published paper, prepared the extracts. This technician was also responsible for carrying out the subsequent translation step with these extracts. Similarly, Flanegan says that for more than twenty years he has been able to keep two senior cell technicians in his lab who are responsible for growing the HeLa cells, making the media, ordering supplies, and maintaining the tissue culture facility. These two technicians are also responsible for training new individuals who join the lab and for maintaining institutional memory of how various experimental protocols have been adapted. Flanegan says that he depends on having experienced, senior people in his lab who can work with new students and new postdocs to learn the protocols: "Having someone that is there year-in and year-out, who knows how to do it and do it right, you are going to be more successful in maintaining that uniformity."[50]

In addition to keeping sameness in the lab, continual preparation of HeLa cell–free extracts is another practice that both Flanegan and Barton mention as key. Both professors use HeLa cell–free extracts as central research tools in their laboratories to dissect the various steps of poliovirus synthesis. For example, half of the experiments carried out in Barton's lab require HeLa cell–free extracts. Therefore, Flanegan's and Barton's labs make extracts on a weekly or monthly basis. Barton explains that he alternated between a month spent making extracts and a couple of months spent doing experiments: "My general rule was to always have the set of extracts that I was using and then another set of good extracts in the freezer ready to go. . . . I would always make sure I had one in the can . . . because you couldn't depend on being able to go back and crank one out."[51] Barton believes that the continual preparation of extracts allows him to maintain the skill set and ongoing diligence required to make good extracts—"to hold yourself to what you know to be the important implicit or explicit variables."[52] Paul agreed that the more often you make HeLa cell–free extracts, the more likely it is that your samples will be reliable.[53]

Diligence and attention to detail are the final disciplines all the virologists stressed. Paul, Flanegan, and Barton all emphasized the vital importance of following all the steps of the extract protocol and not taking shortcuts. As Barton explains: "Some people think that you can just go through this recipe and go right to the end to make virus. But there are a certain number of steps to kind of go through, milestones to achieve that are easier than others . . . every extract that you make is going to translate and poly-protein process at different magnitudes. And so it is easy to follow that as a quality control indicator to ask, am I making extracts, are they translating, am I poly-protein processing? . . . Some labs think you can bypass all that original quality control analysis, and then [they're] hitting their head on the wall and asking, Why is it not making virus? Virus production requires all of the previous endpoints to work."[54] Paul agrees that "it is a matter of trial and error and patience. . . . With all these things you have to be very careful. It is not the kind of experiment for someone who is a sloppy worker."[55]

At the same time, Barton believes that diligence in making good extract is not only learned through lab training or adoption of particular lab cultures but can also be a function of an individual's personal characteristics. He says that diligence "kind of varies based on a person's inherent ability to pay attention to detail."[56] He notes that while a number of people in his lab can make the extracts, one makes them more reliably and consistently while another doesn't. Some people are less disciplined in their work habits, Barton says, and "we talk about this all the time [in my lab], you might be having a problem because you didn't come in on Sunday. But often people have their personality, and that is what they are stuck with, and then it's up to them to dial it up or dial it down, [whereas] some people are more anal-retentive, and they do it the same way every time."[57]

As the polio virologists' unstinting attention to detail and procedure demonstrates, it is extremely difficult to make HeLa cell–free extracts, which suggests that—even using the so-called "blueprint" provided by the Wimmer lab's *Science* paper—it would be hard for anyone to artificially synthesize poliovirus using this published method without prior training in specific labs that study poliovirus synthesis.[58] As this case study illustrates, successful replication of the published 2002 poliovirus experiment hinges not only on the availability of the genetic sequence of the virus, commercial pieces of DNA, or the posting of the publication on the internet but also on the ability to master the mundane yet idiosyncratic biological techniques and adhere to specific laboratory disciplines (table 3.1).

The popular assumption that the poliovirus experiment could serve as a "blueprint" for bioterrorism is incorrect. If the Wimmer lab and other expert virologists experience repeated difficulties in making the HeLa cell–free extract required for this synthesis, it is unlikely that a motley crew of terrorists working in a makeshift laboratory in Kandahar would be successful using this particular protocol. Even an

TABLE 3.1
Managing contingencies: Laboratory know-how and disciplines in 2002 poliovirus synthesis experiment

HeLa cell growth
"Sameness": keep same technicians; keep same protocols; buy stockpile reserves of good serum; test serum; grow own cells vs. farm them out to core labs
Attention to detail, diligence: carefully monitor cell passaging; notice visual, sensory cues in cell growth

HeLa cell extract preparation
"Sameness": use same Dounce homogenizer
Continual preparation of extract: maintenance and awareness of skills in using Dounce homogenizer
Attention to detail, diligence: quickly dounce cells or keep them on ice; visual, sensory cues during douncing; follow all steps instead of taking shortcuts
Deal with failures: persistence to repeat prep and troubleshoot if process fails to work

Quality of RNA
Sameness in purchase of nucleases for degradation of HeLa cell RNAs
Care in handling, work with RNA to prevent acquisition of nucleases
Keep all solutions, reagents, environment nuclease-free
Care in purifying RNA

Translation step
Dialysis vs. nondialysis step or carefully titrate magnesium salt concentrations
Keep solutions, inorganic reagents, and reaction nuclease free

experienced, Ph.D.-level biological researcher who was not specifically trained in one of these specialized laboratories would likely have great difficulties replicating this experiment due to the unique forms of know-how and laboratory disciplines needed to get the experiment to "work." Whereas the biotech revolution frame would see the *Science* article as a tool that could readily and perhaps successfully be used by terrorists, the biosocial frame points to a more modest and contingent technological and threat trajectory for those interested in replicating the experiment or adapting it to create more complicated genomes for bioweapons purposes.

Editing Out a Different Bioterror Threat: Transfection and Infection

In contrast to the laborious method for reproducing the 2002 poliovirus experiment, there are older and much easier ways to synthesize the virus that have not received much attention in policy or public discussions focused on threats from emerging biotechnologies. These alternative synthetic methodologies use two standard virology techniques: transfection and infection. For transfection, one acquires viral RNA, either naturally or through artificial synthesis, which is then coated with a chemical compound and mixed with whole HeLa cells. Through addition of growth media, including serum and control of pH, poliovirus can be produced in the HeLa cells in about twenty-four hours. Since this method uses whole HeLa cells to create virus, it bypasses the inherent difficulties involved in making the extracts.[59] As Flanegan explains: "If you just wanted to make infectious RNA by making it synthetically, I would just take the RNA and make a standard transfection experiment that has been around forever and essentially always works and it is used in lots of labs. All you have to do is find someone who can do a standard transfection, which is very widely used, and you wouldn't have to worry about developing the HeLa S10 extract at all."[60]

Transfection with RNA still involves attention to detail and sterility, due to the inherent sensitivity of RNA to nucleases and the need to eliminate contamination from HeLa cells.[61] But, as Flanegan states, transfection with RNA is a much more widely used technique in virology—one that doesn't require as much specialized and localized laboratory know-how and disciplines as those required for working with HeLa cell–free extracts in poliovirus synthesis. Although transfection is a slow process, repeated rounds of transfection would produce a significant amount of virus. In addition to using viral RNA, viral DNA can also be used for transfection to create poliovirus.[62] In this method, the viral DNA is directly mixed with whole HeLa cells. Although DNA is easier to work with than RNA, since it is more chemically stable, poliovirus production is much slower using DNA compared to transfection with RNA.[63]

At the same time, another way to make virus is through infection, by adding intact poliovirus (obtained from nature or research/medical samples) to whole HeLa cells. In contrast to transfection, which takes at least twenty hours or more to produce virus, infection can yield significant quantities of virus in only seven hours, since the virus is extremely infectious.[64] Also, the intact poliovirus is relatively hardy and easier to work with than RNA. Yet, interestingly, these lower-tech and more widely available approaches to viral synthesis typically have been ignored (or at best marginalized) in media reports and policy discussions, even though one could argue that transfection and infection pose fewer technological hurdles and sets of specialized know-how for bioterrorists wishing to synthesize a dangerous virus. This indicates the vital importance of understanding how different technological practices can pose varying impediments (some high, some low) for technology transfer and use.

This marginalization of techniques like transfection and infection in security policy deliberations is a result of the current media and policy focus on a biotech revolution frame, which emphasizes threats from new and emerging biotechnologies over old, standardized ones. The biotech revolution frame focuses policy attention and responses on future technological and threat trajectories as well as on new enemies, potential terrorists such as "biological hackers" and "biological Unabombers." In this kind of threat conceptualization, an old technology such as infection or transfection is an afterthought at best.

An in-depth look at the poliovirus synthesis experiment, as well as transfection and infection, reveals that the replication and diffusion of biotechnology is a complex phenomenon involving material and social components unique to a given technology. For example, the diffusion of the technique for making good HeLa cell–free extracts within the virology community appears to be influenced by a number of different local and social conditions, even after more than twenty years in existence and an abundance of materials and published protocols. That virologists in the same laboratory (or competitor labs) with the requisite skills set and practices could not replicate this work indicates a role for some natural and material factors. At the same time, the virology researchers themselves also stress the importance of proper laboratory skills and enculturation factors for success with this experiment, which could involve certain tacit aspects of biological work that, as sociologist of science H. M. Collins has argued, perhaps cannot be articulated and transferred without enculturation within specialized technical communities. It could also indicate that certain tacit aspects of this particular biological technique have remained useful only within an esoteric community of virologists and therefore have not been subject to social processes involved in the transfer of this skill across a broader subset of virologists or biologists. By contrast, transfection and infection are biological techniques that have been around for similar time periods and conditions, yet appear to be much more widely diffused across the virology community, which suggests a different set of social and material factors shaping their diffusion and the need to understand the origin of these differences to inform security policy deliberations. Thus, we should not assume, as the biotech revolution frame does, that all biological techniques circulate at the same rate. Rather, we should be attuned to how we should always analyze the co-production of the social and technical in the replication and diffusion of biological work.

The 2003 φX174 Bacteriophage Synthesis
A Brief Experimental Overview

A bacteriophage is a type of virus that infects bacteria. The φX174, or phiX, bacteriophage, consisting of a ~5,300-nucleotide-long genome, is a small, circular virus that infects *Escherichia coli* (*E. coli*).[65] PhiX was first characterized in the 1950s by biologist Robert Sinsheimer's lab at the California Institute of Technology.[66] Then, in 1967, biologists Mehran Goulian, Arthur Kornberg, and Sinsheimer showed that the phiX DNA could be naturally synthesized with the addition of an enzyme (DNA polymerase) and other components, using the intact genome as a template.[67] This work was scientifically significant because it showed that viral DNA could be replicated outside of a cell; publicly, this controversial feat was described as the creation of "life in a test tube."[68] In 1978, the phiX genome was also the first DNA to be completely sequenced.[69] Thus, like poliovirus, it was an extremely well-characterized species by the time a method of artificial synthesis was considered.

In 2003, biologists Hamilton Smith, Clyde Hutchison, Cynthia Pfannkoch, and Craig Venter published a paper in the *Proceedings of the National Academy of Sciences* outlining how they had created phiX synthetically. This work was a continuation of the Venter Institute's ongoing interest in elucidating the requirements for a minimal genome.[70] Similar to poliovirus synthesis, the phiX synthesis began by designing short DNA pieces (42 nucleotides long), based on the published genome sequence, that were purchased from a commercial DNA synthesis company (fig. 3.3).

The experiment involved four key steps for synthesis. First, each strand of the 42-nucleotide DNA pieces was pooled and purified to eliminate segments of incorrect length. Second, a phosphate group was added to these purified DNA strands. These DNA strands were then ligated, or chemically bound, under strict annealing conditions to promote the pairing of the correct sequences. Third, the joined segments were assembled into full-length genomes using a technique called polymerase chain assembly (PCA). PCA is a type of modified polymerase cyclase reaction, a molecular biology technique that amplifies small pieces of DNA. Finally, to create the infectious genome, the full-length linear synthetic DNA was formed into a circle.

To determine if the synthetic method had produced an infectious species, the Venter Institute researchers used electroporation, the application of an external electric field, to incorporate synthetic phiX into *E. coli*. The subsequent visual presence of plaques indicated that the synthetic phiX was infectious to *E. coli*. Synthetic phiX DNA isolated from the plaques was then sequenced in order to check for sequence accuracy. Phage DNA from one of the plaques indicated a sequence identical to one of the original sequences found in GenBank (the National Institutes of Health's genetic sequence database); however, synthetic DNA isolated from other plaques revealed some mutations, which were a bit greater than expected. These mutations were speculated to be due to sequence errors in the original short pieces of

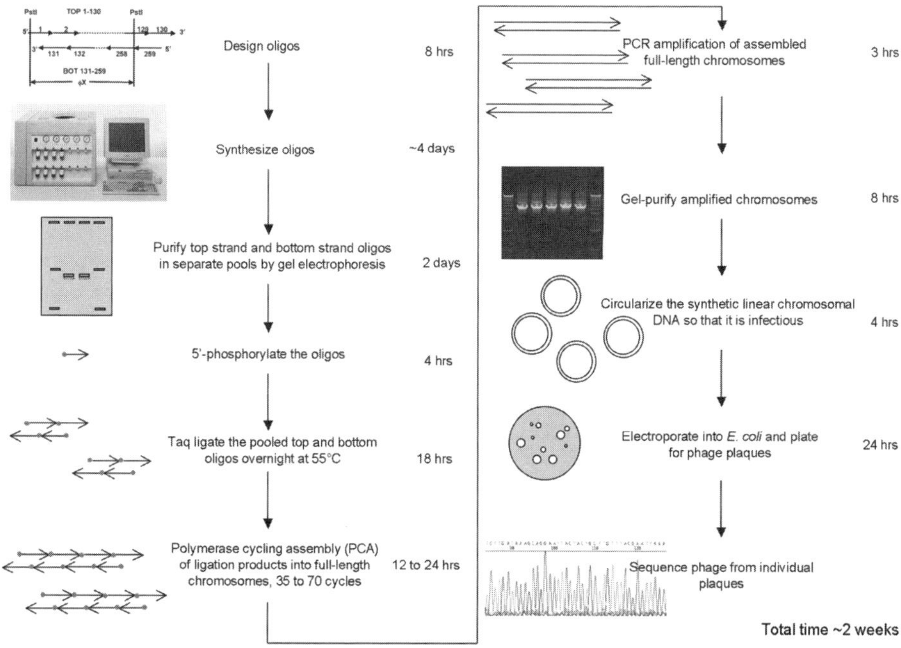

Fig. 3.3. Steps in the global synthesis of infectious phiX174 bacteriophage from synthetic oligonucleotides. Reprinted by permission of Smith, Hutchison, Pfannkoch, and Venter, "Generating a Synthetic Genome." Copyright 2003, National Academy of Sciences, U.S.A.

DNA purchased for the experiment. Ultimately, using this protocol, researchers were able to produce the artificial synthesis of infectious phiX in approximately two weeks; thus, this procedure was touted as being more efficient than the poliovirus synthetic method. This efficiency was achieved because several repair and selection steps in the intermediate stages of synthesis were eliminated using the Venter protocol.

Contingency and Expert Knowledge

In my interviews with the Venter Institute researchers, I also found more experimental contingency than is represented in standard public or policy accounts of the phiX synthesis.[71] Although the synthesis was ultimately carried out within a two-week period (the feature widely emphasized in public and policy descriptions of the experiment), work on the project had begun nearly seven years earlier, in 1996.[72] At that time, one of the researchers, biologist Clyde Hutchison, on sabbatical at the J. Craig Venter Institute, began working on the phiX bacteriophage as a model for synthesizing a larger bacterial genome; Hutchison had studied the natural properties of phiX for more than forty years. During the mid-1990s, he had been working with the Venter group to sequence the bacteria *Mycoplasma genitalium* and conduct comparative studies of that genome with the bacteria *Haemophilus influenza,* which was the first nonviral genome the Venter group had sequenced. As Venter notes, "It was the first time we had two sequenced genomes. It immediately raised all kinds of questions about how many genes were necessary for life, and I think almost immediately we started talking about a minimal genome."[73] Hutchison adds that "early on in that [discussion] there was the idea that one way to find out what a minimal genome was, was to synthesize it. And that idea is the 1999 *Science* paper."[74]

Hutchison notes that the phiX sequence he chose to synthesize was the one that came out of his 1978 sabbatical work in biologist Fred Sanger's lab. As Hutchison explains: "The other thing that made it nice for the [artificial phiX synthesis] experiment is that I had in my freezer DNAs that were made contemporaneous with the sequencing in the seventies. And so we took those out, and these are made from the strains that I had brought back from Cambridge, and we sequenced a number of those. And they all had these base pair differences from what is in GenBank using modern sequencing."[75] Craig Venter emphasizes the significance of having these DNAs on hand: "That is really important because it wasn't like trying to look at something forty years later that had changed from being grown forty years ago." Thus, the researchers could readily compare their synthetic phiX to natural strains of it that Hutchison had retained from his 1970s work on the bacteriophage.

For the experiment, Hutchison initially tried using a published synthesis protocol from Stemmer et al., who had developed a modified technique of polymerase chain reaction (PCR) to build a ~3,000-nucleotide plasmid, a circular piece of DNA, from a set of commercially available DNA pieces.[76] Hutchison decided to synthesize the phage via PCR primarily because phiX could not be cloned.[77] As he explains, "A lot of parts of this genome [phiX] are toxic or can't be cloned into *E. coli,* and that is a general problem with cloning a virus in the host that it normally infects."[78] This explains why Hutchison could not use the conventional synthetic approach of cloning smaller DNA fragments and then putting them together, as the Wimmer group had done in its synthetic poliovirus protocol. As synthetic biologist Tom Ellis notes, "[Synthetic] assembly methods are not interchangeable . . . researchers who run into problems with one technique have to start from scratch."[79]

According to Venter, the initial synthetic phiX approach was very simple: "We basically designed a series of overlapping oligos [pieces of DNA], sent those off, ordered them [from a commercial DNA company], threw them together in a tube, did some PCR."[80] Hutchison adds, "We tried to just copy what Stemmer had done. And so we tried to use that [modified PCR technique] to make a linear piece of DNA which at both ends had a unique restriction site so that we could take that piece, cleave it, circularize it, and we should be able to have infectious phiX."[81] In applying Stemmer et al.'s method to phiX, Hutchison was able to modify the method to produce synthetic DNA that was the length of the natural phiX genome. But when he put the synthetic DNA into *E. coli* to check for the infectivity of the phage, he didn't obtain any plaques, signifying that the bacteriophage contained deleterious mutations and was therefore not viable. As Hutchison explains:

> We didn't fully understand what was going on at the time. The main problem in assembling DNA that works, in the case of a virus, is to make DNA that is infectious. You do that by putting together many oligonucleotides [pieces of DNA], which in the assemblies that we had done are on the order of about forty nucleotides long. When you order oligos [pieces of DNA] from the manufacturers, which is what we did, actually only half of the material that you get is the correct species. . . . There are things [DNA] that are shorter, and things that are about the right length but with one base shorter in the middle. . . . So, if you are putting together two hundred oligos, and each one of them has some probability of a mistake, then it becomes very hard to assemble enough molecules so that any one of them are perfect.[82]

In assessing the early, failed phiX synthesis, Hutchison said, "I considered the real reason: that the error rate in the oligos [DNA] was so high that we weren't getting any molecules that were accurate."[83] Later, the Venter researchers determined in their 2003 paper that the magnitude and consequence of this error rate was such that the probability that a strand of their phiX genome would completely assemble correctly by random would be quite small: "In reality, only ~50% of the molecules in preparations [that is, from automated DNA synthesizers] such as those used in our work have the correct chain length. . . . These incorrect molecules will either block assembly of the oligonucleotides or result in mutations in the assembled DNA."[84]

This problem of high error rates in DNA synthesis has been noted in the technical literature.[85] It stems from the chemical process involved in creating pieces of DNA, which generates many truncated and mutated fragments due to inefficiencies and/or inaccuracies in the coupling reactions (for example, how phosphate groups are added to the DNA strands) as well as random chemical side reactions. In fact, Venter says, "That is the problem with the whole field [of synthetic genomics]. If the starting material was 100 percent accurate, it would be like Legos, you'd just put them together and everything would be simple."[86] But, as Venter notes, "Seeing that we knew that we were unable to achieve phiX through a simple, quick-and-dirty experiment, we knew it was going to need real intensive work."[87] Due to other work priorities, however, Hutchison did not have time to troubleshoot the early phiX synthesis experiment, so he set the failed project aside.[88]

In 2002, six years after the initial phiX work, Hutchison decided to revisit the experiment as part of the Venter Institute's ongoing effort to synthesize a minimal genome. During this second attempt at synthesizing phiX, Nobel laureate Hamilton Smith and staff scientist Cynthia Pfannkoch joined Hutchison on the project. Hutchison emphasizes the importance of this team—arguably some of the world's foremost experts in handling DNA.[89] In the beginning, Pfannkoch and Smith tried replicating his work but had trouble getting it to work. As Smith told Hutchison, "We were impressed that you actually got a full-length piece, because we [Smith and Pfannkoch] weren't able to get one."[90] As a result, Venter says, "It was clear that we had to develop a whole new process for getting there." The group started looking sequentially, examining the issues, and came up with twenty different strategies from which the final process evolved.[91] Thus, the revised Venter Institute experiment also involved a multitude of troubleshooting efforts.

The team initially focused on the problem of purifying the starting material. As Hutchison says, "We started from a position of concluding that the reason [for the failure] was the errors in the oligos and thought that if we purify the oligos by length, then we won't have so many incorrect things."[92] Purification of every single piece of DNA, however, would be time-consuming and laborious. To remove truncated species from the reaction in an efficient manner, Pfannkoch developed a novel method of gel-purifying a pooled set of the DNA pieces, separating them into top and bottom strands.[93] Although this resulted in a fairly straightforward way to purify the DNA, the insight was far from straightforward. As Hutchison remarks, "It may have been obvious, but I didn't think of it. I thought it was a clever idea."[94]

Once this purification problem was solved, the small pieces of DNA were ligated into larger DNA fragments using a stringent annealing process that Hutchison had developed in the 1970s. He says that adding the annealing step resulted from his earlier thinking about his 1970s work: "I had thought about that kind of thing before when I was developing methods for site-directed mutagenesis . . . that I would do this thing of annealing through a temperature gradient so that the most stable structures form first. And that is what we were trying to do here, to get things to compare perfectly to form, and the pieces that have a mistake will be among the leftover components."[95]

Subsequently, however, the researchers had problems when they tried to create the entire phiX genome by just combining these larger sets of DNA pieces into approximately seven hundred base-pair fragments. Although the Venter Institute researchers hoped they could get the synthetic phiX merely by using ligation, as Smith admits, "I think we right off tried to go for broke to get it [ligation] to work by just throwing everything in there. But when it doesn't work, that's when you start thinkin.' "[96] To understand why they were experiencing problems in their ligation of the full DNA strand, Smith carried out a computer simulation of the reaction.[97] Hutchison says the simulation "is one of the most interesting aspects in the paper—the theoretical discussion of what is going on there—I think this [simulation] is something other people had not thought about, or at least it had not been described in the literature."[98]

Through this simulation, the Venter Institute researchers learned that the assembly of the larger DNA fragments deteriorates very rapidly. The simulation showed that because they used pooled DNA purification, the concentrations of the DNA pieces in the starting mixture were not equal and would get used up quickly as the ligation reaction progressed. The ligations did not go through to completion because "if you don't have an exact molar amount of each piece [DNA], you get truncation," Smith explains.[99] As the researchers note in their paper, "If the oligonucleotides [DNA] vary by as little as twenty percent, essentially no full-length assemblies are made."[100] Smith goes on to explain this disconnect between the theory and practice of ligation: "Theoretically, if everything is balanced, I can ligate the entire molecule and never use PCR. . . . In practice you never achieve that, primarily because you can never adjust the pieces to be exactly equimolar in amount, so you run out of one or more pieces as you are ligating and then you end up with truncated ligations. Our average ligation products were probably around 500 to 1,000 in length."[101]

Thus, the simulation revealed that they could not use straight ligation to assemble the full phiX genome. As Hutchison notes about the importance of these simulations, "I think this is something other people had not thought about, as far as I can tell, or at least it had not been described in the literature."[102] These simulations were based, in part, on Smith's prior computational research. So, instead of relying exclusively on ligation, the researchers decided to use ligation to join the approximately 500- to 1,000-nucleotide DNA fragments together to create the full-length genome by using a modified version of PCR, called polymerase chain assembly (PCA).[103] After thirty-five cycles of PCA, the full-length synthetic phiX genome was created. Finally, thirty-five cycles of PCR were used to increase the amount of full-length synthetic phiX for subsequent analysis.

Although the final experimental protocol did result in the intact phiX bacteriophage, that was not its only product. As a result, researchers had to use a plaque assay to identify which genomes were intact—meaning that it was still not easy to make a larger bacterium or virus using this genome assembly method. The assay involves injecting the synthesized phage into agar plates of *E. coli* and waiting for large plaques to form on the plates; large, robust plaques typically signify accurate, infectious phage. As Clyde Hutchison explains, "If you pick the ones [plaques] that grow well, they are completely accurate. . . . They are fully infectious."[104] Since the phiX experiment produced one plaque-forming genome per ten thousand colonies, a plaque assay allows rapid visual identification of fully infectious genomes generated from the synthesis reaction without having to go through laborious and lengthy sequencing.

Successful use of the assay, however, requires insertion of the synthetic DNA into *E. coli* to produce plaques. Inserting synthesized fragments of a virus or cell, instead of the whole genome, into *E. coli* does not generate plaques, since fragments of DNA are not "infectious" to the bacteria. In these cases, the assay is useless as a screening device. The limitation of this visual assay for creating a larger genome (~10,000 base pairs), Hutchison explains, is that in the final product about 1 in 10^5 molecules form plaques, because of remaining errors, "so you would probably really have trouble assembling enough molecules, so you'd probably need to do it in at least two pieces, and you wouldn't be able to apply the biological selection [plaque assay] on those halves."[105] Thus, one would have to sequence tens of thousands of colonies to ensure that the correct sequences were generated and then use cloning techniques to connect the DNA pieces (that is, if the entire organism could be cloned). As the Venter researchers caution in their paper: "Our methods will permit serial synthesis of gene cassettes containing four to seven genes in a highly robust manner. However, without selectivity [that is, plaque assay], these cassettes will contain mutations (~two per kilobase) derived from errors contained in the oligonucleotide pool. Thus, without error correction, they would currently be unsuitable for assembly into a chromosome for an entire organism."[106]

The inability to use a plaque assay would greatly increase the amount of time, complexity, and effort required for synthesis of larger genomes.[107] Smith illustrates the problem in explaining his group's attempt to apply this phiX synthetic method to synthesize another larger genome artificially: "We wanted to make a somewhat bigger molecule that was of some interest, so we picked mouse mitochondrial DNA, which was about sixteen kilobases [16,000 nucleotides]. We decided to make it in three different sections of about six kilobases each and then use the phiX assembly method to assemble the six kilobase sections. And we did that, we assembled the six pieces. But we ran into the same problem that we couldn't clone them and sequence them in *E. coli*. So that got stalled and is still in the refrigerator."[108] As Hutchison notes, "Most of the strategies that people use today involve making pieces that are much smaller than phiX, of the order of 500 to 700 bases [nucleotides], clone them, sequence a few to get one that is exactly right, and go on with those."[109]

Moreover, simply because the Venter group obtained an infectious bacteriophage does not indicate that an infectious virus could be produced with the same technique, because plaque assays only show infectivity in an artificial medium; they do not show infectivity in a host. In order to confirm viral infectivity, one would need to sequence each plaque and then carry out animal model studies; this would further increase the complexity and time required for synthesizing a viable viral genome. Although one of the synthetic phiX plaques revealed a correct sequence, other plaques revealed anywhere from one to five different mutations; these mutations revealed that some strains of the synthetic phiX DNA had a lower infectivity than the natural DNA. For more complex organisms, such mutations could become significant issues for viability. Although Smith speculates that the original commercial pieces of DNA are the source of the mutations, there might be additional errors being introduced across the synthetic process leading to the observed mutations. Only sequencing at each step of the reaction would allow for determination of mutations. As Venter notes, "[DNA] sequences are of relative accuracy. The only way you prove that the sequence is accurate is if it results in the exact same genotype and phenotype that it derived from."[110] Table 3.2 summarizes the contingencies involved in the phiX synthesis.

In light of these issues, Smith points out the limited diffusion and applicability of their whole genome approach: "I don't think any of the gene companies try to assemble large pieces in one shot. Most of them make pieces that are 1,000-base pairs [nucleotides] or less, then clone those and sequence them, so if they wanted to make something the size of phiX, they would make it in half a dozen pieces, which would then be verified by sequencing."[111] This does not mean, however, that the Venter approach is a poor or invalid method for genome synthesis; it was a good model for the Venter Institute's ongoing basic research work to create a minimal genome. Rather, the contingencies revealed in the phiX experiment merely indicate the need for caution in extrapolating these results to other experimental contexts.

TABLE 3.2
Contingencies in 2003 phiX experiment

Contingencies
Team of experts required (Hutchison, Smith, Pfannkoch)
Experts brought prior know-how and understanding to experiment:
Hutchison: prior working knowledge of phiX; development of annealing technique in past lab work
Smith: prior working knowledge of computer simulations for biological reactions
Pfannkoch: prior working knowledge of gel purification of DNA fragments
Although synthetic protocol was based in part on an older scientific publication, a "quick-and-dirty" application of these past protocols was not sufficient; required intensive trial-and-error problem-solving across all steps of the experiment
PhiX cannot be cloned in *E. coli,* which necessitated an alternative synthetic route
Ligation efficiency dependant on decision to purify oligos for this experiment
Visual assay needed in order to screen plaques for viable phiX; does not work for species that do not infect *E. coli* or for fragments of virus/cells
Oligo error rate: presence of mutations; decrease in infectivity of synthetic phiX
PhiX synthetic protocol not necessarily applicable to create other synthetic genomes

In spite of these known contingencies, Venter says, the general assumption is that one can just order pieces of DNA from a synthesis company, put them in a test tube, and create a lethal genome like smallpox. "It doesn't work with phiX, something that is one-twentieth the size of smallpox," he says from his own experience.[112] One U.S. government official who was involved in reviewing the phiX experiment before its publication noted that he did not necessarily consider the phiX experimental method to be an enabling technology for bioterrorism. "For a state, yes; for a terrorist, no—the technological threshold is too high for a terrorist in a Kandahar cave."[113]

Beyond Polio and PhiX: The 2008 Artificial Synthesis of *Mycoplasma Genitalium*

In January 2008, the Venter Institute published a synthetic genome experiment outlining the complete synthesis of *Mycoplasma genitalium,* a ~583,000-nucleotide genome.[114] This experiment was one of many firsts: It was the largest synthetic DNA and the first synthetic bacterial genome constructed through artificial means. Although this experiment built on the knowledge obtained in the 2003 phiX experiment, it primarily did so through the failure of that particular protocol to synthesize larger genomes. With that knowledge, the 2008 Venter synthetic approach largely returned to modified versions of older synthetic methods, which rely heavily on small DNA synthesis, cloning for the genome assembly, and verification of accuracy by sequencing.

While this synthesis was a major advance due to the size of the genome, the experiment took several years to come to fruition and remained a tedious multi-stage process in which the Venter team (now expanded to ten researchers, plus additional help from three companies that specialize in gene synthesis) had to build the genome a quarter at a time.[115] During this building process, however, the team found that *E. coli* had difficulty reproducing the progressively larger DNA segments, so they turned to the yeast *Saccharomyces cerevisiae* as the cloning host instead of *E. coli*. In their approach, the Venter group synthesized twenty-five DNA fragments that were inserted into yeast cells to create the full-length genome. In spite of the success of this experimental method, questions remain about the ease and applicability of this synthetic method for other genomes. For example, working with yeast can pose problems such as high recombination activity and the propensity for large DNA segments to rearrange; these factors could be detrimental to construction of other viable genomes. And it remains unknown whether the synthesized genome is functional or viable in cellular form. As one gene synthesis employee stresses, "Even if a long string of DNA could be made in the lab, it could fall apart once stuck into a cell. There are many other factors that go into getting these synthetic genes to survive in cells."[116]

Although the Venter Institute was able to produce a correct genome sequence using a synthetic method, the researchers note that the experiment was fraught with possibilities for error: "An error could be present in the sequence that was supplied to the contractors. The contractors could produce cassettes [DNA fragments] with errors. Errors could occur during repair of the assembly junctions. Propagation of assemblies in *E. coli* or yeast could lead to errors. In the latter two instances, errors could occur at a late stage of the assembly. At various points during the genome assembly, clones were sequenced. Most of the assemblies were exactly correct; however, in our *E. coli* clones, we encountered at least one example of each of the error types described above. Several errors were repaired by rebuilding assemblies, but in some cases other methods were used."[117]

As Venter himself later admits, "99% of our experiments failed."[118] Thus, even with the laboratory experience that had been generated from previous synthesis experiments, creating the genome was not a simple, straightforward combination of materials and equipment. To deal with the error problems, the ten Venter Institute researchers worked closely with three commercial gene synthesis companies: Blue Heron Biotechnology, GeneArt, and DNA2.0. In particular, Blue Heron played a key role in the project, serving as the primary supplier of the synthetic DNA used by the Venter Institute for this project.[119] As a Blue Heron press release notes, "Blue Heron was selected to play this key role because of their extensive expertise synthesizing the most difficult DNA constructs and their manufacturing capacity. Blue Heron provided 84 of the 101 synthetic DNA fragments used in the project, representing over one-half million base pairs of material. Of these eighty-four constructs, a few difficult cases required Blue Heron to develop new, innovative, approaches to synthesis.[120]

In talking about these difficulties, John Mulligan, president of Blue Heron, states that gene synthesis is a very complex manufacturing operation, compared to the synthesis of small DNA pieces, for several reasons: every part that is synthesized is unique; there are multiple steps in the gene synthesis process; biological behavior is unpredictable; chemical reactions are inconsistent; and there are high failure rates throughout the process.[121] As a result, Blue Heron has instituted stringent quality control at each step of their synthetic gene production, involving considerable time and effort. Even so, Blue Heron has experienced high failure rates across their gene synthesis process. Thus, Mulligan states that gene synthesis requires particular forms of expertise that come in the form of either highly specialized scientists in individual laboratories doing the synthetic work (for instance, the Venter or Wimmer approaches) or specialized companies like Blue Heron that have "industrialized" the gene synthesis process.

Even with their "industrialization" of gene synthesis, Blue Heron's process is by no means "routinized" or "standardized." Mulligan says that creating a synthetic genome in his company remains complex work—and the complexity is not necessarily related to purely biological issues. In order to simplify the work, for instance, Mulligan brought a team of Stanford Business School faculty to Blue Heron to help the company develop a more automated process for its commercial gene synthesis work. To Mulligan's dismay, these Stanford faculty said Blue Heron's method was the most complicated manufacturing process they had ever seen and would not be easily amenable, from an organizational perspective, to a routinized process.[122] According to Mulligan, the problems that remain in gene synthesis are not necessarily resource or money problems, because his company has access to sufficient amounts of materials and capital. Rather, the challenges are intellectual, requiring time, teams of experts, and new (still unknown) techno-organizational processes that stem from trying to simplify what remains a very complex scientific process. These challenges, however, are not captured in simple schematics such as figure 3.4 that are used in policy discussions.

Although small DNA fragments (fewer than a thousand nucleotides) can be readily synthesized, the assembly of longer DNA molecules raises vast technical challenges, many of which are not well understood and can require substantial problem-solving. A 2009 *Trends in Biotechnology* article noted the complexity—

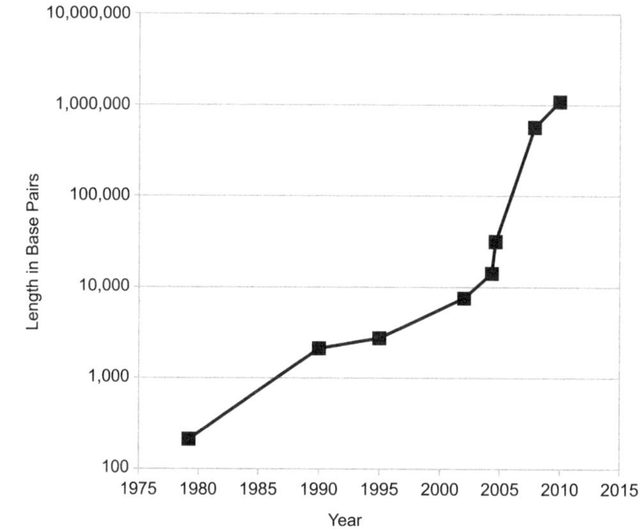

Fig. 3.4. Longest published synthetic DNA. 2010. Reprinted by permission of Robert Carlson.

and tradeoffs—involved in gene synthesis work: "Most multi-gene-engineering projects involve *ad hoc* methods of DNA assembly. . . . Employing custom cloning strategies to use restriction sites within natural sequences are labor intensive and difficult to automate. Molecular biologists often reach a tacit compromise between obtaining a desired sequence and the number of steps in the cloning process they are willing or able to undertake in constructing a sequence."[123] The article goes on to conclude that the "idealistic vision of large scale, affordable gene synthesis has not yet materialized in spite of rapid progress."[124] As a result of the complexity of gene synthesis, some commercial gene synthesis companies have folded; others have been unable to deliver some orders they had accepted.[125] Instead of a proliferation of gene synthesis companies, the industry is consolidating into the hands of a small number of firms.[126]

A Sociotechnical Understanding of the Poliovirus and phiX Experiments

Most policy discussions have tended to use and emphasize simplified, step-by-step diagrams such as those shown in figures 3.1 and 3.3 to explain the ease with which the phiX and poliovirus synthetic methods and related synthetic protocols could be applicable to terrorism. The biotech revolution frame, with its focus on the presumed drivers of biotechnology, does not acknowledge the costs and challenges constituting the production of different kinds of biological products. In reexamining the poliovirus and phiX experiments with attention to unpacking the micro-level practices that underpinned them, however, one can see much contingency and complexity involved in the development of the appropriate laboratory know-how and practices for these synthetic protocols to work as published. As described earlier, scholars in the field of science and technology studies point out that scientific practice, with its troublesome, contingent, and messy means of production, often differs from its clean and orderly public representations. Therefore, an analysis of the broader context of scientific work is critical to understanding the various social dimensions that in turn remain critical to the development and replication of a particular experiment or technological artifact. The power of the biosocial frame lies in this analytic focus.

The biosocial frame requires us to examine the behind-the-scenes dimensions of scientific practice in order to understand fully what would be required to replicate specific scientific work. In the poliovirus experiment, certain tacit components were evident in all of the polio virologists' descriptions of the "art" of using the Dounce homogenizers to break open HeLa cells; technicians learned this tacit knowledge through hands-on work with others who were expert in this practice. But the details of *how* the Wimmer lab conducted the experiment have never been elucidated in media or policy accounts—until now. As S&TS scholars Karin Knorr-Cetina, Michael Lynch, and others have noted, formal scientific communications or other kinds of codified knowledge do not typically reveal this kind of nuance.[127] The power of the biosocial frame is to probe the role of tacit practices in scientific work.

In addition, the biosocial frame directs our attention to the local, specialized knowledge that underpins successful completion of experimental work. In the phiX experiment, Hamilton Smith and Clyde Hutchison brought a wealth of knowledge from past experimental work to inform and guide their development of the synthetic protocol. This expert knowledge does not, however, necessarily remove all contingency in the lab, as demonstrated by David Barton's inability to replicate the HeLa cell extracts as published in the Wimmer lab's 1991 *Science* paper.[128] This contingency can be connected to local laboratory cultures that can prove difficult to replicate in new contexts.

The biosocial frame similarly points us to other kinds of "hidden" knowledge that results from the standard practices that scientists have adopted as part of how they view and conduct their work. More specifically, nowhere in the phiX publication is there a detailed discussion of the need to develop the concept of DNA purification to eliminate truncated species, nor of the development of a computational model to understand what problems were occurring in the ligation step. The experimental protocol as published does not give the appropriate weight to the importance of these steps; it took interviews with the scientists to discover this.

What's more, mundane aspects of laboratory work can often prove crucial to obtaining a successful end product. David Barton notes that while cell extract work is important in poliovirus synthesis experiments, "making extracts is not an experiment. It doesn't get you anywhere in and of itself."[129] Because extract work is not considered "real" science, Barton says, his lab has spent little time trying to isolate the important factors for making extract: "We haven't done a controlled study of how good extracts differ from bad extracts. We don't care why bad ones don't work. . . . My lab stopped optimizing [the extract] long ago, since we found a method that works."[130] Similarly, Ehrenfeld says that she considers extracts to be merely a reagent, albeit a capricious one. In her mind, the laboratory focus should remain on the more important scientific aspects of the project, like testing hypotheses, rather than on preparation of a reagent.[131] However, making a viable extract is critical to replicating the Wimmer experiment as published.

A closer look at the poliovirus and phiX synthesis reveals a number of sociotechnical factors at play in these experiments. In both, the material and informational components (published protocols, DNA pieces) on their own played a limited role in their ultimate success. Getting these two synthetic approaches to work required development of particular intellectual insights, laboratory practices, teamwork, and troubleshooting efforts. Furthermore, these experiments were not based on cutting-edge technologies but were rooted in more evolutionary and well-established laboratory practices and techniques.

As an example, the poliovirus synthesis used extract-making and other laboratory skills (and associated lab personnel) that had been part and parcel of the Wimmer lab for more than twenty years. Similarly, the phiX experiment was not based on a completely new and unforeseen technological capability. Instead, it relied on the modification of an existing experimental protocol that used a variant of the widely available technique of the polymerase chain reaction; the phiX experiment also used specific biological knowledge and skills that the Venter Institute researchers had obtained through their cumulative years of bench work on DNA and phiX. Moreover, both experiments reveal a more limited and at times localized adaptability of the methods to other applications or contexts. In the poliovirus case, attempts at making good HeLa cell–free extracts and replicating the artificial poliovirus synthesis experiment remain difficult and time-consuming, even for experienced virologists who specialize in poliovirus synthesis. In the phiX method, the importance of the plaque assay in identifying infectious genomes poses difficulties in applying the synthetic protocol to other genomes. In cases where the plaque assay cannot be used, the synthetic method cannot be used for larger genomes, and the presumed two-week efficiency of this method is lost.

In broader terms, these local laboratory practices illustrate the difficulty of obtaining accurate bioweapons assessments solely by reading published scientific reports or by examining the material aspects of biotechnology. For example, a 2007 policy report stated that poliovirus is "relatively easy to synthesize because it has a small genome made up of positive-stranded RNA and because a large amount of data is available on sequences of known virulence."[132] Based on purely material factors and codified knowledge, this claim would seem to be correct. As we have seen, though, the *process* of making HeLa cell-free extracts—using a variety of tacit skills, rituals, and other disciplines—plays an important role in making good extracts and producing viable synthetic virus in the lab, though it is not discussed in published explanations. When we consider these sociotechnical aspects of the process, we see that Wimmer's synthesis was far from trivial.

Conclusion

While the shortcomings of the biotech revolution frame are clear, how would the biosocial frame give us a more accurate analysis of bioweapons threats from synthetic genomics? We can look to the poliovirus and phiX experiments to answer that question.

To begin with, an analyst using the biosocial frame would understand that published scientific experiments and protocols obscure the messiness of laboratory work. Thus, the analyst would consider the often circuitous, disordered, and contingent aspects of experimental work in assessing threats from synthetic genomics experiments and would weigh the qualitative, sociotechnical aspects of biotechnology, such as the development of laboratory skills and disciplines, the constitution and maintenance of interdisciplinary communities of scientific practice, organizational structures, institutions, and the contingency and complexity of laboratory work.

More specifically, an analyst using the biosocial frame would ask questions such as: Who was involved in developing the experiment? What was their background and experience? How was this background brought to bear on the experiment? What kind of user is required to get a particular technique to work? Does it require a disciplined, careful researcher, or can a sloppy researcher get the work done? Does it require a team effort? If so, what distinct sets of knowledge are required to replicate the experiment successfully? How should such a team be organized? How do the users shape the way materials, resources, and infrastructure are brought to bear on the experiment? What other contingencies and intellectual problems constitute the experiment? All of these questions would be rooted in understanding—at a detailed, micro level—the scientific practices that underpinned the experimental protocol in question.

In addition, an analyst using the biosocial frame would ask: What kind of laboratory organization and culture are required to get a particular technique or protocol to work? How much is a technique tied to local laboratory practices? What are the mechanisms, factors, and people required to translate this technique or practice to a new context? What constitutes the training and translation process? What factors, both technical *and* nontechnical, shape the diffusion of this technique or technology? What failures constituted the experiment, and how were new knowledge and practices developed to get the experiment to work? What other past scientific practices and experiences were embedded within the protocol to get the technology to work? These questions would lead to a much deeper understanding of the factors shaping the development, translation, and diffusion of a particular technology.

Clearly, this alternative frame could lead to a different kind of bioweapons threat assessment. For instance, assessing the threat from a particular synthetic genome would require more emphasis on the sociotechnical factors required to synthesize a pathogen at the laboratory bench, along with the additional sociotechnical factors needed to produce, weaponize, and deliver the pathogen for a mass casualty attack. To date, most government and nongovernment reports on synthetic genomics refer only briefly to the art of synthetic genomics work.[133] These reports and discussions fail to consider fully what skills are involved, how they are developed and situated in particular laboratory practices, and what socio-organizational elements would be required to develop and transfer the technology to terrorists or states for use. These studies still use the biotech revolution frame and thus assume that the march of time and biotechnology will automatically remove the need for craft- or skill-based knowledge related to synthetic genomics. As this chapter illustrates, a qualitative, sociotechnical approach opens a whole new set of useful considerations to elucidate the "how" behind laboratory work and its resulting threats: How are biotechnologies developed? How are they replicated? How are they translated? How do they diffuse? How can they be adopted to work in particular contexts? To date, these questions have been ignored in the biotech revolution frame and thus in the policies that have resulted from the use of that frame.

Soviet Bioweapons Know-How and Proliferation Threats

> The men and women of the [former Soviet] nuclear, chemical and biological institutes don't carry automatic weapons in their hands, they possess the knowledge and the ability to develop weapons that could kill millions.
>
> *Senator Richard Lugar, 1998*

In the 1990s, with the collapse of the Soviet Union, U.S. intelligence analysts and policymakers issued reports alleging that certain terrorist groups and "rogue" states, as well as Russian criminals, had approached former Soviet weapons facilities and personnel in search of material and expertise relating to weapons of mass destruction.[1] As a result, a new set of U.S. government initiatives, called the Nunn-Lugar Cooperative Threat Reduction Programs, was launched in 1991 to mitigate the WMD proliferation threats from the former Soviet Union.[2] While the original policy focus was on the former Soviet nuclear establishment, additional Nunn-Lugar efforts in 1998 began to engage the former Soviet bioweapons program.[3] Consisting of over forty facilities, the vast Soviet bioweapons complex was involved in conducting research on several disease agents, producing them on a large scale, and weaponizing them into a variety of delivery systems. During the Cold War, the Soviets had also worked to develop genetically engineered strains of bacteria and viruses to use as biological weapons.[4]

The Nunn-Lugar nonproliferation programs also reached out to coopt former Soviet weapons scientists who were seen as possessing dangerous WMD know-how. The effort was prompted in part by U.S. intelligence indicating that Iranian government officials had been aggressively recruiting former Soviet biological weapons scientists. Iran was reportedly offering salaries of as much as $5,000 per month to relocate to Iran, lucrative contracts for consultancy work, and scientific and educational exchanges.[5] Iran was a modest but successful recruiter, as a result of which the U.S. security policy community focused in the late 1990s on human-centered proliferation threats, along with the pathogens, equipment, and infrastructure of the former Soviet program.[6]

Since 1998, the U.S. Departments of Agriculture, Defense, Energy, Health and Human Services, Homeland Security, and State as well as the Environmental Protection Agency and the Civilian Research and Development Foundation have created a robust set of "brain drain prevention" programs to halt the proliferation of biological weapons know-how from these former Soviet scientists. The cost of these programs has grown to more than $600 million for multiyear biotech research and commercialization projects that employ anywhere from five to fifty former bioweaponeers on each project.[7] These projects, at various former Soviet research institutes, have been designed to keep the bioweaponeers busy, pay them a reasonable wage, and give them opportunities for new livelihoods so that they won't be as tempted to aid rogue states or terrorist groups. To date, the U.S. government has funded projects with bioweaponeers from all of the core former Soviet biological weapons facilities, with the exception of a few Russian biodefense facilities that remain closed to U.S. engagement.

Proponents of these programs have argued that such efforts have engaged former weapons scientists with valuable bioweapons know-how as well as opened up many former Soviet biological weapons facilities to U.S. and international oversight, thereby eliminating or reducing proliferation threats. In fact, Iranian recruiters no longer troll for scientists at these former biological weapons facilities. Bioweapons expert Milton Leitenberg has also pointed out that the U.S. intelligence community is not aware of any former Soviet bioweapons scientists who have gone to North Korea or Iraq: "The great majority of Russian bioweapons-relevant scientists that emigrated did so to the United States, the United Kingdom, Germany, France, Australia, Sweden, Finland, Israel, etc., and not to states of bioweapons proliferation concern."[8]

Nevertheless, since their establishment, these brain drain prevention programs have been subject to controversy over how best to measure their nonproliferation benefits. The people who design and implement these programs typically count the number of Soviet biological weapons scientists employed through U.S. assistance in the same way that the Nunn-Lugar program counts the number of pathogen collections secured or facilities and equipment dismantled or destroyed.[9] As weapons proliferation expert Jacques Hymans writes, this metric assumes that "proliferation is as good as accomplished when the [former] Soviet scientist's plane touches down in Damascus or Tripoli."[10] Critics, however, contend that counting bodies is a meaningless way to measure actual threat reduction. With the ubiquity of internet access, they say, the former Soviet bioweaponeers can sell their knowledge online, no matter where they physically work or live.

On top of that, it is not always clear who exactly should be counted in this tally. By way of example, a 2007 U.S. Government Accountability Office report stated that one U.S. government agency had overstated the number of weapons scientists receiving support from its programs by counting both the weapons and nonweapons scientists it employed in its totals.[11] Some critics say that brain drain prevention programs are merely a guise for foreign aid, which has no nonproliferation benefit.[12] Still others have worried that American funding of brain drain programs merely allows countries like Russia to save its own state resources to develop new bioweapons capabilities that could one day pose a threat to the United States.

In light of these criticisms, the White House and Congress have continually pressed U.S. government agencies that design and implement these programs to provide better metrics for assessing their nonproliferation benefits and to establish a secure and sustainable exit strategy with respect to these scientists in the future. Part of the current problem that policymakers face is that there have been no in-depth academic or government studies on the threat posed by these former Soviet bioweaponeers.[13] Such a study would have to evaluate several elements, including the character of the knowledge and know-how associated with making biological weapons. To date, policymakers have not had a good understanding of how to define, comprehend, and evaluate such weapons know-how. The science and technology studies community, however, has studied such know-how issues—also called tacit knowledge—at length as well as other social dimensions of scientific and technological work.

Drawing on these science studies perspectives, in this chapter I examine the present-day brain drain threats posed by individuals involved in the former Soviet biological weapons program.[14] Using a micro-level case study, I explore the following questions: Was specific know-how involved in developing Soviet biological weapons? If so, what are the characteristic features of this type of weapons know-how? How can these brain drain prevention programs be designed and implemented to mitigate proliferation of this know-how tangibly? How can an appropriate exit strategy for these programs be designed? The answers to these questions illustrate the importance of using a biosocial frame to understand the sociotechnical character of bioweapons development and transfer in order to design appropriate nonproliferation policies and programs.

I conclude the chapter by examining how the biotech revolution frame and its associated technological narratives are contributing to significant changes in these

U.S. nonproliferation programs. Until recently, most of the policy debates centered on how to define and measure the nonproliferation efforts that target this former Soviet weapons know-how; there was little discussion about the importance of the proliferation potential of this specialized weapons know-how to create a mass-casualty biological weapon. New U.S. government initiatives launched since September 11, 2001, however, address the more global character of bioweapons-related threats, which are seen to extend beyond weapons scientists from the former Soviet bioweapons complex. These new engagements implicitly embody and reflect the biotech revolution frame, with its focus on potential "biological Unabombers," the material aspects of biotechnology, and the presumed ease of globalization and diffusion of new biotechnologies. Through this lens, one can see a policy devaluation of former Soviet bioweapons expertise, with rising attention and nonproliferation resources devoted to targeting more ubiquitous, yet ambiguous, "dual-use" or "weapons-relevant" threats. If one understands the inherently social character of biotechnology and the way in which weapons knowledge and social context are co-produced, however, these policy moves are questionable. The way we understand and frame bioweapons threats has important implications for how we structure nonproliferation policy programs and resources.

Soviet Biological Weapons Development: The Stepnogorsk Scientific and Experimental Production Base Case Study

To understand the role of tacit knowledge in bioweapons development, we will examine the Stepnogorsk Scientific and Experimental Production Base (SNOPB), one of the Soviet Union's premier biological weapons facilities. The facility, located in the small town of Stepnogorsk in northwest Kazakhstan, was officially established in 1982 by a secret edict from Communist Party Secretary General Leonid Brezhnev.[15] As with many Soviet bioweapons facilities, the Stepnogorsk facility was a covert part of a larger dual-use civilian biopesticide facility. Although the facility was officially established in 1982, plans to build the entire civilian and military complex were already being developed in the 1960s. The civilian part, a biopesticide production plant called Plant Progress, was built first. The construction of the facility started in the late 1970s.[16] The Stepnogorsk facility was created to develop pilot and large-scale production methods for a variety of Soviet biological weapons and to serve as a biological weapons mobilization facility in case of war. From 1983 through 1987, the facility developed the Soviet Union's most potent anthrax biological weapon.

The Stepnogorsk facility is an appropriate case study because: (1) U.S. government officials have established an exit strategy at Stepnogorsk for existing brain drain programs; (2) the facility is unique in that it included research and development (R&D), production, and weaponization activities, allowing an understanding of the complete Soviet biological weapons development processes; (3) the facility has undergone important personnel and structural changes throughout its lifetime; (4) the former director of the facility, Kanatjan Alibekov (Ken Alibek), defected to the United States in 1992 and speaks openly about the facility's biological weapons activities during the Soviet period; and (5) it is a facility I have previously analyzed.[17] Because many former Soviet bioweaponeers in Kazakhstan are still reluctant to talk openly about offensive biological weapons activities during the Soviet period, this study is necessarily based on limited unclassified information. The conclusions, however, illustrate that to understand the difficulties of constituting and transferring bioweapons technologies, we must first understand the science and technology studies concepts about know-how in biological weapons production.

Stepnogorsk Scientific and Experimental Production Base and Anthrax 836: Old Weapon, New Design, New Problems

When the Stepnogorsk facility first opened, the Soviet Ministry of Defense gave it two priority tasks: improving the potency of and organizational capability for large-scale manufacture of the Soviet Anthrax 836 biological weapons.[18] Prior to the Stepnogorsk facility's work, the ministry had already developed an 836 formulation that used special drying methods to embed spores of *Bacillus anthracis* in animal-based carrier media. The existing 836 recipe, however, was not ideal for military use because the added weight of the media made the material quite heavy and prone to settle rapidly upon dissemination. This created problems for production and transport of the agent to the battlefield and meant that the agent might not be easily inhaled by the enemy. Therefore, the Ministry of Defense decided it was necessary to improve the existing 836 technology. Defense scientists went back to the drawing board and developed a paper-based concept for a new 836 weapon.

The new weapon would abandon the use of the existing media and incorporate a unique encapsulation technology based on beads of polyvinyl chloride (PVC).[19] In addition, the heat-protective properties of PVC would enhance viability of the anthrax bacteria during and after dissemination.[20] The potency of the new weapon would be defined by its "Q50" number—the amount of biological weapons agent necessary to cover 1 square kilometer of territory with a dose lethal to 50 percent of the population in the area. A low Q50 level is ideal for battlefield employment of a biological agent because it would allow a small amount of lethal agent to cover a wide area. The older Anthrax 836 weapon had a high Q50 level—approximately 16 kg/km^2. The Soviet Ministry of Defense calculated that its new anthrax weapon would yield a lower Q50 of 4–5 kg/km^2 for the anthrax agent, ideal for battlefield use. The ministry tasked the SNOPB with turning this concept into a working and reliable biological weapon. The ministry developed the technical task, which stipulated that the facility be able to produce no fewer than 250 tons of anthrax per year, with a Q50 level of no more than 5 kg/km^2.

In order to facilitate work at the SNOPB, the Ministry of Defense provided the facility with extensive technical papers and plans. This information included a classified report (approximately 400–600 pages) summarizing previous Ministry of Defense work in developing the Anthrax 836 strain as a biological weapon. The report described different parameters, equipment, and biosafety conditions for the cultivation and production of the Anthrax 836 strain. Other documents detailed procedures for filling and assembling bombs and warheads, procedures for transporting these munitions from the facility, and the various suppliers for all the raw materials. Interestingly, however, the report excluded certain details about the development of the ministry's existing 836 weapon, since some of this information was restricted to Ministry of Defense access only.[21] Although the Ministry was a customer of the Stepnogorsk facility, the Kazakh facility was officially under the authority of the Biopreparat Administration, a separate Soviet ministry that also developed biological weapons. Therefore, the Ministry frequently viewed the Stepnogorsk facility as a direct competitor to its defense laboratories, resulting in frequent battles over money and scientific taskings.

In spite of the extensive reports and documents provided by the Ministry of Defense, the original Stepnogorsk staff experienced problems in applying this information to their facility. The technical documentation on Anthrax 836 was specific to its growth in Ministry of Defense fermenters and equipment. As a result, Stepnogorsk technical staff had trouble replicating previous ministry anthrax work in the facility's 20,000-liter fermenters.[22] In fact, Stepnogorsk staff found that they could use the Ministry of Defense documentation only as a guideline; they had to adapt its production protocols and develop new materials (such as new types of nutrient media) and methods to fit the Stepnogorsk system. As Alibek states, "This [Stepnogorsk] equipment was established and put together to manufacture things in a totally different way. Technological parameters described in that [Ministry of Defense] report wouldn't be usable because you have different equipment, and you need to develop different techniques for different equipment."[23]

Stepnogorsk staff encountered other problems in the scale-up from laboratory cultivation to large-scale production. Alibek explains, "You can't use just small equipment and then after you finish this work you start working in big reactors. It wouldn't work. It is very difficult to scale up from 10 liters to 20 [metric] tons because you can't create the same parameters unless you change the characteristics. . . . You have technological problems, safety problems."[24] Similarly, another former Soviet bioweapons scientist recalls that viruses contaminating the large fermentors would often kill the anthrax bacteria.[25] All these technical issues required not only additional bench work on the science and development but also new efforts to solve a multitude of engineering tasks across the spectrum of weapons development. For example, the need to turn the virtually dormant facility into one capable of mass-producing weaponized anthrax resulted in major engineering problems.[26]

Initially, although all the relevant infrastructure and equipment were on site, none of the equipment was in working condition. In part, this was because some of the equipment had not been assembled properly or even used prior to the 836 work.[27] Stepnogorsk staff had to check the installation of all equipment and conduct tests on it under specified parameters and real-world conditions to ensure proper functioning. First, they had to check the biosafety engineering systems, such as autoclaves, disinfectant chambers, fume hoods, air handling and filtration systems, negative pressure systems, and the hermetic seal of the building. Next, they needed to test the larger technological systems, such as the fermenters. This involved checking the antifoaming and agitator blocking systems as well as all connectors and heat-exchange units. In total, this involved testing and repairing thousands of pieces of equipment.

Other engineering problems then surfaced in integrating the various individual pieces of equipment and infrastructure into an efficient technological process. Portions of the Stepnogorsk facility (assembly lines, bunkers, storage buildings) were first constructed in the late 1970s. This was followed by construction of the main biological weapons production buildings. Because these buildings were constructed at different times, Stepnogorsk staff had to integrate the existing buildings, along with assembling new batteries of equipment such as fermenters and drying, milling, and bomb-filling machines. Other new infrastructure, such as underground storage and pipelines, was also added.[28] Alibek explains: "The major issue and problem was coordinating all of the seemingly unrelated entities and pieces of equipment to work as a relatively well-oiled machine. . . . A disbalance in one system (for example, engineering, technological parameters, scientific work) could result in significant trouble."[29] Getting the multiple material and social components of the

SNOPB bioweapons complex to function properly was critical to developing the Soviets' potent anthrax weapon. As Alibek has noted, "The most virulent culture in a test tube is useless as an offensive weapon until it has been put through a process that gives it stability and predictability. The manufacturing technique is, in a sense, the real weapon, and it is harder to develop than are the individual agents."[30]

To deal with these varying scientific and engineering problems, many more technical staff were hired to work at the Stepnogorsk facility. Some of the new employees were local; others came from biological weapons facilities in Russia. Within its first year, more than two hundred new employees were added to the facility.[31] Eventually, at its peak, 970 employees worked there, one-third of whom were directly involved in biological weapons activities. Interestingly, none of the new employees was hired from the civilian part of the Stepnogorsk Plant Progress, which employed scientists and engineers working with *Bacillus thuringiensis,* a type of bacteria closely related to anthrax.[32] Alibek explains that he adopted this policy to keep the SNOPB's biological weapons activities secret. To support the 836 work, the facility expanded to include more than twenty buildings and support structures, a complex that ultimately spanned two square kilometers.

In spite of these technical and engineering hurdles, the Stepnogorsk facility fulfilled its Ministry of Defense mandate. In 1987, approximately five years after the facility was commissioned, workers at the complex developed a new production method that allowed production of three hundred metric tons of anthrax per year, at a rate of approximately two metric tons per day.[33] Such a sizeable amount of biological agent could be loaded on a number of Soviet delivery systems in the event of war with the United States. That same year, Soviet bioweaponeers successfully tested the new Anthrax 836 weapon on Vozrozhdeniye Island in Uzbekistan; the Ministry of Defense then certified the weapon for use in the Soviet arsenal.[34]

Transfer and Development of Weapons Know-How at the SNOPB

Although it had been under construction since the 1970s, the Stepnogorsk facility was not active until it was commissioned in 1982. As a result, even by 1983, the facility possessed only a few dozen employees, including just four or five engineers. Virtually none of these original employees possessed prior biological weapons experience or knowledge in large-scale weapons production. This lack of experienced personnel contributed to the early problems in adapting Ministry of Defense technical documentation to the Stepnogorsk facility and getting the facility on line.

Because of these early Stepnogorsk technical difficulties, the Ministry of Defense decided in 1984 to transfer sixty-five biological weapons specialists from defense facilities in Sverdlovsk and Kirov to the Stepnogorsk facility over a six-month period. These individuals had specialized expertise in research and manufacturing techniques for weaponized anthrax bacteria. Namely, Alibek's deputy, Col. Gennady Lepeshkin, was a biosafety engineering expert. Lt. Col. Boris Kozhevnikov was an expert in concentration, drying, and testing techniques, whereas Lt. Col. Kiryenko had expertise in cultivation, and Lt. Col. Nikolai Chernyshov was a specialist in drying and milling techniques. Other defense transfers had expertise in aerosol methods and in filling and assembling biological munitions.

Alibek used these defense staff in the facility's managerial positions, making them deputy directors, department chiefs, laboratory heads, senior engineers, and senior scientists. Other Ministry of Defense majors, captains, and senior lieutenants took key technological, manufacturing, and biosafety positions. Alibek recalls that "depending on their knowledge, I would establish them in such a way so that these people would be responsible for some basic, critical points of production, critical equipment, critical processes."[35] These former defense personnel also served as master trainers and provided the initial on-site scientific training, lasting two to three months, for all new biological weapons technical recruits.

At the height of the facility's operation, roughly 125 of its 300-plus biological weapons specialists were senior, or highly experienced, bioweaponeers.[36] The remainder were technicians or engineering and support staff with varying skills related to biological weapons activities. These biological weapons specialists were organized in interdisciplinary teams across the various technological processes involved in R&D, production, and weaponization. The Stepnogorsk facility had no separate divisions for research and scale-up production. For example, joint organizational divisions were established for cultivation that brought together scientists, engineers, and other technicians. These interdisciplinary groups worked together on various aspects of the research, development, and production processes. Alibek says, "I developed this in such a way that we didn't have separate divisions for research and separate divisions for scale-up because I felt that as soon as you establish different entities, you increase the opposite. . . . In this new structure, they would interact."[37]

Alibek favored this arrangement to ensure that multiple staff were capable of assuming different technological functions and to facilitate production activities in the event of war. In order to promote interactions between the scientific and technological parts of the facility, technical personnel were allowed to have open discussions and collaborations. Extreme secrecy and compartmentalization, a characteristic of work at other Soviet biological weapons facilities, were absent within the walls of the Stepnogorsk facility. As Alibek explains, "When you talk about science and technology, you cannot keep everything separate. If you only provide the necessary information, you can get into trouble. It was permitted to collaborate and cooperate, at least in my facility. In our facility everything was interconnected, from all standpoints, so it would have been stupid to impose any secrets between different departments, divisions, and labs."[38] Thus, in order to promote bioweapons advances at the SNOPB, Alibek developed a different type of organizational style and structure, what historian of science Peter Galison calls "human architecture," from that in other Soviet bioweapons facilities—one that allowed for active cooperation and collaboration within the Stepnogorsk facility.[39]

At the R&D end, teams of specialists were involved in the storage, cultivation, small-scale fermentation, and aerosol testing of the anthrax agent. As an example, traditional research microbiologists worked with the 836 strain to establish ideal growth conditions. Once the strain moved to the development phase, which involved aerosol testing, additional specialists with expertise in aerobiology and explosives engineers joined other physical scientists in an effort to understand and control the dissemination dynamics during the testing phase.[40]

Industrial microbiologists and process engineers were involved in the large-scale biological weapons production activities within the Stepnogorsk facility. Weaponization of the agent (namely drying and milling) involved Stepnogorsk microbiologists and chemical and mechanical engineers. It also involved off-site collaborations with engineers at Ministry of Defense munition design bureaus and other Soviet biological weapons facilities.[41] Even the open-air testing on Vozrozhdeniye Island consisted of small, ten- to fifteen-person interdisciplinary teams of Stepnogorsk specialists who worked with resident ministry support personnel.[42] Alibek says that testing was a prerequisite for establishing the military utility of a Soviet biological weapon. Throughout the weapons activities at the facility, its scientists and engineers also maintained scientific exchanges and collaborations with other Soviet biological weapons facilities in Obolensk and Leningrad.[43] These interactions helped to solve research problems and improve the development of the facility's anthrax formulations as well as expand its scientific capabilities.[44]

Tacit Knowledge and Anthrax 836 Development

Tacit knowledge refers to the unarticulated, personally held knowledge that one acquires through a practical, hands-on process, through either "learning by doing" or "learning by example."[45] As I describe in more detail below, tacit knowledge appears to have played an important role in the SNOPB's development of the Soviets' new Anthrax 836 biological weapon. This tacit knowledge involved learning by example, from the knowledge and skills acquired through the transfer of sixty-five experienced Ministry of Defense bioweaponeers. It also involved significant learning by doing, via painstaking, trial-and-error problem-solving using the materials, techniques, and infrastructure unique to the Stepnogorsk facility.

Building on this tacit knowledge definition, sociologist of science H. M. Collins has proposed a useful set of categories of tacit knowledge, which he labels as "concealed knowledge," "mismatched salience," and "ostensive knowledge."[46] Concealed knowledge is a type of know-how that is purposefully held back from other researchers (for instance, when a researcher does not want to share his or her tricks of the trade with others); it can also refer to hands-on knowledge that is not written down in experimental protocols. Mismatched salience refers to a situation in which an experiment requires different types of know-how but no single researcher involved is aware of the totality and complexity of that know-how. To illustrate, researcher A does not realize that researcher B needs to be told to do things in a certain way, and researcher B does not know the right questions to ask; the know-how problem is solved when A and B watch each other work. Ostensive knowledge relates to visual or sensory types of know-how that cannot be conveyed through words, diagrams, or photographs. Collins uses these three categories to describe how different kinds of tacit knowledge can underpin scientific and technological work and how some are more difficult than others to acquire and transfer. In the development of the 836 weapon, we can see how these tacit knowledge categories shaped the development and transfer of bioweapons knowledge at the Stepnogorsk facility.

Although the facility did receive several hundred pages of technical documents involving previous Ministry of Defense anthrax work, Alibek notes that some classified information was not sent to Stepnogorsk. He attributes this to turf issues and competition at Sverdlovsk, the Ministry of Defense, and the SNOPB. As a result, this type of intentionally concealed tacit knowledge, as Collins describes, would be conveyed only through personal communication with the original developers of the Anthrax 836 weapon. Therefore, it is probable that some technical problems encountered by early, inexperienced Stepnogorsk staff when working with the anthrax bacteria resulted from a lack of information on certain parameters or protocols in ministry documents. The arrival of the experienced defense staff at the facility likely solved these problems. One could argue, however, that had turf issues not come into play, this concealed knowledge could have been conveyed explicitly to Stepnogorsk personnel instead of being sent through Ministry of Defense staff.

Beyond the concealed knowledge, however, additional tacit knowledge was evidently involved in solving other engineering and industrial problems at SNOPB. These types of problems, which would also not have been specified in the Ministry of Defense documentation, relate to Collins's categories of mismatched salience and ostensive tacit knowledge. To solve various engineering problems related to the unique infrastructure at SNOPB, workers adopted a trial-and-error process that deployed knowledge obtained through previous hands-on experience from working with fermentation, biosafety, drying, and milling equipment. Again, the arrival of the experienced ministry staff facilitated the deciphering of this ostensive tacit knowledge and the adaptation of existing ministry protocols to work at the Stepnogorsk facility. Thus, the ministry staff served important roles as what Polanyi describes as master trainers to new biological weapons technical recruits, transferring additional tacit knowledge that Collins would describe as mismatched salience and conveying experimental details that recruits lacking prior biological weapons experience would not know how to elicit.[47] The Stepnogorsk facility also developed and transferred what sociologists of science Alberto Cambrosio and Peter Keating would call incorporated, tacit knowledge via periodic exchanges and collaborations with other Soviet bioweaponeers.[48]

In addition to this individual, personally held knowledge, other S&TS scholars have also described communal types of tacit knowledge developed and embodied among various members of a scientific laboratory or technological complex. Namely, sociologists of science Donald MacKenzie and Graham Spinardi emphasize the importance of close working relationships among various interdisciplinary specialists in the development of nuclear weapons and describe how the British nuclear program faced difficulties in its own nuclear weapons development because British scientists were not involved in all aspects of the Manhattan Project.[49] In addition, MacKenzie and Spinardi note the difficulties that U.S., British, and Soviet nuclear scientists faced in solving a variety of unexpected and multifaceted technological problems that emerged due to the newness of the technology and the specific context in which each nuclear program was developed.

Similarly, much of the SNOPB's delay was related to solving new scientific and engineering problems that were neither anticipated nor specified in existing Ministry of Defense documentation and were unique to the facility. Thus, even the ministry staff was required to learn by doing: to develop new ways to translate existing protocols to a new biological weapons facility and to train new recruits in these adaptations. The delay was also due to the difficulty of working with live organisms that did not necessarily tolerate unfavorable growth or storage conditions.

In her study of the Los Alamos National Laboratory, anthropologist of science Laura McNamara describes the communal nature of tacit knowledge as the integration of heterogeneous bodies of knowledge through the design, engineering, and testing cycle to produce a working nuclear weapon.[50] McNamara's description seems to imply that prolonged interaction among different types of scientists across the weapons chain leads to the production of a new type of communally synthesized tacit knowledge that cannot be separated into individual components and is therefore more difficult to transfer. The development of the Anthrax 836 weapons required the synthesis of diverse sets of interdisciplinary expertise as well as new forms of work organization to facilitate this knowledge development and sharing. Thus, even with the transfer of experienced Ministry of Defense staff, it took five years to develop the new 836 technology at the SNOPB, even though the weapon was based on an existing weapons technology.[51]

Benjamin Sims, a sociologist of science at Los Alamos National Laboratory, has highlighted the importance of what he describes as "transactional knowledge" in weapons development.[52] Sims defines transactional knowledge as the organizational and management skills necessary to coordinate practices across multiple technical communities, such that the knowledge of each community can effectively contribute to a larger technological goal. For example, Sims finds that one of the greatest challenges Manhattan Project leaders faced was organizational coordination, which had never before been attempted on such a large scale and which led directly to modern methods of program management. Sims argues that in examining proliferation patterns, it is important to look beyond whether a nation merely has the appropriate technical experts and weapons-related materials; one must also assess whether the country in question possesses the experience in building the interdisciplinary collaborations required to sustain a large-scale research and development program.[53] He highlights the need to analyze how countries develop, organize, and manage different expert communities for weapons development.

At the Stepnogorsk facility, Alibek succeeded in creating a new type of transactional knowledge environment through specific managerial decisions that promoted close working relationships among the R&D, production, and weaponization divisions. As a former Stepnogorsk senior scientist noted: "I consider myself lucky to have worked with Alibek. He had an intelligent, open-minded approach to problem-solving and an unusual way of defining and implementing tasks. I have to note that the scientific personnel at Stepnogorsk responded very well to his management style and produced high-quality work on time. As for me, I enjoyed much more working at Stepnogorsk than at my former organization."[54] Alibek's organizational changes were an innovation in Soviet bioweapons development, which had a direct impact on the quality and type of science developed there.[55]

At the same time, testing was a critical component of the unique knowledge base at the SNOPB, as McNamara says it was at Los Alamos National Laboratory. This testing consisted both of periodic biological weapons production runs and open-air testing, which incorporated what sociologist of science Trevor Pinch calls "prospective" and "current" testing of technologies.[56] Prospective testing is a form of testing on prototype models that takes place before a new technology is formally released into use. The idea of such testing is to find out if the technology works as specified in its design and to monitor it for a range of possible uses. Current testing occurs once a technology is in use. It may be carried out in order to assess performance, to make improvements, to compare it with rival technologies, or to ascertain any special operational difficulties. For instance, a new Soviet biological weapon such as the Anthrax 836 weapon was not certified as reliable and militarily useful until it went through successful open-air tests on Vozrozhdeniye Island.[57] This testing on "Voz" Island confirmed the successful integration of explicit and tacit knowledge by the interdisciplinary team at the SNOPB and led to full-scale production runs three or four times per year to ensure that the facility remained fully mobilized for weapons production. The testing also reinforced the resident tacit weapons knowledge, because all biological weapons personnel participated in these large-scale test runs.

With all of these technological considerations, the Stepnogorsk case shows that it was difficult to develop the 836 weapon to operate in a new context, even with generous funds, resources, critical infrastructure, conducive organizational and management structures, and experienced personnel at the facility's disposal. This does not mean that potent biological weapons are too difficult to be produced by any state, merely that important tacit knowledge and related social dimensions of scientific and technological work tied to specific material contexts were critical to the development of the Soviet's mass-casualty anthrax weapon. Knowing these factors provides analysts and policymakers with new focal points for assessing other state or nonstate actor weapons programs. Given that social factors were so central to the SNOPB's success, how should we assess the present-day proliferation threats posed by its weapons scientists?

"Brain Drain" Threats from SNOPB Bioweaponeers

The first step in assessing proliferation threats from the Stepnogorsk bioweaponeers is to look at changes in the weapons knowledge base at the facility over time.

Starting in 1987, when the major Anthrax 836 work was completed, the Stepnogorsk facility began to downsize.[58] Gradually, some of the original design, production, and testing teams returned to the Ministry of Defense and other Soviet biological weapons facilities. Mounting concerns over Western intelligence and potential inspections prompted the Soviet government to destroy and dismantle critical weapons infrastructure at the Stepnogorsk facility.[59] In 1990, the unique 300-cubic-meter explosive aerosol test chamber was destroyed, and biological agent-filling lines for weaponization were sent back to Russian facilities.[60] With the collapse of the Soviet Union, more drastic personnel and infrastructure changes occurred at the Stepnogorsk facility: starting in 1993, the facility was mothballed and all weapons activities ceased; more bioweaponeers returned to Russia.[61]

What effect did these infrastructure changes have on the remaining tacit knowledge resident in these Stepnogorsk bioweaponeers? At the time of this writing, in 2012, it has been nineteen years since weapons work ceased at the SNOPB. Because of active oversight by U.S. government officials at the complex since 1997, the implication is that there has been no practice or use of specific weapons-related knowledge by Stepnogorsk scientists and engineers, particularly in the use of large fermentation, weaponization, and aerosol-testing equipment.[62] What's more, the facility stopped training new bioweaponeers in 1993, and only a few dozen former biological weapons specialists currently remain on site.[63]

Since 1997, U.S. government assistance has also contributed to further changes in the infrastructure and knowledge base at the Stepnogorsk facility. Initially, U.S. nonproliferation programs focused on dismantling the facility. By September 2000, all internal weapons-related infrastructure had been destroyed, and in 2007, the associated buildings were demolished.[64] Since this U.S.-funded work commenced at the facility, there has been stringent oversight and confirmation that no weapons-related activities have occurred on site during the dismantlement. Furthermore, since 1997, U.S. nonproliferation programs have provided financial assistance for redirection projects for former Stepnogorsk personnel. All of these projects have involved civilian research activities, with Stepnogorsk staff working with nonbiological weapons agents. U.S. government oversight throughout the course of these projects has provided assurances that Stepnogorsk bioweaponeers have not traveled to rogue states to transfer their biological weapons expertise personally. Therefore, during this fifteen-year period, these former Stepnogorsk scientists have not used their specific knowledge of anthrax and other biological weapons.

Nonetheless, one could argue that perhaps the greatest residual proliferation threat comes from the former Ministry of Defense scientists from the Kirov and Sverdlovsk biological weapons facilities who went to Stepnogorsk. These individuals were highly experienced and had translated their biological weapons know-how at multiple, diverse locations under challenging conditions. Science and technology studies scholars have emphasized the importance of translation in getting technologies to work in new contexts.[65] Given their experience and senior positions, moreover, these senior bioweaponeers likely had the privilege of seeing how their work (and that of their subordinates) fit into part of the larger weapons development process at the Stepnogorsk facility. To reduce the threat they may pose, the best policy would be to disband the remaining Stepnogorsk personnel, particularly the remaining former ministry scientists, and fund work for them on nonbiodefense research, so that their bioweapons-related skills would decay.

The notion that tacit knowledge can be lost if not used or transmitted within a generation was first posited by Polanyi, and MacKenzie and Spinardi have further explored the potential decay of tacit knowledge in nuclear weapons development from lack of use.[66] More recently, sociologists Benjamin Sims and Christopher Henke have studied how U.S. nuclear weapons labs have attempted to adapt in the absence of nuclear testing and found that both Los Alamos and Livermore national labs have developed concerted programs and practices that attempt to preserve tacit knowledge resident within and among the labs.[67] These programs, known collectively as the Stockpile Stewardship Program, consist of a variety of computational, experimental, training, and archival practices along with the preservation and new building of key infrastructure.[68] This collective of social and material structures, funded at a level of roughly $5 billion per year since 1995, aims to maintain technical practices at the nuclear weapons labs.[69] Still, nuclear weapons scientists have become increasingly skeptical of the Stockpile Stewardship Program's ability to pass on the nuclear weapons knowledge embedded in design, development, and testing to a new generation of nuclear weapons specialists. As MacKenzie, Spinardi, Sims, and Henke illustrate, effective nonproliferation policies depend on understanding both the preservation and erosion of tacit knowledge.

Polanyi, MacKenzie, and Spinardi seem to suggest that an entire generation would need to pass in order for tacit knowledge to be lost. But this view does not take into account potential gradations in the decay of tacit knowledge or variations in different types of tacit knowledge that Collins has outlined, such as ostensive knowledge. As an example, one could argue that certain sensory-based knowledge in technical work, such as how something looked or felt, could be forgotten in shorter periods of time. This type of knowledge would best relate to what engineer Eugene Ferguson describes as the visual and kinesthetic nature of engineering knowledge, or what sociologists of science Alberto Cambrosio and Peter Keating refer to as the visual art of working with hybrid biological cell lines.[70]

If one considers that certain types of tacit knowledge could degrade over shorter periods of time, then this has significant policy implications for the Stepnogorsk bioweaponeers, who have not been actively using their weapons know-how for the past nineteen years. In this case, one could argue that the proliferation threat of these bioweaponeers has diminished over time. Since much of the work carried out at the Stepnogorsk facility was done in a communal and interactive setting, the tacit knowledge related to Anthrax 836 was distributed across its research and development, production, and testing communities. Therefore, with the exception of Ken Alibek or Gennady Lepeshkin, who were involved in all aspects of bioweapons development in their careers, it is unlikely that one Stepnogorsk bioweaponeer would possess all of the knowledge necessary to replicate the 836 weapon or, by extension, any military-grade biological weapon. Breaking up the remaining Stepnogorsk bioweaponeers to work on nonbiodefense-related work would continue to degrade the communal tacit knowledge within its teams, so that this group knowledge would become much more difficult to transfer to possible proliferators.

Discussions about tacit knowledge and proliferation threats would be incomplete without considering a more cynical conclusion that may result from such an analysis. Critics of U.S. nonproliferation programs have argued that many former Soviet scientists claim to have been involved in bioweapons work and to possess biological weapons know-how but provide little evidence to substantiate these claims. Due to initial sensitivities about the Soviet biological weapons program, U.S. government officials have not pushed these purported weapons scientists to explain in more detail the nature of their former activities.[71] When the U.S. nonproliferation program was created in the early 1990s, such an approach was logical in order to engage these former bioweaponeers quickly and to build trust with their collaborators. With the passage of time and a new understanding about how some of these facilities operated during the Soviet period, it is now time to change the approach to dealing with some of these facilities and scientists.

We know that the current U.S. policy of counting bodies makes it difficult to differentiate between scientists who were actively involved in bioweapons work and people who were merely support or administrative staff. This means that the U.S. government may be supporting individuals who were never in fact involved in bioweapons work, thereby diverting funds that could be better spent on bioweaponeers who pose real proliferation threats. Individuals whose claims of expertise are never verified may be using their purported tacit knowledge to obtain or sustain power in the furtherance of political, economic, or social objectives.[72] These challenges for the brain drain prevention programs highlight the fact that there have been few studies conducted either inside or outside the government that examine the implications of tacit knowledge for weapons development or technology transfer.[73] Such studies would help policymakers understand the sociotechnical dimension of bioweapons proliferation and lead to better design and implementation of nonproliferation programs.[74]

More specifically, as MacKenzie and Spinardi did, intelligence and policy analysts could conduct in-depth interviews with former bioweaponeers who worked in different state programs at different times and during different stages of biological weapons development, such as research, production, weaponization, and delivery. A comparison of various processes in biological weapons development could help clarify the components of tacit knowledge, differentiate between the individual and communal types of such knowledge, and ascertain whether there is evidence that such knowledge erodes over time.[75] A complementary investigation of current advances in biology could determine the extent to which new tools, techniques, and equipment are replacing certain aspects of formerly tacit biological weapons knowledge. The results from such studies would provide more nuanced answers to the fundamental questions about which former bioweaponeers should be funded and for how long and how best to structure their work to lessen their retention of bioweapons know-how. The answers will vary, depending on the facility and its resident personnel, but would identify critical points for focused intervention and more meaningful measures to evaluate nonproliferation progress.

However, tacit knowledge may be only one of many social factors affecting biological weapons proliferation and bioterrorism. For instance, sociologists of science and technology Trevor Pinch and Wiebe Bijker argue that to understand how a specific technological artifact is created, we must look at the particular social groups that shape the choices about its meaning, development, and use. This social group analysis of how technologies develop provides another useful framework for evaluating bioweapons threats.[76] In the Soviet case, we learned that the Ministry of Defense, as the consumer, laid out specifications for Anthrax 836 that the Stepnogorsk facility was required to meet. The Soviet obsession with secrecy kept the facility from hiring additional technical staff from an adjoining civilian biopesticide facility, even though these individuals likely possessed the relevant knowledge and necessary skills. This need for secrecy also influenced the ministry's decision to relocate Soviet anthrax production to the SNOPB, an existing dual-use facility, instead of building an entirely new facility from scratch. As a result, the Stepnogorsk facility had to be retrofitted to support biological weapons production, which required solving new scientific and engineering problems. Thus, requirements and concerns from social groups such as the Ministry of Defense helped shape the development of the Anthrax 836 technology at Stepnogorsk.

The above considerations lead us to ask what social groups could be involved in shaping other state or terrorist development of biological weapons and how their demands might differ from those encountered at Stepnogorsk. Terrorism experts have generally argued that terrorists tend to be technologically conservative with regard to the weapons they develop and use. By contrast, the Ministry of Defense was technologically aggressive, using the most advanced technology in existence at the time for its Anthrax 836 weapon. This juxtaposition suggests that a more nuanced analysis of how social groups shape bioweapons development by states and nonstate actors is needed.

Finally, it is clear that secrecy practices at the Stepnogorsk facility shaped the production of knowledge there. To preserve secrecy of the Soviet bioweapons program, for example, the facility was established in the remote steppes of Kazakhstan. This decision forced Stepnogorsk management and workers to use existing—albeit ill-suited—infrastructure, personnel, and resources to develop the Soviets' anthrax weapon. Thus, the decision to maintain external secrecy resulted in a lengthy and laborious process for developing bioweapons at the facility. Other types of external secrecy imposed on the production of knowledge included the Ministry of Defense's refusal to share key scientific information from existing anthrax weapons work at other defense facilities. Interestingly, this secrecy was imposed by officials from a fellow weapons institute, individuals who should have been doing everything in their power to help the Stepnogorsk facility to further Soviet bioweapons efforts. This counterintuitive example illustrates how secrecy can be a double-edged sword and not always beneficial to bioweapons efforts.[77] This finding is consistent with other socio-organizational problems found in modern biotech industry work.[78]

Moreover, the Stepnogorsk case shows that a variety of secrecy practices can shape the production of knowledge. For instance, inside the walls of the SNOPB, secrecy practices varied. One aim was to maintain separation of knowledge by not hiring staff from the adjacent civilian facility, but Alibek also chose to ignore and reinterpret existing Soviet secrecy practices covering the organization of scientific work within the SNOPB. Alibek broke down the practice of work compartmentalization and encouraged interdisciplinary collaboration among his staff. These complex and malleable secrecy practices at play within a particular weapons facility play an important role in shaping the production of bioweapons work.

The Future of U.S. Brain Drain Programs

Since September 11, 2001, the biotech revolution frame and its associated technological narratives have suggested that these brain drain programs move in new directions. New criticisms and questions have emerged as to whether former weapons scientists possess unique knowledge and skills that should be the sole focus of these nonproliferation programs, or whether any nation with WMD-relevant knowledge, materials, or industry that could be accessible to states or terrorist groups should also be considered.[79] For example, a 2009 Institute of Medicine and National Research Council study entitled *Global Security Engagement: A New Model for Cooperative Threat Reduction* emphasized that in recent years there has been an evolution in how WMD threats have been defined. The report explains that "over time, policymakers came to understand that not only those with direct, past weapons experience pose a risk, but also those capable of creating weapons threats pose a risk and should be included in programs."[80] In talking specifically about new biological threats, the report goes on to state, "The universal availability of information and the highly dual-use nature of many technologies, particularly in the biological and chemical fields, make it possible to develop a WMD without having previously worked directly in a state WMD program."[81]

This new global outlook for nonproliferation began to materialize in 2006 when a new State Department Biosecurity Engagement Program was launched.[82] This program was pursuant to a National Security Council–mandated, interagency-approved U.S. government strategy for strengthening global security with the aim of preventing terrorists and proliferators from acquiring WMD-related expertise, materials, and technology. As the State Department strategy paper for this initiative noted, "The threat of bioterrorism is increasing due to gradual lowering of the technical and financial barriers to purchase the materials, technologies, and expertise to develop biological weapons that are linked to the worldwide growth in biotechnology . . . particularly in states with rapidly expanding bioscience sectors that never had biological weapons programs."[83] To illustrate this thesis, a State Department official chose to highlight the words of Abu Ayyub al-Masri, a member of al-Qaeda in Iraq, who said, "We are in dire need of you [scientists]. The field of jihad can satisfy your scientific ambitions, and the large American bases [in Iraq] are good places to test your unconventional weapons, whether biological or dirty, as they call them."[84]

From a modest allocation of $4 million in fiscal year 2006, the congressional appropriation for this new State Department global biosecurity engagement program has grown to over $90 million over the past three years.[85] In fiscal year 2007, biosecurity activities were launched in more than twelve countries throughout Asia, the Middle East, and Latin America.[86] According to a September 2008 report, these new biological engagement programs comprised 41 percent of the State Department's entire Nunn-Lugar budget; for fiscal year 2011, that figure had risen to 48 percent.[87] Moreover, traditional programs such as the International Science and Technology Center (ISTC) in Moscow and the Science and Technology Center (STCU) in Ukraine, which were primarily focused on the former Soviet WMD threat, are being transformed to address these emerging global WMD threats and terrorist challenges as well.[88]

The growth in these global activities is prompting significant and continuing funding reductions for the State Department's former Soviet bioweapons brain drain efforts.[89] In 2009, for instance, ISTC and STCU funding decreased 10 percent, and funding for former Soviet biochem engagement programs decreased 8 percent from fiscal year 2008; these numbers have continued to decrease for fiscal year 2011.[90] In comparison, in 2006, more than one-half of the State Department's Nunn-Lugar–related budget was applied to biothreat reduction projects in the former Soviet Union.[91] State Department officials report that funding for ISTC and STCU projects in the former Soviet Union will decrease at a rate of 25 percent per year through 2012, the anticipated close-out date for support of former Soviet weapons scientists from these centers.[92]

Furthermore, in fiscal years 2004–2009, the U.S. Department of Defense's bioweapons proliferation prevention program has reduced its biological research engagement with Russia while expanding its involvement with other nations of the former Soviet Union.[93] A 2007 National Research Council report noted, however, that only 10 percent of the budget being considered by the Department of Defense for the future will be allocated for funding brain drain–type research activities.[94] This report also noted the shrinking budgets of State Department and other interagency bio-engagement efforts with Russia and the former Soviet Union.[95] As the National Research Council report highlights, "Although the economic situation in Russia is stabilizing, the future of a number of larger biological institutions is in flux; and many former weapon scientists remain trapped in uncertain circumstances that could raise serious proliferation concerns."[96]

However, this same report supports the Defense Department's shift to engage a "second tier" of younger, nonweapons scientists and specialists, because "many will have dual-use skills that could become a future concern unless they are committed to peaceful and transparent activities."[97] As the report recommends: "The engagement of 'former weapons scientists' often in preference to non-weapon scientists, needs to receive less emphasis. An ever growing number of scientists throughout the world who have never been involved in military-related activities are developing dual-use capabilities. Of course it is important to continue to engage former weapon scientists who have special skills of concern, but the primary criteria in selecting scientists for engagement should be two-fold: their potential dual-use capabilities and/or their contributions in strengthening the scientific, public health, and agriculture infrastructures for addressing infectious diseases in their countries."[98] Some have questioned whether civilian scientists in these other nations have enough skills or knowledge to pose a significant proliferation risk, at the expense of mitigating proliferation from highly skilled weapons scientists from the former Soviet bioweapons complex.[99] Privately, however, some U.S. government officials associated with these Nunn-Lugar programs have said they see these new global biological engagements as the nonproliferation priority for the future. As a 2008 Congressional Research Service report notes, "This new global focus may serve to shape the second decade of U.S. threat reduction and nonproliferation assistance."[100] For the fiscal year 2011 budget request, the U.S. Department of Defense is asking for $209 million for its Biological Threat Reduction Program. The bulk of these funds will be used for collaborative biosafety and biosecurity activities in Azerbaijan, Armenia, Georgia, Kazakhstan, Ukraine, and Uzbekistan.[101]

One can see that these changes in policy direction reflect the underlying biotech revolution frame, which has assumed a democratization of expertise with biotechnology developments. The assumption is based on the frame's focus on codified knowledge, material end products, the accessibility of biological materials, the globalization and diffusion of technology, a future orientation, and assumptions about linear or exponential technological trajectories. With this democratization of expertise, weapons knowledge is no longer seen as consisting of a special kind of know-how developed through particular kinds of material, social, and organizational practices. As a result, these decreases in nonproliferation funding to former Soviet scientists suggest that specialized bioweapons knowledge is seen by policy officials as less dangerous than the ill-defined "dual-use" threats. This conclusion logically flows from a reliance on the biotech revolution frame and its associated technological narratives and policy practices.

As we have seen in this chapter, though, a biosocial analytic frame demonstrates that the development of a mass-casualty biological weapon is a nontrivial undertaking; the social dimensions and context of bioweapons work matter. Nonetheless, policy decisions about global threat reduction rarely involve consideration of the sociotechnical nature of bioweapons development and biotechnological work. This omission is unfortunate, because the frame analysts and policymakers use to understand bioweapons threats has a big impact on the decisions they reach about the development of nonproliferation policies and programs.

PART THREE

ANALYTIC FAILURES IN BIOWEAPONS ASSESSMENTS

OVERVIEW
"Curveball" and the Iraqi Mobile Bioweapons Threat

In February 2003, Secretary of State Colin Powell spoke to the United Nations, outlining the case for U.S. invasion of Iraq. In his speech, Powell warned of the dangers from Iraq's purported WMD programs. Using specially declassified intelligence information, Powell highlighted—with dramatic visual imagery—Iraq's continued development of biological weapons, emphasizing its alleged development of a mobile biological weapons capability (fig. O.1). Powell took time in his speech to emphasize the credibility of the intelligence underpinning these claims, arguing that these mobile biological factories could produce enough anthrax bacteria and botulinum toxin to kill thousands of people.

From a series of postwar investigations conducted by government and nongovernment sources,[1] we now know that CIA analysts relied primarily on secret information provided by an Iraqi defector known as Rafid Ahmed Alwan al-Janabi, code-named "Curveball," to inform the bioweapons assessments that underpinned Powell's UN speech.[2] These investigations, however, also revealed that Curveball was a fabricator.[3]

In most standard media and policy accounts, the Iraqi mobile lab story begins in late 1999, when Curveball arrived in Germany seeking asylum. During subsequent interrogations by German intelligence, Curveball claimed that he was a chemical engineer who had worked in the design and operation of Saddam Hussein's secretive mobile bioweapons laboratories. German intelligence passed these reports to U.S. intelligence. On receiving Curveball's reports, the CIA's bioweapons analysts took a particular interest in the mobile lab claims. With this new

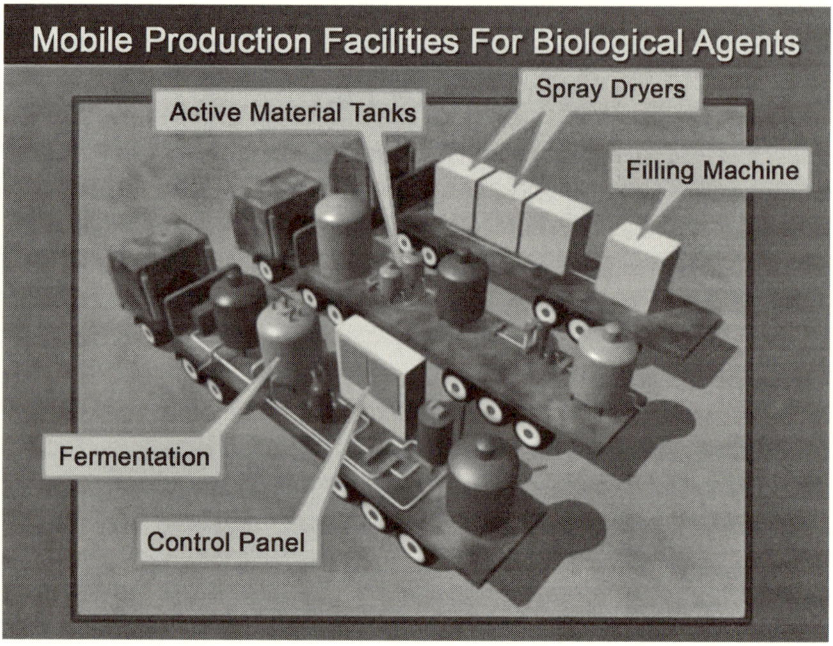

Fig. O.1. Trucks outfitted for purported biological weapon use. From Colin Powell, "Iraq: Failing to Disarm. Biological Weapons," Address to the United Nations, 5 February 2003, slide 20. http://2001-2009.state.gov/secretary/former/powell/photos/2003/17323.htm.

intelligence information, subsequent classified CIA reports and briefings to policymakers began emphasizing a more worrisome assessment of Iraq's covert bioweapons capabilities. Prompted in part by this and other examples of Saddam's supposed advanced weapons, the United States launched Operation Iraqi Freedom in March 2003 to disarm Iraq of its suspected weapons of mass destruction.

Only a few weeks after the start of the war, in a dramatic turn of events, Kurdish and U.S. military forces in Mosul and Erbil seized three trailers suspected of serving as the mobile bioweapons laboratories.[4] The discovery of these trailers seemed to vindicate Curveball's claims and the U.S. intelligence community's threat assessments about Iraq's mobile bioweapons capabilities. In a May 2003 press interview, President George W. Bush touted these findings: "We found the weapons of mass destruction. We found biological laboratories. You remember when Colin Powell stood up in front of the world, and he said, Iraq has got laboratories, mobile labs to build biological weapons. They're illegal. They're against the United Nations resolutions, and we've so far discovered two. And we'll find more weapons as time goes on. But for those who say we haven't found the banned manufacturing devices or banned weapons, they're wrong, we found them."[5] Within a year's time, a diverse collection of government and nongovernment analysts had discredited the purpose of the captured trailers and all of the intelligence evidence about the mobile biological labs presented in Powell's UN speech. We now know that Iraq's bioweapons program ended back in 1996 and that it is unlikely that Iraq ever had a mobile bioweapons capability.[6]

Not only were the Iraq bioweapons assessments proved wrong, but the CIA also misjudged Iraq's chemical and nuclear weapons capabilities. These intelligence failures were even more significant because, as intelligence expert Dennis Gormley writes, "Ironically, compared to other contemporaneous intelligence challenges, Iraq actually offered a set of favorable circumstances for gathering and analyzing intelligence on Saddam Hussein's WMD programmes. . . . American intelligence had the benefit of a target long accessible not just through space imaging and signals intelligence systems but also through United Nations inspectors on the ground."[7] With such rich intelligence resources, it is surprising that all of the CIA's WMD assessments on Iraq were incorrect. Yet even if Hussein took great efforts to obscure his WMD intentions and activities, an independent group of former U.S. intelligence officials appointed to review the classified data used in the flawed Iraq intelligence assessments found major deficiencies in intelligence collection and analysis on Iraq. As this group explained, "The Intelligence Community did not have conclusive evidence on what the Iraqis were working on, what they had achieved, which programs were ongoing, who was working them, or what the doctrines for use might be. Conversely, the Community saw no evidence that WMD programs were slowed, put on hold, or even nonexistent."[8] Within the U.S. intelligence community, however, the erroneous Iraqi WMD assessments have been described as resulting from a "perfect storm," a rare moment in history during which the confluence of poor information, judgment, and actions led to the intelligence failures.[9] With respect to the mobile lab case, most investigations of its intelligence failures have concluded that the key assessment problems resulted from Curveball's singular, cunning fabrications plus a combination of bad analysis, management, and politics.[10]

Given the acknowledged failures in the Iraq assessments, policymakers and intelligence professionals have recognized the need for intelligence reform. Recently, recommendations for change have centered on the need for more intelligence collection on WMD issues, better oversight of the analytic process, and the creation of new organizational structures for analysis.[11] Others have emphasized changes in analytic practice, such as the need for multiple sources, more written caveats on information limitations, skepticism of source information, and better technical expertise to inform assessments.[12] Although some of these reforms do hold merit, they have not dealt with the fundamental analytic shortcomings stemming from the frames and practices that intelligence analysts have used since the end of the Cold War to construct knowledge about bioweapons threats. Although this omission is glaring from studies of and policy responses to the Iraq intelligence failure, it is not surprising. Former assistant secretary of state for intelligence Carl Ford remarks: "People just can't come to accept that if you spend $20 billion a year [for U.S. intelligence], that we would miss something like Iraq WMD. That has to be an anomaly. I think that the best analysis that the [U.S. intelligence] community has done recently has been on Iraq. It wasn't on China, it wasn't on Korea, it wasn't on the Middle East. It was on Iraq WMD. And that's sort of an example of our analytic work at its best. And that people don't want to hear. They want to assume that we messed up but that everything else is okay. But I think that you need to look at it and begin to ask whether there is a fundamental problem."[13]

This overview and the chapters that follow illustrate how the fundamental problems in the Iraqi bioweapons assessments were due to analysts using the biotech revolution frame. Relying on this frame led CIA analysts to privilege the authority of material and technical factors within intelligence reports and assume, incorrectly, that Iraq's bioweapons capability had grown more sophisticated with the march of time. Analysts relied so heavily on this frame's simple understanding of bioweapons technologies that they disregarded contrary evidence, the absence of evidence, and alternative explanations for intelligence on the mobile bioweapons labs. The biotech revolution frame, however, tells only part of the story. Errors in CIA analytic judgments also stemmed from the way the biotech revolution frame was coupled with particular CIA organizational practices that reinforced and magnified the extent to which bioweapons analysts trusted and relied on this frame and its technological narratives in their assessments.

In her book *Whole World on Fire: Organizations, Knowledge, and Nuclear Weapons Devastation,* Lynn Eden examines how particular institutional frames and practices can shape knowledge in weapons assessments. Eden confronts the puzzle of how U.S. nuclear war planners developed detailed knowledge about the blast damage caused by nuclear weapons but systematically ignored the more devastating effects of mass fire damage in their calculations and plans. Eden argues that to understand this disconnect, one must examine how knowledge is constructed in organizations. In her analysis, Eden highlights two key concepts she calls "organizational frames" and "knowledge-laden organizational routines." Eden defines organizational frames as the bounded approach by which organizations choose problems, develop strategies to solve those problems, and place constraints and requirements on possible solutions; this involves using only certain kinds of information, technologies, and experts. Eden then defines knowledge-laden organizational routines as the resulting practices by which organizations go about finding solutions to the problems they have decided to solve.

With these organizational frames and routines, Eden argues that organizational capacity to work on nuclear problems developed along certain lines, lines that reinforced the kinds of knowledge, expertise, research programs, and practices brought to bear in these assessments. As a result, these analytic approaches became a taken-for-granted way of doing assessments; what was lost in the process was an understanding of how those frames and practices privileged the solving of a narrow, and ultimately incomplete, set of problems with respect to the damage resulting from nuclear weapons. The negative consequences, Eden says, are that "certain expertise will not be brought to bear on problems, the organization will not be structured in certain ways to carry out investigations, and organizational routines will carry certain kinds of knowledge but not others kinds."[14] Thus, Eden's work argues for the importance of understanding the institutional social context in which analysts work to produce knowledge and the ways that this context can leave out important considerations for analysis and policymaking.

The Iraq bioweapons intelligence failure is a salient example of how analysts within organizations such as the CIA have used particular frames and practices to structure work, which in turn have shaped the kinds of knowledge they produced about bioweapons threats. In the Curveball case, CIA analysts missed important contextual considerations in evaluating Iraq's purported mobile bioweapons capability by relying on the biotech revolution frame and problematic analytic practices. The next section provides a brief historical overview of U.S. suspicions about Iraqi mobile bioweapons and explains how Curveball became such an important resource for CIA analysts, even as other intelligence and nongovernment officials questioned the reliability of such intelligence.

Iraqi Mobile Bioweapons Suspicions (1991–1999)

Immediately after the Gulf War in 1991, Iraq repeatedly denied that it had an offensive biological weapons program. During this time, the CIA knew little about Iraq's bioweapons capabilities.[15] This situation changed with the onset of intrusive on-the-ground inspections by the United Nations. As described in chapter 2, between 1994 and early 1995 the UN weapons inspection team known as the United Nations Special Commission (UNSCOM) obtained substantial material evidence indicating that Iraq had possessed an offensive bioweapons program prior to the Gulf War.[16] Although Iraqi officials continued to hide details of their past bioweapons activities, UNSCOM's findings bolstered concerns within the CIA and throughout the U.S. intelligence community that Iraq was maintaining a covert bioweapons program.

Beyond that, in December 1996, U.S. intelligence received a human intelligence report of two Iraqi notes, handwritten on Iraqi Military Industrialisation Commission letterhead, suggesting that Iraq had once considered a mobile bioweapons production capability in the late 1980s.[17] These notes were related to earlier unclassified information that the U.S. intelligence community had received from UNSCOM, which had interviewed General Amir Al-Saadi, Hussein's chief science advisor.[18] Although Al-Saadi admitted to UNSCOM that he desired mobile biological labs for the Iraqi offensive bioweapons program, he stated that he ultimately decided against pursuing this concept for pragmatic reasons; Iraqi bioweapons scientists had determined that a functional mobile capability was too difficult, cumbersome, and impractical.[19] Thus, no specific drawings or plans for a mobile bioweapons lab concept were ever made by Iraq, and no mobile facilities were ever built.

After this Al-Saadi revelation, however, UNSCOM conducted a series of investigations to determine if they could find evidence of a hidden mobile bioweapons capability. According to UNSCOM inspector Gabriele Kraatz-Wadsack, "In '97 I went with Scott Ritter [UN inspector] because he got intel information [about mobile bioweapons labs]. We went to [Saddam Hussein's son] Qusay's car shop in person to look at all the refrigerated trucks . . . and Scott even looked in a railroad compartment. We investigated and he looked at railroads . . . but we never found any evidence."[20] In spite of this lack of evidence about mobile bioweapons labs, the CIA's bioweapons analysts continued to be concerned about the potential covert expansion and advancement of Iraq's bioweapons program through mobile laboratories or other "underground" or hidden means.

In addition, in the mid-1990s, a foreign intelligence service had issued a classified report from a human source who had attended an Iraqi chemical weapons conference, indicating that Iraq was considering a mobile capability for its chemical weapons program.[21] The Iraqi concept of chemical weapons mobility would entail positioning large stockpiles of chemical precursors and other materials at different sites. One set of production equipment would then move around Iraq to the locations where the materials were stored, and production would occur at the fixed sites, not on the road. According to the source, Iraq considered a mobile chemical weapons program to save money, although in the end, the Iraqis also deemed this concept unreliable, inefficient, and not cost-saving. Yet when this initial foreign intelligence report was posted in the CIA's classified intranet system, the CIA's bioweapons analysts took special interest in it.[22]

From August 1998 through November 2002, UN inspections were halted due to Iraqi noncompliance. During this gap, CIA analysts assumed that Iraq was continuing its bioweapons efforts unabated. In 1999, one year after Iraq kicked out UN inspectors, two U.S. National Intelligence Council reports noted that there existed no reliable U.S. intelligence—neither human intelligence, nor signals intelligence, nor satellite imagery—to indicate that Iraqi bioweapons activities had resumed or expanded.[23] At the same time, however, these and other intelligence reports repeatedly pointed to Iraq's persistent strategy to deny, deceive, and conceal information about its past WMD programs to UN inspectors. With this in mind, the CIA's analytic community judged that Iraq's denial and deception efforts were so sophisticated that they *must* have mobile biological laboratories. As one analyst states, "If you had followed since 1988 . . . there was a history and track record of [Iraqi] lying, hiding, and obfuscation. . . . Based on all the [intelligence] reporting it is following a pattern of continued obfuscation. We know the infrastructure is there and the people are there, so according to our best judgment these things are going on."[24] Here this analyst is explicitly pointing to material factors and simple body counts as critical measures of bioweapons capability. Another former U.S. intelligence analyst adds: "There were so many suspicions about that country [Iraq] and what they were doing at the time. Mobile labs are a typical evolution, you might say, in thinking when you send over inspectors for years and you don't find anything. So you say, well maybe they [Iraqis] are moving them [bioweapons] around, maybe they are in boxcars or in trailer trucks. So we never saw one, but someone, somewhere along the line came up with this idea. . . . Maybe they [Iraqis] are just rolling these things [mobile labs] all over the place."[25] In drawing on the biotech revolution frame and its associated technological narratives, CIA analysts constructed an understanding of Iraq as an enemy with a covert and portable bioweapons capability. Thus, through the 1990s, U.S. intelligence attention remained on the covert, quantitative, and material possibilities constituting Iraq's bioweapons capabilities. It was within this analytic context that Curveball and his claims surfaced.

The Rise of Curveball (1999–2002)

In late 1999, Rafid Ahmed Alwan al-Janabi, an Iraqi citizen, arrived in Germany seeking asylum. During subsequent interrogations by the Bundesnachrichtendienst

(BND), Germany's intelligence agency, Alwan claimed that he was a chemical engineer who had worked in the design and operation of Saddam's secretive mobile bioweapons laboratories. Alwan stated that Iraq had started a mobile bioweapons program in 1995, ultimately creating seven mobile production units in specific locations; one of those units had supposedly begun production of bioweapons agents as early as 1997.[26] With these claims, the BND quickly named a bioweapons technical analyst as the chief interrogator responsible for running the debriefing sessions with Alwan and for submitting these reports to BND management.[27] Over the next year and a half, the BND interrogated Alwan fifty-two times about Saddam's mobile bioweapons program, ultimately generating over a hundred reports from him.[28]

In early 2000, the BND passed these reports to the DIA operations base in Munich. The DIA then forwarded the reports to the Counterproliferation Division within the CIA's Directorate of Operations and to bioweapons analysts at the CIA's Weapons, Intelligence, Nonproliferation, and Arms Control Center (WINPAC), located within the Directorate of Intelligence (fig. O.2); both of these CIA units were responsible for technical issues related to the collection and the analysis of biological weapons threats, respectively. WINPAC analysts, however, were given primary responsibility for judging raw intelligence reports and producing finished intelligence reports for policymakers. Once in CIA hands, Alwan was given the codename "Curveball."

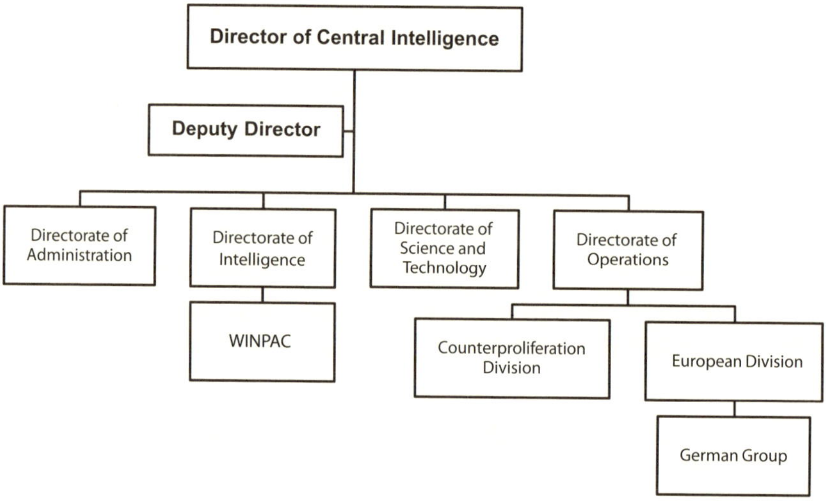

Fig. O.2. CIA organization chart, 2002–2003. Kathleen Vogel.

Upon receiving Curveball's reports, WINPAC's bioweapons analysts were impressed that his information seemed very technical, including dimensions, temperature ranges, equipment dials, and other engineering details about the mobile labs. CIA analysts prized these technical "facts," which they judged could be objectively verified independent of an Iraqi context. In his reports, Curveball sketched examples of the purported laboratory equipment on the mobile facilities and made a model of one of the lab depots.[29] As one former analyst described Curveball's early drawings: "His background was more engineering, so the drawings were more engineering-y as a opposed to bio. . . . With his engineering background he was from a State establishment for heavy equipment manufacturing . . . so they were making things and putting them on the trailers . . . and he talked about dials, some were temperature dials, some were pressure dials, he never said he knew what was in there. . . . He said that they called them [biological agents] by codenames A, B, C."[30] According to Curveball, some of the Iraqi mobile labs consisted of three commercial tractor-trailer trucks that could be connected to form a single efficient bioweapons production unit. Once the units were in production, Curveball stated, Iraqi technicians could adjust flow rates, temperatures, and other variables to produce five different biological agents.[31]

The BND would not allow U.S. and foreign intelligence analysts and collectors direct access to Curveball. CIA analysts had only limited access to Curveball's BND debriefers or details about their debriefing sessions; U.S. intelligence also never received the full transcripts of the BND's debriefing sessions.[32] The technical details of the purported mobile bioweapons labs in the BND reports, however, captivated the WINPAC analysts. Early on, to evaluate further the feasibility of Curveball's mobile lab descriptions, WINPAC analysts employed technical experts (in-house and contractors) to study the reports. Based on abstract technical considerations alone, these experts assessed Curveball's reports to represent "workable" engineering designs for mobile bioweapons laboratories.

In early 2000, WINPAC analysts also used satellite imagery to evaluate the credibility of the purported location of depot sites for the mobile labs that Curveball had mentioned. For example, satellite photos from the National Imagery and Mapping Agency identified Iraqi buildings at the Amiriyah Serum and Vaccine Institute that could house such mobile production plants as well as increased activity and construction at these sites, although there was no evidence of mobile labs or other illicit activity present on the imagery.[33] As one of these analysts admitted, "When we reviewed the imagery we couldn't find any evidence of the [mobile BW production] plants being there."[34] But, as one CIA bioweapons analyst explained, "We were able to identify the sites he [Curveball] had named to be agricultural sites housing these mobile plants. Stuff that looked like more corroboration to us at the time."[35] With these considerations, the CIA's bioweapons analysts added these imagery data to their Iraqi mobile bioweapons file. In finished intelligence reports to policymakers about the purported mobile labs, WINPAC analysts emphasized that "the reported locations of these plants have been identified in imagery, but Iraq has most likely dispersed these units since the source defected."[36]

WINPAC analysts, however, did not pursue in-depth investigation of possible legitimate civilian activities at these suspect sites. Namely, from the late 1990s to 2002, Iraq conducted some large human and animal vaccination campaigns that involved increased activity at purported mobile bioweapons sites like the Amiriyah Serum and Vaccine Institute.[37] Nonetheless, WINPAC analysts did not spend resources or effort to investigate these civilian activities as an explanation for the "suspicious" activity noted on the imagery. Instead, the increased activity in the satellite imagery was simply interpreted by the CIA's bioweapons analysts as potential mobile bioweapons-related activities.[38] By early 2000, WINPAC analysts had concluded that Curveball's information—and thus an Iraqi mobile bioweapons threat—was plausible based on the cumulative weight of imagery, previous classified intelligence, and Curveball's technical descriptions.[39] According to a former U.S. intelligence analyst, there was nothing "obviously wrong" in this cumulative body of evidence.[40]

Beginning in 2001, analysts received new human intelligence sources that were added to the growing Iraqi mobile bioweapons file. In June, an asylum seeker who was an Iraqi chemical engineer, often referred to as "the second source," provided a human intelligence report stating that Iraq had "transportable facilities for the production of biological weapons mounted on trailers at a special armaments factory in Iraq, and that there were other Iraqi sites where biological weapons were produced. The report noted that protective gear had to be worn in these transportable facilities, which were housed in partially underground buildings that were surrounded by a fence."[41] When analysts turned once again to satellite imagery to find the purported sites named by the source, they were unable to locate the transportable bioweapons systems. Similar to the Curveball reports, analysts assumed that this lack of evidence was due to deception—that Iraq was hiding its activities from U.S. satellite overflights—instead of the absence of weapons activities.[42]

In addition, in March 2002, an Iraqi major associated with the Iraqi National Congress (INC), often referred to as "the INC source," provided a human intelligence report stating that the Iraqi intelligence service was attempting to procure mobile biological research labs that would allow Iraq to conceal its research work from UN inspectors.[43] Although this report did not specifically discuss biological weapons, CIA analysts added the report to the Iraqi mobile bioweapons file as another piece of evidence.[44] They also obtained seven other intelligence reports concerning suspect Iraqi bioweapons activities. Some of this information was related to findings from UN inspections. As Rolf Ekeus, former UNSCOM chairman, explains, "Iraq did have a number of trucks to transport frozen materials around, some of these, some in convoy were picked up by overhead imagery."[45] According to a UN biological weapons inspections unit, other refrigerated trucks were found to be used to transport foodstuffs such as milk, meat, ice, and other perishable items to military units.[46] Yet none of these trucks identified by UN inspections concealed bioweapons activities. This information, however, was still interpreted by WINPAC analysts as suggesting a potential Iraqi mobile bioweapons capability and was placed in the growing Iraqi mobile bioweapons file.

WINPAC analysts also obtained intelligence from a fourth human source. This source, known by the code name "Red River," was an Iraqi official who had spied for British intelligence. Red River provided eight human intelligence reports on purported Iraqi mobile units starting in 2000.[47] In one report dated September 2002, Red River stated that "Iraq had manufactured mobile production systems mounted on road-trailer units and on rail cars."[48] He admitted, however, that his information was hearsay from a "new sub-source" with links to Iraqi opposition groups; he had not witnessed or confirmed these mobile systems himself.[49]

Despite the evidence from additional human sources and imagery data, WINPAC analysts turned overwhelmingly to Curveball's intelligence to assess a purported Iraqi mobile bioweapons capability. Curveball ultimately supplied 119 human intelligence reports.[50] As already mentioned, other classified information was added as supporting evidence for Curveball's claims. There is no indication, however, that CIA analysts conducted contextualized analyses to verify these other classified pieces of human source and imagery data. Because technical experts were able to assess that Curveball's technical and physical descriptions appeared to be plausible, WINPAC analysts deemed Curveball's reports likely to be true and judged him to be a credible human source.[51]

Although other CIA and intelligence analysts were brought in for various briefings and assessments of the purported mobile labs, WINPAC analysts had the lead authority in drafting the reports, determining what additional expert knowledge was needed to evaluate Curveball's claims, choosing what information was relevant to include in the assessments, and communicating this information to senior intelligence and policy officials. As such, the mobile lab assessments remained within the exclusive purview of WINPAC analysts, who were designated as the

CIA's technical experts on weapons assessments.[52] WINPAC's judgments were then accepted across the U.S intelligence community. As a Senate report indicates, "Additional reporting from Curveball, and additional human intelligence (HUMINT) sources that analysts believed corroborated his reporting, was instrumental in the IC [intelligence community] shifting its characterization of Iraq's mobile BW [bioweapons] production program from an assessment in December 2000 that stated, 'according to credible US military reporting Baghdad now can produce biological agents in transportable plants' to the 2002 NIE's [National Intelligence Estimate] assessment that 'Baghdad *has* transportable facilities.'"[53] Yet the impact of Curveball's reporting went beyond the Iraqi mobile labs case. More generally, Curveball's reporting was crucial to revising the CIA's overall assessments on the state of Iraq's bioweapons program, which intelligence analysts determined to be continuing and becoming more advanced. As one CIA bioweapons analyst indicates, "The big factor changing [bioweapons] assessments that we had since the Gulf War was this body of [human source] reporting we got on the mobile bioweapons program."[54]

Internal CIA Debates about Curveball (Fall 2002)

In September 2002, as Iraq WMD issues began to take center stage in the George W. Bush administration and in the public press, the CIA's management within its Directorate of Operations requested that its European Division, and more specifically its German group, obtain more information about and access to Curveball from the BND. This was the first time that the Operations management had formally requested that its European Division and German group assess the Curveball case from an Operations tradecraft perspective, that is, through the methods used by Operations personnel to assess the veracity of the claims and integrity of a human intelligence source. In examining Curveball's reports, Margaret Henoch, the European Division's German group chief at that time, grew concerned that Curveball's reporting had not been subjected to a rigorous tradecraft evaluation, particularly because there were troubling issues throughout his reporting. In e-mailing her concerns to Operations management, Henoch emphasized that "the [foreign intelligence service] ha[s] developed some doubts about him. We have been unable to vet him operationally and know very little about him."[55] WINPAC analysts, however, continued to focus on the technical details that Curveball provided to inform their assessment of his credibility and argued that critics such as Henoch and others were not aware that "WINPAC had multiple sources reporting on the program."[56]

By early 2001, however, the Directorate of Operations' Counterproliferation Division had received additional messages from German intelligence indicating problems with Curveball; he was becoming an erratic source. Also, contradictions in Curveball's reporting emerged during this time; he retracted some of his previous claims and could not say whether the mobile labs functioned or if they were even bioweapons-related. By September 2001, the BND had lost contact with Curveball.[57] When he resurfaced in 2002, the BND reported that he continued to be a "handling problem."[58] In April 2002, British intelligence had also raised concerns about Curveball's conduct and change in reporting, stating that "elements of [Curveball's] behavior strike us as typical of individuals we would normally assess as fabricators."[59] WINPAC analysts, however, had set those inconsistencies aside because they could not be reconciled with the seemingly plausible technical details Curveball had originally provided.

Beyond Curveball's behavioral issues, British and Israeli intelligence services also raised questions about the accuracy of the information Curveball had provided in his reports.[60] In 2001, both intelligence services provided imagery to WINPAC about Djer al-Nadaf, a facility Curveball had described as part of the mobile lab program. Photos of the site, dating back to May 1997, indicated the presence of a wall in precisely a location that ruled out the entry and exit of a mobile trailer; this wall had existed when Curveball claimed to have worked at the site and to have seen the movement of mobile facilities from this location. Instead of requesting that Curveball be asked about this discrepancy (or bringing in other tradecraft techniques to help evaluate it), WINPAC analysts chose instead to interpret the findings as evidence that the wall was merely temporary or fake and could be altered to allow the passage of mobile trailers.[61] Furthermore, in May 2002 CIA Operations issued a fabrication notice about the INC source that had been used to corroborate Curveball's reporting.[62] With all of these issues, Henoch and her supervisor, European Division chief Tyler Drumheller, grew more concerned about Curveball's reliability.

In October 2002, Henoch organized a meeting with WINPAC analysts to raise her concerns about these intelligence cables. WINPAC analysts dismissed her doubts and ignored her queries about whether Curveball might be a fabricator; a sustained argument between Henoch and WINPAC ensued.[63] At a subsequent meeting between Henoch and WINPAC to air these concerns, "the [CIA's] BW analyst . . . questioned whether the [German] group chief had sufficient knowledge of Curveball's reporting to be able to make an accurate assessment of his reliability."[64] As Henoch continued to raise criticisms, one of WINPAC's [bioweapons] analysts responded by invoking claims of expertise and authority on weapons issues, telling her, "You are simply not qualified to judge the complicated, technical aspects. That's our job."[65] WINPAC and Henoch remained at an impasse on the Curveball case.

By December 2002, with Iraq dominating the news and the Bush administration's attention, CIA upper management was seeking formal clarifications on the Curveball debates between Henoch and WINPAC analysts. The CIA's Office of the Deputy Director took on the issue of resolving Curveball's reliability and the use of his reporting in finished intelligence reports. In meetings with CIA management, Henoch outlined the concerns of her group and division based on tradecraft considerations: that the BND had experienced handling problems with Curveball; that neither U.S., nor German, nor other foreign intelligence entities had been able to verify the information Curveball had provided; and that some foreign intelligence services had become worried that Curveball might be a fabricator.[66] In addition, Henoch was concerned about the significant "improvement" in Curveball's reporting over time and the subsequent decline of his reporting after he received the equivalent of a German "green card."[67] According to Henoch, this might reveal that Curveball was "more forthcoming and cooperative when he needed resettlement assistance; now that he does not need it, he is less helpful, possibly because when he was being helpful, he was embellishing a bit."[68]

Henoch and Drumheller continually emphasized that no one in the U.S. intelligence community had subjected Curveball's information to stringent tradecraft tests. They said this was a particular concern because of the volume of his reports, the concerns and inconsistencies in his reporting outlined by foreign intelligence services since 2001, and the fabrication notices emerging from other human intelligence sources used to corroborate his claims. Tyler Drumheller recalled, "So we said [to the CIA's bioweapons analysts], we're not saying that he is a bad case, we're saying he might be a bad case, that his intelligence shouldn't be used until it gets sorted out."[69]

WINPAC continued to vouch for the reliability of the technical and physical details Curveball had provided, while Henoch countered that Curveball could have obtained such information from open sources. For example, Henoch argued that Curveball's identification of Djer al-Nadaf and other sites present in satellite imagery "was of dubious significance because it merely established that Curveball had been to the location, not that he had any knowledge of bioweapons activities being conducted there."[70] Henoch recalled, "I remember saying at the time, you could drive by the CIA and you'd know where it was, but it wouldn't mean that you worked there."[71] Moreover, when WINPAC analysts claimed that they had been able to verify some of Curveball's technical details through the Internet,

Henoch replied, "Exactly, it's on the Internet. That's where he [Curveball] got it too!"[72] Henoch and Drumheller stressed to CIA upper management that Curveball had not been adequately vetted and called him "an unvalidated source."[73] They were adamant that formal intelligence reports and assessments should not rely on his information.[74]

In rejecting these Operations arguments, WINPAC analysts insisted that it would be impossible to verify Curveball's claims because German intelligence would not give them access to him. WINPAC analysts maintained that the only way to evaluate Curveball was based primarily on his physical site and technical claims—information only technical experts could adequately assess. Yet WINPAC analysts reinterpreted gaps and inconsistencies that emerged in Curveball's descriptions to fit existing assumptions about an Iraqi mobile bioweapons capability. As Drumheller explains, "Any anomalies they [bioweapons analysts] couldn't explain, they'd say, 'Well, that's denial and deception, that's the Iraqis trying to hide it.' "[75] This use of the absence of evidence as information with which to construct judgments about an advanced, covert Iraqi bioweapons program is consistent with the technological narrative of a biotech revolution frame that assumes the elusive enemy is always hiding and on the move with a secret bioweapons capability.

After this December 2002 meeting including CIA management, WINPAC analysts, Henoch, and Drumheller, the executive assistant for the CIA deputy director issued a memo on the Curveball reliability debate. CIA management ultimately endorsed WINPAC's authority over the Curveball case due to the technical and physical details underpinning WINPAC's assessment, including "the detailed, technical nature of his [Curveball's] reporting; [technical intelligence] confirming the existence/configuration of the facilities he described (one Baghdad office building is known to house administrative offices linked to WMD programs); UNSCOM's discovery of military documents discussing 'mobile fermentation' capability; confirmation/replication of the described design by U.S. contractors."[76] Simply put, the biotech revolution frame trumped Operations' tradecraft expertise. Curveball's technical reporting became the central piece of intelligence that led to Colin Powell's infamous UN speech.

Conclusion

WINPAC's assessments of Curveball and the Iraqi mobile bioweapons threat show clear evidence of the biotech revolution frame at work in these CIA judgments. WINPAC analysts were fixated on the technical, material details in Curveball's and other human source reporting and relied on technical expertise, satellite imagery data, and the internet as tools to interpret this reporting. In addition, WINPAC analysts privileged codified, classified knowledge about the purported Iraqi mobile bioweapons labs present in intelligence reports from Curveball and other human intelligence sources. This led to assumptions about an abstract technological trajectory for Iraqi bioweapons development that fit naturally into existing U.S. technological threat narratives of the late 1990s and early 2000s. These narratives, all set within the context of the biotech revolution frame, emphasized a growing, advanced, covert, and diffuse set of bioweapons threats.

But this case still raises puzzling questions about how WINPAC analysts constructed knowledge about Curveball and the Iraqi mobile bioweapons threat. Namely, why didn't the CIA Operations Division validate Curveball? Given UNSCOM and the Directorate of Operations' German group expertise, why didn't CIA analysts seek their help in evaluating Curveball's reporting, other human intelligence source reporting, and other classified data? Why did WINPAC receive such early and consistent authority over the Curveball case? Why did CIA upper management find WINPAC's technical judgments so compelling? Why did WINPAC analysts so trust the classified reporting about the Iraqi mobile bioweapons threat, even in light of the problems that emerged in this reporting over time? Although these questions are central to understanding the Iraq intelligence failures, they also point to the need to explore how scientific and technological knowledge about weapons are co-produced within a specific, organizational context.

Thus, we must examine the organizational social world surrounding the WINPAC analysts and how it affected the way they constructed knowledge for their Iraqi mobile bioweapons assessments. In drawing on Lynn Eden's notions of organizational frames and routines, the next three chapters of this book provide an in-depth examination of the social context in which the CIA's bioweapons cadre worked; this context fundamentally shaped how WINPAC analysts collected, synthesized, and disseminated information for their assessments.

Chapter 5 explores how the CIA's construction and ordering of expertise for the conduct of weapons assessments have changed over time and how they shaped what WINPAC analysts considered relevant, if incomplete, information for their mobile bioweapons assessments. Since the end of the Cold War, which coincided with changes in CIA analytic structures, WINPAC analysts, who are technical analysts, have had primary authority for weapons assessments. As a result, reliance on the biotech revolution frame pervades and dominates bioweapons assessments. Chapter 6 discusses how problems with expertise in weapons assessments have also been compounded by the CIA's widespread use of current intelligence reporting, an analytic practice that focuses on the production of short, time-sensitive reports to policymakers. Its prevalence has hampered in-depth analysis on bioweapons threats and exacerbated the bias of the biotech revolution frame in bioweapons assessments. Finally, chapter 7 describes how secrecy and classification practices created and privileged different kinds of knowledge about an Iraqi mobile bioweapons capability throughout the CIA and the U.S. policy community. This probe of expertise, current intelligence reporting, and secrecy reveals the peril that can result from overreliance on the biotech revolution frame and insufficient consideration of how organizational analytic practices can create pervasive problems in the production of knowledge about bioweapons threats.

Sociologist Benjamin Sims has argued that disasters, whether technological or analytic, provide unique opportunities to study how knowledge is formed, because they "open up for examination (sometimes quite literally) networks of social and material relations that appear settled . . . bringing to the foreground the central importance of technologies, people, and work practices that ordinarily reside in the background."[77] The CIA's Iraqi mobile bioweapons assessments offer such a window into taken-for-granted work practices and contextual factors that can powerfully constrain analyses and lead to poor judgments in the production of knowledge about weapons threats.

Expertise and Analytic Practice

> The thing that was really missed in Iraq was that we failed to understand that Iraqi society—political, social, and civil society—changed in the 1990s. It entered a vortex of total corruption; consequently, producing WMD was the last thing it was interested in or even was capable of.
>
> *David Kay, former head of Iraq Survey Group, 2007*

Given the priority, time, and resources the United States and its allies devoted to collecting and analyzing intelligence on Iraqi WMDs from 1991 to 2003, David Kay's explanation of the U.S. intelligence failures is shocking. Kay is essentially saying that the U.S. intelligence community missed a crucial factor—Iraq's internal collapse—that prevented Saddam Hussein from advancing, or even sustaining, his WMD programs. Absent consideration of this societal change, the United States drew a conclusion about Iraq's WMDs—on which it based an invasion—that has since been proven wrong. How did analysts within the intelligence community fail to see this critical change and factor it into their weapons assessments?

The short answer is a balkanization of knowledge and expertise within the CIA. The CIA analysts' assessment of Curveball, their Iraqi source held by Bundesnachrichtendienst (BND), the German intelligence agency, reveals an information and expertise divide within the CIA's Directorate of Operations and in the Directorate of Intelligence. Accompanying these divides, CIA analysts relied on the biotech revolution frame—one focused on the simple material and technical aspects of a mobile biological weapons capability—and failed to situate Curveball's claims in the larger Iraqi context. In addition, the Curveball case reveals how the CIA was unable to develop more holistic forms of knowledge in weapons assessments. Finally, the flawed Iraqi bioweapons assessments show how various types of in-depth subject matter and methodological expertise were devalued in the CIA's analysis and collection efforts. Disconnects and tensions in how these various types of knowledge and expertise were defined, prioritized, organized, and integrated over a span of three decades led CIA analysts to privilege Curveball's Iraqi mobile bioweapons claims and thereby assume an advanced Iraqi bioweapons capability.

To understand how these events occurred, we look to the science and technology studies field and its methods for examining the formation and contestation of expertise and how those modes in turn shape the production of technical knowledge. An important conceptual tool in science and technology studies is consideration of the knowledge claims of both the winners and the losers of an expert debate, rather than the assumption that the winner is a priori correct. By examining both sides and laying out the important frames and practices that structure each side's position, we can see the different, conflicting ways each side produces knowledge and understands the world. Such examination demonstrates how controversies are resolved not necessarily by who has the "correct facts" but by who is able to define the terms of what counts as legitimate and relevant knowledge. In understanding the success of the "victors," science and technology studies scholarship considers the larger social context that has shaped how distinct sets of expertise obtain authority.

To date, existing studies of intelligence analysis failures have not used specific, in-depth case studies to explore how the definition and organization of expertise in the CIA shapes analysts' work.[1] On top of that, existing studies of bioweapons assessments have largely focused on narrow technical issues or the deficit of technical expertise in the intelligence community, rather than considering the broad organizational practices that shape the intake of knowledge and expertise for intelligence assessments. The Curveball case offers the opportunity to do both: to present a historical, systemic understanding of the organizational practices that have shaped notions of expertise in the CIA and to take a micro-level look at how larger organizational practices shaped analytic work in a specific case. We will see how the creation and management of expertise within organizations can powerfully shape analysis in subtle, often unrecognized ways—with outcomes that can prove detrimental for intelligence assessments and policymaking.

S&TS scholar Michelle Murphy's concept of "regimes of perceptibility" provides a useful lens through which to understand the CIA's failure to consider Iraq's societal change in assessing Curveball's veracity and reaching a conclusion on Iraq's WMDs. Murphy defines a regime of perceptibility as the way in which a community of specialists perceives the world.[2] By studying how these specialists produce knowledge, which she calls historical epistemology, Murphy finds that the things specialists see (and don't see) in their understandings of the world are not accidental but are produced through specific epistemological traditions and work practices that involve both social and material factors. As these regimes of perceptibility become institutionalized, they become what Lynn Eden describes as taken-for-granted frames and routines for constructing knowledge in organizations. Drawing on published literature and interviews with former and current U.S. intelligence practitioners, this chapter traces how CIA analysts produced knowledge in the course of their Iraqi mobile bioweapons intelligence assessments.

Technical and Social Science Information and Expertise

As mentioned in the overview to this section, the technical details in Curveball's descriptions of the purported Iraqi mobile labs captivated the CIA's bioweapons analysts. In spite of some inconsistencies that emerged over time in Curveball's reporting, these analysts consistently judged him to be a credible human source because of his technical claims. As a result, the CIA's bioweapons analysts spent little time exploring the broader context underpinning Curveball's reporting or an Iraqi mobile bioweapons capability in general. For instance, in interviewing a former U.S. intelligence analyst after the known intelligence failures, I asked a practical question of whether the analyst had considered how Iraqi bioweapons scientists and technicians would have worked, lived, and moved (for instance, in smaller trailers or trucks) as the mobile bioweapons labs operated under cover in the Iraqi desert or railways.[3] The analyst replied, "I personally never thought of any stuff like that, it just never occurred to me."[4]

This analyst also agreed that there had been serious professional disagreements about Curveball between the CIA's bioweapons analysts and the managers of the Directorate of Operations' European Division (Tyler Drumheller) and German group (Margaret Henoch). As one government report documents, "The [CIA's] BW [bioweapons] analyst . . . questioned whether the [German] group chief had sufficient knowledge of Curveball's reporting to be able to make an accurate assessment of his reliability."[5] The analysts repeatedly emphasized the technical nature of the reporting and insisted that they were the only experts qualified to evaluate Curveball as a source.

But Henoch didn't buy their supremacy or their insistence on the technical nature of the work. She had studied history and engineering at Northwestern University and had conducted technology assessments at Stanford Research Institute for several years before being hired by the CIA. In that job, her projects involved examining the technical capabilities of Soviet weapons systems using unclassified information.[6] Henoch had experience conducting in-depth technical assessments on sensitive Soviet technologies that did not rely on human source intelligence but instead used painstaking open-source information on technical systems. In addition, Henoch's father had been a nuclear physicist at Los Alamos National Laboratory, one of the main American nuclear weapons laboratories, so Henoch had grown up with an understanding of weapons scientists and the importance of situating them in their work context and personal lives. As a result, Henoch was very surprised to learn that Curveball's intelligence file had not included any additional background information about him or his employment history.

More to the point, in her twenty-year career in the CIA's Directorate of Operations, Henoch had worked in positions that proved relevant to the Curveball case. In a variety of counterintelligence positions both at CIA headquarters and overseas, Henoch had served as both a working-level officer and a manager, including a stint as chief of counterintelligence for a division in the Directorate of Operations. Henoch's responsibilities had involved monitoring intelligence activities for inconsistencies and problems that would indicate deception or other difficulties with a human source providing information. Additionally, she had worked on WMD-related issues as part of her CIA work portfolio and had served as chief of the counterproliferation division in a large overseas station, where she had overseen the recruitment and validation of individuals who provided reliable intelligence.

These experiences taught Henoch that evaluating a human intelligence source's knowledge and credibility about weapons issues involved not only technical issues but also a wider range of personal and contextual information. Because Curveball's intelligence file lacked a broader array of corroborating evidence, Henoch was reluctant to accept the validity of Curveball's reports without additional vetting. When, however, the Curveball debates between Henoch and the bioweapons analysts rose through the CIA hierarchy, upper management sided with the analysts' technical arguments. To understand this outcome, it is important to examine not only how the biotech revolution frame was in play but also how the organization of expertise for weapons assessments within the CIA changed over time. These organizational changes have shaped who is deemed to have the proper expertise and authority to rule on WMD issues.

Starting in the 1960s, technical intelligence analysts were located within the CIA's Directorate of Science and Technology, an organizational division distinct from the Directorate of Intelligence, which was organized in offices of political, economic, and military analysis. CIA management separated its technical experts into a distinct directorate because many of the analysts who originally came to the CIA were World War II veterans who had worked on technical issues or had come from the U.S. national laboratories and missile development centers.[7] In the 1960s, however, close working collaborations existed between analysts in the Directorates of Intelligence and Science and Technology, such that final assessments of a country's weapons capabilities were situated within the context of a larger political or strategic issue. In describing his experience as a CIA analyst at that time, Richard Kerr, former deputy director of the CIA, says, "As a young [military] analyst I was kind of a penman for them [technical analysts]. . . . You acted on a technical issue as someone who knew how to put their information in an analytic context. My experience was that that worked well as long as you gave them credit for what they were doing. So, it was very much a collaborative process."[8] Thus, although technical and social science analysts were located in separate directorates, the CIA supported practices that involved close working relationships between both kinds of experts to construct weapons assessments.

In the 1970s, however, the Directorate of Intelligence was reorganized from more general categories of analyses (political, economic, social) to focus on specific countries and/or regions.[9] For example, the Directorate of Intelligence created distinct East Asian and Soviet offices under this new structure. The separate Science and Technology Directorate was abolished, but there remained a distinct technical analytic office within the Directorate of Intelligence. Under this new organizational structure, technical analysts were more closely linked to other regional and national analytic units. According to Kerr, "That's probably the period of time when you had the greatest depth of expertise on countries because you had the full range of capabilities and then you had a technical office [within the Directorate of Intelligence] to rely on as well."[10] Former CIA officer Arthur Hulnick has noted that this organizational structure made "more detailed analytic research feasible."[11] In the 1970s, CIA technical analysts also worked closely with outside technical experts at U.S. government laboratories in which weapons technologies were being developed and tested. Thus, a wealth of internal, multidisciplinary expertise for weapons assessments existed in the CIA through the 1970s. CIA management also established and supported work practices that involved in-depth collaborations between different CIA and outside experts to inform intelligence assessments.

In the 1980s, the technical weapons analysts remained within the Directorate of Intelligence, although they were organized into a new unit, the Office of Scientific and Weapons Research, whose work included analysis of chemical and biological weapons. Here, weapons assessments were still subordinated to the larger political or strategic context. Kerr explains that in the analytic environment of that time, "the political analysts always had a dominant say in how you were going to present it [intelligence assessment]—even very technical issues like throw weights of missiles . . . because in most of the issues you dealt with in the Soviet Union, many of the issues that were weapons-oriented also had major political implications. . . .

So you had people like the head of the [Intelligence Directorate's] Soviet analysis shop . . . even though he wasn't in the office that did the assessment of technical characteristics of the missile, he was the person who went to the arms control group in the White House. So he ended up representing their [technical analysts'] views."[12] As Kerr points out, in the 1980s, the CIA's politico-military analysts were given the authority to synthesize various types of expert knowledge for weapons assessments; they also served as the main interface with senior politically appointed officials. This means of organizing weapons analyses was markedly different from that of the Curveball case.

After the end of the Cold War, the CIA downsized its analytic capabilities. By the early 1990s, the Office of Scientific and Weapons Research (OSWR) in the Directorate of Intelligence was disbanded, and many of its technical analysts retired. Richard Kerr explained the significance of these personnel changes: "A lot of people in that office came out of Lawrence Livermore [National Laboratory] and Los Alamos, and they were people who had developed nuclear weapons, and they were getting a little long in the tooth and were not replaced by the same kind of people."[13] With these retirements, the Directorate of Intelligence lost crucial understandings of weapons know-how. In addition, other OSWR analysts were shifted to other analytic units within the CIA. By way of example, some technical analysts went to newly created units such as the Office of Weapons, Technology, and Proliferation, which was outside the existing geographically based analytic offices. Richard Kerr points out that these personnel changes also had an impact on analysis: "When you change an office like that and spread its analysts around, you tend to lose those people and that [technical] capability."[14] What began happening in the 1990s, then, was a loss of tight working relationships between technical and social science experts and of the specialized tacit knowledge that had informed the CIA's weapons assessments.

Also in the early 1990s, an increasing concern about WMD proliferation to rogue states prompted the CIA to create a new functional unit called the Nonproliferation Center.[15] The center was created in a special administrative line, separate from the other intelligence directorates. Consistent with the technological threat narratives emerging from the U.S. policy community at the time, the CIA created the center as a way of signaling the seriousness of the diffuse, technologically advanced weapons threats facing U.S. national security. One of the center's top priorities was to "facilitate the U.S. Intelligence Community's collection, analysis, operations, and R&D efforts against foreign offensive biological warfare . . . and chemical warfare . . . activities."[16] The center was given the authority to coordinate WMD assessments across the multiple agencies of the U.S. intelligence community and served as the primary CIA representative to senior U.S. government officials on WMD issues. The Nonproliferation Center's first director was Gordon Oehler, a physicist and former head of the OSWR; several of his former technical analysts were hired by the new center as well.[17] The center also recruited a variety of technical and political experts who had been working in the CIA's other analytic and clandestine units. With the creation of the Nonproliferation Center and its newly designated authorities, the CIA's WMD assessments began to prioritize a technical focus. No longer subordinate to the CIA's political or military analysts, WMD analysts in the Nonproliferation Center now had direct access to policymakers.

In 1997, a summer study by the President's Foreign Intelligence Advisory Board emphasized that more intelligence resources were needed on bioweapons proliferation issues. The board recommended that the Nonproliferation Center be granted new authority to oversee intelligence spending and collection priorities on chemical and biological weapons issues.[18] Later that year, with support from Congress, CIA Director George Tenet established a new structure and focus for the Nonproliferation Center.[19] With these changes, the CIA also prioritized the hiring of analysts with technical expertise. Through the 1990s, the Nonproliferation Center's authority on WMD issues grew.

In 2001, the Nonproliferation Center as an organizational entity was disbanded and replaced with a new and larger center, the Weapons, Intelligence, Nonproliferation, and Arms Control Center (WINPAC). In an administrative change from the Nonproliferation Center, WINPAC was established within the CIA's Directorate of Intelligence, which was the CIA's main analytic arm.[20] With its creation, WINPAC centralized all of the CIA's technical weapons specialists in both nonproliferation and arms control issues under one organizational unit. With a staff of seven hundred, WINPAC became one of the largest analytic units in the Directorate of Intelligence.[21] WINPAC is the analytic unit that assessed Curveball's claims.

The creation of the Nonproliferation Center and WINPAC has led to an increasing institutional consolidation, segregation, and prioritization of technical expertise on WMD issues within the CIA, along with an incorporation of the biotech revolution frame and its related technological threat narratives. In contrast to the Cold War period, later WMD assessments became increasingly detached from an overarching geographic or national context in these new functional analytic units. Kerr explained the effect of this abstraction on weapons assessments: "Techical people tended to look at the problem as a technical challenge and then say if I were to assess this [weapons] development at a particular point in time, I would say they [enemies] are doing these kinds of things, which leads me to believe that they are at this [particular] phase in the development. So, from their point of view, it's kind of a cumulative additive problem. Every piece of evidence kind of adds to the judgment."[22] Kerr, however, goes on to highlight the potential sources of error that can result from this type of calculation:

> Countries develop nuclear weapons; they [weapons] don't develop themselves. So, unless you start at a country basis and understand why they are developing, what kind of resources they are putting in, how they're going to control them, how they fit into the military. . . . It seems [to me that] to talk about a weapon in the abstract is very misleading. . . . And the problem is, of course, that the technical people [WINPAC analysts] ended up being the people responsible for writing the [Iraq WMD] National Intelligence Estimate and the major judgment. I mean they were the people who were kind of deferred to in terms [like] here's how you develop a weapon, here's what phase you are, here's what you have to do in the logical steps of weapons development.[23]

Certainly, all knowledge-forming arrangements are constrained; nationally or regionally focused analysts also introduce their own biases into assessments and can miss important transnational and technical issues. But what Kerr usefully identifies here is how these CIA organizational changes have affected the way weapons assessments are conceptualized and conducted and the knowledge that results.

The CIA's organizational changes and overall downsizing during the 1990s also shaped the extent to which regional or country analysts considered WMDs as part of their central work portfolio. As Richard Kerr explained, "When these technical analysts were sent off to other offices . . . to do other kinds of jobs, then the regional offices tended to shrink in size and become more focused on the classic politics, economics, and social issues."[24] As a result, political and military analysts no longer prioritized their own complementary work on weapons issues. As one former CIA analyst noted, "Most of the [regional] analysts are social scientists. . . . [For example,] they look at politics in Ukraine or Cuba. They look at very nuanced, very complicated global issues that oftentimes don't have technical aspects. . . . They aren't heavy on science and technology except for WINPAC. There is that weird kind of split."[25] With this organizational split, regional or national analysts came to defer to technical analysts on judgments of WMD assessments.

Kerr also argues that the growing importance of special analytic centers focused on WMD issues has tended to devalue regional expertise on weapons issues and has led to an acceptance of technical expertise as irrefutable: "I think consumers [policymakers] have always been willing to take technical judgments as more authoritative because they couldn't argue with them. I mean anybody can argue politics . . . but the weight of a SS-9 [missile] warhead is a little different kind of a problem. So they tended to defer to the technical people, but earlier the regional offices had a much stronger confidence so they tended to argue with the technical people as the intermediary. . . . I think that there was a lot of debate about technical issues between technical people and nontechnical people before it was written down. My impression is that has changed."[26] With these changes, Richard Kerr explains that "over the years, what you have is a changing set of where the expertise lies, how you coordinate across those organizational lines, and who drove the analysis to a considerable degree."[27] As a result, efforts to integrate regional and national information in weapons assessments became highly contingent on WINPAC leadership and analyst outreach. According to the 2005 WMD Commission report, which examined the problems behind the Iraq intelligence failures, "Functional units such as WINPAC have highly varying relations with the regional components, such as NESA [Near Eastern and South Asian Analysis]."[28] NESA was the CIA's geographic analytic office responsible for Iraq.

This shift from a geographic to a functional focus as an organizing principle for understanding WMDs was also occurring within the Directorate of Operations, the CIA's clandestine arm, beginning in the mid-1980s. As Tyler Drumheller explained, "About 1985, when [CIA Director William] Casey began with the counterterrorism center, and then they had the counterintelligence center, they started setting up these separate entities."[29] Continuing this trend, in 1996 the CIA created a new organizational unit called the Counterproliferation Division.[30] Originally housed within the Nonproliferation Center, its purpose was to assist with the collection of intelligence on WMD proliferation threats. Later, the Counterproliferation Division was moved to the Directorate of Operations to create a more transnational and functional focus for collection efforts on WMD proliferation issues.[31]

Margaret Henoch reflected on why the separate Counterproliferation Division was created: "I think that as technology became more interesting, people felt that they needed to focus more on the technology, instead of the people using it."[32] Thus, the clandestine side of the CIA also began to reflect this technical emphasis in its collection efforts on WMDs. Tyler Drumheller noted the problem with that technical focus in the case of Curveball: "I believe that you need to work across the geographic divisions in intelligence. Even these transnational issues are affected at their very basic levels by local issues. Because Curveball was a German source, he was affected by our relationship with Germany."[33] In the Curveball case, however, instead of consulting with their Operations colleagues with German expertise, Counterproliferation officers worked with WINPAC analysts, their technical counterpart in the Directorate of Intelligence.

Since their early origins within the Nonproliferation Center, Counterproliferation officers have often had close working relationships with WINPAC analysts, and WINPAC analysts have spent time on work rotations in the Counterproliferation division, including during the period when Curveball was active. As one former U.S. intelligence analyst notes, "When the Curveball stuff was going on, one of our folks was sitting in the DO [Directorate of Operations Counterproliferation Division] at the time doing this, so we were working very closely together and he was telling us all the bits and pieces."[34] The strong affinities between WINPAC and the Counterproliferation Division meant that they both viewed Curveball's reporting in a largely technical framework that precluded a more holistic interrogation of Curveball and a more comprehensive, country-based understanding of Iraq's mobile bioweapons capabilities.

After the failures of the WMD analysis, the director of the CIA commissioned an independent study of the process, chaired by Richard Kerr. In his report, Kerr noted a glaring disconnect between technical and country knowledge in the prewar intelligence assessments of Iraq's WMD programs: "The national intelligence produced on the technical and cultural/political areas [in Iraq] . . . remained largely distinct and separate. Little or no attempt was made to examine or explain the impact of each area on the other. Thus, perspective and a comprehensive sense of understanding of the Iraqi target per se was lacking."[35] Later, Kerr et al. concluded, "Analysis of Iraq's WMD programs, therefore, provides an excellent case study for an assessment of the limitations of relying too heavily on technical collection systems with little acknowledgement of the political/cultural context in which such [weapons] programs exist."[36] The CIA's gradual shift toward technical supremacy of information and expertise led to a stark separation between technical and country knowledge in its Iraq bioweapons assessments. As a result, the CIA failed to undertake a holistic integration of different types of knowledge and expertise that would have provided an alternative way to assess Saddam's bioweapons capability.

Divides in Analytic and Operational Expertise

Most governmental and nongovernmental commentaries on the operational problems in assessing Iraq's mobile bioweapons capability focus on the lack of good intelligence to inform analysis. However, interviews with participants at the time and an analysis of their communication show that there was indeed sufficient operational knowledge and expertise available within the CIA to evaluate Curveball's claims more rigorously at a much earlier stage; it was simply not valued and integrated into WINPAC assessments. In fact, important knowledge within the Directorate of Operations, the CIA's main reservoir of human intelligence expertise, was marginalized in the Curveball case. Had it been more central to the debate, it could have reduced WINPAC's confidence in Curveball's technical claims.

Organizationally, the Directorate of Operations managed the clandestine collection of foreign intelligence for the CIA, including the gathering of secret and open-source information using human and technical means (such as signals or imagery). From this gathered information, the Directorate of Operations produced "raw" or "unfinished" intelligence reports. Analysts in the CIA's Directorate of Intelligence then used these raw reports to create their assessments and prepare finished intelligence reports and briefings for U.S. policymakers.[37]

Because WINPAC analysts viewed Curveball's reports (and the ensuing assessments of Iraqi mobile labs) through a technical lens, they saw little reason to draw on nontechnical expertise or knowledge to evaluate Curveball's claims. This problem extended to the operational evaluation of Curveball as a source: WINPAC did not bring in the Directorate of Operations' European Division and its associated German group from the beginning to evaluate Curveball's reports; nor did WINPAC include them in subsequent meetings about Curveball with other U.S. and foreign intelligence officials. It was not until the fall of 2002, more than two years after WINPAC began receiving Curveball's initial reports, that the European Division and the German group were tasked to work on the Curveball case. Even so, WINPAC analysts subsequently dismissed the Directorate of Operations' officials concerns about Curveball and reiterated the superiority of their own technical judgments on the purported Iraqi mobile labs.

Tyler Drumheller, however, argues that WINPAC analysts should have focused more on what *kind* of source Curveball was—a human source and not a piece of hardware—to determine what kinds of expertise were needed to assess Curveball's claims. According to Drumheller, a less technical focus would have led analysts to spend more time, resources, and effort to scrutinize Curveball's personal reliability and the methods the BND had used to interrogate him. Drumheller explained that WINPAC "didn't know where he actually worked, what his actual job was . . . whereas we looked at him with more of a skeptical [eye], you know, how he was handled, how he was questioned."[38] Drumheller says these details were critical for determining how the BND had assessed Curveball and how that might have affected their reporting: "The way the Germans did this interrogation is, they tended to use sort of leading debriefs, which we don't do, but it's their style. And, so, when they [the Germans] were debriefing him, they said, 'Gee, did you ever see anything about mobile labs?' "[39] In his book *Curveball,* journalist Bob Drogin describes how German debriefers would supply Curveball with textbooks and other technical sources as well as ask him leading questions such as "Did they [Iraq] use German trucks for the mobile program?" Or, in showing pictures of captured trailers, the German interrogators would ask Curveball, "Is this the kind of trailer you told us about?"[40] According to Drumheller, these kinds of leading questions provide opportunities for human intelligence sources to probe their debriefers and adapt their reporting to what they perceive as the debriefers' interests, leading to fabrication of information.

According to Henoch, "If WINPAC had done this correctly, what they should have done was to come back to us to say, oh, this is the BND guy. They [WINPAC] should have sent some low-level person over to the low-level German desk and said, 'Do you guys know anything about this? Is there any way you can help us make sure this is okay?' And then we would have said, 'How about this, this, and this?' and off it would have gone."[41] Henoch notes that when her office first began receiving Curveball's information, a working-level operations officer who had extensive expertise related to Germany was well aware of the caveats needed when dealing with German intelligence. Drumheller adds that had they collaborated with WINPAC, the Directorate of Operations would have pushed for direct access to Curveball and used the CIA's own operations experts to interrogate him in Germany. Henoch explains how she would have interrogated Curveball: "I would have done a literature search and found articles that referred to it [mobile labs] and then compared his [Curveball's] information. And if his information seemed to track word for word, then I would have gone back to him and confronted him on it, because most people are cowards and they haven't thought through it. . . . It's sort of like what you would do with a student who plagiarized something. But no one ever confronted him [Curveball] on anything."[42]

Even without direct access to Curveball, there were other Operations methods available to assess Curveball's reliability. As Drumheller notes, "We didn't know they [WINPAC] knew his name. They never told us his name, but there were people in the DI [Directorate of Intelligence] who knew his name. That would have made a huge difference because we [Operations] could have traced him."[43] For example, postwar investigations determined that Curveball had been out of the country during several periods when he claimed Iraqi mobile bioweapons production had occurred.[44] Had Operations officials known his name, they could have tracked his whereabouts and established early on that his claims of having worked at purported mobile lab sites were inconsistent with his travel record. They could also have confronted him with the inconsistencies. As Drumheller explained, Curveball could have been asked, "Were you in Djerf al Nadaf [purported mobile depot] on this day? What day did the accident happen? He would say, 'Well, around this time.' Okay. That's very interesting because we have reports from Moroccan immigration that you were in Morocco at this time, how can you explain that?"[45]

Drumheller explains that Operations could have helped German intelligence use alternative methods to test Curveball's reporting on specifics about mobile bioweapons depots, Iraq, the Iraqi bioweapons program, technological issues, past historical events, or facts about his own purported resume that the CIA could definitively confirm.[46] Giving an example, Drumheller described one possible approach to test Curveball: "Okay, you worked for Basil Al-Saadi. Where is his office? What does he do? What does he look like? What is his daughter like?"[47] Margaret Henoch adds: "I would have asked him for a really detailed background: Where was he born? Where did he grow up? Where did he live? What did he major in in college? What did he study? Where were his jobs in college? What were his jobs after college? Where were you last summer before you came here? How did you get out of Iraq? Tell me what route you took. I would have made him walk through a minute-by-minute personal history. It was obvious that no one had ever asked that, and that is like the basics."[48] In addition, Henoch argues that the Counterproliferation Division could have tried harder to verify Curveball's technical background: "This guy says he was educated, he went to this college. Here is what he should be like. Then you [Counterproliferation Division] are supposed to figure out, does he fit that [technical] profile?"[49]

Henoch also says the Counterproliferation Division could have worked more closely with other foreign intelligence services to ascertain Curveball's technical and educational background: "You go to the [foreign intelligence] services and say, 'Did you have somebody who went to this college at this point in time at this place, could we talk to him?' . . . If you can't prove or corroborate that he was there, then you're done, I would say."[50] Alternatively, Henoch says they could have worked with their counterparts in foreign intelligence services to learn more about Curveball or his associates: "He was an émigré, people probably knew he wasn't in Iraq anymore. . . . You knew that there had to be somebody from that [biological] facility who had [also] come out of Iraq. So you would go to the Brits, the Israelis, the French, the Italians, the Turks, and said, 'Have you guys got somebody who has ever claimed to work at this place?' And if they say, 'Yes,' you say, 'May I ask him a question about a guy? Is he who he says he is?' And they say, 'Well, he was a loser engineer.' At which point you say, 'Okay, thanks,' and stop putting out his reporting."[51]

Henoch goes on to note that in Operations work, an émigré is formally classified as a different type of human intelligence source from defectors. Human sources officially designated as defectors have been vetted by special intelligence committees that have evaluated the source's reporting and have gone through a process to determine that the source has enough value to be given the official label of defector and supported for the rest of his or her life. An émigré, by contrast, has not gone through this process. Henoch states that most émigrés are typically bad or unreliable human sources, so they are usually treated as suspect unless rigorously vetted. Yet Curveball, as an émigré, was never operationally evaluated as a human source. But postwar investigations and interviews conducted by the Iraq Survey Group—established by the Pentagon and CIA to hunt for Iraqi WMD after the start of the 2003 war—indicated that information collection on Curveball was possible before the war. For example, the Iraq Survey Group interviewed Curveball's work supervisors and childhood friends (some of whom were living outside Iraq prior to the war), who said Curveball had been a poor engineering student, was a low-level technical worker, and had a reputation as a thief, liar, and con artist.[52]

To further check his credibility, Henoch proposed testing Curveball's truthfulness by showing him pictures of suspected sites and trailers, along with "control" pictures, to see how he would describe each of them. Henoch recalls that during her career she had witnessed seemingly legitimate Soviet human sources who had deployed disinformation campaigns to thwart U.S. intelligence. But with Curveball, WINPAC analysts and their defense intelligence counterparts believed that such "testing" was unnecessary, so it was never conducted as part of the mobile lab assessments.[53] In considering the variety of omissions evident in the assessment of Curveball, the 2005 WMD Commission noted, "The lack of direct access to Curveball made it more difficult to assess his veracity. But such lack of access does not preclude the Intelligence Community from attempting to assess the source's bona fides and the credibility of source reporting."[54]

In reflecting on the Curveball case, Drumheller argues that WINPAC analysts did not understand that collecting and evaluating clandestine information requires a kind of expertise that analysts do not possess. He says that there is both an art and a science to handling a source and that for over fifty years the Directorate of Operations has developed a methodology for validating its sources that sets it apart from other agencies of the [intelligence] collection community. Being an Operations case officer, he says, is like being a lawyer or doctor: it takes a depth of knowledge and experience. "You learn what makes a good source," Drumheller adds.[55] Henoch says that WINPAC analysts relied too heavily on their own limited abilities to assess Curveball: "Normal people don't commit espionage. Defectors are in a horrible situation, and they're crazy. Just definitionally they're insane. If you start with that, and if you start with the fact that there's a way to have an adversarial and yet not hostile, nasty relationship, then you're going to get more truth. It's like a used car salesman. You like them, but you know that he's ripping you off.

So you're not going to say, 'Thanks, that's got to be a good deal.' You're going to get a mechanic."[56] Because of her knowledge of the behavioral problems common to defectors, Henoch says that she was not bothered when she learned that Curveball had shown up drunk to German intelligence meetings. She was more disturbed, however, to find out that no one in U.S. intelligence had spent the time and energy to investigate his background to determine his reliability as a human source.

Years before Curveball came along, Henoch had noticed what she believed was WINPAC's interest in running its own operations: "When I was chief of a Counterproliferation branch, I noticed that WINPAC had started to sort of become its own agency, for lack of a better word. . . . It wanted to do operational stuff, it wanted to do analysis. . . . It was a bunch of analysts who wanted to collect information . . . people who didn't really understand operations."[57] Although WINPAC analysts do work rotations in the Directorate of Operations' Counterproliferation Division, Drumheller argues that it doesn't make them qualified as Operations personnel:

> If WINPAC analysts want to spend time at the DO [Directorate of Operations], they should go through the operations course and become case officers. And, they [WINPAC] don't see it that way, they think it's just go to the embassy and ask questions, they don't realize that that's the problem. Some of the DO work seems very simple . . . you go to a cocktail party, you talk, you get a report. But that's just the tip of the iceberg. It's a year of training [to become a case officer], it's two or three [additional] years, because then you really are not considered a fully sort of journeyman case officer until you've had a full tour overseas under supervision. . . . To learn how to live with cover, you've got to develop a feel.[58]

These comments reveal important epistemological divides between operations officials and analysts that hindered a more holistic assessment of Curveball and his Iraqi mobile bioweapons claims. Although WINPAC analysts received Curveball's intelligence reports from their technical counterparts in the Directorate of Operations' Counterproliferation Division, WINPAC's analysts had overlooked or discounted pertinent operational expertise that was resident in the CIA. The disconnect in this case was a result of historical, organizational changes in how CIA collectors and analysts had worked, whereby weapons analysts had become isolated intellectually and physically from diverse sets of operational knowledge and expertise. That had not always been the case.

In the 1960s, senior analysts in the Directorate of Intelligence often organized collection strategies on weapons issues, working closely with collectors. During this time, CIA analysts were intimately involved in deciding what information should be collected and how it would be done using particular collection techniques and technologies. As Carl Ford, a onetime assistant secretary of state for intelligence who had also served as a CIA collector and analyst, explains, "What had happened in the old days was that the office responsible for analysis not only did the analysis but they also made provisions for a collection management process, providing direction to the collectors on what information they needed."[59] This initiative, in part, was influenced by the fact that several CIA analysts during the 1960s and 1970s had previously worked in various U.S. weapons programs and had a good sense of what explicit and implicit information should be collected to assess weapons developments. Ford says that analysts recognized that collectors were "the best people to tell you, 'If that's what you want, here's what you'll have to do, and here's how much it costs.' "[60]

As a result of the close relationship between collection and analysis, former CIA analyst Richard Kerr says that analysts "knew what they were getting; they knew what they were not getting. They knew what they needed, and they knew how to get what they needed."[61] Also, during this time, because the CIA had its own major in-house collection organization, these collection specialists often relied on CIA analysts to be "their instruments of understanding of what they needed, how they needed it, how they'd like it."[62] Ford explains the collaboration:

> In the past this process was a collaborative process, where the analyst would tell the collector the kinds of information, both direct and indirect, that was needed in order to better answer a particular key question. . . . "Here's how we think you [the collector] might find that out, how you might go about getting that information," . . . and the collectors would decide what they needed to do in order to collect that. There were times when the analysts would sit down with collectors and find out that they had important details but didn't understand what we wanted from them. Or they [the collectors] would say, "That's easy, I can get that for you." [Or] the collector says, "Well, that's not possible, but what about this?" It was the same for both human and technical collectors. There was a constant back and forth about what we needed to make a good guess about that particular subject.[63]

The 1960s were a time of close working relationships between collection and analysis, reflecting the value placed on integrating operations and analytic expertise in producing intelligence assessments.

Over time, however, as senior analysts retired and as collection became more bureaucratized and independent from the CIA due to the establishment of the

National Security Agency, the National Reconnaissance Office, and other non-CIA collection agencies, the relationship that had existed between collectors and analysts began to change. By the mid-1970s, collection became a process largely separate from analytic work; priorities for collection were set by "collection managers" located within separate organizational units in the CIA, who would identify and define a list of priority intelligence targets each year.[64] According to Ford, these collection managers were not very helpful to collectors or analysts, because they often stated the obvious or were too general in their suggestions. He says, moreover, that the disconnect between collection managers and analysts led to divergent goals: "The collection managers would have a meeting, and the analysts would go and sit down, and there would be an hour's discussion for the year, and they [the collection managers] would go off and build their list [priority collection list]. And it [the collection list] became less and less important to the analysts. It just became a bureaucratic exercise."[65] As organizational changes made collection and analysis increasingly separate, there was less understanding by both analysts and collectors of the value of a close, integrated working relationship for intelligence assessments.

After the Cold War, some close analyst-collector working relationships did still exist, however. As an example, Margaret Henoch describes a fruitful working relationship she had as a collector with an analyst in the early 1990s: "I had a guy who worked for me in my last post, he was a DI [Directorate of Intelligence] guy. And if we'd get a report in, I'd say, 'Phil, take a look at this, tell me what you think.' And he'd say, 'Well, do you realize you didn't answer these questions?' And we'd be like, 'Give me more questions.' Or he would come in with something, and I'd say, 'Well, okay, what about this, what about this one?' "[66] But with the increasing bureaucratization of intelligence, this type of close collaboration was more difficult to maintain consistently. Over time, collaborative interchange of knowledge and praxis between collectors and analysts became more ad hoc and less standard institutional practice, which reduced the effectiveness of collection, as Ford explains: "The collectors aren't mind readers. They don't know what the analysts need and want. And if you leave out that part, you really have put the collectors in a very difficult position. Without having that discussion about what we need in order to answer the question, you leave it up to the collector to do it for themselves, and that's not their specialty. They are having to guess how you might answer some of these very complex questions. They do a great job at collecting, but sometimes the information isn't any good because it's not what we need, or it's from the wrong place. I can't blame the collector for that, because nobody told them how to go about doing it."[67]

With less collaboration, bureaucratic priorities and routines influenced much of what was collected for analysts, thereby shaping their assessments. On top of that, according to Ford and Kerr, the "art" behind the development of a collection-analytic strategy has been seriously impaired by the loss of institutional practices that actively support close working relationships between collectors and analysts.

In examining analysis and collection for bioweapons assessments, another key issue is reconciling collection needs with existing collection capabilities and priorities. Contemporary collection budgets and priorities, which devote resources and attention to large technical collection systems such as satellites, are not specifically focused on how to answer the questions most critical to bioweapons assessments. One problem is competing for time and targeting with the other surveillance missions for which a satellite is deployed. Another is winning recognition that understanding bioweapons threats involves the robust collection of human and other types of social, political, and economic intelligence.

In addition, the separation between collectors and analysts has in turn created gaps in the hidden knowledge that plays a role in collection work. In the past, for example, when analysts worked closely with collectors, they better understood the role of reports officers, or "processors."[68] These specialized workers in collection organizations act as intermediaries between collectors and analysts; they transform collected clandestine information (human intelligence, imagery, signals) into a "raw intelligence report" that is readable and usable by analysts.[69] More concretely, reports officers decode signals, analyze satellite imagery, translate foreign transcripts, obscure sensitive sources and methods, and streamline other cumbersome data.

Reports officers also served as important reservoirs of contextual knowledge about an issue or country for case officers (spies); in contrast, case officers are responsible for recruiting and handling human sources. During the Cold War, for instance, reports officers focused on a specific country or region, spoke the language, read the press from their area, and understood the national character. They knew the country's institutions and knew where to turn to get secret information. In contrast, case officers had more people skills and were more operations-oriented. As Margaret Henoch explains: "The case officer likes to talk to people, is fairly good at it, should be intuitive about when somebody is talking to you, should be able to strike up a conversation. . . . A case officer would know how to deal with people from the region. . . . And the case officer knows the techniques, understands when he may be being jerked around, knows the bullshit of clandestine meetings, and can do the baroque stuff of recruitment."[70] These complementary expertise and skill sets often led to close working relationships between the reports officers and case officers tasked to collect and evaluate human source intelligence. In addition, the reports officer served as the interface between the case officer and the analyst for targeting and refining collection efforts. Not only did reports officers interpret and translate complex raw intelligence, they were also able to make important editorial determinations about what operations information was relevant to pass on to analysts.

Starting in the early 1990s, however, the relationship among case officers, reports officers, and analysts changed; due to managerial decisions, the role of the reports officer became more marginalized in the collection and analysis process. As reports officers lost rank and status within the CIA, managers and analysts lost sight of the distinct knowledge and expertise reports officers possessed. As a result, Henoch says that few individuals who join the Directorate of Operations want to be reports officers because the culture doesn't reward that: "I have a very good friend, and she used to say, 'Well, you know I'm pond scum,' because she was a reports officer. And it was that way."[71]

Because they work for the collectors, moreover, reports officers are also physically and intellectually separated from analysts. As a result, reports officers can be unaware of specific pieces of information that they should look for in the collected intelligence and include in their reports to analysts. Ford notes: "Processors [reports officers] have far more knowledge than ever comes out in the formal intelligence reports, but since they don't know what it is that the analysts need to know, they don't report it. But if you call them on the telephone or go out and see them, they say, 'Oh, I didn't know you needed to know any of that.' Invariably, when a second look is taken, especially in response to analysts' questions, the processors find more data."[72]

The current lack of contact between reports officers and analysts means that reports officers may not understand what information is valuable to particular analysts; analysts, in turn, may not be aware of the techniques and larger set of information available to the reports officers. A lot of collected information that may have analytic utility often ends up on the cutting room floor.[73] For example, if WINPAC analysts had better understood the role of reports officers, they could have paid more attention to how collectors from the U.S. Defense Intelligence Agency (DIA), who first received Curveball's reports from German intelligence, largely worked as informal reports officers. In this capacity, the DIA translated and redacted German intelligence reports on Curveball but did not conduct further operational evaluation of Curveball's information before passing the reports to the CIA.[74] This information would have been valuable in assessing Curveball's reliability.

Although working relationships do still exist between reports officers and analysts, they appear to vary greatly. According to one former U.S. intelligence analyst involved in early Iraq bioweapons assessments: "In the First Gulf War, I had a really good friend at the NSA [National Security Agency]. Occasionally, we would find people like [Rihab] Taha [former Iraqi bioweapons scientist] traveling to some trade show. My friend at NSA didn't think it was worth putting it in a cable, because nobody cared about it except me, but he told me and I told the DO [Directorate of Operations] that Taha is going to be in a meeting in Europe on this date, it might be an opportunity to meet her."[75] In this case, access to key collected information depended on the serendipitous professional friendship that already existed between the intelligence analyst and the NSA worker. As Richard Kerr notes, "A lot of it turns on your ability to socialize with the system and make it work for you. . . . That's human factors."[76] But most analysts do not realize the depth of knowledge that reports officers can bring to the intelligence process.

Because reports officers and their work are often obscured or marginalized elements in the intelligence process, they serve as what Steven Shapin calls "invisible technicians," whose importance in the production of knowledge is often overlooked.[77] Some official CIA diagrams of the intelligence process even represent the work done by reports officers with an image of a computer terminal rather than a person.[78] Margaret Henoch has stated that the term *processor* has been used more frequently in recent years to refer to reports officers, because it reflects changes in how these workers and their work are viewed in the knowledge-making part of intelligence. Henoch explains that "a reports officer is now very often just 'processing' information. A processor is somebody whose input is not asked for, who doesn't really have any expertise. They are just an editor."[79]

In looking back at the Curveball case, it is clear that there were serious disconnects in the integration of operational and analytic knowledge. When the Directorate of Operations' European Division and German group debated with WINPAC analysts about Curveball's reliability in the fall of 2002, both sets of experts relied on different frameworks and methodologies; comparing, contrasting, and integrating these differences would have been difficult, time-consuming, and resource-intensive. One can also see, however, that if more aspects of operational knowledge and expertise were brought to bear much earlier on, they could have helped provide additional valuable (albeit challenging) information to WINPAC analysts for assessing Curveball as a human source and making judgments on Iraq's mobile bioweapons capabilities.

Individual versus Communal Knowledge

The way in which individual and communal knowledge are prioritized is another concern for intelligence analysts. Although analysts consider finished CIA intelligence products to be collective judgments and each product is subject to review by different analytic offices, in reality, individual analysts often play a strong role in shaping how knowledge is created and presented in these products. Ford has described CIA analysts as operating primarily under a "sole-practitioner" model, where each analyst is directly responsible for a very small, discrete functional or geographic area.[80] Under this existing model, analytic managers mete out work to individual analysts. Each analyst works autonomously and is responsible for creating a stream of analytic products on that issue area.

Although exceptions do occur, most analytic work done by CIA analysts uses this individual orientation. As Ford explains, "So, if you have a thousand analysts, they'll [CIA management] break up the problem into a thousand pieces, but if you have twenty analysts, they'll break it up into twenty. . . . Each one of them [analysts] will come up with their own individual [analytic] program."[81] Even analysts within the same specialty, like WMD, will work largely independently. Ford further explains this autonomy in analysis:

> Right now, analysts are free to do his or her own thing when it comes to topics and methodologies. They're all writing about important subjects, yes, but the political analyst is writing about the political motives for the Iranian nuclear program. The economist is writing about what it will cost, the military people are writing about possible targets, the technical people about the power of the weapons, and so on. All important subjects, but nobody is saying, "Okay, let's put all these experts together and come up with an in-depth answer to the policymakers' single most important question." What happens is people say, "Let's write about Iran nukes." And what you end up with is four or five superficial answers, none of which is very helpful to the policymakers. Rarely do our [intelligence] papers add up to more than the sum of their parts.[82]

Analysts do discuss their work with colleagues and participate in ad hoc collaborative projects in the course of their careers, but there is often no consistent, overarching collaborative structure and mechanism for most analyses unless there is a specific institutional or managerial directive.

In part to boost collaboration, centers like the Nonproliferation Center and WINPAC were created to increase analytic competence and serve as focal points for WMD issues. But their analyses are still structured under the sole-practitioner model. For instance, Ford explains that when these centers were created, "All they've done is they've taken ten people here, ten people there, forty people there, and set them in one room, and they're doing exactly the same thing, and that is they're doing sixty separate projects."[83] This outcome is not surprising, as the formation and maintenance of a sustained, interdisciplinary team for the production of knowledge requires organizational work of its own. Intelligence practitioner Rob Johnston explains that "successful [analytic] teams have very specific organizational and structural requirements. . . . Without specific processes, organizing principles, and operational structures, interdisciplinary teams will quickly revert to being simply a room full of experts who ultimately drift back to their previous work patterns. . . . The experts will not be a team at all; they will be a group of experts individually working in some general problem space."[84] And that structure does not produce the same kind of knowledge as would the same number of people organized into a team, working collaboratively over a sustained period of time to answer a complex policy-relevant question.

The ability to maintain a team-oriented framework for analysis is also hindered by the types of achievements the CIA values for professional advancement. Under the sole-practitioner model, the CIA rewards and promotes individual analysts for the projects and reports they initiate, research, and write by themselves. This creates an organizational culture that tends to value autonomy in analysis rather than collaboration. One former intelligence practitioner points out that such autonomy creates an organization in which there can be significant variability in analytic work: "Each analytic office within the DI [Directorate of Intelligence] is run as its own autonomous unit. . . . One analytic unit can be perfectly optimized and functioning at peak performance, while just down the hall another unit in the same office can be tremendously dysfunctional."[85] This autonomy makes across-the-board, system-wide improvements in intelligence analysis difficult. As a result, intelligence scholar Rob Johnston has observed that methodological improvements (as well as problems) in analysis are often localized to individual domains.[86]

As Ford further explains, however, this autonomy can also make analysts protective of their own best practices and reluctant to share them with their fellow analysts: "Analysts establish their own personal rules for analysis and need not share these rules in any detail with their fellow analysts or supervisors, either before or after they complete a project. They consider such information proprietary. Moreover, little or no incentive exists to foster openness. . . . Any assistance offered is purely voluntary. The organizational incentives that do exist promote a competitive atmosphere, not teamwork."[87] In Ford's view, analysts operating under competition do not merely passively hinder the development of communal knowledge on an intelligence problem; they can be responsible for actively blocking new knowledge from being developed.[88] Max Weber, in his classic analysis of bureaucracy, found that preoccupation with these kinds of protective measures is an inherent characteristic within institutions, because administrative units strive to maintain a competitive advantage over rival units.[89] Additionally, former deputy director of the CIA Richard Kerr has noted that the proprietary focus on analysis can create an analytic work culture in which analysts and their managers view the repository of relevant knowledge and expertise to be resident solely within a particular analytic unit, such as WINPAC, with little recognition of the importance of outside experts.[90] Although competition in intelligence analysis is often lauded for its ability to introduce new and challenging lines of thinking, the organizational focus and incentive structures for individual analytic work can hinder internal and external motivations to share or incorporate different types of expertise among analyses and analytic products.

In fact, current CIA organizational practices have no consistent method for recognizing multiple contributors to a single analytic product. As Ford explains: "Right now, we have no structured design to say that one analyst did 40 percent of the work on a project, and another did 60 percent. Or, that the 40 percent part was done better, so that person gets a bigger reward, and the 60 percent part wasn't nearly as good, so that person gets less. The system is not set up to do it that way. What happens is if, if I [as a CIA analyst] talk you into doing a project with me, I'm going to get 90 percent of the credit and you're going to get 10 percent, if you're lucky. So why would you volunteer to work with me? Since it wasn't your idea, you don't get the face time with the policymakers or one of the other incentives that make the system work."[91] Former CIA analyst John Gentry has previously noted that "most analysts work most of the time on individual assignments; management regularly claims that it cannot adequately assess the work of individuals who work on teams."[92] Although some collaborations on CIA analyses do occur through formal managerial directive, they otherwise tend to be arranged informally among colleagues who are friends (or friendly colleagues) and carried out on their own private time in an ad hoc manner.

Although analysts often describe how their analytic products are "coordinated" with other analysts, implying collaboration, this is not necessarily true collaborative work. As an example, even if economic or regional analysts are directed to coordinate with technical analysts on weapons assessments, this often does not involve in-depth interrogation (or development) of the assessment with other analysts, because, under the sole-practitioner model, each analyst has his or her own high-priority reports under way. So a WINPAC analyst may seek review and comment from other analysts on his or her draft report, but these other analysts are often not involved in the initial construction of the assessment, nor do they have the authority or knowledge to question the underlying assumptions or methodologies (for instance, the biotech revolution frame) the technical analyst has used once an assessment is produced.

In this context, intelligence expert Stephen Marrin finds that although the coordination process shapes the report, "the expertise of the primary drafter of the piece usually has primary influence on the accuracy of the final piece."[93] Because the starting assumptions and conceptual frame of the analytic work are not typically questioned, so-called coordination often largely involves fact-checking or agreeing on appropriate prose, rather than discussing and debating the conceptualization and construction of the assessment. Intelligence scholar James Bruce writes that coordination should be an important part of the analytic process, where significant errors or problems in analysis can be detected and corrected. Bruce, however, goes on to note, "But this important feature of self-correction [in coordination] is lost when the focus shifts from epistemology to language."[94] Although the nature of coordination depends on the analysts and managers involved, an organizational practice that supports a sole-practitioner model does not typically promote in-depth interrogation of methodologies as a routine part of the coordination process.

The lack of organizational collaboration can even extend to a lack of assistance with data storage and retrieval, meaning that analysts receive little staff support to help them work with large amounts of complex data from classified and unclassified databases. Although some analysts within the CIA have intelligence assistants, can draw on defense contractors, or work with other units for analytic support, the data collection, analysis, and writing for intelligence products is largely done by individuals. As Ford explains, "We have made sole practitioners, each with their own account, individually responsible for retrieving the information they need. Most often, analysts end up using only a tiny fraction of the available information, the most easily observed pieces that flood in daily."[95] Even when analysts are asked to conduct more in-depth, collaborative analyses, there are limitations to what they can undertake, because "every one of those ideas has to be ones that a person can do by themselves or convince another person to work with them and then convince the [organizational] structure that such an arrangement is acceptable," according to Ford.[96] As a result, there are very few two-person—let alone multiperson—collaborative projects (outside of specific managerial directive). As a result, analytic projects tend to be narrow and limited in scope to what an individual analyst can accomplish.

With the focus on individual work comes the expectation that improving analytic competence means improving an analyst's area or subject matter expertise rather than his or her analytical approach or techniques. As Ford says, "If you sit around among analysts and look at how they define expertise, it will be the Chinese language, or something like 'I read another book on China, have you seen the *China Quarterly* article on X?' All of it's in terms of becoming more knowledgeable about China or proliferation or about chemical weapons. It's the content of your specialty."[97] As a result, few organizational incentives exist for analysts to reflect on methodologies or other fundamental forms of analytic practice and how these shape the production of knowledge in assessments.[98] When it comes to weapons assessments, however, the central questions for policymakers—for instance, does Iraq have a mobile bioweapons capability?—often consist of both technical and nontechnical issues that virtually no individual alone could answer adequately, particularly as the CIA is currently structured into separate functional and geographic lines of expertise.

In looking at the Iraqi mobile lab assessments, we can see that a small number of WINPAC analysts largely handled the evaluation of Curveball using a competitive, sole-practitioner model. Each analyst was responsible for identifying, analyzing, and producing the range of intelligence reports and assessments on Curveball and the Iraqi mobile bioweapons threats sent to policymakers and other members of the U.S. intelligence community. With the exception of the Directorate of Operations' Counterproliferation Division, WINPAC analysts did not collaborate closely with experts from other CIA units or with other U.S. intelligence agencies to assess Curveball and his Iraqi mobile bioweapons claims. In fact, WINPAC's analytic autonomy hampered the incorporation of alternative types of expert knowledge (operational, nontechnical) in evaluating such threats.

From January 2000 through October 2002, moreover, WINPAC analysts kept Curveball's reporting and their methodologies for assessing it largely proprietary. Although WINPAC coordinated its assessments with other CIA units and U.S. intelligence agencies, analysts from those agencies did not have direct access to Curveball's reports or to subsequent Operations reports indicating problems with Curveball as a source. Thus, WINPAC operated largely as an autonomous unit with respect to assessing Curveball and the Iraqi mobile bioweapons threat. When the Directorate of Operations' European Division and German group were finally given access to Curveball's reporting and raised questions about his reliability and WINPAC's methodologies for assessing him, WINPAC analysts took offense. Instead of welcoming alternative views to refine their assessments, WINPAC analysts viewed these perspectives as threats to their analytic work. The competitive atmosphere that ensued hindered more in-depth consideration of operational knowledge in the mobile lab assessments. This competitive atmosphere was reinforced by CIA upper management, who set WINPAC and Operations' German experts on opposing sides, instead of fostering an environment in which both sets of knowledge and expertise could have been combined in a collaborative fashion.

Generalists versus Specialists

Connected to the problem of individual versus communal knowledge is the issue of how expert knowledge is defined, supported, and ordered for intelligence analysis. Within the CIA, generalists (those who are hired and trained to work on a broad and changing set of issues) are given priority over specialists (those hired and trained with in-depth expertise to work on a particular subject matter for an extended period of time). This reflects a change in organizational practices within the CIA over a twenty-year period. In the Curveball case, the use of generalists as analysts affected what was available and deemed relevant as expertise in CIA's mobile bioweapons assessments. The generalist mindset also shaped the way CIA management supported WINPAC's assessments.

In 1951, intelligence scholar and practitioner Sherman Kent argued that to conduct strategic intelligence, the CIA's analytic cadre required "people to whom research and rigorous thought are the breath of life, and they must accordingly have tolerance for the queer bird and the eccentric with a unique talent. They must guarantee a sort of academic freedom of inquiry . . . a deference to the enormous difficulties which the search for truth often involves."[99] In his book *Sharpening Strategic Intelligence,* Richard Russell writes that Kent envisioned a CIA whose analysis was comparable to the rigorous research done by a major university's faculty and would draw on the best classified and unclassified information available.[100] So, early on, CIA leaders considered the development and maintenance of long-term, in-depth expertise as critical to the conduct of intelligence analysis.

Before the 1970s, this vision was not far from reality. Weapons analyses were conducted by a combination of technical and nontechnical experts who often came to the CIA midcareer, after receiving a Ph.D. or related terminal degree and working for lengthy stints in civilian or military organizations or academic disciplines. For example, on weapons issues, the CIA often hired analysts with experience developing weapons technologies who brought particular understandings about the role of know-how and the minutiae of weapons development and weapons systems into their assessments. During that time, the CIA placed a high value on expertise and the ways it could inform analysis of weapons threats. Ford notes that at that time, "experts were so important because they had actually built a nuclear weapon before. They had built or been in a bioweapons lab. That's something that you can't get anyplace else, rather than being there and being an expert in that particular field. Because you can then say, 'Well, here's what you need to know. If the thing [weapon] you are looking for uses a lot of water, then look at the water bill, look for new pipes, look for this or that.' Knowing things like that requires knowledge of the target, knowledge of the problem, knowledge of the culture, knowledge of the system."[101] When these midcareer experts were brought into the CIA, their extensive knowledge base was then available for application to the analysis of weapons threats.

On top of that, expertise of this sort came not just from CIA employees. CIA analysts also worked closely with specialized technical experts at U.S. government laboratories developing weapons technologies in order to understand foreign technological developments. Dennis Gormley, head of intelligence at the U.S. Army's Harry Diamond Lab during the 1970s, recalls how his lab provided additional kinds of expertise to the CIA:

> Harry Diamond Laboratory was a government laboratory that had twelve laboratories and about a thousand scientists and engineers in it. It did 80 percent of its work, as distinct from farming it out to a contractor and just being a contract agent for it. So we did everything from build fuses for ICBMs [intercontinental ballistic missiles] and SLBMs [submarine launched ballistic missiles] to hardening electronic systems in a major weapons system to sustain, to operate in a nuclear environment. We had an entire lab that replicated the Soviet development process; they [Harry Diamond engineers] became, over time, Russian engineers. I spent a good deal of my time bringing CIA analysts through Harry Diamond Laboratories to learn about technology and how technology operates so that they could become better analysts of the analogs that they were viewing within the Soviet Union. And so that was an enormous resource available to the CIA during the era. I had a close working relationship with CIA and DIA, and we trained oodles of people who came through and got tours of the laboratory, would ask questions, would have continuing contacts with engineers who were specialists on particular technologies.[102]

Instead of providing short-term ad hoc contracts, government laboratories such as Harry Diamond provided specialized know-how and other complementary technical knowledge within the context of close, long-term partnerships with the CIA. With this organizational practice of prioritizing internal and external expertise, the CIA was able to draw on a vast array of stable, in-depth subject matter expertise for conducting intelligence analyses on weapons issues.

Starting in the late 1970s and more acutely after the Cold War ended, changes in organizational practices regarding internal and external expertise began altering how CIA managers and analysts sought and used expert knowledge in intelligence assessments. For instance, the close, long-term partnerships between U.S. government laboratories and the CIA began to disappear. As Dennis Gormley says, "The U.S. government consciously made a decision in the '70s to basically outsource everything [to defense contractors]. And today, as a consequence of that decision in the '70s, what it had was this crushing effect on tacit knowledge [know-how]. No longer does the CIA have access to this specialized skill base."[103] And, as noted earlier, many in-house CIA experts who had conducted rigorous weapons analyses in the 1960s and 1970s began to retire in the 1990s and were not replaced by people with similar weapons know-how.

In addition, with the collapse of the Soviet Union, the changing security environment in the 1990s also played a role in diminishing the organizational practice of inculcating expertise. With the rise in number of potential state and nonstate threats after the Cold War, CIA management preferred to hire and train analysts who could be generalists, because management believed them to be better suited to respond to an unpredictable security environment. Former CIA analyst Richard Russell explains that, because security crises are often unanticipated, they often force intelligence managers to "surge" their analysts to deal with the crisis of the day. In this context, Russell finds that "in promotion panels they [intelligence managers] consequently tend to favor generalists who are more versatile and willing to bounce from hot topic to hot topic than individuals who would prefer to stay put and work on 'slower' accounts for longer periods of time and to develop a specialty."[104] As a result of these changes, says Ford, "expertise seemingly became less and less important to the people who were making the personnel decisions. Next thing I knew, our world-class economists had left, the most experienced political people were gone, the technical people from the labs had been pushed out or retired, and OSR [Office of Strategic Research], the military office I had been assigned to, was disbanded. Apparently, those in charge decided that generalists could do the same job as the experts they were replacing."[105] Connecting the devaluing of in-depth subject matter expertise with larger organizational changes within the CIA, Henoch further adds, "When we [the CIA] stopped a geographic focus and went to adding functional focus. . . . The trouble with functional foci is that they were manned by people who were not experts."[106] Although technical experts can bring in their own biases and blind spots, they do possess knowledge critical for weapons analyses.

The CIA's generalist culture has encouraged people to move around and switch jobs often. The thinking, Ford says, was, "You don't have to have a nuclear engineer on staff in order to do nuclear analysis or economic or political or whatever. You could do it simply by having smart people that had gone to the best [undergraduate] colleges. . . . Generalists were good enough."[107] As another former CIA weapons analyst comments: "They [CIA] don't particularly like experts. If you're a good analyst, you should be a general analyst. . . . If you're well trained, you should be able to do anything. That's the sort of thinking."[108] On the Operations side, Tyler Drumheller has also noted this shift in the value placed on expertise: "Well, right now the people that run it [the CIA] are the people that came up through that system, people who follow a very set pattern. They work in a branch, they move to a certain place. There is sort of an idea that you don't want to become too much of an expert, you want to be a generalist, you want to be flexible. . . . Where the DO [Directorate of Operations] goes back and forth is whether you want to have people who are experts in one area of the world or one issue, or you want to have generalists. It's the same argument as the analysts."[109] Throughout the CIA, then, fungibility and broad knowledge—rather than in-depth subject matter expertise and skill-based knowledge—are the new priority.

Since the 1990s, the pervasiveness of generalists has changed the composition of the CIA's analytic cadre. Writing in 2007, Richard Russell noted that, although the CIA's Directorate of Intelligence claims to have experts, "few if any analysts are nationally, much less internationally, recognized experts in their field."[110] This is a dramatic change from the Cold War period, when many CIA analysts were known and respected within their professional disciplines. In addition, although exact data are classified, Russell estimates that only about 10 percent of the CIA's analysts have doctoral degrees—a larger percentage having master's degrees.[111] Although bachelor's and master's degrees embody useful subject matter knowledge for analysis, individuals with these degrees typically have not conducted the complex, extended, in-depth research projects requiring close attention to methodological practices that are required for doctoral degrees.

Furthermore, rewarding generalists through promotion has further hindered the development of internal subject matter experts in analysis. In 2001, former CIA inspector general Frederick P. Hitz noted, "Since the Cold War ended, agency analysts have tended to be eighteen-month wonders who hopscotch from subject to subject without developing any broad, long-term expertise in any one area."[112] Intelligence scholar Stephen Marrin has also noted that such frequent work changes prevent an analyst from developing knowledge about specific disciplines and applying sophisticated methodological tools to complex intelligence data.[113] Instead of inculcating internal and external expertise in order to assess existing and emerging threats, the CIA has largely hired, supported, and promoted individuals who do not have extensive subject matter expertise. Development of in-depth expertise on particular topics is also stymied by the need for analysts to rotate positions frequently.

This impact of a generalist culture within the CIA is reflected in WINPAC and its assessment of Curveball. In his book *Curveball,* Bob Drogin writes that there were only six WINPAC analysts covering all bioweapons issues *globally* when the Curveball reporting emerged.[114] Subsequently, during the heated internal debates over Curveball's reliability that arose in the fall of 2002, Drumheller notes only two WINPAC bioweapons analysts who were directly involved.[115] One of them was not available to work on Curveball for the entire period, having been assigned to work in the Counterproliferation Division within the Directorate of Operations during part of the time of Curveball's reporting.[116]

An Iraq bioweapons team was formed very late in the leadup to the 2003 war, but by then much of Curveball's reporting had already been published and disseminated in reports and briefings to U.S. policymakers and other members of the U.S. intelligence community. In addition, the Iraq bioweapons team was quite small and had few analysts with extensive experience analyzing Iraq's bioweapons program. As one former U.S. intelligence analyst recalls,

> When the drum started beating in the fall of 2002, they made an Iraq-only team, and I was put on that team because there were people sitting in the DO helping with that, people doing the Curveball, a couple of main people there were drafting the NIE [National Intelligence Estimate] and doing other stuff. . . . They shifted a lot . . . because before that, Iraq was part of the Middle East team . . . but then things are going on, we are going to need a surge, bring some more people from here and there. . . . They said, "You have experience, so why don't you go up to this, because you have the background." . . . Not many other people on the team did, because they had only been there a couple of years.[117]

The lack of background on bioweapons issues within WINPAC was noted by Drumheller and Henoch. As Drumheller states, "The woman who ran that group [the WINPAC bioweapons team], she was one of the drafters on the first NIE. She has no background in the [technical] area, except she's sort of trained by WINPAC."[118] Another bioweapons analyst working on the Iraq portfolio had an undergraduate degree in biology before being hired by WINPAC. Because this analyst spoke Italian, she was originally assigned to assess bioweapons programs in Libya, a former Italian colony; later, Iraq was added to her portfolio.[119] As Drumheller points out: "You think all these people at WINPAC are a bunch of engineers and physicists, [but] the WINPAC chief is a liberal arts major. The Agency believes you can cross-train people and put them in anything, but she had no more expertise in this [bioweapons] than any of the case officers working on it. Except that she read lots and lots of things. It's one of the great weaknesses of the agency. It's the same as the people that run . . . the Bin Laden operations; they are not experts on Arabic stuff and on the Koran. . . . They just read lots and lots of intercepts."[120] That generalists were assessing Curveball's reporting means that the dominant biotech revolution frame, with its focus on counting materials, technical information, and abstract technological trajectories, was a simple one for these analysts to use in constructing their assessments about an Iraqi mobile bioweapons capability. The analysts' lack of in-depth technical background and weapons know-how precluded their ability to question Curveball's technical claims or even to know what would be needed to assess those claims more rigorously.

As an example, the generalist background of WINPAC's bioweapons analysts affected their consideration of whether to bring in relevant outside experts to evaluate Curveball's claims. Before Colin Powell's UN speech in the fall of 2002, the CIA briefed a select audience of UN inspectors, showing them some of Curveball's drawings about the purported Iraqi mobile bioweapons labs. These inspectors were biological experts who had spent considerable time assessing Iraq's past and present bioweapons capabilities. From their on-the-ground experiences in Iraq, these UN inspectors were surprised to see what they considered an erroneous depiction of an Iraqi mobile bioweapons capability in the CIA's briefing.

The UN inspectors' critique of the CIA briefing stemmed from their own past internal assessment of how a covert Iraqi mobile program might operate. In the summer of 2002, before UN inspections resumed, the UN bioweapons inspection team held a group discussion on how they might be able to detect covert bioweapons activities in Iraq. From this discussion, they produced an approximately ten-page draft paper on Iraqi mobile bioweapons capability, which they sent to Hans Blix, the chairman of the UN inspections team. UN bioweapons inspector Peter Prosser recalls this exercise: "We wanted to have a picture in our own mind of underground facilities, mobile facilities. If we were on the ground in Iraq, what would we tell inspectors to look for? What does it look like? I mean, you want to know if you're looking for a big eighteen-wheeler truck, are you looking for two or three smaller ones? How can we do it, how can we configure it? Is the truck going to have any external signs? Is it going to be big pipes up here or down there? You know, these are just basic, common-sense things that you do before you even start an inspection."[121] With this study under their belt, UN bioweapons inspectors questioned the CIA's presentation of an alleged Iraqi mobile bioweapons capability. Former UN inspector Kay Mereish explains: "What was presented in the diagrams technically was incorrect . . . from the [prior] group discussion that we [UN inspectors] had, from the knowledge about fermentation, what it requires, the set up. I mean, there is a lot of things that gives you the idea to ask, What is this? Why did you think this is there? and Is this possible? and all those questions. They [CIA briefers] could not answer any technical question that is essential for the operation of what they have in the diagram. . . . That briefing was very much what they think they had on the mobile labs."[122]

Although WINPAC's bioweapons analysts hired some external defense contractors to validate Curveball's claims, it does not appear that these experts consulted UN inspectors or tried to evaluate an Iraqi mobile bioweapons capability beyond cursory, abstract technical details. As one former U.S. intelligence analyst recalls, "Our experts, and that's not me because I don't know about fermentation, but our experts looked at this stuff [Curveball's reporting] and figured out that if you have these temperatures and pressures it's probably these things."[123] On top of that, there is no evidence that WINPAC analysts consulted or worked closely with former U.S. and Soviet bioweapons scientists to draw on their specialized weapons know-how in assessing Curveball's reporting or to help craft information that could be used by German debriefers in subsequent sessions with Curveball. Even though WINPAC's mobile lab assessments emphasized some technical details, the generalist background of the analysts and managers involved in the assessments led them to accept a simple understanding of biotechnology—by relying on the dominant biotech revolution frame's understanding of Iraq's bioweapons capabilities—and forgo more in-depth and holistic means by which to evaluate Curveball's technical details; it also shaped what additional outside expertise would be considered relevant to validate Curveball's claims.[124]

In addition, the CIA's generalist culture led WINPAC bioweapons analysts to assume they knew how to evaluate Curveball as a source and did not need to seek additional expertise from the Directorate of Operations. As one former U.S. intelligence analyst says, "One of the things that was very appealing about him [Curveball] was that he didn't know every single detail. So, here is a chemical engineer, he said there were dials, valves, and stuff like that. He didn't know anything else. . . . When you deal with sources a lot, people who know everything look suspicious."[125] As Henoch noted, however, WINPAC analysts relied on their own limited understanding of operations work and did not probe Curveball's knowledge and reliability in other areas, which a rigorous operations evaluation of a human source should always involve.

Henoch also argues that the pervasive generalist mindset has shaped how CIA upper management viewed the value of operational expert knowledge in weapons assessments when it became a political issue. In late 2002, for example, when Henoch questioned Curveball's reliability based on operational concerns, she was reproached by Jim Pavitt, deputy director of the Directorate of Operations. As Henoch recalls, "So, when he [Pavitt] said, 'Well, you weren't qualified to judge this,' my job was not to judge the technical piece. . . . Pavitt didn't even understand to hear me say, 'I'm not arguing with what he [Curveball] said technically, I am arguing with who he is,' and he just didn't hear that. . . . I would make the argument that they [CIA management] don't understand the business [intelligence]. In bringing in the bland [generalists], you had a bunch of people who didn't know what business they were in."[126] Here, Henoch is arguing that Pavitt and other senior CIA officials who have risen through the ranks as generalists have developed blind spots and biases related to generalist forms of knowledge. At this same time, this incident also suggests that Pavitt's deference to technical authority on weapons issues stems from the increasing disconnects between operational and analytic knowledge that have developed in the CIA over time, as well as separations between technical and social forms of knowledge.

Conclusion

In popular discussions about how intelligence is produced, the CIA and other intelligence and policy organizations have used a schematic known as "the intelligence cycle," which consists of five key steps (fig. 5.1): (1) planning and direction, where policymakers set the intelligence priorities; (2) collection; (3) processing; (4) analysis; and (5) dissemination, which involves conveying final intelligence reports to policymakers. With its cyclical representation, the key stages of the production of knowledge—collection, processing, and analysis—seem to flow in a smooth and straightforward fashion. Left out of this neat and simple representation are the messier frames, work practices, and hidden forms of knowledge and expertise that actually structure intelligence work and, ultimately, knowledge itself.

In their book *Leviathan and the Air Pump,* Steven Shapin and Simon Schaffer propose that "solutions to the problem of knowledge are solutions to the problem of social order."[127] In essence, Shapin and Schaffer argue that the way individuals (and groups) are organized and rewarded for work fundamentally shapes the knowledge they produce. In looking at the Curveball case, social ordering clearly

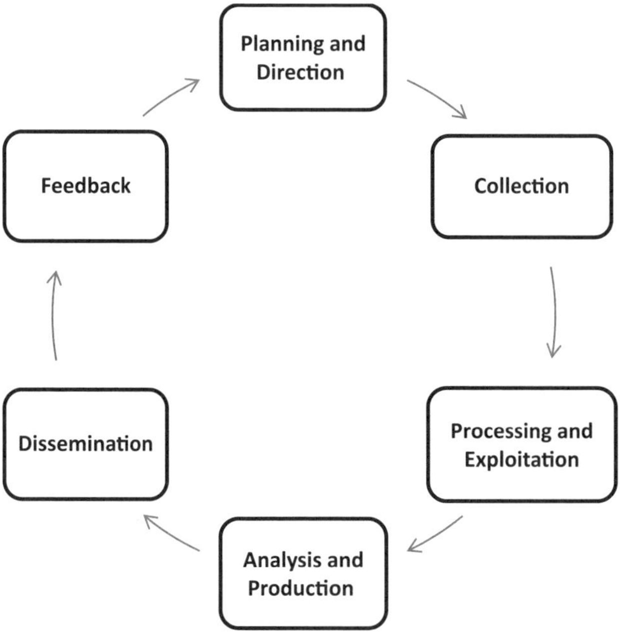

Fig. 5.1. The Intelligence Cycle. Adapted from a similar graphic in U.S. Central Intelligence Agency, "Work of the CIA," 27.

underpinned the way the Iraqi mobile bioweapons assessments were conducted, including a privileging of technical forms of knowledge, problems in integration of operational expertise, the rewarding of individual analytic work, and a privileging of generalist expertise. These outcomes reflect fundamental changes in CIA organizational structure, practices, and rewards that have occurred over the past twenty years.

For instance, WINPAC's focus on technical information in its Iraqi mobile lab assessments reflects CIA organizational changes that have isolated technical analysts from other types of experts. Furthermore, WINPAC's reliance on technical expertise and information sources (technical drawings, satellite imagery) demonstrates how the popular biotech revolution frame described in chapter 2 has also shaped CIA thinking. These institutional frames and practices created a regime of perceptibility among WINPAC analysts, whereby alternative forms of information and knowledge—even those within the CIA's own Operations units—were simply not considered important or relevant to the Iraqi mobile bioweapons assessments.[128] By understanding how these organizational practices can shape analysis, we can see how WINPAC analysts came to believe that Iraq had mobile bioweapons capability and how their judgments garnered and sustained such privilege and authority within the CIA. Social ordering of knowledge and expertise has important implications for collection and analytic work practices and the assessments and policymaking that follow.

These conclusions, however, do not imply that the ordering of knowledge and expertise within the CIA during the Cold War period remain the only, or even the best, solutions to the problems underpinning bioweapons assessments. Even during what Richard Kerr and Carl Ford seem to describe as the "Golden Age" of intelligence assessments, when the highest concentration of experts and integrated knowledge was brought to bear on assessments of Soviet capabilities, there remained serious intelligence failures for various reasons. But a historical understanding of CIA analysis shows that the organizing principle for intelligence analysis during the Curveball case was not the only model possible for weapons assessments, making clear the important factors that have been excluded in this post–Cold War shift in CIA culture.

The challenge, then, is for analysts and their managers to reflect on how different forms of knowledge and expertise can inform bioweapons assessments and the subtle ways in which different organizational practices can favor (or exclude) various kinds of knowledge. In short, the problems of knowledge within CIA assessments go beyond a fix of merely plugging in appropriate subject matter expertise or increasing collection efforts. Instead, the flawed mobile lab assessments show that the CIA needs to reexamine the frameworks, expertise, social ordering, values, and taken-for-granted organizational practices that guide the production of knowledge in such assessments. By unpacking these issues at the institutional level, analysts, managers, and policymakers can see different possible policy responses for these knowledge-based problems in intelligence. The next two chapters focus on current intelligence reporting and secrecy and reveal additional organizational practices that profoundly shaped the production of knowledge about Curveball and his mobile lab claims.

Current Intelligence Reporting and CIA Analytic Practice

> Basically, on a day-to-day basis, it's like working at CNN, only we're CNN *with secrets.* Actually, it's more like CNN's Headline News.
>
> *Anonymous CIA analyst*

In his State of the Union address of January 28, 2003, President George W. Bush revealed for the first time that U.S. intelligence agencies had amassed damning information about Iraq's continued efforts to develop weapons of mass destruction: "The United States will ask the U.N. Security Council to convene on February the 5th to consider the facts of Iraq's ongoing defiance of the world. Secretary of State Powell will present information and intelligence about Iraq's illegal weapons programs, its attempt to hide those weapons from inspectors, and its links to terrorist groups."[1] Lawrence Wilkerson, Colin Powell's chief of staff at the time, recalls that Bush's address was the first time he had heard about Powell's upcoming speech. Wilkerson says, "It was the next day that the Secretary [Powell] walked in my office and said, 'Go out to the CIA and get me ready.' "[2]

Over the next seven days, Wilkerson worked day and night with top CIA officials to prepare Powell's February 5 speech at the UN. Wilkerson notes that when Director of Central Intelligence George Tenet and his experts revealed the evidence regarding Iraq's mobile bioweapons program, "They presented it in a very dynamic, dramatic, *we know this is accurate,* way."[3] Tenet is well known for reportedly telling President Bush that intelligence about weapons of mass destruction in Iraq was "a slam dunk case."[4] At the time, Wilkerson judged the mobile bioweapons intelligence to be the most concrete and uncontested evidence of all of the U.S. intelligence on Iraq's WMDs, because "there wasn't a dissenting note ever thrown out anywhere in the whole thing. If there was a leg of that thing that Powell depended on to stand up, that was it."[5] Given that the mobile bioweapons intelligence appeared solid, after questions about the other Iraq WMD intelligence were resolved, Wilkerson turned his attention to the visual aesthetics of Powell's presentation. CIA graphic artists had constructed drawings of the purported Iraqi mobile bioweapons labs to be included in Powell's presentation to the UN (fig. 6.1).

Wilkerson remembers the time and effort spent on these visuals and the difficulty of trying to sequence and sync the graphics with the narrative. By the second day of the project, he felt that the CIA team wasn't up to the job and turned to National Security Advisor Condoleezza Rice for help from the White House media team. "These were the people who put on the extravaganzas that the White House puts on. So, I mean, these are Hollywood, New York–class people. They took over the graphics, synching it with the text," he says.[6]

Powell's UN speech had the effect he was hoping for, impressing American journalists with its dramatic, history-making message. The following day, the country's leading newspapers endorsed the veracity of Powell's claims. In an editorial titled "Irrefutable," the *Washington Post* wrote, "After Secretary of State Colin

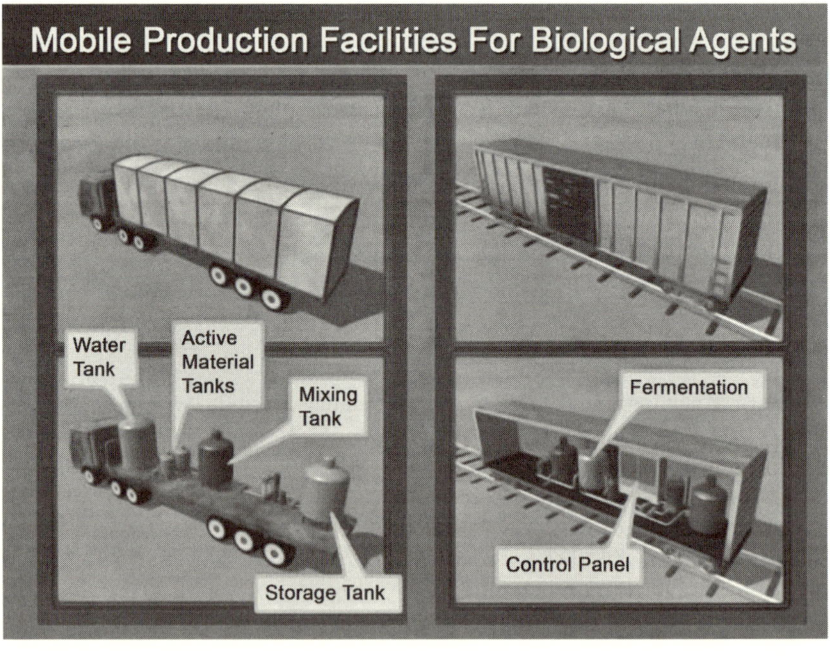

Fig. 6.1. Detail of where material is carried in purported mobile production facilities for bioweapons work. From Colin Powell, "Iraq: Failing to Disarm. Biological Weapons," Address to the United Nations, 5 February 2003, slide 21. http://2001-2009.state.gov/secretary/former/powell/photos/2003/17324.htm.

L. Powell's presentation to the United Nations Security Council yesterday, it is hard to imagine how anyone could doubt that Iraq possesses weapons of mass destruction."[7] The *New York Times* wrote, "The secretary offered much evidence that Iraq has weapons programs to hide. . . . Mr. Powell began his discussion of Iraq's weapons program by talking about biological arms, about which the United States has the most information. . . . It will be difficult for the skeptics to argue that Washington's case against Iraq is based on groundless suspicions and not intelligence information."[8] The connection between intelligence and journalism in Powell's UN speech, however, was not limited solely to this media coverage. As I describe in more detail below, the media-like atmosphere surrounding the preparation and presentation of Powell's UN speech was a fitting culmination of the journalistic style that typified the CIA's assessments of Iraq's purported mobile bioweapons program.

Current intelligence reporting refers to an analytic practice through which the intelligence community conveys to policymakers newly collected classified information focused on important day-to-day events and immediate, pressing policy issues. This reporting comes in a variety of formats, including daily oral briefings and video feeds to policymakers, ad hoc memoranda, and electronic and printed daily reports. The printed reports include the President's Daily Brief, the Vice President's Supplement, the Senior Executive Intelligence Brief (SEIB), the Senior Executive Memorandum, and the National Terrorism Brief.[9] These daily intelligence reports and briefings are often based on newly collected classified information and generally do not involve significant in-depth research. The CIA's own guide to intelligence states that current intelligence "may be disseminated without complete evaluation, interpretation, analysis, or integration."[10]

Intelligence practitioners and scholars have often argued that current intelligence reporting is too dominant and has too big an influence on how intelligence analysts spend their time.[11] Intelligence scholar Loch Johnson notes that 80 to 90 percent of the analytic resources of the U.S. intelligence community are devoted to current intelligence reporting.[12] Thus, in terms of sheer volume, time, and effort, the practice of current intelligence reporting structures the way many intelligence analysts work and the kinds of products they provide to policymakers. With the immediacy of this type of focus, Mark Lowenthal, former assistant director of central intelligence for analysis and production, has warned that the intelligence community has "gotten out of the knowledge-building business."[13]

Current intelligence reporting, however, has not always been such a dominant and pervasive intelligence practice. In previous decades, only a small portion of intelligence analysts would have been concerned with producing current intelligence reports.[14] In the 1990s, however, the CIA's Directorate of Intelligence began to shift the prioritization of analytic work to current intelligence reports to increase the relevance of the CIA's products to policymakers.[15] As one CIA analyst recalls, "We used to have groups that did current reporting and different groups that did longer term products. We still have some of that but it is very limited. I couldn't say what happened exactly, but we're all doing current production now."[16] Commenting on this shift in analytic practice, former intelligence official Carl Ford remarks, "A lot of people understand what's happened, and they know the statistics, but they never have really understood the implications of that evolution [for analysis]."[17]

As the U.S. intelligence community has shifted its focus to current events, both the analysts and their reports have taken on the characteristics of contemporary journalism. In a recent, unclassified ethnographic study conducted by the CIA, for example, several analysts describe themselves and their work in largely journalistic language. As one analyst says, "I think of myself as a writer for the most important newspaper in the world."[18] Another analyst reflects, "It took me awhile to figure out that this place [the CIA] runs more like a newspaper than a university."[19] But not all are content with this change. As one analyst complains, "About fifteen years ago, I would have described myself as a scholar. Now, I'm a reporter. I've got fifteen people trying to change my work into bullet points. Presumably no one has time to read anymore."[20] The pressing, news-oriented climate pervasive in intelligence analysis has led some critics to refer to the CIA pejoratively as "CNN with secrets."[21]

Given all the media analogies, what does it mean for analysts to think of themselves as reporters? Or for the CIA's analytic work environment and products to be compared to CNN's Headline News? To help answer these questions, we turn to sociologist Herbert Gans's book, *Deciding What's News,* which examines the practice of journalism in American newsrooms.[22] Like journalists, CIA intelligence analysts have adopted particular heuristics and work practices to produce current intelligence reports for policymaker consumption, a result of organizational practices that have elevated the value of current intelligence reporting over more in-depth, strategic analytic products. The shift has grown out of a new metric—responsiveness to policymaker security concerns—and is measured by the volume of headline-grabbing current intelligence reports the CIA provides to policymakers. Although such reporting provides timely information about weapons threats to policymakers, it fails to produce an in-depth understanding of the complex, multidisciplinary character of these threats.

In the following section, we will see just how the journalistic practices that underpin current intelligence reporting hinder the robust analysis of weapons issues. We will also see how current reporting practices and products were central to the CIA's assessments of the Iraqi mobile bioweapons labs and thus not only caused analytic problems but also reflected, contributed to, and reinforced the knowledge and expertise problems that plagued the Curveball assessments described in chapter 5. This chapter illustrates the problems that self-reinforcing, taken-for-granted organizational practices can have on the conduct of intelligence analysis and the knowledge it produces about security threats.

Current Intelligence Reporting as Journalistic Practice

Gans writes that although news reporting relies on empirical methods, it differs from other kinds of social science analyses due to the time pressures associated with news deadlines and the need to attract and keep audiences. As an analytic practice, he explains, "what distinguishes journalism from literary and social-science studies is the deadline. . . . This is one reason why news is basically descriptive; temporal and other resources that social scientists can devote to complex analyses and explanations are not often available."[23] To work within these deadlines and promote efficiency across the story selection and production process, Gans finds that journalists adopt a set of unwritten rules to guide their practices. These unwritten rules include quick heuristic tools to filter through and prioritize information; other rules for news production are based on developing practices and procedures that make the process efficient and standardized. Attention to what attracts and keeps news audiences is also a key part of the story selection and production process.[24] He further explains that the pressure of producing and delivering a news product every day fundamentally shapes the way reporters and news managers decide what is newsworthy: "Considerations [for news stories] do not exist only because they are efficient, but become significant because they are also efficient. . . . Efficiency is thus a function of the deadline, for while no one knows whether the audience wants the latest news or whether it would pay more for less efficiently produced news, the news must be on the air or in the readers' mailboxes at a prearranged time."[25]

Similarly, the Directorate of Intelligence, the CIA's main analytic branch, relies on an analytic model that incorporates its own set of unwritten rules and production processes to promote efficiency in current intelligence reporting practices and deadlines.[26] As I illustrate below, these rules include heuristic tools that enable quick judgments about human sources and items worthy of reporting to policymakers; these heuristics privilege the biotech revolution frame. Intelligence scholar Stephen Marrin has commented that "current intelligence production is the least analytical because time constraints do not permit so-called 'analytic tradecraft' to be applied. . . . Short deadlines require analysts to apply short-cuts, and as a result most current intelligence analysis is based more on informed intuition than structured or rigorous methods."[27] In addition, the production of a current intelligence report is characterized by a set of organizational routines throughout the intelligence review and approval process that inhibits in-depth analysis of the complex set of social and technical factors shaping weapons development. Moreover, the need to be relevant and responsive to policymakers underpins the entire current intelligence reporting process and further shapes how CIA analysts are trained, validated, and promoted.

The Daily Life of a Current Intelligence Reporter: Heuristics for Story Selection

In describing the daily work priorities facing intelligence analysts, former CIA analyst Larry Johnson stresses, "Today your first responsibility as an analyst is to keep track of what's happening right now."[28] This emphasis on the present is reflected in how an analyst typically starts his or her work day, with a focus on anticipating and selecting a new current report to write from the new intelligence information. By way of example, a CIA analyst might start his or her morning by reviewing the new "raw" intelligence information that has come in from a variety of signal, imagery, and human sources; often, analysts have a hundred or more intelligence reports to sort through each day. One former U.S. intelligence analyst explains that the raw intelligence "comes to your desk in electronic form and you learn how to put in your search terms, like you do for your daily Google. . . . So, you come in in the morning, you start reading all the stuff that has been accumulating."[29] From these newly collected pieces of intelligence information, analysts must evaluate whether there is an item worthy of being crafted into a short current intelligence report for policymakers' consumption. Intelligence analysts rely on heuristic tools to help them make quick decisions about this new information because, as intelligence scholar Stephen Marrin explains, for current intelligence reports "the analyst has only a couple of hours to do background research, come to a conclusion regarding the implications of the incident for American interests, and convert this information and analysis into acceptable language for publication."[30]

To help filter new intelligence information, analysts often rely on prior current intelligence reports and related analytic products to evaluate what might be an important piece of information to send to policymakers. As one CIA analyst explains, "I've looked at our previous products, and I've got a good idea of the pattern; so, when I sort through the traffic [raw intelligence], I know what I'm trying to find."[31] Another analyst notes, "The current data ought to fit a certain pattern. If it doesn't, I know something is wrong."[32] One former U.S. intelligence analyst adds that it would be reasonable to report that a country had a biowarfare program "because you had some good old information and you saw some new activity going on."[33] Thus, in gathering and sorting their information, CIA analysts depend on prior analytic products to serve as a baseline against which to evaluate new information. They often use what could be characterized as the formula "Old Information plus New Information equals Threat" to decide what might constitute an important item to include in a current intelligence report for senior policymakers.

In addition, CIA analysts use other heuristics to guide them in choosing sources for their current reports. Although they are expected to be "all-source analysts" and use both classified information (including different kinds of intelligence, such as human, signals, and so forth) and open-source information, in practice they often prefer to use classified sources for current intelligence reports. As one analyst states, "If the traffic [raw intelligence] comes from operations [clandestine side], I tend to pay more attention to it than to information in the open literature."[34] Another intelligence analyst adds, "What we bring to the party is information no one else has."[35] A third analyst concurs: "Our value-added is classified sourcing. Everybody has access to the Web and CNN."[36] Thus, from the beginning of their work day, analysts privilege newly acquired clandestine information in determining what items are worthy of including in current intelligence reports. Just as Gans finds that journalists depend on their own sources for news stories, intelligence analysts depend on classified sources to shape their decisions on information priority for daily intelligence reporting.

Among clandestine sources, analysts especially value human intelligence. As Roger George and James Bruce write, "Information collected by human intelligence (HUMINT) . . . can be a priceless resource uniquely available to intelligence analysts," because human sources can provide eyewitness accounts and confirm other types of information.[37] But not all human intelligence is equal; some sources are reporting information for the first time, while others have reported before but their information has never been fully corroborated. Many human intelligence reports that land on analysts' desks contain various disclaimers about their sources. One former intelligence analyst states that what analysts rarely see but always want to see is "a reliable source, which means somebody who has been reporting for a while that has been checked, vetted, and most [of his or her reporting] has turned out to be true."[38] Nonetheless, Ford says that analysts value human intelligence sources in current reports because policymakers do: "There is a tendency for policymakers to put an extra value on human reporting because it's a story, it's familiar, and it has a lot more details that they can read and absorb. So they always love the human sources. And analysts treasure those [human sources] because of that."[39] Because of pressing deadlines and the paucity of "reliable" human sources, analysts often have to make quick judgment calls on more tentative human intelligence sources for a current report.

In addition, analysts use their own individually developed rules, daily practices, and intuitive frames to determine what belongs in a current intelligence report. Time constraints play a role too, according to one CIA analyst: "I don't have time to worry about formal analytic methods. I've got my own system. It's more intuitive and a lot faster."[40] Another analyst explains how the analytic process for creating a current report is very pragmatic: "You read all this stuff, you have your expertise, and you make judgments."[41] According to CIA expert Richards Heuer, analysts draw on established frames to help their decision-making: "The current intelligence analyst's task is often extremely concept-driven. The analyst must provide immediate interpretation of the latest, often unexpected events. Apart from his or her store of background information, the analyst may have no data other than the initial, usually incomplete report. Under these circumstances, interpretation is based upon an implicit mental model of how and why events normally transpire in the country for which the analyst is responsible. Accuracy of judgment depends almost exclusively upon accuracy of the mental model, for there is little other basis for judgment."[42] This mental model, however, is also shaped by an analyst's ongoing use of other heuristics such as the privileging of classified information, reliance on prior analytic assessments, and simple "addition" formulas of old plus new intelligence. As a result, intelligence expert Dennis Gormley notes that "analysts today rarely expose their thinking to more rigorous forms of appraisal by employing scenario development, red teams (in which a problem is viewed from the perspective of a competitor or adversary), or structured augmentation tools. The latter are simply of little use when the demands of time dictate dependence on individual intuition rather than methodological rigor."[43]

Intelligence analysts also make reporting decisions based on their intended audience—namely, the policymakers. Determining what constitutes a good current intelligence report "comes with experience and understanding what people want downtown," according to one former U.S. intelligence analyst.[44] This requires watching the news and reading the papers to keep up with national news. As this former U.S. intelligence analyst explains, "You have to watch what is going on in the news, because you know people [policymakers] are going to be interested in this. The weird thing is that if it is in the newspaper, it ends up being even more interesting, even though it is open stuff, because then everyone focuses on it."[45] Intelligence analysts also consider whether policymakers have asked follow-up questions or shown recent interest in previous current intelligence reports on a subject, and whether the analyst can provide a new slant on an issue known to be of interest to policymakers.[46]

Thus, analysts draw on a variety of practices to help them process information within their pressing work environment. Using simple and quick heuristics and established frames helps analysts filter through the massive amounts of data that come into the CIA to select an item for a current intelligence report. Intelligence scholar Rob Johnston summarizes: "Operating under difficult time constraints . . . the analyst often finds himself or herself trying to produce daily products using the most time-efficient strategies available."[47]

The Daily Life of a Current Intelligence Reporter: Buying, Selling, and the Assembly-Line Production of Intelligence

Once an analyst decides to propose a daily intelligence item for a current report, he or she must then "sell" the idea to his or her management. If the manager "buys" the idea, the analyst will prepare the report that will then be sent to a higher administrative level. Because current reports are limited in space and content, higher management must decide what intelligence items for the day are worth passing on to busy policymakers. At the same time, analysts want their analytic products to reach as many customers as possible. As one former analyst explains,

> When you see all the papers at the Agency, you wonder, who is reading them? Who's reading them are all the congressional staff downtown. All of these papers go to the oversight committees, they all go downtown, to the NSC [National Security Council], and all over the place. If a congressional staff has read something, you will get a call. You are always throwing stuff out there, studies on things of interest. I have a really good friend who was just last year the staff director for the Senate Subcommittee on [name deleted to preserve anonymity]. He and the rest of his staff read this stuff voraciously anytime it came in, because they were looking for bits and pieces that would appeal to his senator's fancy. This is how it works; everyone reads all this stuff and it bubbles up to the top.[48]

This buying and selling of ideas for a current report is akin to the marketplace for news that exists within news organizations. According to Gans, journalists also have to sell their ideas to their bosses because "news organizations consist of people who are competing for the same scarce resource"—air time or magazine space.[49] As a result, Gans writes, "story suggestors identify what they deem most salable—the most novel, dramatic, or unusual components of a story idea—in the hope of making a sale to a selector, who cannot buy everything that is being sold."[50] Although the marketplace does weed out some reporting, Gans writes that many news stories virtually sell themselves because buyers and sellers come from similar journalistic backgrounds and have a shared understanding of what they deem newsworthy. Similarly, as I describe in more detail below, intelligence managers in the CIA's analytic branch often come up from the analytic ranks and are promoted due to their production of current intelligence reports and briefings that "sell" with policymakers.

The CIA's most prominent and prestigious current intelligence report is the President's Daily Brief (PDB), a highly classified, 10- to 12-page government document produced each morning for the president.[51] The PDB is intended to provide the president with new international intelligence warranting attention, including economic, political, social, or technical issues. James R. Woolsey, who was President Clinton's first director of central intelligence, states that "If there's something new and exciting and important, it has a good chance of making the PDB. . . . It's like making the front page."[52] Thus, one CIA analyst notes that every office wants its work to make it into the PDB.[53] But different presidents have made different use of this daily briefing document. Dwight D. Eisenhower and Lyndon Johnson gave PDBs great importance, whereas Ronald Reagan, George H. W. Bush, and Bill Clinton did not have as much interest in them. However, national security scholar Kenneth Lieberthal writes that George W. Bush assigned such importance to the PDB that "within the IC [intelligence community], getting an item into the PDB became a major goal of analysts. In the CIA, analysts who got an item into the PDB that President Bush found interesting or useful were rewarded."[54]

Typically, an item included in a PDB is restricted to about one page in length, although for technical issues a background paper may be prepared for the intelligence officer assigned to brief the PDB to the president.[55] In the years leading up to the 2003 Iraq War, the PDB format was such that it emphasized short, attention-getting pieces of analytic work. An example of a PDB item declassified by the Bush administration is shown figure 6.2. This was the first PDB released to the public by a president still in office.

On any given day, intelligence analysts usually have to have to decide by 9:00 a.m. whether to write an item for the PDB.[56] Once an item, or paper, has been approved for inclusion in the PDB, the analyst responsible must then go through a protracted internal and external approval process, the "First Customer Process"

Declassified and Approved
for Release, 10 April 2004

Bin Ladin Determined To Strike in US

Clandestine, foreign government, and media reports indicate Bin Ladin since 1997 has wanted to conduct terrorist attacks in the US. Bin Ladin implied in US television interviews in 1997 and 1998 that his followers would follow the example of World Trade Center bomber Ramzi Yousef and "bring the fighting to America."

> After US missile strikes on his base in Afghanistan in 1998, Bin Ladin told followers he wanted to retaliate in Washington, according to a [redacted] service.

> An Egyptian Islamic Jihad (EIJ) operative told an [redacted] service at the same time that Bin Ladin was planning to exploit the operative's access to the US to mount a terrorist strike.

The millennium plotting in Canada in 1999 may have been part of Bin Ladin's first serious attempt to implement a terrorist strike in the US. Convicted plotter Ahmed Ressam has told the FBI that he conceived the idea to attack Los Angeles International Airport himself, but that Bin Ladin lieutenant Abu Zubaydah encouraged him and helped facilitate the operation. Ressam also said that in 1998 Abu Zubaydah was planning his own US attack.

> Ressam says Bin Ladin was aware of the Los Angeles operation.

Although Bin Ladin has not succeeded, his attacks against the US Embassies in Kenya and Tanzania in 1998 demonstrate that he prepares operations years in advance and is not deterred by setbacks. Bin Ladin associates surveilled our Embassies in Nairobi and Dar es Salaam as early as 1993, and some members of the Nairobi cell planning the bombings were arrested and deported in 1997.

Al-Qa'ida members—including some who are US citizens—have resided in or traveled to the US for years, and the group apparently maintains a support structure that could aid attacks. Two al-Qa'ida members found guilty in the conspiracy to bomb our Embassies in East Africa were US citizens, and a senior EIJ member lived in California in the mid-1990s.

> A clandestine source said in 1998 that a Bin Ladin cell in New York was recruiting Muslim-American youth for attacks.

We have not been able to corroborate some of the more sensational threat reporting, such as that from a [redacted] service in 1998 saying that Bin Ladin wanted to hijack a US aircraft to gain the release of "Blind Shaykh" 'Umar 'Abd al-Rahman and other US-held extremists.

continued

For the President Only
6 August 2001 [redacted]

Declassified and Approved
for Release, 10 April 2004

Fig. 6.2. Bin Ladin Determined to Strike in U.S. Example of President's PDB, Declassified and Approved for Release, 10 April 2004. National Security Archive, George Washington University, www.gwu.edu/~nsarchiv/NSAEBB/NSAEBB116/index.htm.

(fig. 6.3).[57] As described below, this production process consists of an established routine intended to promote efficiency, much like the stress-filled, assembly-line process that Gans describes within news organizations.

When an intelligence analyst receives approval from his or her upper management for the PDB item, he or she sends the proposal to the CIA office responsible for producing it. If the PDB staff agrees to it, then the analyst works on drafting a formal intelligence report on the item for the next PDB. Once complete, the analyst sends the draft through a "coordination" review process inside and outside the CIA. As one former intelligence analyst explains, "If I mention Germany, France, or any other country, or any other subject, I then have to find the [CIA] experts in

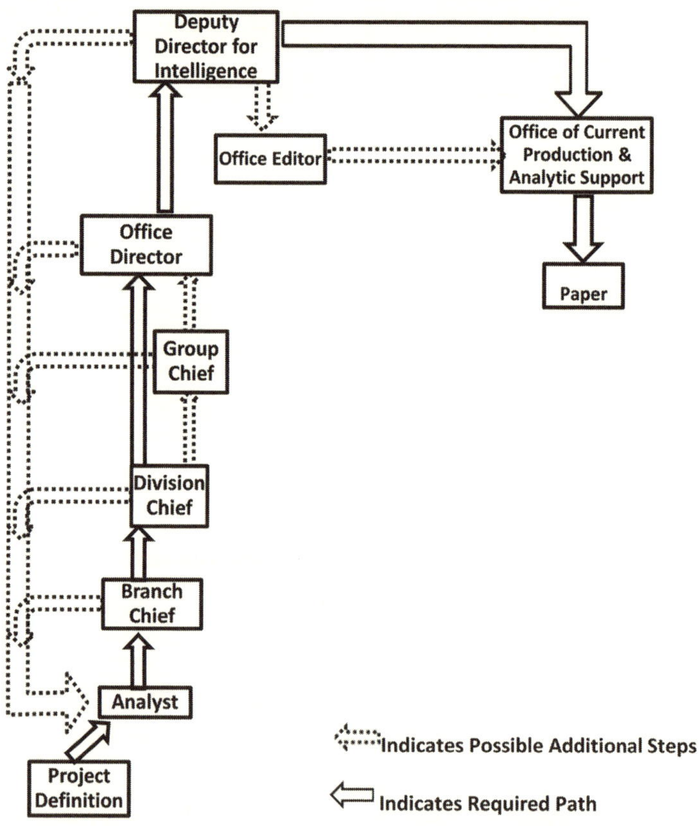

Fig. 6.3. Passage of Paper through the Review Process. From Gentry, *Lost Promise.* Reprinted by permission from Rowman and Littlefield Publishing Group.

that and send it to them to get their chop on it, and then I have to send it out of the building—the DIA, NSA, State, et cetera—so they can chop on it also."[58] During the 1990s and early 2000s, the U.S. intelligence community comprised thirteen separate agencies. Although each intelligence report would not usually have to be coordinated with all thirteen agencies, many individual reports require clearance with at least two agencies.

Although coordination varies by office personnel and their management, the coordination process is focused on getting a report approved for release. As a result, in many cases, coordination, as a bureaucratic exercise, often focuses on the prose and facts presented rather than on an extended interrogation of claims, assumptions, methodologies, and arguments underlying the report.[59] As one former U.S. intelligence analyst describes the coordination process:

> You would check with people. If it [intelligence] is about a front company, more often than not they [other internal/external analysts] would have seen the same things you did. But I might have it only in relation to bioweapons stuff, or they might have seen it for conventional arms. They [other analysts] generally provide a larger context. Sometimes they really don't have much to add, but you always check . . . for something like, "Here is a [foreign] front company that seems to be getting a fermentor for Iraq. Do you know anything else about this company?" Sometimes they know and sometimes they don't. It's just very basic stuff like that. Or, if you are talking to the DO [Directorate of Operations], you ask them, "Have you seen this company before?" [They say,] "Oh, yeah, well, maybe we have."[60]

In contrast to an extended collaborative relationship with operations officials, the coordination process devolves to simple fact-checking. In addition, due to the everpresent deadlines, formal analytic methodologies are often not used to verify the intelligence behind a current intelligence report as part of the coordination process. As one analyst notes, "It doesn't matter if I'm writing a piece myself or if I'm coordinating a piece with some group. We don't sit around and test hypotheses, because we're too busy writing. We've got some serious deadlines here."[61]

Editorial staff for the PDB can have significant power in terms of what reports are selected, how they are presented in the PDB, and whether the analyst needs to revise or expand the report. As one analyst says, "A lot of times the editors hold your life in their hands, because they kind of decide whether what you wrote is crap. And I've had questions from my counterparts [editorial staff], and they say it doesn't meet the threshold in their minds, and so sometimes they will tell you that they need more [human] source, and can you say a little more about what kind of access he has, direct or indirect. So sometimes you can do that with the DO [Directorate of Operations] and put that in the piece."[62] The coordination process for creation, review, and approval of a PDB item is similar to what Gans describes as "seriatim journalism," where news stories are passed, in assembly-line fashion, through several hands for review and approval before they are published.[63]

As Gans explains, however, within this focus on a serial production and review process, the writer's assumptions, hypotheses, and analytic practices are typically not questioned or interrogated by the reviewers; the priority lies in getting the prose in the report approved through the production chain.[64] One Senate report has highlighted that work by senior intelligence analysts is neither scrutinized nor "substantively reviewed before it goes up the chain to the policymaker."[65] In part, this lack of scrutiny is related to the value placed on professional autonomy—Ford's sole-practitioner model—within the CIA's analytic cadre and is analogous to the professional autonomy in news production, where, according to Gans, "writers are entitled to select their own facts, draw their own conclusions, and come up with their own evaluations, although they may be edited later."[66]

Part of the PDB production process can also include the incorporation of graphics and other visual representations into the article. In this way, as one analyst explains, assembling a PDB item "is much like writing a daily newspaper article. If you want graphics, then you have to see the graphics people. It is a newspaper, it is done every day like a newspaper."[67] According to one analyst, CIA graphics designers welcome work on WMD issues, because "they love this stuff, and the weirder the better. If you say I want a map of Baghdad, they couldn't give a shit about that. They are [professional] graphics artists with lots of clearances, and they like doing this stuff [WMD graphics]. You work with them saying, 'Here's what we have from the source, here's what we want to show.' "[68] Since the early 1990s, the newspaper-like quality of the PDB has included attention to format details such as "snappy" headlines to draw policymakers' eyes to "hot news" articles of the day.[69] One analyst illustrates this comparison with a particular newspaper format: "Imagine *USA Today* with spies—bullet points, short paragraphs, the occasional picture. You know, short and simple."[70]

From the moment an analyst walks in the door, the entire process for drafting, clearing, and finalizing an item for the PDB can take almost twenty-four hours, which obviously can consume an analyst's day. Moreover, tensions mount if the report is delayed in the coordination process. As one former U.S. intelligence analyst describes, "They [managers/editors] start yelling at you, 'Where is it? Where is it?' And you are waiting on coordination, and this can go on until one or two in the morning, depending on how contentious it [the PDB item] is."[71] In describing these heated disagreements that can arise in the PDB process, one former U.S. intelligence analyst explains with a hypothetical example:

> Suppose Sunkist is a company in Yemen. And I write that a Yemeni company is supplying bioweapons stuff to Iraq. If, then, the Yemeni [CIA] analyst disagrees—that there is no way that a Yemeni company would ever do something bad—then you have a giant mess, because then we have to agree to language [in the report]. And so it gets escalated, and you have to go up your chain. A lot of times it gets to fairly high levels, and I have been in these coordination meetings until two or three in the morning. Sometimes in the current [intelligence] things, people will make a footnote, which means that you disagree but usually that means another agency has disagreed, but not internally, you have to get past the internal [CIA] disagreements. So you'd be up until two or three in the morning fighting over words. And the [PDB] briefers come in at three in the morning, so sometimes you have to call your section chief. This happens a lot, not just in our section.[72]

With these potential hassles, former intelligence analyst Roger George has noted that "few analysts welcome coordination, as it involves time and trouble 'wordsmithing' their work to satisfy other analysts."[73]

Because the PDB is typically delivered to the president by 8:00 a.m. and the PDB briefers arrive around 3:00 a.m., internal disagreements must be resolved very early in the morning if an article is to be included in that day's PDB. Managers or section chiefs are brought in to break particularly difficult impasses. But their focus is often not on whether a report should be removed or subject to additional analysis but rather on finding consensus on the report's language so that it can be approved for dissemination to policymakers. This focus on language rather than quality of content is analogous to the atmosphere of conformity that Gans says exists in the media: "Because news organizations are assembly lines on which people must work together to manufacture a product against a deadline, they almost always generate conformity."[74] Gans says that conformity pertains to story formats and other news production practices and can extend into the values and ideology expressed in news stories. In the CIA, conformity in analysis pertains to reaching consensus on appropriate report language or on the exercise of managerial power so that a PDB or other current report can be released. Thus, the analytic priority largely focuses on meeting the deadline to get the current intelligence report out, rather than on taking the time needed to get to the heart of the intellectual disagreement.

Once the current report is delivered, the president's response to a PDB item is also important to CIA analysts. More specifically, we know that during the George W. Bush administration, additional policy assignments to CIA analysts came directly out of the morning PDB meetings.[75] "If you are a CIA analyst, this is what we get our jollies out of: I got a question [about the PDB item] from the president, I got a question from the vice president," says one former U.S. intelligence analyst. "It is nice to get a question from lesser people like the secretary of state or [Secretary of Defense] Rumsfeld, but getting questions from these two [the president or vice president] is like, this is what you live for."[76] Such a question from a "policy principal" then triggers another round of current intelligence reporting production, because "if they [the president or vice president] ask a question, it requires a formal response, which means you have to take all day drafting it, which means that you have to look through stuff again, you have to read it again, you have to coordinate it again. It is a whole day."[77] Intelligence practitioner Mark Kauppi corroborates that "an analyst's day is driven by the tyranny of current intelligence and the latest taskings."[78]

Follow-up questioning from senior policymakers ends up affecting what kinds of analyses and products are developed, because an analyst who is busy responding to questions cannot be working on something else at the same time. For instance, as one analyst explains, "You have a certain number of people working on biological warfare issues. And if every day you keep asking them one question, they can't be looking at the twenty-seven other questions they are supposed to be looking at, [so] you are taking resources away from everything else."[79] Thus, the priority for most analysts lies in being responsive to the policymakers' questions (or issues) of the day, as opposed to devoting analytic talent to in-depth, long-term assessments. Former National Intelligence Officer Paul Pillar has described this frequent tasking of analysts by policymakers as one of the subtle ways intelligence can become politicized.[80] Furthermore, a recent U.S. government report finds that this initial current intelligence report-policymaker question–follow-up current intelligence report cycle can lead to the impression of corroborating classified reports on an issue for which, in fact, there exist very few sources.[81]

Alternatively, if the president and vice president do not request a follow-up question from a PDB article, the analyst then seeks out another new intelligence item than can be proposed for the next day's PDB, policy briefing, or other current report. This procedure is similar to that practiced in news organizations, where news production never ends; someone is always planning the next news story.[82] The

PDB, however, is only one type of current intelligence report; most of what analysts produce for their offices are various other types of current intelligence reports. Under these work conditions, analysts spend the bulk of their time selecting, sorting, and editing new intelligence information for more current intelligence reports rather than on longer, in-depth analytic assessments or products of greater strategic focus. Thus, as intelligence scholar Kenneth Lieberthal concludes, the emphasis on current intelligence reporting encourages analysts to focus on specific, current items "at the expense of developing deep understanding of major issues."[83]

The constant stream of products and the fast-paced work environment are stressful for analysts and even seem to restructure how they think of themselves and their work. In describing the tensions of current intelligence reporting, one CIA analyst notes that "I haven't been doing this very long, but I wish I had been a journalism major instead of poli-sci. The pace is excruciating."[84] The unrelenting pace of the work environment can lead to burnout; currently, CIA analysts have, on average, five to seven years of analytic experience.[85] One analyst complained that "they [CIA management] would tell us, 'You need to do a long-term paper, but you also need to do current production—you need a bunch of both.' And you'd say, 'How is that possible?' They'd say, 'Just figure it out.' You were expected to work X hours a day, and you did because it was the right thing to do, and you ended up getting burned out. Today, people don't stay there very long. The number of people who have been there longer than five years is not much."[86] At the CIA, such burnout—comparable to that of news reporters at high-intensity media outlets—leads to problems in retaining analysts. Indeed, once they have received all their top secret clearances, CIA analysts often leave the agency for more lucrative pay and flexible work schedules offered by defense contractors.[87]

The rapid turnover of CIA analysts inhibits their development and appreciation of expertise (including expertise on analytic methodologies, as described in chapter 5). The lack of appreciation for expertise and the emphasis on current intelligence reporting are also evident in the way analysts are trained. Several intelligence scholars have noted that CIA analysts spend the bulk of their training time developing writing, communication, and briefing skills rather than learning and evaluating different research and analytic methods.[88] At present, the intelligence community values and rewards the mastery of current intelligence reporting at the expense of such analytic techniques. Thus, there exist few incentives for analysts to learn new techniques or to create longer, in-depth analytic products. As Ford explains:

> Most offices and agencies consider time away from the direct practice of analysis, as time spent not "working." Learning how to analyze more effectively, if it

> is acknowledged at all, is either done on an analyst's own time, or is wedged into short periods away from regular analytical duties. Moreover, when analysts return from formal training, it is not unusual for them to find that their newly acquired skills clash with the practices of the office, and they receive little encouragement to try something new or experimental. Time pressures, not the soundness of the methodology, takes precedence. Not surprisingly, most analysts end up allocating little time to honing their "craft" of analysis.[89]

In another reflection of this journalistic environment, CIA analysts are typically rewarded for the number of intelligence "pieces" they produce rather than the substantive depth or quality of their finished product.[90] As one analyst explains, for example, analyses are often referred to as "productions," and an analyst's list of written work for the yearly performance review is called a "rag sheet."[91] According to one U.S. intelligence analyst, when analysts are up for their yearly reviews, the CIA's promotions evaluators typically ask, "'How many PDBs did you do? How many briefings did you do? To whom? And did you write a long-term paper?' There is always a fight about this. You have to do the current intel, the daily things, but then you also are supposed to be thinking larger and writing a big paper. A lot of times, so much crap is going on that you don't have time to sit down and write a big paper."[92] This analyst further comments, "There is always some discussion about, well, maybe we should take people off-line for six months so that they can do some research and writing, but if people see them doing that, they are going to be asked to do other things, so there is always this competing stuff."[93]

In spite of calls for longer analytic products, the rewards for current intelligence items remain a priority, to include recognition for briefing preparations. As one analyst reflects, "In the middle of my career they decided that doing briefings on current hot topics should count as much as a current production thing, which is good, because a lot of times you are doing two or three PDBs a week and two, or three, or four briefings while this is going on."[94] In addition to the report count, the CIA rewards its analysts for in-person meetings: "Sometimes, when you write something or even a paper, they [policymakers] will say, 'Come down and talk to us about it,' so they started giving credit for that."[95] Briefings and other in-person meetings provide analysts with opportunities for "face time" with policymakers, which the CIA views as an important reflection of the relevance and value of analysts' work.[96] As Pillar explains, face time is "part of how you measure success. One of the worst things for an intelligence agency or an intelligence officer is to be irrelevant."[97]

Although there are periodic discussions among analysts about the need to get out from under the tyranny of intelligence based solely on current needs, doing so has proven difficult. As one former U.S. intelligence analyst remarks, "We used to sit around and say, 'Well, you know, people should free us up so that we can do these long-term research papers because they want to have our long-term insights.' But then, all the time they [managers] would say, 'Where is the PDB? Where is this? Where is that?' . . . and that is what has to feed the policy machine every day, and so you end up making the choice."[98] Likewise, feeding the policy machine is what is desired, valued, and rewarded within the CIA. Former analyst Richard Russell has observed during his CIA career that in evaluating analysts for promotion, managers "tend to reward those analysts who work on issues that command daily current intelligence headlines."[99] And, as another analyst explains, "if you would talk to some analysts who have backwater accounts and they are not writing anything for the president, so they are sitting there doing research and coming up with a long-term paper on the chemical industry of Waziristan or whatever. And I can tell you they are all sitting there saying, 'I wish I could write a PDB,' because that is what the place lives for."[100]

Current intelligence reporting has always been an element of CIA analytic practices, but its prominence and priority emerged in the 1980s and became intensified in the 1990s. During that time, the director of the CIA's Office of Training and Education declared to a new class that "analysts in fact do not do analysis. Instead, he argued, they are in the 'investigative journalism' business."[101] As former CIA analyst John Gentry notes, this comment was significant because this office was the CIA's main training center for intelligence analysis. This privileging of current reporting in CIA analytic practice intensified with the end of the Cold War. As explained in chapter 2, in the post–Cold War era, the U.S. government struggled with how to prioritize a range of new national security threats. During this time, a variety of high-level policy discussions emphasized the need for a leaner and more responsive intelligence community.[102] In turn, U.S. intelligence analysts were given opportunities to increase their understanding of policymaker security concerns through short-term rotations in the executive branch and in Congress. As one intelligence analyst notes, "This brought the intelligence community closer to its 'customer' and asking more, 'What does the customer need?' "[103] Although these experiences were beneficial to understanding policymakers' concerns, they led CIA analysts and managers to emphasize the relevancy and responsiveness of intelligence analysis to policy, which increasingly was defined as a constant stream of current intelligence reports instead of more rigorous, in-depth analytic products.

Current Intelligence Reporting and the Iraqi Mobile Bioweapons Labs

We have seen how CIA analysts' heuristics and current reporting bias shaped the way they collected, assembled, and presented information—and their work on the Iraqi bioweapons threat was no different. WINPAC bioweapons analysts privileged classified information and built on existing mental models such as the biotech revolution frame. Analysts also used a cumulative addition formula in assessing intelligence information, along with an awareness of policymaker interests, to form quick and reinforcing judgments about an Iraqi mobile bioweapons capability. In addition, their focus on keeping the production process going meant that important questions and debates about the veracity of these claims were excluded from current intelligence reports and related analytic documents provided to policymakers. Thus, when Lawrence Wilkerson was preparing Colin Powell's UN speech, the CIA's bioweapons analytic cadre had already concluded that Iraq had mobile bioweapons labs.

In focusing on Curveball, the CIA's bioweapons analysts employed a set of heuristics, one of which involved a focus on the technical details in Curveball's reporting. Analysts used internet data, satellite images, and readily accessible technical experts to check on some aspects of Curveball's technical and physical descriptions. A predominant focus on material aspects of Curveball's reporting (engineering designs, dials), codified knowledge (an Iraqi intelligence note on the mobile lab concept), and assumptions of a covert, growing Iraqi bioweapons program indicated analysts' use of the biotech revolution frame as a heuristic to evaluate Iraq's mobile bioweapons capability. In doing so, the CIA analysts deemed Curveball's information to be "workable" for mobile bioweapons production.[104] Beginning in 2001, moreover, in a cumulative manner, analysts added details from a few new human intelligence sources to the growing Iraqi mobile lab. There is no indication, however, that the analysts conducted in-depth analyses to verify these various classified intelligence reports; rather, the data that fit the equation and mental model of an Iraqi mobile bioweapons capability were readily adopted. In contrast, information that did not fit the model (UN weapons-inspection findings, Directorate of Operations' questioning of Curveball) was ignored or refuted.

In the spring of 2000, shortly after the CIA began receiving Curveball's reports, the CIA's bioweapons analysts began producing current intelligence reports for senior policymakers.[105] One early example was a May 19, 2000, DIA report, *Iraq: Biological Warfare Program,* which stated, "Baghdad reportedly has developed mobile biological agent production facilities to mask ongoing production efforts.

This project, allegedly the most ambitious BW-related Iraqi denial-and-deception effort thus far, will complicate identifying Iraq's offensive BW infrastructure."[106] Vice Admiral Thomas R. Wilson, then director of the DIA, recalls that at the time, the early Curveball reporting "was considered high priority."[107] By December 2000, three important intelligence reports—all based on current intelligence—included concerns about Iraq's bioweapons program and its mobile bioweapons capabilities.

The CIA's bioweapons analysts, along with the Nonproliferation Center, the National Imagery Mapping Agency, and the DIA, produced a *Special Intelligence Report,* a very brief, highly focused analysis of a topic of major significance prepared for high-level policymakers, entitled *New Evidence of Iraqi Biological Warfare Program.*[108] This report was based on the entire set of current intelligence reports and corroborating information from Curveball that analysts had collected over the year.[109] The report noted that "credible reporting from a single source suggests" that Iraq has produced biological agents but cautioned, "We cannot confirm whether Iraq has produced . . . biological agents."[110] The report explained, however, that "the Intelligence Community assesses this reporting to be credible because the source has provided a wealth of specific detail, much of which we have been able to corroborate with other intelligence. This Defense HUMINT Service reporting has provided significant insights into many facets of Iraq's BW program."[111]

Also in December 2000, the National Intelligence Council produced an NIE entitled *Worldwide Biological Warfare Programs: Trends and Prospects, Update.* This report noted that "new intelligence acquired in 2000 . . . causes [the intelligence community] to adjust our assessment upward of the bioweapons threat posed by Iraq. . . . The new information suggests that Baghdad has expanded its offensive bioweapons program by establishing a large-scale, redundant, and concealed bioweapons agent production capability."[112] The "new information" referred to more than one hundred classified reports the CIA had received by that time from German intelligence about Curveball.[113] Although the NIE draft was revised in three successive rounds of e-mail coordination with bioweapons analysts across the intelligence community, a postwar U.S. Senate Select Committee on Intelligence investigation found that the coordination process "did not significantly change any of the overall assessments, and only offered more detail and 'refined our assessments.' "[114] There were no additional studies conducted by other intelligence agencies to interrogate the CIA's judgments.

At the request of the National Security Council, the intelligence community also produced in December 2000 a U.S. intelligence community assessment entitled *Iraq: Steadily Pursuing WMD Capabilities.*[115] The CIA's bioweapons analysts contributed key current intelligence gleaned from Curveball, and the report concluded: "We cannot confirm whether Iraq has produced . . . biological agents, although in the case of biological weapons, credible reporting from a single source suggests it has done so on a large scale and had developed a clandestine production capability. . . . According to reporting from a single source, Iraq has constructed seven transportable—via trucks and rail cars—plants, some of which have produced BW agents."[116] Yet, by this time, almost a year after Curveball had first begun reporting, only cursory corroborations and technical evaluations had been conducted of his mobile lab claims. As described in chapter 5, there had been no attempts by the CIA's bioweapons analysts to work with the Directorate of Operations to evaluate Curveball as a human source more rigorously or to try to evaluate the suspected Iraqi mobile bioweapons labs by alternative means.

In September 2001, the CIA's bioweapons analysts still had no operational evaluation of Curveball and limited additional human intelligence confirmation, yet they produced another current report for senior policymakers entitled "Iraq: Mobile BW Agent Production Capability," in *Senior, Publish When Ready*; the *SPWR* is routinely supplied to senior policymakers in the National Security Council and the White House.[117] This *SPWR* read: "Sources indicate Baghdad continues to pursue a mobile BW capability to produce large amounts of BW agents covertly."[118] Also in September, WINPAC bioweapons analysts issued another *SPWR*, "Memorandum to the Secretary of Defense," highlighting the conclusions from the classified reporting by Curveball while emphasizing the overarching pattern of Iraqi deception in its weapons programs. The report states, "Mobile BW information comes from [several] sources, one of whom is credible. . . . We have raised our collection posture in a bid to locate these production units, but years of fruitless searches by UNSCOM indicate they are well hidden."[119] In October 2001, WINPAC bioweapons analysts followed up with a report entitled *Iraq: Mobile Biological Warfare Agent Production Capability,* which stated: "The establishment of mobile BW agent production plans and continued delivery system development provide Baghdad with BW capabilities surpassing the pre–Gulf War era."[120]

Contemporaneously, amid the production and coordination of these Iraq reports, the CIA's bioweapons analysts were also working on short, internal communications regarding a potential Iraqi bioweapons threat related to smallpox and to U.S. agriculture.[121] As one former U.S. intelligence analyst explains, Vice President Richard Cheney was particularly interested in receiving intelligence information about "bioweapons in general and Iraq specifically. . . . They [the vice president's staff] were always interested in biological weapons, which is kind of cool, and there were a lot of people on Cheney's staff that we would talk to, and we would either send them papers or go down to talk to their staff fairly often."[122] As this analyst goes on to explain, "It is very obvious when you live with this every day: if I see anything, I should write it up because Cheney will want it. The VP's office was very big on biological warfare issues, so they just liked that in general, so they were always asking for stuff. . . . It was either Scooter [Libby] asking something or Cheney asking something. And when you get taskers like that, you have to spend the day researching it, writing it up, and coordinating it, and sending it away."[123]

For its May 2002 issue, *Vanity Fair* magazine wrote an article on one of the other human sources the CIA used to corroborate Curveball's claims. Early press coverage on this article prompted CIA analysts to spend time writing two papers entitled *Iraqi Defector in the New York Daily News Article* and *Assessment of the Iraqi Defector Cited in the Vanity Fair Article on Iraqi WMD*.[124]

In July 2002, the CIA's bioweapons analysts produced another current intelligence report entitled "Iraq's Expanding BW Capability" in another *SPWR*, in which the CIA judged that "Baghdad has transportable production facilities for BW agents . . . according to defectors."[125] Although the report cited three human sources, Curveball's reporting was the predominant source of information. The report included drawings produced by CIA graphics artists, based on Curveball's information and other current intelligence reports. As one former analyst describes, "In there [the long report], I know that there were drawings. It was a fairly technical report, but its audience was policymakers. . . . There were drawings in the [prior] PDBs based on the information given to us and our interpretations, because people like these things, it is making the stuff real to people, and this is the way to do that. It's just a way of getting your point across."[126]

Drawing on past CIA assessments, in August 2002 the Defense Intelligence Agency issued a report, *Iraq: Biological Warfare Program Handbook*, which stated that "Baghdad has reportedly rebuilt its full offensive BW program in well-concealed, underground, mobile or difficult-to-locate facilities."[127] During the summer of 2002, CIA analysts prepared a briefing for George Tenet, the director of the CIA. Tenet went to the Oval Office to brief Bush and Cheney personally about the mobile program and show them illustrations of the trailers prepared by CIA artists. Curveball's reports generated a lot of excitement within the White House. As one National Security Council (NSC) staffer later recalled, "We really thought the trailers were the smoking gun. When I saw that [Curveball's intelligence reports], I thought, 'We got him.' . . . Finally, the agency was giving us something concrete."[128]

Starting in the fall of 2002, WINPAC's bioweapons analysts drafted a new round of current reports based on material used in previous reports. In September

2002, the WINPAC bioweapons analysts helped prepare a briefing for George Tenet to deliver to the Senate's Intelligence and Armed Services Committees and, subsequently, to the Senate Foreign Relations Committee. In the briefing, Tenet stated: "We know Iraq has developed a redundant capability to produce biological warfare agents using mobile production units."[129] This information was largely based on Curveball's reporting—he was described as "a credible defector who worked in the program"—as well as that of the fourth UK source.[130] In October 2002, the CIA published another report, *Saddam's Timelines for Using WMD*. Although it emphasizes that Iraq was using fixed facilities to produce bioweapons agents, the report states that "Iraq could also use its mobile facilities to produce some bacterial agents."[131]

Then, in October 2002, a newly issued NIE reflected a marked shift in the U.S. intelligence community's consensus about the state and progress of Iraq's bioweapons program, based largely on Curveball's reports.[132] The genesis of the October 2002 NIE stemmed from congressional concern about the Bush administration's plans to invade Iraq. In September, the Bush administration had requested that Congress pass a resolution granting the United States authority to use military action against Iraq. In response, the leadership of the Senate Select Committee on Intelligence issued an immediate request to the CIA director to draft an NIE on Iraq's WMD programs. At the time, there had been no prior NIE focused specifically on the status of Iraq's WMD programs. Such NIEs typically take months to complete, but this one was finished in three weeks.[133] However, because an NIE is a synthesis of previous intelligence reports—themselves often based on earlier current intelligence reports without additional substantive investigation or methodological interrogation—Ford has argued that such NIEs seldom add anything new. He says they should be considered just another type of current intelligence report, because they have not incorporated more rigorous, in-depth analytic scrutiny to assess prior reporting.[134]

In this case, CIA analysts put together the NIE section on Iraq's bioweapons program using a compilation of previous intelligence community publications.[135] Regarding a purported mobile lab capability, the NIE stated assertively that "Baghdad *has* mobile facilities for producing bacterial and toxin BW agents; these facilities can evade detection and are highly survivable. Within three to six months these units probably could produce an amount of agent equal to the total that Iraq has produced in the years prior to the Gulf War."[136] These mobile lab claims were then used to judge that "all key aspects—R&D, production, and weaponization—of Iraq's offensive BW program are active and that most elements are larger and more advanced than they were before the Gulf War."[137] Intelligence analysts from the DIA and the State Department's Bureau of Intelligence and Research have stated that Curveball's reporting provided the majority of information in the intelligence community's assessments about the purported Iraqi mobile bioweapons labs.[138]

Three days after the October 2002 NIE was published, the director of central intelligence published an unclassified version of the assessment in the white paper *Iraq's Weapons of Mass Destruction Program,* which stated: "Baghdad has pursued a mobile BW search and production capability to better conceal its program. UNSCOM uncovered a document on Iraqi Military Industrial Commission letterhead indicating that Iraq was interested in developing mobile fermentation units, and an Iraqi scientist admitted to UN inspectors that Iraq was trying to move in the direction of mobile BW production. Iraq has now established large-scale, redundant, and concealed BW agent production capabilities based on mobile BW facilities."[139] A month later, in November 2002, the CIA's bioweapons analysts issued another report, largely based on Curveball's reporting, entitled *Iraq: Biological Warfare Agents Pose Growing Threat to U.S. Interests.* This report stated that Iraq's bioweapons program "is more robust than it was prior to the Gulf War" and argued that technological advances increased the potential Iraqi bioweapons threat to the United States.[140] Once again, no new in-depth, independent analyses had been conducted between the publication of these back-to-back reports.

Even CIA internal controversies that erupted between WINPAC's bioweapons analysts and the Directorate of Operations personnel did not lead to additional in-depth analytic scrutiny. For example, when CIA management organized a meeting in December 2002 to address the tensions between the WINPAC bioweapons analysts and the Directorate of Operations, management decided to settle the dispute instead of issuing a call for further analysis and evaluation. CIA management decided to judge Curveball's evidence as credible based largely on the bioweapons analysts' heuristics for source evaluation and selection.[141] Thus, in the same way that Gans describes how news organizations make decisions, CIA management focused on settling the internal argument so that policymakers could use the information. They did not consider the argument to be evidence of the need for further inquiry and evaluation of Curveball's information. Subsequently, in the preparation of Powell's February 2003 UN speech, CIA analysts drew on their existing analytic reports, including drawings of the purported mobile labs by CIA graphics artists.[142] Also in February 2003, the CIA's bioweapons analysts issued a report, *Iraq: Options for Unconventional Use of CBW,* which outlined how Iraq might use chemical and biological weapons against the United States and its allies.[143] In the leadup to the March 2003 war, a series of current intelligence reports on the Iraqi mobile bioweapons labs, packaged and presented in different formats and for different audiences, laid out the case for lethal, advanced Iraqi WMD threats.

Throughout this period of CIA interest in an Iraqi mobile bioweapons capability (1996–2003), policymakers were keenly interested in Iraq and bioweapons issues. In 1995, President Clinton issued Presidential Decision Directive 35, which prioritized intelligence attention to "rogue" states and WMD proliferation; in this context, Iraq was a high policy priority.[144] As a result, intelligence analysts focused their current intelligence reporting efforts on these issues. One former U.S. intelligence analyst explains that during this period, "anything in Iraq will be of interest to the principals downtown."[145]

As noted in chapter 5, the Nonproliferation Center was created by the CIA director in the early 1990s in response to policy priorities on WMD proliferation; biological weapons analysis was one component of the center's work. Subsequently, in 2001 WINPAC was formed to gather all technical analysts working on proliferation and arms control into one administrative unit. Although these two centers were created to provide better collection and analysis on WMD issues, John Lauder, former Nonproliferation Center director, says that events of the day overtook more thorough reflection during the 1990s and into the early 2000s:

> There was a sense that we were getting gobbled up by the problem of the moment. And that really became a factor after WINPAC got formed. . . . With the change in administration, there was a sense that the president was the primary customer. The President's Daily Brief is the premier product of the IC [intelligence community], and as a result we skewered the whole way in which the community worked. My impression is that it was a contributing factor to the Iraq WMD problem. I also critique myself in that I should have fought harder against the current intelligence tendency. But when I look back on it at the time, the phones were ringing, and you have to deal with the issues of the moment.[146]

As another former CIA analyst working in the early 2000s with WINPAC added, "Most WINPAC analysts are so caught up with day-to-day stuff that they don't really have time to think about the big picture. . . . They're current intelligence analysts, that's what they do."[147] This individual also noted that analysts doing a lot of current intelligence reporting tend to work primarily with classified sources and prioritize the new information they get from collectors, rather than working with more complex and varied sources that include unclassified information or collaboration with outside experts. Thus, from their creation, the Nonproliferation Center and later WINPAC—the two analytic centers with the authority to produce reports and communicate with policymakers about Iraqi bioweapons threats—relied largely on the analytic practices and heuristics of current intelligence reporting.

In the aftermath of the Iraq War, current reporting also shaped how the CIA's bioweapons analysts approached their postwar assessments of Iraq's bioweapons program. A few weeks after the start of the March 2003 invasion, U.S. and Kurdish military forces captured three suspected mobile bio-facilities in Mosul and Erbil. The first U.S. military teams on the scene included some individuals with technical backgrounds who took a variety of measurements and pictures of the trailers and wrote a detailed report that they sent back to CIA headquarters. The CIA, through German intelligence, sent some of the trailer photos to Curveball for evaluation. In looking at the photos, Curveball replied that while he hadn't worked on those specific trailers, some of the equipment looked like components he had installed in another mobile lab facility.[148] As stated in chapter 5, however, there were no control tests given to Curveball with these photos to try to check the credibility of his claims. Instead, with the trailer information and Curveball's statements, WINPAC analysts concluded that the captured trailers were the "smoking gun" necessary to identify them as Iraqi mobile bioweapons facilities.

Policymakers then asked the CIA to write an unclassified white paper based on the captured trailers. In addition to working with their fellow DIA analysts to draft the paper, WINPAC analysts brought in CIA graphics artists to provide some additional illustrations for the report.[149] The resulting six-page coauthored DIA-CIA white paper, "Iraqi Mobile Biological Warfare Agent Production Plants," included graphics from Powell's speech (slides 21 and 22) as well as photos of the captured trailers, with a new CIA graphic to show how bio-production equipment could fit into the captured trailers (fig. 6.4).[150] In the white paper, the analysts carefully laid out their argument describing the discovery of the trailers and how the trailers (and their equipment) corroborated the evidence used in Powell's speech, prewar intelligence, and human source reporting. No mention was made, however, that some of the human sources had already been discredited as fabricators by that time. Nor was there any mention of the internal CIA debate that had already taken place between WINPAC analysts and Directorate of Operations personnel. In addition, WINPAC analysts conducted no additional, rigorous, alternative analyses to evaluate the trailer findings. Thus, although the white paper

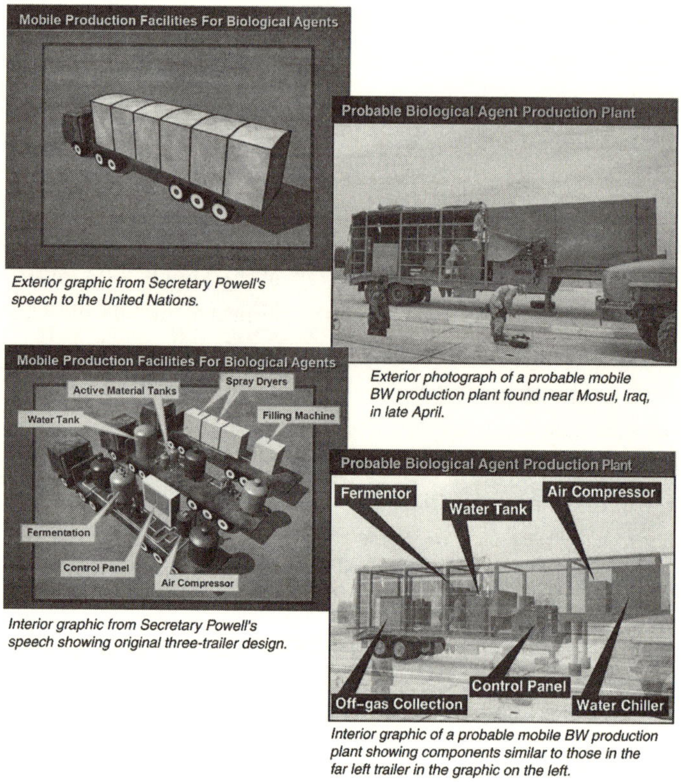

Fig. 6.4. Reported mobile bioweapons plants compared to trucks found in Iraq. From U.S. Central Intelligence Agency and U.S. Defense Intelligence Agency, "Iraqi Mobile Biological Warfare Agent Production Plants."

was released and touted as a rigorously researched analytic product, it bears all the markings of a report drawing on current intelligence analytic practices.

When the white paper was ultimately released in May 2003, CIA and DIA analysts worked with the CIA public affairs office to hold a ninety-minute "open mic" session to answer questions from the press and public about the trailers. In a press conference on the white paper, intelligence officials stated that the trailer's hardware presented no direct evidence of weapons use (for instance, presence of pathogen residue). They even said that a technical assessment alone "would not lead you intuitively and logically to biological warfare."[151] The best evidence of likely biological warfare use, they said, was the trailers' close resemblance to prewar descriptions of mobile bioweapons plans given by Iraqi sources.

Yet even before the white paper was released, some government analysts had begun to question the assessment of the trailers as Iraqi mobile bioweapons facilities.[152] To settle these rising internal disputes, a team of ten independent contractors sponsored by the Defense Intelligence Agency was sent to Iraq at the end of May 2003 to provide a more definitive assessment of the trailers. The team consisted of experts in fermentation, biological science and engineering, and biological weapons, many of whom had had twenty-five years of experience in their fields.[153] The team spent days scrutinizing the trailers, taking the equipment apart and examining it, and taking hundreds of photos. "Within the first four hours it was clear to everyone that these were not biological [weapons] labs," one team member said.[154] As another team member described this assessment, "We just looked at the practicality of it—could this system actually grow organisms, collect them, and make material that could be used for biological weapons. Ultimately, it was decided that you could, probably, if you wanted to grow organisms in either of those contraptions, but you could probably grow more bacteria in a sleeve of agar plates than in those facilities."[155]

The team's conclusions reached Washington one day before the CIA's white paper was released, in the form of a three-page classified field report.[156] Although the report remains classified, team members cite the Iraq Survey Group's unclassified conclusions as reflecting the same findings,[157] which concluded that the captured trailers were impractical for biological agent production and more consistent with the generation of hydrogen gas.[158] Although these contradictory findings were available to WINPAC analysts before the May 2003 DIA-CIA white paper emerged, there is no indication that WINPAC analysts conducted additional research to assess this alternative interpretation or revised their paper to incorporate these findings before releasing the white paper to the public.

Current Reporting, Expertise, and Analytic Practice

The underlying problems of the balkanization of knowledge and expertise within the CIA described in chapter 5 magnify and reinforce these current intelligence reporting practices. For instance, bioweapons analysts who are rewarded for their individual analytic products largely reinforce the CIA's focus on the production of individual analytic knowledge as opposed to the development of a more complex multidisciplinary team effort. Moreover, current intelligence reporting contributes to the existing passive analytic practices within the CIA, because it relies on an analyst receiving new intelligence information as the primary catalyst and structure for its analytic work and products. Ford has described this as a "catcher's mitt" strategy for analysis: "The way a current report starts is, something [intelligence] comes to you, and it causes you to react and to say, 'Oh, I've got to find out more about this and write this up for the boss.' And you might do a little study and even some research, but it's based off of something that comes in and was large enough and obvious enough that you said, 'This is kind of important.' "[159] But instead of seeing this priority on the reporting of new streams of information as potential problems for analysis, many in the intelligence community still value this catcher's mitt approach. As Ford relates, "I've actually heard people say, 'Since you can never analyze this stuff [intelligence information] closely enough to make a difference, we're just going to have to collect a lot and hope that if we collect more, all the answers will eventually come out.' "[160]

With this focus on collected intelligence, current reporting analysts typically work with what Ford has described as "obvious data"—intelligence data easily discernible through key words or report titles. In contrast, however, Ford notes how in-depth research and analysis involves a very different starting point and approach:

> Research almost always starts out by asking, "What's the question?" I don't have to have any current reporting in hand, it really doesn't matter. My boss [a policymaker] wants to know the answer to this particular question . . . and he or she doesn't care that if I am to answer that question, I must answer fifteen others before I can get to his/her answer. And, when I come up with something, nobody else will have done it; it will be new knowledge. That's research. . . . You will also find that each question requires a slightly different approach. There is no "one size fits all." And anyone who has gone through an archive and looked for data on any subject, whether it's science, medicine, history, political . . . if they've had to go look for data that nobody had ever found before, they know exactly what I'm talking about. But apparently our people [intelligence analysts] have no experience with that.[161]

But if one is reporting on what new intelligence has been collected, as current intelligence reporting is structured, there is no need to interrogate the information further or to design a research strategy. As former CIA analyst and methodologist Stanley Feder notes, systematic analysis that comes from a designed research strategy does not fit into an existing CIA organizational culture that "sees an 'analyst' as someone who writes reports, often evaluating and summarizing available information."[162]

Ford uses a hypothetical example to explain how analysts' exclusive work with obvious data can introduce problems into weapons assessments:

> Over a period of, let's say, three or four years, there will be eight obvious bits of information that seem to be suggestive of a biological weapons program. The analysts will be using only those eight pieces as the substantive data for their assessments, because as they see it, their job is to guess what these pieces of information can tell them. Unfortunately, there are very few problems in the world where having eight pieces takes you very far. In many cases, with that few pieces you can't even tell if the data you have is relevant to the question you are attempting to answer, let alone be a sound basis for arriving at an answer. Indeed, at that point in the process, trying to "connect the dots" is the biggest mistake an analyst can make. The "dots" may give you a place to start but rarely provide a completely satisfactory answer. If you just connect the dots, guess what? You're going to be wrong more times than not, and you're going to say that Iraq has constituted a biological weapons program because the eight dots say they are.[163]

In reflecting this "connect the dots" strategy, one former U.S. intelligence analyst has described his/her judgment-making process for an analytic report: "I can't make a judgment call based on one piece of information, I have to have two or three corroborating pieces of information. . . . But sometimes you get a piece that is so compelling and you may not have it specifically corroborated . . . but it is so compelling that you look at stuff around it, and [you say,] 'Based on what I know, this is probably true,' and 'I will stick my neck out, and here is what we have, and this is what we think is going on.' "[164] Similarly, if we look at WINPAC assessments of the Iraqi mobile labs case, we see that the bulk of the information used to make them centered largely on one unvalidated source—Curveball. Although there were a few additional human sources used to corroborate Curveball's information, these sources provided only a small number of reports compared to those of Curveball, and in any case these sources were later deemed to be fabricators.[165] In the Iraq mobile lab case, WINPAC analysts primarily relied on "obvious" intelligence for their analyses, without a sense of an overarching research design for long-term analysis of the supposed threat.

In the Curveball case, we can also see that WINPAC's mode of analysis was largely passive; their Iraqi mobile lab interest and stream of reporting were driven largely by the emergence of Curveball as a source. Moreover, the key sources of information used in WINPAC's mobile lab assessments were his numerous reports and other pieces of collected data. WINPAC based their judgments largely on the obvious pieces of data (technical details, buildings) that these collection reports provided and did not probe additional information (in either operations or analysis) to inform their assessments. Little effort was made to generate new collection or analytic knowledge about the purported labs. As former CIA deputy director Richard Kerr says of WINPAC's analysis, "No one laid out a plan for what was wanted or needed. So, to a considerable degree, what the analysts did is do what they have historically done. They wrote on things they thought were important. And they followed up every time a news item came out and somebody [policymaker] asked about it. But, in my view, there was not a creation of a systematic work plan or strategic plan for what kind of information would we need if we go to war with Iraq."[166]

The prioritization of current intelligence reporting has altered the production of knowledge in weapons assessments. Kerr recalls that during the Cold War, for example, CIA analysts were "doing major research papers on nearly every aspect of a country's development, whether it was technical, political, or economic."[167] At that time, current intelligence reporting represented only a quarter of the CIA's analytic work, with the remaining analysts working on various types of applied and basic research projects set up to integrate more complex sets of expertise and methodologies. But, as described in chapter 5, the existing generalist model for expertise that began to take hold in the post–Cold War environment has diminished the recognition and value of in-depth expertise in various aspects of intelligence work. With this shift, as Ford argues, "it's not that surprising when you come down ten or fifteen years without many experts around, and without very good collection management, you would end up doing mostly current reporting."[168] Although the drive for current intelligence reporting is arguably catalyzed by policymaker demands, a lack of knowledge and other expertise problems reinforce the reliance on current reporting as a dominant analytic practice in the CIA.

Conclusion

In constructing their Iraqi bioweapons assessments, WINPAC analysts largely functioned as a kind of "WMD beat reporter," gathering new intelligence information and reporting it to policymakers according to set deadlines and without subjecting it to more in-depth investigation or methodological consideration. The assessment of the intelligence community and policymakers regarding Iraq's mobile bioweapons capability rested largely on intelligence gleaned from Curveball, enhanced by CIA-generated images, and copied and disseminated in a range of classified documents. Given the *USA Today*–type cultural environment that dominates current intelligence reporting, it is not surprising that the mobile lab drawings became a powerful "image bite" in the world of intelligence community communications and analysis and came to play such an important visual role in mobilizing support for Powell's UN speech. In the absence of other, more tangible data on the purported mobile labs, the drawings and their associated current intelligence products essentially became the standards by which to interpret Iraqi mobile bioweapons capabilities. Although intelligence and policy practitioners recognize the challenges of current intelligence reporting, this chapter illustrates how problematic and pervasive these practices can be in the production of knowledge regarding weapons assessments and the serious implications they make for intelligence used in U.S. national security policymaking.

Secrecy and the Production of the Iraqi Mobile Bioweapons Threat

> The secret . . . is one of man's greatest achievements. . . . The secret offers . . . the possibility of a second world alongside the manifest world.
>
> *Georg Simmel*

Secrecy is an essential characteristic of intelligence work. Intelligence scholar and practitioner Abram Shulsky and coauthor Gary Schmitt argue that the element of secrecy is what distinguishes intelligence from other types of knowledge.[1] Intelligence practitioners often use a twofold explanation for describing the importance of secrecy in intelligence: various secrecy and classification practices have been developed for keeping sensitive information from falling into enemy hands, and secrets collected on enemies by the intelligence community are valued for what they can reveal about hidden intentions, plans, and capabilities. Both secrets and the practices to construct and maintain secrecy critically shape how practitioners conceptualize, define, and structure intelligence work.

Recall that "Curveball" was the code name for the Iraqi human source that was central to the CIA's assessments of an Iraqi mobile bioweapons threat; WINPAC was the analytic unit in which the CIA's bioweapons analysts produced these assessments. In this chapter, I examine how different facets of secrecy, as organizational practices within the CIA, came to privilege Curveball's reporting and WINPAC's analytic judgments about a purported Iraqi mobile bioweapons capability throughout the U.S. intelligence and policy communities.

At the CIA, secrecy is a fundamental priority and one that begins in the hiring process.[2] A would-be analyst must undergo a variety of intrusive background checks (a polygraph test, medical and psychological exams, financial and credit investigations, and so forth) to make sure that he or she can be trusted with classified secrets. This in-depth scrutiny is required before a prospective analyst can be offered a job by the agency. Upon passing these background checks, a hired analyst is given a specific security clearance that pertains to the sensitivity of the information he or she will be working with. The more sensitive the information, the higher the level of security clearance the analyst must have to be able to see it.

Similarly, classified information and finished intelligence reports receive a label to denote where they lie in the hierarchy of secrecy. As an example, classified materials labeled "SECRET" are ones that, "if disclosed in an unauthorized manner, could reasonably be expected to cause serious damage to national security."[3] Other classification designations can include "CONFIDENTIAL," "TOP SECRET," and "NOFORN" (no foreign nationals). Additional "secret" labels involve cryptonyms given to human intelligence sources (like "Curveball").[4] Informal secrecy also underpins most CIA work; the CIA encourages analysts and other employees not to tell outsiders that they work at the agency or that they have a specific level of security clearance.[5]

To store and retrieve all this classified information, the U.S. intelligence community has developed distinct information systems. CIA analysts log into a restricted, classified intranet system called the Secret Internet Protocol Router Network (SIPRNET), which transmits classified information within the CIA and to other intelligence and military agencies.[6] The classified database most used by CIA analysts is called Corporate Information Retrieval and Storage (CIRAS). With CIRAS, analysts can perform most electronic searches and retrievals for source documents from CIA archives as well as from other CIA entities and other agencies of the U.S. intelligence community.[7] In addition, CIA analysts store various types and levels of classified information in office safes and other secured storage units, such as Sensitive Compartmented Information Facilities (SCIF).

Within these restricted electronic or physical spaces, CIA employees must follow specific security practices. For instance, viewing certain classified information requires not only the appropriate security clearance but also a "need to know" that information in order to carry out official duties. As one government report indicates, however, these need-to-know restrictions are not standardized: "In practice, these individual decisions follow agency-specific policies (or unstated habits) that vary widely across the Intelligence Community."[8] Thus, a combination of formal and informal social and material practices exists within the CIA to limit access to classified information. CIA anthropologist Rob Johnston notes that such practices create an atmosphere in which CIA employees send "nonverbal messages . . . that this is a position of secrecy and high importance."[9] The ubiquity of secrecy practices within the CIA produces and reinforces a social structure and environment where secrets—and the ability to access them and work with them—are highly valued.

Most policy-relevant discussions of the relationship between secrecy and the production of knowledge in intelligence work have focused on access: who is approved, or "cleared," to see specific pieces of classified information. While such discussions are important, they result in a narrow understanding of only the secrecy practices and regimes that prohibit the release of intelligence information to enemy hands. Historian of science Peter Galison has emphasized the anti-epistemology of intelligence work, which is focused on "how knowledge can be covered and obscured."[10] Most intelligence officials and policymakers also focus on this aspect of intelligence. This epistemological framework, however, does little to explain the important "generative" effect secrecy practices can also have—how they help shape what is known, not simply what is obscured or covered.[11] For example, this chapter's opening quotation from nineteenth-century German sociologist Georg Simmel emphasizes the work involved in the construction and use of secrets and how they produce a parallel world of meaning. I would add, however, that secret worlds are not completely cut off from the outside, but rather are co-constructed with the manifest world and have tangible effects on the real world.

In studying the production of technical knowledge, historian of science Steven Shapin emphasizes the importance of how knowledge is created in particular contexts—that "locality and spatial situation need to be attended to in order to understand how scientific knowledge was made, how it secured credibility, how it travelled."[12] In other words, we must examine the ways in which complex social and material practices in institutional contexts shape what is included and excluded in the production of secret knowledge and how these practices affect what is known. To illustrate the generative effect of secrecy practices in the CIA, this chapter examines three primary issues involved in analysts' and policymakers' understanding of the Iraqi mobile bioweapons threat: (1) the value of classified secrets; (2) secrets and the compartmentalization of knowledge; and (3) secrets, relationships, and social order.

When it examined the Iraqi mobile bioweapons assessments, the CIA made some information secret to guard against Iraqi espionage or espionage by other enemies. But other CIA secrecy practices were employed as techniques of authority, privilege, and control in order to shape what other intelligence and policy officials knew about the mobile labs. The secrecy practices that underpinned the CIA assessments were socially and materially constituted; formal and informal; contingent, purposeful, and entrenched. They shaped identities, trust (or distrust), and organizational relationships. These factors led to different people having different knowledge about the Iraqi mobile bioweapons threat, both inside and outside the CIA. Specifically, WINPAC analysts' secrets and secrecy practices privileged and reinforced a simple material and technical focus in their intelligence assessments of Iraq's purported mobile bioweapons capability at the expense of more complicated but empirically grounded ways of knowing. This chapter illustrates how the use of particular secrecy practices can create parallel worlds of knowledge about security threats that can ultimately prove detrimental to intelligence collection and analysis.

The Value of Classified Secrets

As we have seen, WINPAC analysts took particular interest in classified information that emerged in the late 1990s suggesting Iraqi interest in a mobile bioweapons capability. In early 2000, these analysts were also eager to receive Curveball's reports from German intelligence. Because Curveball alluded to secret designations in his reporting, such as code names for biological agents, WINPAC analysts deemed his claims about an Iraqi mobile bioweapons capability to be compelling.[13] Indeed, the 2002 NIE noted that "Iraq uses code words to compartmentalize BW [bioweapons] program elements. . . . A report from the HUMINT [human intelligence] source code named Curveball who provided most of the IC's [intelligence community's] understanding of the mobile production capability states that letters were used to describe agents produced in the mobile plants."[14] In addition, analysts noted the secret mobile bioweapons sites that Curveball named in his reporting and used satellite imagery to confirm these locations. Later, these bioweapons analysts drew on a limited number of human intelligence reports from three other Iraqi sources in order to corroborate further Curveball's secret claims.

At the same time, CIA analysts repeatedly pointed to Iraq's persistent effort to conceal information about its WMD programs from UN inspectors as a reason to suspect continued and expanded bioweapons activities in Iraq. Even after UN inspections resumed, the continued lack of overt evidence of Iraqi mobile labs appeared to harden the notion within the CIA that Iraq's secrecy practices were so sophisticated that they *must* have mobile biological laboratories. This trust in the secrecy of Saddam's purported bioweapons program was reflected in the 2002 NIE, which stated, "We judge that we are seeing only a portion of Iraq's WMD efforts, owing to Baghdad's denial and deception efforts."[15] Thus, CIA analysts used the absence of evidence as a type of information and confirmation of sophisticated secrecy being used by Iraq to cover up its weapons activities. The CIA's concern about a covert bioweapons program dated back to Iraq's efforts to hide its bioweapons infrastructure and to conceal the status of its bioweapons program before the Gulf War. WINPAC analysts had failed to assess the program adequately before the Gulf War, so they remained concerned that Iraq was still hiding and developing more than they could see.

CIA analysts also drew on their past intelligence work experiences, in which they had seen the role of secrecy in hiding other state-level WMD programs. One former U.S. intelligence analyst recalled his experience assessing Libya's chemical weapons program and discovering a hoax Libya had perpetrated to hide its operations at the Rabta chemical plant: "It would have been about 1990. We knew they were making chemical [weapons] agent. And, the [U.S.] politicos said, 'We'll go in and bomb them.' So they [Libya] created a huge hoax. They put rubber tires out and set fire to them, and so when our satellites took pictures [of Rabta], all they saw was a big fire. We had received reporting saying that the Libyans had a couple of accidents [at Rabta]. So, we hear this, and we say, 'Yahoo! They did it [caused a fire accident] to themselves!' "[16] Analysts surmised from early intelligence information that a suspected Libyan chemical weapons site had been destroyed by an accident. But the analyst quoted above points out that "all deception is based on reality. Later, in going through this [intelligence] stuff, looking at the information, volumes of information that was available . . . after a few weeks, with more imagery, we determined that it [the fire] was a huge hoax to keep the U.S. from going in and bombing them."[17] This analyst argues that by not considering the possibility of deception, the CIA had produced an incorrect intelligence assessment of Libya's chemical weapons program. In addition, by the late 1990s CIA analysts had already been faulted for missing the covert bioweapons programs of the former Soviet Union and Aum Shinrikyo (although, as described in chapters 2 and 4, analysts' interpretations of what they missed in these programs were also in error). During this time, analysts and policymakers relied on what I described in chapter 2 as a biotech revolution frame, which emphasizes the technical and material dimensions of biotechnology and the problem of "technological surprise" in assessing bioweapons threats. Thus, the possibility of Iraq hiding a sophisticated, covert "breakout" bioweapons capability was a plausible narrative that logically flowed from analysts using this frame and drawing on past experiences.

In November 2002, UN inspections in Iraq resumed with a new inspection unit, the United Nations Monitoring and Verification Commission (UNMOVIC). Early on, some of these UN inspectors received classified U.S. intelligence briefings about the purported mobile bioweapons labs, which included diagrams. As former UNMOVIC inspector Kay Mereish explains, "That briefing was very much what they [the intelligence community] think they have on the mobile labs. Then later on, we got a series of briefings on specific sites. They would say, 'We believe it was in the following location and here are the coordinates, here is the name, here is the imagery.' "[18] From these briefings, UNMOVIC teams went and checked the named sites for evidence of mobile bioweapons activity, but none was ever found at any of these sites.

Mereish describes these UN inspections: "We went to sites that they [the U.S. intelligence community] would claim there was a mobile facility. One of the important sites that was said [by U.S. intelligence to exist] was actually close to Tikrit. It was supposedly one of the hottest sites for a possible mobile production hiding location. What we found was a mobile workshop."[19] But this finding was not exactly what the intelligence briefings had suspected. Mereish goes on to explain that the captured "mobile workshop" was an old tractor-trailer that had belonged years ago to the Iraqi Agriculture Department and was used to help farmers fix their tractors and other farm equipment. As UNMOVIC inspector Peter Prosser further explains the function of these mobile workshops, "If you've got a combine harvester that breaks down in the middle of the paddock, well, you can't tow it, you've got to fix it on the spot. You take the mechanic, you take all the tools, and you go out there and fix it on the spot."[20] As Mereish surmised, "So there was only one thing correct from the intell: there *was* something mobile. But it is a workshop, and if you looked, actually there were no tires [on the tractor-trailer]. So it's even not mobile. It had nothing to do with [mobile bioweapons] production."[21] Yet there is no indication that the CIA's bioweapons analysts factored in or investigated these legitimate farming functions uncovered by UNMOVIC to interrogate further Curveball's secret information or other pieces of human intelligence that suggested an Iraqi mobile bioweapons capability.

In addition, at sites Curveball specifically named but that turned out to be biological or agricultural facilities, such as the Amiriyah Serum and Vaccine Institute and Djerf al Nadaf, UNMOVIC inspectors found no fermentation or other bioweapons-related equipment. Specifically, at the Djerf al Nadaf facility, inspectors took a variety of biological samples from multiple on-site locations, but none tested positive for bioweapons residue.[22] Furthermore, secret rooms that Curveball had described in his reporting as bioweapons activity sites turned out to be maintenance bays for seed-handling equipment or other legitimate civilian uses.[23] At one site, UNMOVIC inspectors also failed to find a large garage door that Curveball had described and that would have allowed the purported mobile trucks to enter the facility. In addition, a solid, six-foot-high permanent wall blocked vehicular access to the facility.[24] Nonetheless, WINPAC analysts repeatedly discounted the contradictory UNMOVIC findings as "the result of the inspectors' relative inexperience in the face of Iraqi denial and deception."[25] Thus, the absence of evidence became a type of evidence that WINPAC analysts used to rationalize discrepancies in Curveball's reporting.

Although WINPAC repeatedly discounted UNMOVIC's divergent findings, a close look at anecdotal accounts provided by UN inspectors reveals remarkable revelations about Iraqi military and civilian life pertinent to the Iraqi mobile bioweapons assessments. After Colin Powell's UN speech in February 2003, U.S. and UN officials put tremendous pressure on Iraqi officials to own up to their purported mobile bioweapons labs. Immediately after Powell's speech, for example, UNMOVIC Deputy Executive Chairman Dimitri Perricos had a particularly pointed conversation with General Amir Al-Saadi, Saddam Hussein's chief science advisor. Kay Mereish describes this encounter: "We were in Iraq, and Dimitri had a meeting with Amir Al-Saadi and basically put him on the spot, and he said, 'You saw the [Powell] briefing, so you better give me anything more that might be mobile labs. You need to produce that immediately.' Within two, three days Amir Saadi presented this information to us about what are the mobile facilities within the military, within anything."[26] Mereish relates that General Saadi gave UNMOVIC inspectors numerous pictures and documents describing a variety of mobile laboratory and refrigerated units that Iraq used for food and water testing, bakeries and morgues for military forces in the field, and for other legitimate civilian and military purposes. When UNMOVIC inspectors investigated these vehicles, none found evidence of bioweapons activity.[27]

Mereish explains, however, that to someone without specific technical expertise and looking only at satellite imagery, some equipment at these sites could appear to be of dual use. For instance, some of the trucks had large vessels on board that looked like mixing bowls for a solid missile propellant and could be interpreted as evidence of weapons activities; however, the truck was actually a bakery. Mereish explained that "for the troops in the field, you had to have a meal; you don't ship every day the loaves of bread. So, you carry your bakery, you carry your hospital. There were cold, refrigerated trucks that carried the perishable items, the meat, and so forth for the military to carry their food."[28] Although it is odd to think of the Iraqi military as having food trucks, UNMOVIC's on-the-ground investigations reveal this intriguing, yet mundane, logistical facet of Iraqi military life. Without that contextual understanding, WINPAC bioweapons analysts could understandably but erroneously interpret the mobile units as potential weapons labs. But this example illustrates the importance of analysts going beyond satellite imagery to incorporate on-the-ground, in-depth understandings of the social milieu and local infrastructure in which the suspected weapons systems operated.

In addition to bakeries, Mereish goes on to describe how other mobile laboratories were used for Iraqi government-mandated food analyses and quality control testing:

> From the Iraqi Department of Agriculture and Commerce, a requirement was established for these two mobile labs [showing pictures]. The head of the lab, between 1991 and 1998, she's in charge of quality control of all food imported to the country, which had to be subjected randomly to selective testing [by Iraqi law]. Her laboratory several times was bombed by the U.S. and U.K. during that period of time. So she had a problem that shipments of [imported] tea and sugar and so forth could not be released without that certificate of testing. So she decided, "Maybe I'll have a mobile lab in place of my fixed [lab] facility." . . . They test for mercury, they test for certain things in contaminants in food. Even I was surprised that Iraq had quality control. I mean, it's funny they do. They have rules and regulations that they have to test imported food. I thought, if you imported from Australia, why do you want to test it? Your [Iraqi] laboratories are not better than the producer. But they really do test.[29]

This passage reveals how using the simple biotech revolution frame can miss important social considerations in assessments of suspected infrastructure: even UN inspectors were surprised to learn that an Iraqi government agency had a legitimate, peaceful, and practical need for mobile biological laboratories. This oversight reflects what I described in chapter 2 as an analytic bias resulting from the use of a purely quantitative accounting of materials and infrastructure in weapons threat assessments. Such an accounting framework often fails to recognize and consider how social and cultural factors can shape the development and use of materials and technologies in unexpected ways.

In spite of these intriguing UNMOVIC findings, the CIA's WINPAC analysts continued to discount these data in their assessments. Even after the war had started, when U.S. and Kurdish military forces captured suspected mobile bioweapons trailers near Mosul, the CIA's bioweapons analysts relied on their secret source, Curveball, to confirm the validity of these findings. Thus, throughout the pre- and postwar period, WINPAC analysts placed greater weight on Curveball's secrets than on the ongoing UNMOVIC inspections or other available evidence that failed to identify or corroborate an Iraqi mobile bioweapons capability.

In a 2005 ethnographic study of the CIA, one CIA analyst highlighted the importance of secret information in intelligence work: "There is something special about the word 'secret' in my business. It says that it must be important. . . . We tend to weigh classified material as more important than other sources."[30] In looking at the Curveball case, WINPAC analysts gave Curveball's secret information privileged epistemological status as compared with unclassified reporting. Once certain technical facts about Curveball's reporting were deemed plausible and supportive of an Iraqi mobile bioweapons capability, WINPAC analysts stuck with it, even when contradictory evidence emerged from UNMOVIC inspections. In contrast, WINPAC analysts continually scrutinized and discounted UNMOVIC findings that questioned Curveball's claims.

The value and privileging of secret information extends beyond the walls of the CIA's headquarters in Langley, Virginia. Former Directorate of Operations official Tyler Drumheller explains that secret information, through its very codification in reports, has power and permanence: "Once something's written down on paper and disseminated in the [intelligence] community, [then] it's real, it's a fact. It doesn't matter if it's true or not . . . especially once the policy community reads it. It's very hard to get something out of somebody's head once they've read it. And you can put all the caveats on it you want, [but] it doesn't matter."[31] As described in chapter 6, the high value that WINPAC analysts placed on Curveball's "secrets" was embodied in a series of classified current intelligence reports disseminated throughout the U.S. intelligence and policy communities, which worked to create an early (and reinforcing) belief in an Iraqi mobile lab bioweapons capability. Due to the larger cultural value of secrets in intelligence work, the Curveball case illustrates how classified information can achieve privileged epistemological status in intelligence analysis as compared to other forms of knowledge.

Secrets and Compartmentalization of Knowledge

Secrecy played another role in boosting confidence in Curveball's reporting. Secrecy practices worked to compartmentalize information about Curveball within different sectors of the intelligence community. This compartmentalization promoted Curveball's reliability as a human intelligence source and fed WINPAC's determination that a growing Iraqi bioweapons threat existed. This compartmentalization resulted from (at least) three different issues: (1) security considerations; (2) methods of transmitting and organizing classified information; and (3) management and control. As we will see, each of these secrecy practices has important social and material dimensions. In some cases, compartmentalization shaped knowledge through access restrictions. Namely, security restrictions prohibited some interactions between intelligence analysts and civilian experts regarding the mobile labs, which hindered the integration of classified and unclassified information to assess the potential threat.

In other cases, problems with the storage and retrieval of secret information within the CIA and related intelligence organizations resulted in the inclusion of some classified information known to be fabricated in formal intelligence reports that were distributed to other members of the U.S. intelligence community and policymakers. Other compartmentalization, however, involved specific management techniques used to grant authority to WINPAC analysts. Because of this compartmentalization, secrecy practices designed to protect classified information from enemy hands also created problems inside the intelligence community that hampered intelligence collection and analysis.

Secrecy for Security

Afraid that Curveball's information might be leaked to Iraqi officials, WINPAC analysts kept a tight hold on details regarding his reporting. This secrecy proved problematic for UNMOVIC inspectors in preparation for their return to Iraq in 2002. As described in chapter 5, UN inspectors did not have the opportunity to clarify seemingly erroneous intelligence information they received in CIA briefings. Due to secrecy surrounding U.S. intelligence on Iraq, moreover, UN inspectors were not privy to the identities or expertise of their CIA briefers. Kay Mereish noted, "We don't know their background. I don't know their names. I have no idea who those people are at all."[32] This made it difficult for UN inspectors to follow up with their CIA briefers about the technical discrepancies that arose in their discussions. As a result, UNMOVIC inspectors grew frustrated at the lack of response and clarification from the CIA, particularly when repeated UN investigations of suspect mobile weapons sites—based on highly classified U.S. information—came up empty-handed.

UN inspector Peter Prosser explains why access to intelligence analysts could have helped the Iraqi mobile bioweapons investigation: "You know, when you get a tip about something [in Iraq], you go in there and it could be a school, it could be a post office, or it could be something else. And you really need to go back to the person that provided that information via SIGINT [signals intelligence] or imagery and really have a heart-to-heart talk with them."[33] In his experience working with Australian intelligence, Prosser found this kind of close working interaction very beneficial for analysis. Such an exchange could have been useful for scrutinizing the discrepancies in Curveball's reporting. UNMOVIC official Ewen Buchanan agrees: "If this is the third time that 'Mohammed' has talked about missiles and trees, and we have found nothing, then maybe we shouldn't bother listening to Mohammed anymore."[34]

Instead, the information about the suspected Iraqi mobile bioweapons labs largely flowed one way—from the UNMOVIC inspectors to U.S. intelligence. Typically, the only feedback UNMOVIC inspectors would receive from U.S. intelligence was requests that they revisit a site or visit a new one. However, the compartmentalization of information and access to intelligence analysts that Mereish and Buchanan describe in 2002 was not an established characteristic of UN inspections. As Buchanan explains, "During the old briefings at UNSCOM they [intelligence briefers] would always say 'I don't know,' but they'd write it down and say, 'We will come back to you on that.' "[35] Although legitimate concerns existed within the UN that too much information exchange between UN inspectors and U.S. intelligence might compromise sensitive intelligence information, Buchanan's comments highlight the benefits of the prior exchanges.[36]

The security restrictions on Curveball's reporting also affected the U.S. intelligence and policy communities' perceptions of what classified information was available at the time. As Operations official Margaret Henoch explains, "We all assumed, myself included, that there was something else that they [WINPAC analysts] had that they couldn't use. And this was the stuff that they were going to use [in Powell's UN speech] because the real stuff they had to protect."[37] Later Henoch comments, "They [WINPAC] could not possibly believe Curveball, so there had to be something I couldn't see."[38] Thus, even Operations officials such as Henoch assumed insufficient authorization to view certain aspects of the mobile lab intelligence in the analysts' possession, which highlights a taken-for-granted assumption operating in the intelligence community: the absence of evidence must be due to classification restrictions and not a lack of information or poor information.[39]

Policymakers privy to some of the CIA's mobile bioweapons reporting sometimes made this same assumption. One former high-level U.S. government official states that specific classified details on Iraq's bioweapons program were so highly compartmentalized that she was rarely privy to specific reporting on the issue, even though she received highly classified briefings on other bioweapons issues (at times, including Iraq's bioweapons program). In seeing Powell's UN speech, she assumed that the classified information underpinning the mobile lab drawings was also highly compartmentalized for security reasons, which explains why she had not seen it in prior intelligence reporting.[40] A 2004 Senate report notes this problem of compartmentalization of source information: "In the years before Operation Iraqi Freedom, the CIA protected its Iraqi weapons of mass destruction sources so well that some of the information they provided was kept from the majority of analysts with a legitimate need to know. . . . The CIA's failure to share important information about source reporting on Iraq's mobile biological weapons program . . . left analysts and policymakers with an incomplete and, at times, misleading picture of these issues."[41] Indeed, in the Curveball case, extreme compartmentalization worked to create false assumptions that more highly detailed, classified information existed, when in fact it did not.

This problem of compartmentalization continued even when U.S. military forces captured suspected mobile labs early in the Iraq War. One former U.S. intelligence analyst recounted a conversation with Mereish:

> I've known Kay for years, and I had a meeting with her. It was after we found the trailers [in Mosul and Erbil]. And she was telling me that this is not like a fermentor in Iraq. Well, I told her, "I'm sorry, it looks really plausible to us." She wanted to know more of what I knew, but I was not at liberty to tell her because that is the way it is. She was telling [me] that it was the wrong design of the fermentor. I'm not a fermentation person, but I have talked to our experts, and they are telling me that they [Iraq] could do it like that. She [Mereish] said, "I've been all over Iraq, and I haven't seen any fermentors like that." Well, okay, fine. She does have a Ph.D., and she is very technical. She has been all over the country, and I take her points. She kept saying, "You need to tell me more," and I said, "I'm sorry, I can't talk to you."[42]

This exchange reveals that, early on, there appeared to be contradictions in how to interpret the captured labs and that there was no mechanism sought for CIA analysts to share important intelligence information with relevant experts outside the intelligence community. Even more striking is that in the exchange above, the analyst did not even try to engage Mereish further to understand her concerns regarding the fermentors. At the same time, the analyst acknowledged that Mereish had important, in-depth expertise relevant to assessing the captured labs. In the end, however, the CIA analyst ended the conversation. Apparently, the analyst was more concerned with guarding classified information and assessments—and perhaps his own authority—even if these appeared to be wrong, than with being curious about Mereish's remarks and working to clarify what seemed to be significant contradictions in intelligence.

Other compartmentalization problems can result from protecting human source information. As described in chapter 5, specific Operations intelligence workers known as reports officers determine what information is included in human intelligence reports sent to analysts; these officers can serve in a formal or informal capacity. To protect intelligence sources and methods, reports officers often remove significant identifiers from human intelligence reports before sharing the reports with analysts: sources are often described in general terms in classified reports and are not necessarily labeled with code words or other source-specific information; in addition, other particulars about the debriefing sessions are removed. As a result, human intelligence reports have a tendency to omit details, with much important contextual information removed for security reasons.[43] Intelligence scholars have noted that these practices can leave out important specifics about a source's expertise, access, or other relevant details that could help analysts in their evaluation of the source's claims.[44] These practices can also make it hard for an analyst to identify whether a new human intelligence report comes from a new source or an old, repeat source and to identify or recall sources deemed as fabricators.

This protection of source information played a role in how Curveball's information was presented to the public in Powell's UN speech. When I asked a former U.S. intelligence analyst why the decision was made to use drawings of the mobile bioweapons labs for Powell's speech rather than specific text from Curveball's intelligence reports, the analyst explained that the CIA is usually more guarded with information obtained by human sources than, for example, signals intelligence, because human sources (or their relations) could be killed if discovered.[45] The drawings, therefore, provided an analytic and visual heuristic that served as a more accessible, expedient, and safe means of conveying Curveball's secret claims in both classified and unclassified domains. A more cynical interpretation, however, would suggest that WINPAC analysts used the drawings to create a more convincing version of events rather than include the disparate and contradictory range of sources and materials that actually comprised the intelligence on the mobile labs.[46] In either case, the drawings in Powell's speech failed to convey such discrepancies or the UN weapons inspectors' concern about the absence of confirming evidence in Curveball's reporting.

Organization and Transmission of Classified Information

The transmission and storage of classified information presents another compartmentalization problem in the Iraqi mobile bioweapons case, which began the moment the Defense Intelligence Agency submitted and disseminated Curveball's reports within the U.S. intelligence community. As is the custom for intelligence dissemination, the DIA, as originators of the Curveball reports, added specific tags to the reports to specify which government officials were authorized with "need-to-know" status. Tyler Drumheller explained that "the way it comes in is, the DIA gets it [human intelligence reports], they have their own formats they used called IRRs [Investigative Records Repository], and each one has a list of customers or consumers. At the bottom on the second page, there's a list of who it is disseminated to, and it'll say 'WINPAC,' 'Iraqi Working Group,' the 'CIA DO [Directorate of Operations] Counterproliferation Division,' 'Commandant of the Marine Corps,' the 'White House Situation Room,' or something like that."[47] Everyone who is on the list gets the report—anyone not on the list does not. Therefore, it is critically important to be designated as authorized with a need to know by the originators of the reports. In the Curveball case, however, only a narrow subset of intelligence analysts and collectors were cleared to read foreign intelligence reports on Iraq's WMDs.[48]

Within the CIA, Curveball's reports went to bioweapons analysts in WINPAC and the Directorate of Operations' Counterproliferation Division but not to other potentially relevant analysts and collection officials, unless the original recipients of the reports chose to forward this information to others deemed to have a relevant need to know. Upon receiving Curveball's reports from German intelligence, for example, DIA officials did not include the CIA's European Division and German group in their Directorate of Operations on the initial Curveball dissemination tag lines—an oversight repeated by the CIA's own Directorate of Operations. Although the Operations' Counterproliferation Division was included in the original tag line, due to its collection responsibilities on WMD issues, the division did not flag these reports to its European Division or German group.

Because Curveball was a source handled and debriefed only by German intelligence, Drumheller has argued that the Counterproliferation Division should have recognized the importance of including Operations personnel with German intelligence expertise in discussions about Curveball. Instead, Drumheller relates, "When CPD [Counterproliferation Division] got it [the Curveball reports], they said, 'Well, there's no reason for EUR [European Division] to see this. This has nothing to do with EUR; the Germans gave it to us, it's a German case, but it doesn't have anything to do with Germany.' "[49] These informal practices of ascribing a need to know prevented the Directorate of Operations' European Division and German group from being aware of or involved in the assessment of Curveball when his reporting first emerged in 2000 through mid-2002. This seemingly small oversight in deciding who got to see Curveball's reports later came to have enormous implications for the reliability of WINPAC's mobile bioweapons assessments.

Excluding the European Division and the German group meant leaving out critical operations expertise in assessing Curveball. For instance, the European Division was not included in meetings the WINPAC analysts organized with other foreign liaison services to discuss Curveball's reporting. Drumheller notes:

"They [the bioweapons analysts] had had meetings in Germany, and it was at those meetings that the British said there may be problems [with Curveball]. We didn't know any of that. We didn't know that they [the British] knew his name."[50] This example illustrates the critical importance of the social and material practices related to tagging, which determines who has the need to know and whether and when decisions and practices for tagging get changed over time.

The initial dissemination tags also affect how intelligence reports are stored in classified databases, something that later obscured Curveball's reports from the European Division. Henoch explained that "it [intelligence reporting] is stored in a database, and you can't access it unless you are on the address line. And frequently, it is less conspiracy than incompetence. And my guess is that in the beginning, because they don't understand the way the DO [Directorate of Operations] works, it never occurred to them that because he [Curveball] was in Germany, they should put Europe [the Directorate of Operations' European division] on the address line. He was talking about weapons, so they just put 'Counterproliferation [Division]' on it."[51] Henoch's comment reveals that intelligence databases are also structured to allow access only to those designated with a need to know. Furthermore, because the Curveball reports were initially tagged by DIA analysts with the keyword "WMD," this designation automatically mapped solely to technical offices in the CIA (WINPAC, Counterproliferation Division, among others)—another illustration of the profound disconnects between technical and other forms of expertise in the Directorates of Intelligence and Operations (see chapter 5).

This process of compartmentalization affected not only what Henoch could automatically see but also what she might be able to seek out: "By the time it [Curveball's intelligence reporting] reaches the Agency, it goes into a channel that I wouldn't ever read [WMD]. I just wouldn't read finished intelligence unless it dealt with the issues right in Germany, Austria."[52] So, without a tag of "Germany" or "Austria"—in addition to "WMD"—Curveball's reports would have been invisible in the intelligence channels in which Henoch worked. Even if she had been given the authority to receive Curveball's reports, Henoch's involvement would have depended on whether she was "copied in" for information purposes only or to take some kind of action. Henoch explained that each day she would receive a deluge of newly collected information; unless she had been tasked to act on the Curveball case, she would likely have filed away his reports, given the other demands on her time.[53]

Despite this rigid compartmentalization, CIA analysts have developed internal workarounds involving social interventions to gain access to intelligence information they would not otherwise receive. More specifically, according to

Henoch, the way to get to reporting you're not initially copied on is to find someone to add you to the list at the very beginning: "The first time it comes in from the field, it comes in with one set of address lines. You just have to grab somebody. So you have to get yourself into it. You have to get the first one [intelligence report]."[54] Henoch's remarks highlight the critical importance of socializing within the intelligence community to make sure that one has access to relevant reports. Another avenue onto the list is through an authorizing phone call from upper CIA management. Thus, social practices help spread reports to relevant intelligence officials who may not be authorized with a need to know by the reports' original recipients.

In the case of the Iraqi mobile lab assessments, the secrecy practices designed to protect classified information from enemy hands also hampered intelligence collection and analysis to the extent that the European Division was not even aware of the problems and the lack of vetting in Curveball's reports until the fall of 2002, more than two years after his reports emerged. By that time, Curveball's human intelligence reporting had been incorporated into a variety of formal intelligence and policy reports, which gave it credibility in many sectors of their respective communities. As a result, Henoch explains, the Directorate of Operations' usual role of recruiting and validating the source had been overtaken by events and policy imperatives: "So for anyone to leap in at that moment . . . it was really like, 'I'm sorry, the levees have already broken.' "[55] The repeated circulation of Curveball's intelligence reports and their incorporation into finished intelligence documents formed a kind of validation of Curveball's claims, even though Curveball himself had not been operationally vetted. This phenomenon is corroborated in the book *Documents: Artifacts of Modern Knowledge,* in which anthropologist Anneliese Riles includes case studies illustrating that the practices of document production, collection, and dissemination can construct particular kinds of accepted narratives, even when there exists a disparate or contradictory set of evidence.[56]

The practices for managing classified information also create opportunities for flawed or fabricated information to remain valid within intelligence systems. Because intelligence channels are complex and fragmentary, for example, the CIA has had difficulty recalling a human intelligence report, even if the individual has been identified as a fabricator. Although fabrication notices were issued about some of the human sources related to the Iraqi mobile labs case, the intelligence community as a whole did not have a protocol or mechanism in place at the time to flag the original report as having been invalidated or to note that it had been recalled or reissued. As a result, analysts throughout the intelligence community were forced to catch the warning in their flood of daily intelligence the first time it appeared or to rely on memory (if they had been working on the case at the time) that a fabrication notice had been issued on a particular source. Alternatively, they could have tried to search for it via keywords in intelligence databases. Tyler Drumheller explained that an analyst would have to "Google," for instance, "reports on Iraq WMD before the invasion of Iraq" and then pore through them for a specific one, but even then, the original report may not indicate whether the sources and their reporting remain credible.[57]

For instance, although CIA bioweapons analysts used two other human intelligence sources from Iraq (the INC source and the second source) to corroborate Curveball's reporting in a variety of finished intelligence reports, both were later determined to be fabricators. In May 2002, a fabrication notice was issued about the INC source, but the original report was not recalled or reissued with a fabrication notice attached electronically.[58] So the original human intelligence report remained in intelligence databases and files used by analysts in preparing reports to other intelligence analysts and policymakers.[59] The frequent turnover of CIA analysts, their large portfolios of work, and the constant pressures of producing current intelligence reports likely obscured the fact that fabrication notices had been tied to prior human intelligence reports.

This false mobile bioweapons reporting was ultimately used in the influential October 2002 NIE as well as in Colin Powell's February 2003 UN speech. During meetings for the preparation of these two documents, there were intelligence personnel present and aware of the fabrication notice; however, they did not mention this problem in the discussion of the mobile labs.[60] If the original report had been reissued with a recall notice, this would have provided opportunities for analysts from other intelligence agencies to raise questions about the inclusion of the information, even if the CIA's analysts did not.[61] Yet once a finished intelligence report was issued, the vagueness with which human sources were described in the report would not have allowed quick identification of a flawed source. For instance, in the October 2002 NIE, the evidence for the mobile bioweapons labs was attributed simply to "multiple sensitive sources."[62] As the 2005 WMD Commission report finds, this wording implied that there was more extensive corroboration and confirmation of the mobile lab assessments in the NIE than actually existed at the time.

Although recent efforts have been made to correct these problems, the U.S. intelligence community continues to lack a mechanism to track the sources of finished intelligence materials or briefings.[63] As one recent critique stated, because of the poor tracking mechanism, "there is no way to know which pieces [finished intelligence reports sent to policymakers or other intelligence analysts] relied upon what information."[64] This problem, however, does not necessarily require a new or complicated kind of technological solution; one simple solution would be to include citations—footnotes—with the data used in intelligence reports. Former intelligence official Ford describes how footnotes can prove critical to intelligence assessments: "An old curmudgeon working at CIA while I was still in DIA did the best intelligence report I've ever seen. He was an analyst on Korea when the Chinese entered the war in Korea, and so when I met him, he'd been around for a long time. In this particular case, he was having problems getting people to listen to some of his findings because it contradicted conventional wisdom. So he wrote a paper with everything footnoted—all of his material and pictures, intercepts, HUMINT—so that if you didn't believe him, you could go back in the files and read all the reports yourself and see why he had come to a different conclusion."[65] Ford says the footnotes made the document the most powerful he'd ever read, because

> he [the Korea analyst] could say to the doubters, "You can believe it or not, or you can do nothing about it or not, but here is where the evidence led me." This [report] tells you something that, although the Chinese may be moving in the opposite direction on every other front, for some reason Burma's an exception. It's probably important to know why Burma is the only place in the world where the Chinese are taking this sort of risk, and we should study that. Why aren't we finding out more about that? It might tell us more about the Chinese view of the subject. And showing your work is such a simple thing. Footnotes can also help supervisors critique their analysts' work and help guide them in their intellectual growth. Even if you took the footnotes out before you sent it to the consumer [policymaker], I don't see any problem with it, and indeed if I were a policymaker, I probably would find leaving the footnotes in helpful.[66]

Using footnotes may seem like a simple solution, but it is indeed surprising that an obligatory academic practice is not also standard in contemporary intelligence work.

For over forty years, CIA officials have debated the utility of footnotes in finished intelligence reports; as a result, the internal analytic practice of using footnotes has varied.[67] Since the end of the Cold War and the rise of current intelligence reporting, intelligence managers have often preferred journalistic writing styles, abbreviated formats, and rapid publication of intelligence documents that do not readily lend themselves to detailed citations. The 2005 WMD Commission report finds that during the Iraq WMD assessments, proper sourcing of data used in finished intelligence reports was lacking.[68] In the Curveball report, footnotes could have helped reveal the limited evidence on which the Iraqi mobile lab assessments were based and allowed other intelligence analysts and policymakers to question the information and assumptions underpinning the assessments.

Beyond footnotes, the fragmented dissemination of classified information can allow fabricated secret information to persist for years in compartmented sites and then come to life again. As Drumheller explains,

> At the time when it [a fabrication notice] comes out, everybody that is involved, you get all these notices, and these reports are all numbered, and they're responsible to go collect them all and get them back. They're not supposed to have made Xerox copies, but some people do. [For example,] Somebody has made a copy and has it sitting in their safe and someone [later] finds it and says, "Wow, look at this!" That's hard to guard against. But you can't control people. I mean, there is a system. The system is they're numbered, and they have to account for them, and they have to turn them back in, and they sort of have to say, "No, I didn't make a Xerox." But people do it [photocopy] all the time, because you can't hold them [intelligence reports] forever, you have to turn them back in. People don't take all the security steps that seriously, and so they'll make a Xerox and they'll cut the classifications off the top and bottom and say, "Oh, it's not secret now," and they just store it. Or they'll copy portions of it, which is almost worse, because then someone else later on goes through the files and finds this sort of unattributed bit of what looks like really terrific intelligence, and they start the whole process again. That happens all the time.[69]

This scenario illustrates the importance of the social life of documents in intelligence work and of continual analytic reflection on the use of sources in intelligence reports.

Management and Control

Secrecy and compartmentalization of classified information can also occur for management and other types of control. One classic example of this was featured in historian Michael Dennis's research on the development of the proximity fuze during World War II.[70] As Dennis explains, Merle Tuve, leader of the fuze project, instituted a secrecy policy among his workers that prohibited them from discussing their work over the lunch hour in a local restaurant. Through his archival research, Dennis finds that the primary rationale for Tuve's new lunchroom secrecy policy was a managerial one: to keep tight control over employees so that individual researchers would be focused on their job assignments and accomplish their specified tasks.[71] The secrecy practices, however, so compartmentalized fuze research that Tuve ultimately needed to develop special bureaucratic procedures to be able to reconstruct the laboratory's various pieces of technical work.[72] In this case, new secrecy practices were instituted primarily to keep managerial authority and control over scientific research, but they led to other unintended consequences with adverse work effects.

Moving beyond this historical case, secrecy practices for management and control are evident in contemporary accounts of intelligence work. For example, human intelligence sources are often referred to as "assets" that are "owned" by particular intelligence collectors. As the 2005 WMD Commission report notes, "Collectors of information continue to operate as though they 'own' the information, and collectors continue to control access to the information they generate. Decisions to withhold information are typically based on rules that are neither clearly defined nor consistently applied, with no system in place to hold collectors accountable for inappropriately withholding information."[73] This sense of ownership of classified information can hamper sharing of information among and between intelligence analysts and collectors.

In the mobile bioweapons case, several "owners" considered Curveball to be their asset but had conflicting interpretations of what this ownership implied. Because Curveball was identified in Germany, he was considered to be a German intelligence asset. As such, German intelligence would not allow U.S. and foreign intelligence analysts and collectors to have direct access to him or to full transcripts of his debriefing sessions. At the same time, because Curveball's reports came to the CIA through the DIA, his human intelligence reporting was seen as DIA—not CIA—property. Because the CIA's Directorate of Operations did not own Curveball, its staff was not given the opportunity or authority at the outset to verify his credibility through their own evaluation methods.

The WINPAC analysts assumed that the DIA, as the primary U.S. collection agency handling this source, would have verified Curveball's information before passing it along. Meanwhile, the DIA considered itself to be a conduit of the report and nothing more. Staffers there assumed that asset validation was the responsibility of WINPAC's analysts; if the analysts judged the information as credible, then the source would be considered by the DIA to be validated.[74] Thus, the DIA did not take any steps to try to validate Curveball's reporting before passing it along to WINPAC's analysts. These differences in the ways intelligence agencies choose to own and handle human sources and human intelligence reports are an important consideration in assessing secret information. As Tyler Drumheller explains, because "the DIA doesn't really do a lot of agent handling, the way the Curveball intelligence was handled, . . . it came through the Agency as sort of finished intelligence," even though it had never been operationally verified.[75] Later, when people working for Drumheller and Henoch tried to validate Curveball's reporting, the DIA took offense that another agency—the CIA—would try to do so. In February 2003, after questions about Curveball's credibility had begun to emerge, "the Defense HUMINT division chief said he was 'shocked' by CIA's [Operations'] suggestion that Curveball might be unreliable."[76]

In addition to the DIA, the CIA's Directorate of Operations' Counterproliferation Division also assumed ownership of Curveball's reports, which Drumheller says caused problems, even within the CIA's own Directorate of Operations, because the Counterproliferation Division "may have notified the [German] desk officer that there was a source [Curveball], but they said, 'It's our case,' and then it becomes proprietary."[77] The proprietary nature of human intelligence sources and the resulting secrecy regime meant that the European Division and the German group were not given access to Curveball's files without a protracted management debate.

Finally, WINPAC's analysts assumed ultimate ownership of the Curveball reports and tried to restrict access to the documents. As Henoch says, "The problem was that WINPAC did not want anyone else to see it. They made it very hard to get to."[78] She recalls telling her staff to go figure out the Curveball reporting, and they would come back and tell her the only way they could gain access was for her to call WINPAC and demand it: "And so I called, and that is how we started to get this stuff. In six weeks, we had what we needed. It should have been easier. We shouldn't have had to fight for it."[79] Those six weeks in the fall of 2002 were a crucial window of time when arguments for the case to go to war in Iraq were building within the U.S. government.

This sense of ownership by different agencies and offices stems from the secrecy that sociologist Max Weber describes as a common feature within bureaucracies. According to Weber, secrecy is exerted within bureaucracies so that administrative units can retain a competitive advantage over other units.[80] Given the inherent secrecy of intelligence operations, it is not surprising that different agencies and offices within the intelligence bureaucracy also use secrecy to gain certain advantages and rewards over other administrative units. The sole-practitioner model of analysis that Ford described within the CIA also meant that individual analysts or particular analytic units often kept their analytic methods proprietary. In the Curveball case, it was not until the Directorate of Operations' European Division raised serious and persistent questions about Curveball's reports—in the context of an impending policy justification for war, almost three years after Curveball first began reporting—that WINPAC analysts were called on to explain to their CIA colleagues how they had assessed Curveball's reliability and made their mobile lab assessments. This proprietary privilege also hindered the sharing of other relevant intelligence reports with other bioweapons analysts outside the CIA.[81]

In addition, WINPAC kept secret the problems with Curveball and other human intelligence sources.[82] As a result, these problems were excluded from finished analytic reports distributed to other intelligence analysts or policymakers in the runup to the October 2002 NIE and Powell's UN speech in February 2003. Had these problems been shared, the final analysis might have been different. One bioweapons analyst from the State Department's Bureau of Intelligence and Research said that, had Curveball's reports been removed from consideration, "it would have reduced his confidence in the assessment that Iraq had mobile BW production units."[83] Nonetheless, the intelligence community had "cleared" (signed off on) the text of Powell's speech and the figures involving the mobile bioweapons labs. Due to the secrecy surrounding the internal CIA debates, the larger intelligence and policy communities were not aware of the problems with Curveball's reporting and the other sources used to corroborate his claims during the preparation of Powell's speech.

Even after the war, when the purported mobile bioweapons trailers were found in the Iraqi desert by military forces, WINPAC and DIA analysts continued to assert control over bioweapons intelligence. As mentioned earlier, discovery of the trailers prompted several debates within the intelligence and policy communities about whether these were the long-expected Iraqi mobile bioweapons labs. In order to settle these debates, the DIA sent an independent team of nongovernmental defense contractors composed of technical experts to assess the trailers on the ground in Iraq. A member of this team recalls, "We put together a team of experts, people who understand refrigeration, mechanical structures, electrical, microbiology. Some were engineers, some were scientists. We had a Brit who was an expert in fermentation. It was really an elite group of ten people who went to look at these trailers."[84]

Upon arriving in Iraq, the team spent several days investigating all aspects of the trailers and determined that they were not capable of bioweapons production. However, when the team leader communicated these results back to DIA headquarters and then followed up with a 122-page final report entitled *Final Technical Engineering Exploitation Report on Iraqi Suspected Biological Weapons-Associated Trailer,* the report was stamped "SECRET" and shelved in classified channels.[85] A team member noted the intelligence community's penchant for classifying documents to keep them proprietary, regardless of what should be shared with others: "They can just tell other intelligence members 'We can't release that.' "[86] The managerial decision to classify and shelve the team's report was meant to privilege the existing CIA notion that the captured trailers were indeed the long-suspected Iraqi mobile bioweapons labs.

In contrast to the independent team's report, a joint unclassified DIA-CIA white paper, entitled "Iraqi Mobile Biological Warfare Agent Production Plants," was soon released on the CIA website (see chapter 6). This report argued that the captured trailers *were* most consistent for bioweapons production.[87] When the State Department's bioweapons intelligence analysts and officials saw this unclassified report, they were concerned that it did not include alternative interpretations of what the trailers could be. After Carl Ford, assistant secretary of state for intelligence and research, raised these concerns in memos to Secretary of State Colin Powell, Powell asked for formal CIA clarification.

In response to Powell's query, Ford was summoned to CIA headquarters to meet with CIA Director George Tenet and Deputy Director of Central Intelligence John McLaughlin. Ford remembers that Tenet and McLaughlin invoked secrecy to explain the joint DIA-CIA report's findings. When Ford inquired about the captured trailers, he recalls Tenet saying that there was intelligence information about the trailers that the State Department analysts did not know but that the DIA-CIA report's intelligence and conclusions could be trusted. Ford countered by stating that his analysts were raising valid, serious, and legitimate questions about the data. Ford recalls that Tenet and McLaughlin did not mention Curveball's track record, though by that time they knew of his questionable reliability; instead, "They got angry and mad at me. And they did know a lot more than I did. Unfortunately, if they had told me any of that, it would have made my case stronger, it would have weakened their case. All kinds of things suggested there was something wrong by the end of May of 2003. Here's a case, I think, in which the people at the top, rather than being intelligence advisors, had become advocates for a position in their agency, and it didn't really matter what I thought or anybody else thought. They had told the president, the president went out in public, and anything that smacked of them being wrong was not okay."[88] Ford believes that the CIA management used secrecy and invoked secrecy privileges to justify the DIA-CIA conclusions about the captured trailers.[89] For almost a year after Ford's meeting with Tenet and McLaughlin—and after the trailers were discovered—Bush administration and intelligence officials continued to state publicly that the captured trailers were mobile bioweapons production facilities.

Furthermore, the DIA's other commissioned report, *Final Technical Engineering Exploitation Report on Iraqi Suspected Biological Weapons-Associated Trailers*—based on analysis conducted by a team of independent, nongovernment contractors—remains classified. According to a former team member, "To my knowledge, this report has never seen the light of day. . . . I could not even get this report, to share it with other agencies in the [intelligence] community. I was asked for copies of the report by other customers [policymakers] who knew that I was going to Iraq and what I was doing. The Defense Intelligence Agency has never sent that report to those customers, even though I gave them the names and agencies to which those customers belonged."[90] In addition, the team's report was supposed to be presented in a classified meeting in 2003, but at the last minute, the briefer was reportedly told by the DIA director not to present the report. Only in 2004, one year after the report was written, was the report formally disseminated outside the DIA when posted on the intelligence community intranet.[91]

In 2006, a *Washington Post* reporter published details about the shelved study, based on leaks from intelligence insiders.[92] When the reporter asked DIA management why the contractor report had been held so tightly within their organization, the team leader recalled that the DIA said that the report had to be vetted to determine whether its conclusions were credible. But the team leader pointed out that the DIA had assembled a team of ten external experts, each with at least fifteen years of bioweapons-related experience, to go to Iraq and determine whether the trailers could, in fact, be connected to bioweapons production: "They [the DIA] sent us to do a job. So then we go, and we come to absolutely solid grounds, unequivocal conclusions. They don't like the conclusions, and then they go and tell people in the *Washington Post* five years later that they had to vet it to make sure it was credible. But wait a minute, I thought we were the ones who were making what you wanted to know credible. I don't know where they would find people to make it credible, because we had what I consider to be some of the most elite people in this country."[93] This "vetting" explanation allowed DIA management to question publicly the conclusions drawn by the team as well as keep the classified report buried within its own intelligence channels and away from the eyes of policymakers or the public. As the team leader later remarked about these secrecy practices, "People play games with this information. . . . They tell people things, but they won't tell them everything."[94] This example illustrates how secrecy can mask not only "real" information but also its lack—or even misinformation—to further particular exertions of power and control.

Secrets, Relationships, and Social Order

Another consideration in the world of secrecy is how relationships among the players in the intelligence and policy communities influence who wants to keep what information away from whom. Susan Wright and David Wallace note, "To fully understand the social construction of secrets, we must ask how these relations are formed and by whom, how contests of secrecy develop, by what means, in what settings, with what effects."[95] To understand the secrets and secrecy practices that shaped the mobile lab assessments, we must start with the CIA's relationship with Germany's intelligence department, the BND, dating back to the Cold War. As Tyler Drumheller explains, "The Agency always had odd relations with the BND. . . . There's some hostility there."[96] The United States had helped the Germans set up their intelligence agency after World War II, and as a result, according to Drumheller, the CIA staff viewed the relationship as that of big brother (the CIA) and little brother (the BND). The relationship was further complicated by several well-publicized scandals that involved CIA and BND operations officials in the 1990s.[97] As a result, these officials often had strained working relationships; the BND often preferred working with the DIA.

WINPAC and even the CIA's own Directorate of Operations' Counterproliferation Division did not understand this troubled relationship or certain other internal aspects of German intelligence. As Tyler Drumheller explains, "They [WINPAC analysts, Counterproliferation Division] don't talk to anybody that really knows what's going on inside the German service. If they had asked us, then we could have told them that there are tensions and stresses inside the German service that drive them to want to have a big success that would make them reluctant to go back and correct themselves."[98]

At the same time, the close and historical relationships between staff in the Counterproliferation Division and WINPAC analysts also shaped knowledge about the Iraqi mobile labs—by excluding other types of expertise and knowledge. The 2005 WMD Commission report notes that when the BND developed concerns about Curveball's veracity in early 2001, the Counterproliferation Division shared reports about these concerns with WINPAC, because "the primary BW analyst who worked on the Iraq issue had close relations with the DO's [Directorate of Operations'] Counterproliferation Division. . . . This and other operational information was not, however, shared with analysts outside CIA."[99] The information was not even shared with Operations colleagues in the CIA's European Division. Even when debates emerged within the Directorate of Operations about Curveball, the Counterproliferation Division supported the CIA's WINPAC analysts.

As Henoch relates, "Their boss [in the Counterproliferation Division] absolutely sided with WINPAC. He didn't tell us anything. He didn't help us. He knew Tyler well, he knew me."[100] In addition, the head of the CIA's Directorate of Operations at the time, James Pavitt, supported WINPAC's authority on the Curveball case, even on operational issues. Pavitt himself had a personal connection to WINPAC: in 1995, he founded the Counterproliferation Division within the Nonproliferation Center and served as its director prior to heading up the Directorate of Operations. Thus, Pavitt had developed a close working relationship with WINPAC. In a highly classified domain, such relationships proved significant to the flow and privileging of secret information.

Wright and Wallace aptly point out that "secrets do not develop in a social vacuum. Rather, the construction of a web of secrecy is a social process that defines relationships between those inside and those outside the web."[101] Moreover, the way secrets are kept and conveyed shapes relationships among organizations.[102] In the Iraqi mobile lab assessments, all these relationships among national agencies, American intelligence agencies, and colleagues within agencies determined how certain secrets regarding Curveball and the Iraqi mobile lab threat were kept, constructed, communicated, and promoted in the intelligence and policy communities.

Conclusion

The widespread and competitive secrecy surrounding Curveball—both intentional secrecy and unwitting secrecy—speaks to the dangers of reliance on secrets. In addition, the prominence and value that WINPAC analysts placed on Curveball's secret reporting kept them from considering alternative data, expertise, and analytic frameworks that could have provided a more contextual understanding of how to interrogate and evaluate Curveball's claims of an Iraqi mobile bioweapons capability. In his study of secrets, Simmel noted that secrets are attractive and prized because of the common assumption that "what is denied to many must have special value."[103] Simmel cautions, however, that secrets can become problematic if one does not reflect sufficiently on the importance of evaluating and contextualizing secret information: "From secrecy, which shades all that is profound and significant, grows the typical error according to which everything mysterious is something important and essential."[104] In the mobile lab case, Henoch argues that the veil of secrecy surrounding Curveball was in fact unwarranted: "Really, what was the secret with Curveball? He left his country, they knew he was gone. If he was that big of a threat, they [Iraqis] had people in Germany. He had a work permit, he had a residence. It just doesn't make sense. And it really wasn't a secret, I would say. My name and affiliation with the Agency was a secret, and most people didn't know about that. . . . I got in my car every morning, and I had some kind of bullshit story. . . . But all anyone had to do was follow me. What is a real strategic secret? The simple truth is that there are not that many."[105]

Other former intelligence officials share this view about the dangers of relying exclusively on secret information rather than developing a more holistic, all-source approach to collecting and analyzing intelligence information. As Ford argues, "The more you know about common ordinary things, the better that you are able to hone in on putting together some of the secret stuff that you need to know. And it just simply, it is no longer a part of the analytic process . . . and they [intelligence analysts] don't even understand that anymore."[106] According to another intelligence analyst, "You don't just get a piece of intelligence and say, 'Well, Syria is now working on clam toxins.' Somebody should say, 'Where the hell are they getting their clams from? *How* are they doing this?' "[107] Answering the "how" of such questions, however, requires not only classified information and techniques but, as the UN inspections in Iraq showed, a variety of other kinds of unclassified information and methods as well. It also requires understanding and studying the broader social context in which weapons programs are situated—an approach not valued by analysts who focus on purely material and technical aspects of bioweapons threats.

Beyond that, the CIA's culture of funding and prioritizing "secret collection" makes it difficult to analyze and integrate unclassified social factors that might shape WMD development. As former CIA deputy director Richard Kerr explains: "Clandestine services who do overseas work are stealing secrets. They aren't interested in sociological information and soft stuff that doesn't seem to them to be a secret, and there's some justification to that. But, it [soft information] takes a lot of collection. And that's not something you collect through intelligence. You collect it through other means. Photography won't show it, and signals intelligence won't show it. And clandestine reporting probably shouldn't be wasted on it. But it's a terribly important thing if you're going to understand a country. It's hard to come by. It's slow, tedious, day-to-day, and it's grubby work. It's research."[108] As we saw in chapters 5 and 6, the culture of current intelligence reporting and the state of fragmented expertise that structures the CIA's intelligence collection and analysis also make significant, in-depth, unclassified research a challenge; this is a problem policymakers need to understand. As the final consumers of intelligence, they, too, must understand how relationships in the intelligence community shape the production, analysis, and dissemination of information, and they must be the strongest advocates for the need to meld public and secret information to inform their decisions.

At the same time, reliance on Curveball's "secret information" allowed for and sustained the possibility of an Iraqi mobile bioweapons capability even when empirical evidence was lacking. This alternative "secret world" was so powerful as to be perpetuated in the face of contrary information. Even today, some former U.S. intelligence analysts still believe in an Iraqi mobile bioweapons capability. In commenting on the captured Iraqi trailers in 2007, one analyst argues, "It [the captured trailer] looked a lot like Powell's picture. Now, whether they [Iraqis] took Powell's picture and built something that looked like it, I have no idea, because the Iraqis are very sneaky, and they are also really good at machining things.[109] This analyst continues to perceive Iraq as a devious, deceptive enemy, still hiding mobile weapons activities—even after four postwar years and several postwar investigations to the contrary.

In looking at the value placed on Curveball's information and the various secrecy practices that underpinned the CIA's assessments, one can see how these practices produced "a different map of intellectual geography, a different sense of the horizons of possibility" regarding an Iraqi mobile bioweapons capability.[110] The 2005 WMD Commission pointed out that "the compartmentalization of highly sensitive activities creates unknown islands of information under the 'personalized' security governance of each program manager."[111] These different islands or geographies of information are most clearly evident in the exchange and intake of intelligence between UNMOVIC inspectors and the CIA's WINPAC analysts. Although UNMOVIC inspectors repeatedly failed to find on-the-ground evidence of an Iraqi mobile bioweapons capability, WINPAC analysts interpreted the lack of information as evidence to the contrary. The segregation of these groups due to secrecy practices hindered a more rigorous evaluation of Curveball's claims.

Moreover, these secrecy divides failed to integrate valuable resources into the mobile lab assessments. For example, Henoch remarks that when she finally received Curveball's reports, "really, it wasn't so much getting the stuff, but how you read it."[112] When Henoch and Drumheller read Curveball's reports, they read with an operational eye, keeping in mind knowledge of German intelligence and their debriefing practices, the DIA's style of handling such reports, and Operations tradecraft for evaluating human intelligence sources. Moreover, their experience also made them wary that Iraq might provide false information through deception operations or legitimate "secret" information through a double agent in order to drive U.S. policy and actions. Their expertise on problems with the secrets provided by human sources made them skeptical of Curveball's claims in the absence of further evaluation—as Henoch remarks, "You cannot judge validity by the information alone."[113] Also, in reading Curveball's reports, Henoch attended to what was clearly *absent* in his record, such as background and personal checks, substantive checks with foreign intelligence services, surveillance of his whereabouts, checks on his knowledge of other important Iraqi issues and circumstances. As science and technology studies scholar Brian Rappert notes, an attention to what is left out of accounts is a useful analytic technique, because "absences can provide a basis for inquiring into what our 'revelations' constitute and how they are constituted."[114]

In contrast to Henoch, the WINPAC analysts typically focused on the technical details *present* in Curveball's reporting, details that fit existing assumptions about Iraqi bioweapons capabilities and a growing set of post–Cold War, technologically advanced bioweapons threats. The WINPAC analysts considered the absence of evidence only when UN inspection findings differed from Curveball's claims. In these instances, however, WINPAC analysts did not use the absence of evidence as a reason to investigate Curveball's claims further but as an unproblematic piece of evidence itself. In doing so, they failed to see how these assumptions and methods might cause them to overlook serious problems regarding Curveball and his mobile labs claims in ways that would erroneously shape their assessments.

In addition, CIA management's secrecy practices worked to privilege the analysts' perspective in the "knowledge" on the mobile labs that was conveyed to policymakers. In this way, Brian Balmer argues that secrecy does not merely function as a passive tool that obscures knowledge but can also be "an active tool that allows governments to define reality through the exercise of spatial-epistemic power."[115] In using the term *spatial-epistemic,* Balmer aims to emphasize how secrecy can create and reinforce different understandings of what is known about the real world in different places. For example, CIA management chose to keep hidden the internal debates about Curveball between its operators and analysts. But, as one State Department intelligence analyst comments, without Curveball's reporting "you probably could only honestly say that Iraq would be motivated to have a mobile BW program and that it was attempting to procure components that would support that."[116] Also, in the aftermath of the captured trailers in Iraq, both CIA and DIA management chose to use classification to squelch a contrarian contractor report. In contrast, the CIA and DIA released their own white paper on the unclassified intranet—a much more open and accessible space. The differences in how these different documents and arguments were made visible and available controlled public and policymaker understandings of the Iraqi mobile bioweapons threat.[117]

However, the secrecy practices in place during the Curveball episode were not the only possibilities available, because, as Balmer writes, the "boundaries between secrecy and openness are fluid and negotiable."[118] For starters, more exchange and interaction between UN inspectors and intelligence officials could have been constructed; the Directorate of Operations' European Division could have been brought in to access Curveball's reports from the beginning; debates over Curveball's reliability could have been shared with other intelligence analysts; the CIA's WINPAC analysts, in their analytic products to policymakers, could have laid out their methodological approach and determination of source evaluation in more detail. All of these were not issues that required a set level of secrecy for security reasons but could have been negotiated internally to allow for more sharing of expertise and knowledge on the purported Iraqi mobile bioweapons capability. This conclusion does not imply that secrets are not valuable or that information sharing is the one-size-fits-all solution for intelligence assessments. Rather, this case illustrates the importance of paying attention to the sociotechnical environment of intelligence collection and analysis.[119]

In the Iraqi mobile bioweapons case, the value placed on human intelligence, other "secrets," and different secrecy practices fragmented information and expertise related to evaluating an Iraqi mobile bioweapons threat. This fragmentation, however, not only excluded certain kinds of information but also worked to generate alternative worlds of knowledge that privileged a growing, diffuse, technologically advanced Iraqi bioweapons threat. In addition, these secrecy practices, in play with other CIA organizational practices such as current intelligence reporting and the balkanization of expertise, further compounded the assessment of Curveball and his claims. The examination of these practices and how they combine illustrates the importance of looking at grassroots-level work practices within a larger institutional context in order to understand how knowledge in intelligence collection and analysis is produced with important technical, material, and social dimensions.

PART FOUR

ALTERNATIVE ANALYTIC SOLUTIONS

A New Knowledge Model for Bioweapons Intelligence Assessments

Since the end of the Cold War, the September 11 attacks, and the aftermath of the Iraq intelligence failures, the U.S. intelligence community has focused attention and resources on initiatives to improve intelligence analyses of bioweapons threats. This chapter examines the efforts of three groups: (1) the CIA's Strategic Assessment Group; (2) the CIA / Department of Defense Iraq Survey Group; and (3) the Office of the Director of National Intelligence's Biological Sciences Experts Group. Although formed independently, all three were created to build new knowledge about bioweapons threats to improve intelligence analysis and policymaking. The chronological examination that follows shows how each group was conceptualized and institutionalized and reveals how each successive initiative failed to learn from the successes and shortcomings of its predecessors. While each of these efforts has some merit, they have individually and collectively missed the root of the combined knowledge-based problems outlined in this book: the problematic and pervasive technical frames and analytic practices underpinning U.S. bioweapons assessments. Until intelligence analysts address these more fundamental problems, they will continue to face blind spots in their assessments of bioweapons threats, which will likely lead to future intelligence failures.

After looking at these three initiatives in detail, I outline a new approach to improve the production of knowledge in bioweapons analyses—one drawing on the elements and principles of the co-production framework that stresses the need to consider how technical knowledge and social context are mutually constituted. This new analytic approach, which I call the Strategic Sociotechnical Assessment, builds on certain strengths of the three previous initiatives but also takes into account the important intertwining of social and technical issues that *should* constitute analyses of bioweapons threats. The "strategic" part of my model stresses the need for the development of long-term, in-depth research capabilities within the intelligence community to counter the dominance of current intelligence reporting that pervades intelligence analysis and has thus created thin understandings of security threats. My new analytic model does not guarantee against intelligence failure, for as former deputy director of national intelligence for analysis Thomas Fingar has argued, "Intelligence is not omniscience."[1] It does, however, suggest important steps forward to improve the practice of intelligence gathering and assessment, to the benefit of both analysts and policymakers.

The CIA's Strategic Assessment Group (2002)

In the late 1990s, the CIA launched a new initiative to improve the ability of its analysts to conduct in-depth, strategic-level assessments and to move away from an exclusive focus on current intelligence reporting. This initiative involved the creation of a new analytic unit called the Strategic Assessment Group (SAG), located within the Directorate of Intelligence's Office of Transnational Issues.[2] The SAG was the brainchild of senior CIA analyst James Harris, a Ph.D. economist and China expert interested in improving the CIA's ability to tap into outside expertise for its intelligence assessments. Harris was an important advocate for the SAG's relevance and importance to CIA management and received significant organizational resources and support in the SAG's early years. In addition to winning new personnel and funding, one former CIA analyst notes that Harris got the SAG great office space—a measure of importance within the bureaucracy.[3]

The SAG was established to conduct long-term, strategic assessments of specific security issues as well as a variety of "futures," or forecasting studies.[4] It consisted of approximately fifteen analysts with backgrounds in a variety of technical and social science disciplines. Each analyst was given a specific portfolio for research and allowed approximately one year to conduct a strategic or future-oriented assessment on that issue; the analyst could often propose a topic that interested him or her. The analysts were given resources to consult with a variety of outside experts for their work. At the end of the research period, they typically produced a report for the CIA and often held an unclassified workshop with outside experts on the topic.

In 2002, one technically trained analyst in the SAG chose to focus on the strategic implications of new developments in biotechnology and how they might affect bioweapons development. Although the analyst did not have training in the biological sciences, he had a master's-level education in both physics and Spanish (with a bachelor's degree in comparative literature) and had spent most of his intelligence career as a science and technology analyst conducting technically oriented assessments. He was recognized for his ability to write well and to work with highly technical subject matter in analytic projects. At the outset of this assessment of emerging bioweapons threats, he was interested in gathering data from various experts to create "a generalized road map to show where biotechnology is going in the next ten to fifteen years and, based on that, assess what would be the implications for biological weapons."[5] With this goal, the analyst was drawing on what I have called a biotech revolution frame, with its future orientation and assumed biotechnological trajectories as the conceptual starting point for how the assessment would be structured. Hence, he planned to produce an abstract, aggregated assessment about biotechnologies, not an examination of the varied specificities of how biotechnologies might work in context.

Although the analyst worked largely independently on the project, he consulted with bioweapons analysts from the CIA's Weapons, Intelligence, Nonproliferation, and Arms Control (WINPAC) unit. The analyst also contracted with the U.S. National Research Council's Board on Life Sciences to identify outside scientific experts relevant to the assessment and to help organize an unclassified workshop exploring the intersection of new biology and biological weapons. In developing the project, he asked the Board on Life Sciences to survey twenty-three scientific experts across emerging biotechnology areas such as RNA interference and gene splicing to assess "how they see developments in their field extending out over the next five, seven, ten years and what the implications would be for biological weapons."[6] In constructing his biotechnology road map, the analyst set up the survey of experts to gather information on abstract, fixed biotechnological trajectories and future-oriented threats. In addition to working with the Board of Life Sciences, he was able to take research trips to U.S. universities to consult with additional scientific experts. Throughout the course of the project, he used only technical expertise for the assessment; no social science or other relevant experts were brought in to help contextualize an understanding of the science and technology and its purported threats in practice and context.

As part of the research, the analyst held a two-day unclassified workshop at the National Science Foundation (NSF) in 2003, which included the experts identified by the Board on Life Sciences but also additional outside scientific and bioweapons policy experts, such as science advisor Joshua Lederberg and bioweapons analysts from WINPAC and other U.S. intelligence agencies. At the end of the first day of the workshop, the SAG analyst told the biological science experts in attendance, "For your homework tonight, go home and think about: What's the worst [bioweapons] thing that could happen? What's your biggest worry?"[7]

The next day, the SAG analyst collected the experts' responses and shared them with other members of the team. "Some of them I'll never forget. Some of them were really awful, right out of science fiction," said the analyst of the responses.[8] The experts had imagined bioweapons horror stories, the analyst said, carried out "by a Ted Kaczynski–type [Unabomber] graduate student," thereby shifting the enemy of concern from a specific actor in the real world to a more generic and unknown set of possible malefactors (that is to say, biological Unabombers).[9] As described in chapter 2, this change is consistent with popular biotechnological threat narratives that emerged from analysts and policymakers in the 1990s.

In reflecting on the main conclusions from the study and workshop, the SAG analyst emphasized two key points. One of them was the futility of trying to create a "biotechnology roadmap." As the analyst explained, the technical experts on the project advised that the biotechnology field "was growing so rapidly and it's so dynamic that you can't really predict what's going to happen even over a five-year period."[10] Here one sees reflected the potentially disruptive character of biotechnology as characteristic of the biotech revolution frame described in chapter 2. Yet the scientific experts assumed technological disruption as an enabler of bioweapons threats rather than also considering how such disruptions could frustrate the application of new biotechnological developments, as science and technology policy expert Paul Nightingale and others have noted.[11]

Despite this problem of technology prediction, the SAG analyst noted that the scientific experts consulted on the project advised with certainty that "if you look at the wave front of knowledge in life sciences with the genomics revolution, it is just going to keep expanding, and it's going to do it more and more quickly. You can expect the information revolution that's coming with genomics to just grow and expand."[12] In addition, the experts emphasized that once the plethora of new biological information was released and stored in a multitude of public scientific databases, there would be a "knowledge explosion, and it was going to be made accessible to the general public."[13] These remarks show that the scientific experts surveyed emphasized only codified knowledge in their assumptions of the diffusion and globalization of biotechnologies. The other knowledge component of biotechnology, tacit knowledge, was not mentioned in this discussion. On top of that, no consideration was given to how new biotechnologies might have different, localized mechanisms of technology diffusion and transfer. After the workshop, a short unclassified summary of the meeting, *The Darker Bioweapons Future,* was posted and made public on the internet in November 2003. In addition, a classified version of the report went to the White House.[14]

Initially, due to its penchant for secrecy, the CIA had planned to classify all of the report's findings, even though they were based largely on unclassified information. After some outside experts at the workshop complained about the need to classify the document, the CIA decided to produce an unclassified summary for release to the public. The unclassified summary concluded that "advances in biotechnology, coupled with the difficulty in detecting nefarious biological activity, have the potential to create a much more dangerous biological warfare threat."[15] The report offered the example of the artificial synthesis experiment of the poliovirus to make this point; it did not, however, mention the tacit knowledge issues required for the successful replication of that experiment or other technical complexities that constituted that work (see chapter 3).

The SAG analyst emphasized that the study was valuable for changing some of WINPAC's default analytic practices—at least for a while. As an example, the analyst explained that most of WINPAC's bioweapons assessments had been focused on traditional bioweapons agents and therefore that the WINPAC analysts had not kept up on the latest technological trends and how those might contribute to new kinds of security threats. He noted that the one-year study that constituted *The Darker Bioweapons Future* made WINPAC analysts aware of and attentive to potential threats from advanced bioweapons agents and that the project succeeded in getting some of WINPAC's analysts away from their daily production pressures to become involved, at least peripherally, in more long-term assessments that used outside expertise. With its involvement in the project, the SAG analyst noted that "WINPAC has extended a little bit beyond current intelligence and is looking at future trends and forecasting. I don't know how full fledged that is; it may just be one or two persons, but I know that they are doing that."[16]

The unclassified workshop that the SAG funded and conducted at the NSF also provided a forum for the CIA and other intelligence analysts, as well as civilian scientists and bioweapons experts who did not necessarily hold security clearances, to engage in unclassified discussions about bioweapons threats. In doing so, the SAG analyst noted that the study made WINPAC analysts more aware of the value of drawing on outside expertise instead of relying solely on information and expertise resident within the CIA's classified environment. This intellectual exchange also facilitated the release of most of the SAG's findings in an unclassified report—an important step forward in decreasing the secrecy surrounding some aspects of weapons-related assessments.

The CIA's decision to declassify some of the study's findings was not without its problems, however. Prior to its approval for open release, one of the outside experts involved in the study leaked *The Darker Bioweapons Future* to a nongovernmental organization to post on the internet. The former SAG analyst recalls: "We got into a lot of hot water for that, because you are never supposed to leak anything with CIA letterhead, that's a big no-no. Looking back, it probably wasn't a bad thing. I thought people should be aware of this potential threat. After that [report] there was a congressional report on it, and it raised people's awareness to the extent where they said, 'They're right, and we're not looking at this, and it could potentially be a real problem.'"[17] For this analyst, the primary benefit of presenting an unclassified report summary was that it served as a tool to raise awareness—especially among policymakers—of the security implications of advanced biotechnologies.

Commenting on the debate over the public release of some of the SAG's findings in *The Darker Bioweapons Future,* secrecy expert Steven Aftergood has made three important points: "First, it showed that secrecy is a primal instinct of at least some government agencies. Certainly nondisclosure is the default mode at CIA. Second, it showed that secrecy makes a poor fit with the deliberative process, particularly when a matter of public policy is involved. Finally, the dispute demonstrated that change is possible. There is enough plasticity even in the CIA to bring about a shift in policy and practice."[18] In making these observations, Aftergood noted that although intelligence organizations might initially default to secrecy, external pressure can create opportunities to reconsider standard practices. With this in mind, Aftergood argued, "The task at hand is to generate that pressure."[19] In this case, the pressure to release some information to the public apparently came from the outside experts who had participated in the project and workshop and had been allowed to review the unclassified version of the report.

The research that culminated in *The Darker Bioweapons Future* shows that the CIA made important strides in agreeing to give one analyst the time and support to conduct an in-depth, one-year strategic assessment on bioweapons threats utilizing outside, unclassified technical expertise. This effort, unfortunately, also led to erroneous, generalized conclusions about the threat posed by advances in biotechnology. Given the simple, uncontextualized assumptions about biotechnological trajectories, for example, the study failed to examine the more complex and contingent character underpinning certain types of scientific advances, such as artificial synthesis of the poliovirus. The effort also failed to address more fundamental and pervasive problems in analytic practice related to expertise, secrecy, and current intelligence reporting that were visible in the CIA's flawed Iraqi bioweapons assessments and that have characterized other intelligence assessments.

With respect to expertise, the SAG analyst drew only on technical expertise and circumscribed the project's focus to narrow technical aspects of advanced or emerging technologies. In adopting a biotech revolution frame to structure this study and its survey of technical experts, he assumed that biotechnologies develop in the abstract and have a fixed trajectory. Furthermore, the analyst did not seek out or factor into the assessment examinations a detailed understanding of the skills, disciplines, organization, management, and other localized social practices constituting the biological sciences and biotechnology. Thus, his conclusions largely followed the popular biotechnology threat narratives of the time and failed to provide a more nuanced and holistic understanding of the complex character of the effort needed to turn such technologies into weapons.

WINPAC analysts were not integrally involved in the design and implementation of the SAG study but rather served as part-time participants and consultants on the study and workshop. As a result, they were only peripherally involved in seeing the merit and experiencing the practice of working with outside experts on an unclassified research project. So although the SAG's study took place during the latter part of the internal CIA debates over Curveball (2002–2003), the analyst's findings do not appear to have convinced WINPAC's analysts to tap into additional sets of outside expertise (technical or otherwise) for their Iraqi mobile bioweapons assessments. In addition, the SAG's technical focus in its study—its consultations with technical experts only—and its presumed technological threat outcome might have merely reinforced WINPAC's existing assumptions about advanced Iraqi bioweapons capabilities.

Moreover, the project did nothing to change the CIA's existing analytic culture of sole-practitioner research projects and products. For this assessment, a single SAG analyst proposed and carried out the research. While the analyst drew on outside scientific expertise to inform his findings, he used no other sets of knowledge or interdisciplinary expertise to construct the study or shape the research project as it progressed. This lack is even more striking because the SAG itself, as a CIA analytic office, was made up of analysts with backgrounds in diverse fields, including economics, politics, science and technology, sociology, the military, and area studies. Although an analyst might collaborate with others in the SAG, it appears that in this study that was not the case. The analyst's work on the biotechnology assessment project, therefore, did little to change the individually driven analytic practices that structure much of the CIA's day-to-day analytic work.

In addition, the analyst's project continued the disconnect between the CIA's Directorate of Operations and the Directorate of Intelligence in bioweapons assessments. Because the project was not designed to draw on classified information, the assessment did not involve any consultation or collaboration with the Directorate of Operations; it used only open-source information. The problem with this practice is that future-oriented studies about advances in technology were being carried out without any inquiry into or intelligence collection on their connection with the technological capabilities or activities of existing state or terrorist groups or the actual likelihood that these technologies might be used as weapons in real-world contexts. Finally, the study, with its focus on obtaining outside scientific expertise, did not address the need to develop internal, in-depth analytic expertise within the CIA in particular subject areas relevant to the assessment. More specifically, like WINPAC analysts, the outside experts used in the assessments were only part-time participants and consultants on the study and workshop and were not fully integrated into the entire course of the study. The study, therefore, does not appear to have challenged the culture that privileges generalists within the CIA's analytic cadre.

This SAG also appears to have had limited impact on the CIA's current reporting culture in WINPAC's assessments. The CIA's bioweapons analysts were interested in staying current and would only pull themselves away from their work to meet with outside experts if they didn't have a daily deadline looming over their heads: "It [analysts' participation] depended on if analysts were being pressed for an assessment the next day and were really under pressure to finish it. . . . But if I could get them away for a day, they were happy to do it, because they were getting some of their questions answered too. Among BW analysts in the last couple of years, there was more awareness, and they would go to these things. But, if they were in a crunch, it was much harder to get them away."[20] According to this analyst, all WINPAC analysts did at the time was current intelligence reporting.[21] The SAG analyst noted that only one WINPAC bioweapons analyst was consistently involved as a "collaborator" on the project—and only part time at that. Thus, the strategic assessment on bioweapons threats was a small portion of the CIA's analysis on bioweapons threats compared to the much larger volume and predominance of current intelligence reporting at the CIA, including that related to Curveball. As a result, the study did little to change the priority and rewards of current intelligence reporting as standard analytic practice among WINPAC analysts.

The size disparity between the SAG and the CIA's current intelligence analytic units would soon pose challenges for the SAG's long-term viability. In 2004, the SAG's management changed, and the SAG analyst noted that the new manager "just didn't feel that strategic assessments were that important, and he felt that they were having a difficult time marketing them to the customer base."[22] As a result, the SAG, having lost an advocate within the CIA administration, was shut down in 2005. With the loss of its founder and key internal advocate, the SAG was unable to survive the CIA's priority on current intelligence reporting.

Some secrecy practices were improved. The SAG produced an unclassified summary and linked CIA analysts to outside experts without security clearances, but some problems remained. As an example, existing CIA security clearance practices prevented the SAG analyst from starting the project on time. The analyst who conducted the assessment was hired in 2001—from another agency within the U.S. intelligence community—to work on the project. Even with an active top-secret security clearance, it took the analyst one year after applying for the job to obtain the specific security clearances needed for the task. Furthermore, the official CIA report that resulted from the one-year study remained classified, even though it was based largely on unclassified information and only included one paragraph of classified information. Finally, although the WINPAC analyst who participated in the study did see unclassified information, this exposure was limited compared to the overwhelming majority of classified information WINPAC analysts regularly use in their current intelligence reports.

Table 8.1 summarizes the main features of the SAG's analytic approach, as viewed through a consideration of the frames and practices I have previously discussed. Even with some of the shortcomings outlined below, the SAG's work illustrated how organizational support for long-term, in-depth strategic assessments could be garnered within the CIA. It also showed that a mechanism could be created within the agency's analytic cadre to tap into outside expertise and that substantial input for intelligence assessments could be discussed with relevant outside experts in unclassified settings. Thus, the SAG's work and brief history illustrates some important elements to consider for the creation of new forms of knowledge for intelligence assessments.

The SAG's work also demonstrates how particular forms of knowledge emerge from the existing social context and practices of analysis. Because the SAG's analyst was working within the popular biotech revolution frame, he narrowly focused the research design on purely technical issues (without a contextualization of their social dimensions) and drew only on technical expertise. These outside experts were also working from a biotech revolution frame, using assumptions about the ease of biotechnology diffusion. It is not surprising, then, that the resulting abstracted technological assessment led to the logic of a "darker bioweapons future" with advances in biotechnology.

TABLE 8.1
Knowledge model for Strategic Assessment Group

FRAME
Biotech revolution frame: relies on codified knowledge and material factors in its understandings of science and technology
Assumes fixed trajectories to predict technological development and the bioweapons threat
Abstraction of technology from social context
Assumes potentially disruptive technologies
Assumes abstract enemies

PRACTICES
Expertise:
- Relied solely on technical experts and information; quantitative methods
- One analyst conducted project (sole practitioner model for analysis) but drew heavily on outside experts to inform thinking
- No focus on developing internal experts; maintained existing CIA practice of using generalists as analysts
- Did not work with CIA's Directorate of Operations
- No indication that outside expertise was drawn upon for other WINPAC assessments

Current intelligence reporting:
- Did not do current reporting, only strategic assessments; helped get one WINPAC analyst involved, part time, in analysis that was not driven by current intelligence
- Was given one year to conduct project and conducted external interviews as part of project with much longer time frame than current intelligence reports
- Difficult at times to pull relevant WINPAC analysts from other units away from their current reporting tasks to work on the project
- Effect on larger current intelligence reporting practices in WINPAC was marginal

Secrecy:
- Relied mostly on open-source information for analysis, including outside, unclassified expertise
- Clearance issues for analyst delayed start of project by one year
- Although project findings were intended to be kept classified, an unclassified executive summary was subsequently released to the public; illustrated ability of CIA to reconsider classification practices in specific cases
- Unclassified study did not seem to alter how WINPAC analysts privileged classified information in their work

The SAG, however, could have used a more socially infused technological framework and analytic practices. For instance, its analyst could have brought in a set of social science experts to provide analyses on the tacit dimensions of these new biological science techniques and emerging biotechnologies. These scholars could also have examined the specific conditions and social practices needed to make the new technologies standardized and usable in varying contexts. Had different sets of expertise and practices been brought to bear on the project, one could envision that a different kind of bioweapons future focused on the complexity and contingency of technical work might have resulted as part of this assessment.

The Iraq Survey Group (2003)

In contrast to and independent of the CIA's Strategic Assessment Group, the U.S. Department of Defense created a different kind of analytic unit to improve bioweapons intelligence after the Iraq War. At the start of the war, the U.S. government had deployed special military units to investigate suspect Iraqi locations for WMDs. In these initial efforts, the units inspected many sites but only with the aim of finding WMDs. These units were neither created nor sent out to develop an ongoing analytic assessment of the Iraqi WMD programs. As former UN and Iraq Survey Group inspector Rod Barton explains, "Everyone in the U.S. administration was so certain that weapons were there that the . . . instructions were simply to 'search and find.' "[23] But these early military investigations found no biological weapons or bioweapons activities in Iraq.[24]

With this lack of evidence and mounting pressure to locate the suspected weapons, the U.S. government undertook a new, large-scale, systematic collection of evidence with the goal of better understanding the prewar state of Iraqi WMD programs. To do this, the U.S. Department of Defense created a new investigative unit, the Iraq Survey Group (ISG), an international team of more than one thousand personnel, including military, collection, analysis, and support staff, organized jointly by the Pentagon and the CIA. From June 2003 until September 2004, the ISG carried out an assessment of Iraqi WMD stockpiles, expertise, and other related infrastructure.

The ISG, led by a U.S. military commander, used its unique blend of assets to conduct a new and more extensive investigation of Iraq's WMD programs. Analytic and collection staff included specialists on Iraq and WMD issues from the U.S. government, the United Kingdom, and Australia; several analytic staff members were former UN inspectors. In addition, the ISG had dedicated linguists and debriefers who could conduct in-depth interviews with Iraqi civilians and detainees. The CIA director provided intelligence collection and analytic resources to the ISG and appointed former UN weapons inspector David Kay as special advisor for Iraqi WMD to provide key direction to the WMD investigation. From the outset, the ISG's focus was to put the Iraqi WMD-related findings into a larger political-military context.[25] Therefore, compared to the SAG, the ISG had a larger and more diverse set of experts and analytic resources, organized into teams, at its disposal. In addition, the ISG's analytic approach moved away from the early military-led focus on finding specific weapons materials to a more in-depth, contextualized approach to assessing Iraq's WMD programs.

From the outset, the ISG had three key staff members dedicated to Iraqi bioweapons assessments; they were based in Iraq during most of the fifteen-month investigation. Two of the staff members were CIA bioweapons analysts, one of whom was involved in some of the CIA's prewar WINPAC assessments of the Iraqi mobile bioweapons labs. The third core member was Hamish Killip, a British UN weapons inspector who had conducted fifty bioweapons inspections in Iraq during the 1990s and had worked in the British biodefense program. Later, former UN weapons inspector Rod Barton and another CIA WINPAC bioweapons analyst were added to the effort. In total, the bioweapons team included five or six core staff members at any given time. In addition, several analysts from the CIA and other U.S. intelligence agencies with some relevant biological or Iraqi background knowledge served on the bioweapons team for one- or two-month rotations.

Maintaining the entire bioweapons team over the course of the investigation, however, was difficult. Although the CIA honored Kay's requests for specific expertise, he sometimes had to push the CIA to provide these individuals. Other times, some members of the bioweapons team would be called back to their home offices after serving in Iraq for only a few months.[26] Kay also noted that after the war, "the hunt for WMD was not the primary priority for the IC [intelligence community]. . . . A heavy element was recruiting Iraqis who would be continuing agents for the U.S., and WMD was just sort of an afterthought."[27] Although CIA management initially promised Kay all the resources necessary for his investigations, this promise proved short-lived. As Kay recalls, "That deal lasted until I got on the airplane to Baghdad. And [then] everything became a constant battle for people, and I would try to embarrass the heads of regional [CIA] agencies on videoconferences in which the [CIA] director was involved by saying they refused to send people, and I've got openings here and I need them."[28] In addition, as the Iraqi insurgency problem emerged, Kay found that some CIA analysts and other resources would be taken off the investigation and redirected to increase intelligence collection and analysis on the growing violence. Thus, over the course of the investigation, the composition of the bioweapons team and its available resources varied, posing challenges for the team's assessment work.

Within a few weeks after the war ended, the ISG was involved in evaluating the suspected mobile bioweapons trailers captured by U.S. military forces in Mosul and Erbil. The ISG's approach to assessing the trailers differed from that taken by WINPAC analysts, who had only consulted internal technical experts and Curveball about the trailers, and the U.S. Defense Intelligence Agency, which had selected an independent team of scientific experts to assess the trailers. Instead,

Kay—influenced by the deadlocked arguments on the conflicting technical interpretations of the trailers within the U.S. intelligence community—decided against another technically focused assessment.[29] He also determined that he wasn't going to follow the early postwar military approach, which had been to try to track down the list of over nine hundred potential WMD targets as a way to locate additional mobile labs for confirmation. As Kay explains, "The military's approach was to go and look at these targets and literally open the door—'Is there any WMD in here?' If no, then conclude. That's fine if you have labeled WMD facilities, and if they have not been looted or bombed, but I never saw any facilities that either had not been thoroughly looted or bombed, so I said, 'We are not running around the country, opening doors and looking to see if we can find WMD' . . . the 'Where's Waldo' type of approach."[30]

Instead, the ISG used what Kay has called an "intelligence approach" centered on a more contextual way of assessing the mobile labs and focused on the social and technical aspects of the purported trailers: "If WMD existed, it required people, and these ranged from really bright scientific people, to guns, gates, guards, and drivers. And so, we'll go looking for them. And so, you'd look at people, and you'd look at components, and then, of course, if you got information that said something is somewhere, then you'd definitely go in and look."[31] Thus, Kay's approach started out with a people-centered component that would help target further collection and analysis efforts in the assessment. Kay explained the utility of dedicating significant efforts to that part of the assessment: "If you run down all the people you know and all the people that they know, and everyone tells you a reasonably consistent story, you've got a basis for drawing a conclusion."[32] Instead of focusing on the purely material or technical aspects of bioweapons capabilities, Kay included a significant effort to investigate the human dimension of the suspected mobile labs.

As a result, to evaluate the captured trailers, the ISG's bioweapons team focused on evaluating Curveball as a source. As Kay describes, "We went after the source of information and then tore it apart . . . either of two ways. . . . If Curveball turned out to be absolutely golden and you proved that, then you had another basis to look at the [captured] trailers. But if Curveball turned out to be a pure fabricator, then those trailers, based on his information, were likely to be something else, because he didn't describe anything he knew about [directly]. . . . The trailer issue was entirely based, as it turned out, on one person—this guy called Curveball. So, instead of arguing about whether these trailers were this or that, let's go after Curveball."[33] In many ways, this focus on interrogating Curveball as a human source resembled the approach that the CIA's Directorate of Operations officials Tyler Drumheller and Margaret Henoch had advocated to WINPAC analysts and CIA management before the war.

Because Curveball was sequestered in Germany, the ISG bioweapons team worked to verify his identity through his family and friends in Iraq by sending out individuals or small, nondescript teams for interviews. As Kay explains, "You had to go and find where he worked. And the records for that particular site had been looted, but we recovered some, so we had to go through the records to reconstruct his personnel file, and then you had to go find the people he worked for and interview them. So that period took well over a month."[34] In conducting more than sixty interviews with Curveball's family, friends, colleagues, and acquaintances, the bioweapons team found that his personal and work history didn't reflect his earlier intelligence reporting. Kay notes that "part of his personal history started to fall apart; he wasn't who he said he was."[35] From the interviews, the ISG learned that Curveball had been a poor engineering student and had held low-level technical jobs. More significantly, the ISG learned that he had already been fired from a site by 1995, when he alleged the mobile bioweapons program had started in Iraq, and that he had been out of Iraq for substantial stretches during periods when he claimed to have been working on a mobile bioweapons lab. Also, interviews with some of Curveball's relatives and colleagues depicted him as a "congenital liar," a "con artist," and a "rat."[36]

In addition to these personal interviews, Kay's teams also conducted on-the-ground inspections to verify the information Curveball had given to German intelligence. Kay says that when "you went to the physical sites he had described . . . you realized that the stuff that he had described that was so compelling to the Powell [UN] case was not there . . . insides of buildings that did not exist and had never existed in the building, [nor] doorways he described. . . . Walls had moved."[37] So none of Curveball's intelligence reporting held up to the ISG's on-the-ground inspections. These findings were consistent with what UN inspectors had concluded from their on-the-ground investigations during the months leading up to the 2003 war—findings that WINPAC analysts had ignored. Even with the increasing level of violence from the growing Iraqi insurgency, the ISG conducted the bulk of its interviews and investigations on the Curveball mobile labs case within roughly a three-month period.

In addition to its focus on evaluating Curveball as a source, the ISG also assessed the plausibility of an alternative explanation for the captured trailers—hydrogen production for military use. Although WINPAC analysts had originally dismissed this possibility in an early, unclassified postwar white paper, Kay chose to take another look at the evidence. Once again, Kay decided to do a historical study of Iraq's efforts to acquire hydrogen production capabilities, instead of merely making another technical assessment. Thus, the ISG's bioweapons team learned that Iraq had used mobile hydrogen production units to supply hydrogen gas for weather balloons to artillery units on the field.[38] As Kay explains, "Turns out that in the '80s they [Iraqis] had bought a Swiss system for hydrogen production and the system had essentially corroded from nonuse. But someone [Iraqi] had come up with the idea of instead of buying a new system and trying to get it through UN sanctions, why don't they produce their own? And it had been part of the corrupt military production process, so it really wasn't done [so] much because the military wanted it as much as the people who were doing the production could get money from doing it."[39] Interestingly, the hydrogen production history resembles other Iraqi procurement efforts for legitimate purposes. As described in chapter 7, UN inspectors learned that Iraq had developed its own mobile food testing laboratories and food production kitchens to meet legitimate military needs in the field and overcome civilian losses from the extended coalition bombing campaigns and procurement problems resulting from UN sanctions.

In addition, from the historical study and interviews, Kay discovered some resonant internal sociopolitical dimensions of Iraqi government life that proved helpful in understanding Iraqi WMD activities: not only had Iraq developed indigenous mobile hydrogen production systems, but during the 1990s, rampant internal corruption had become a pervasive aspect of Iraqi government activities, undermining the ability of the Iraqi government to devote necessary attention and resources to WMD activities. Thus, the Iraq Survey Group dedicated a significant portion of its work to understanding the connections between the financial and political state of Saddam's regime and the financing of his WMD programs. Although UN inspectors had noted the corruption before the 2003 war, their narrow analytic focus on material and technical accounting did not offer a mechanism for incorporating these observations and anecdotes into their weapons assessments. The ISG, with its expanded frame of analysis and resources, was equipped to explore these broader dimensions shaping Iraqi WMD development. Its experience illustrates how in-depth interviews about the broader context of sociopolitical life, in conjunction with weapons assessments, elucidated the detrimental effect of political corruption on Iraqi weapons development.

Through historical research, the ISG's bioweapons team was also able to establish that the location in Mosul where one of the captured trailers had been found was indeed a site that had produced trailers for Iraqi hydrogen production. Armed with this information, the ISG was then able to compare the available technical information about the putative bioweapons trailers to Iraqi hydrogen production processes; the ISG found them to be consistent. At the end of this extensive inquiry, which included social, technical, and on-the-ground contextual evaluations, the ISG concluded that hydrogen production, *not* mobile bioweapons production, was the most consistent and likely explanation for the captured trailers.[40]

The ISG had substantial resources at its disposal (if not consistent personnel) as well as the benefit of military occupation of the area under investigation, yet it still worked in a difficult, violence-laden, postwar environment. Nevertheless, its bioweapons team was able to conduct extensive research, interviews, and on-site investigations using few people and within only a few months.

The ISG differed from the CIA's Strategic Assessment Group in some important respects. First, although the ISG may have started out with expectations of finding hidden Iraqi biological weapons, some members of its bioweapons team grew skeptical, as on-the-ground investigation and in-depth interviews suggested a different picture. Instead of continuing to accept the prevailing threat frame, which had assumed an advanced, covert Iraqi mobile bioweapons capability, some members of the ISG began to question this assumption and to look for alternative understandings of Iraq's prewar bioweapons capabilities. This shifting of frame allowed the ISG team to consider and seek out other, nontechnical sets of evidence in order to shape its collection, analysis, and evaluation efforts. Beyond that, Kay's approach—which rejected a purely material, technical focus and included in-depth interviews and an understanding of the social context surrounding Curveball and his reporting—opened up new lines of inquiry and information. Thus, the ISG's qualitative interviews with Iraqis were not merely anecdotal data but a dedicated methodological effort that actively sought, evaluated, and integrated new data with other types of classified and unclassified information to obtain a more rigorous and holistic understanding of Iraq's bioweapons efforts. This change underscores the importance of having a leader, such as David Kay, who was able and willing to stimulate and sustain new forms of analysis that combined social and technical considerations.

In terms of analytic practice, the ISG also benefited from its ability to work not merely as sole practitioners but also in teams organized to share and develop new knowledge. Although varying in composition, the teams were composed of a variety of experts in intelligence collection and analysis, who often worked side by side in Iraq.[41] The ISG was given access to both classified and unclassified data for its assessments. Former UN weapons inspectors were key members of the team and provided important historical and on-the-ground understandings of Iraq's past bioweapons activities. Because most core members of the bioweapons team had technical backgrounds, the ISG's expertise was mostly technical. Although the team also had linguists at its disposal, it would have benefited from additional sets of nontechnical expertise. As mentioned earlier, the team also included some CIA analysts who had been involved in WINPAC's prewar Iraqi mobile bioweapons intelligence assessments, but even these largely technical specialists, given the mandate, attention, and resources, were able to use a new frame and analytic practices focused on the social context of weapons development when that became necessary. As a result of these changes, new understandings of Iraqi WMD efforts emerged.

There remained, however, several challenges that posed problems for the ISG's work. For example, the bioweapons team faced instability in its staffing. In addition, some of the CIA analysts who worked on the bioweapons team were involved in the current intelligence reports on Curveball. For some time thereafter, these analysts were reluctant to concede the mounting evidence suggesting problems with Curveball's reporting and the CIA's mobile bioweapons assessments.[42] Debates about these issues ensued between these analysts and others on the bioweapons team and ultimately led to one of the CIA's WINPAC analysts quitting during the ISG's investigations.[43] In addition, there were also problems in the coordination of interviews and other parts of the investigations that hindered some of the ISG's work.[44] Hence, after the ISG submitted its findings, the team was disbanded; it was set up only to provide an in-depth assessment of one particular state's bioweapons activities for a set period of time. After its mission was completed, the team's collective expertise and unique knowledge were soon scattered. Support for and awareness of the benefits of a teamwork approach to analysis disappeared after the team finished its report.

Due to the ISG's mandate, the pressures placed on it to provide current intelligence reporting were minimal. Although Kay regularly provided updates to the CIA and other government officials about the ISG's ongoing findings, the team itself was focused on in-depth analysis of Curveball and the claims of an Iraqi mobile bioweapons capability. For three months, the analysts collected and assessed new information that pertained to a number of social and contextual factors relevant to the mobile lab assessment. The final report of the assessments was produced more than a year after the investigations had begun. Although the ISG analysts were under pressure to find information related to Iraqi WMDs, this pressure led the team to seek out new information sources and methodologies for understanding Iraq's bioweapons programs—methodologies that would yield significant new data and insights into Iraq's weapons activities within only a few months. In contrast to the passive analytic practices of current intelligence reporting, ISG team members were actively shaping collection strategies for their analysis and combining a variety of different sources to produce new knowledge in their final assessments on particular Iraqi WMD targets.

As part of its new analytic approach, the ISG drew on both classified and unclassified information. Instead of merely accepting the secret information that Curveball had provided about the purported Iraqi mobile labs, Kay chose to interrogate Curveball as a source. To do so, the ISG went beyond relying on classified reports in classified databases and classified satellite imagery and instead pursued interviews and on-the-ground investigations in Iraq, which yielded an important social and historical context in which to assess Curveball's "technical" claims; through this new analytic work, Curveball's claims were ultimately determined to be false.

Table 8.2 summarizes the main facets of the Iraq Survey Group model. Key elements in the ISG's creation of knowledge included its ability to work as a team; to seek out new information and methodologies; and to integrate a variety of technical and nontechnical, classified and unclassified information. The ISG was given special resources (both financial and personnel), and its work was conducted in a unique military-led postwar context. But an examination of how the ISG was able to produce more accurate knowledge about Iraq's bioweapons program highlights the importance of the new analytic frames and practices in the team's work and final conclusions. Although launched as an independent effort, the ISG work

TABLE 8.2
Knowledge model for Iraq Survey Group

FRAME
Partly biosocial due to leadership mandate: relies on understanding broader social, contextual factors shaping Iraqi bioweapons development

PRACTICES
Expertise:
- Mostly technical
- Operations and analytic staff worked together closely during assessments
- Team included experienced UN weapons inspectors
- Team had available Arabic linguists and other support staff
- Team effort
- At times, instability of staffing; some CIA staff were "experts" on the Curveball reporting that posed problems for the assessments

Current reporting:
- In-depth research conducted over a few months; final assessment spanned one year
- Although Iraq Survey Group provided regular reports to U.S. government, it was also given time to evaluate all of its investigation efforts for a final assessment

Secrecy:
- Used both classified and unclassified information for its assessments
- Published an unclassified report of more than 1,000 pages

was a significant improvement over that of the SAG, in that it employed what could be considered a biosocial frame, involved more types of multidisciplinary experts who worked in teams, and largely avoided current intelligence reporting pressures. Also, the ISG was able, for a period of time, to draw WINPAC analysts out of their offices at CIA headquarters and conduct in-depth, on-the ground empirical research instead of merely receiving intelligence reports passively to form assessments. Finally, the ISG's work culminated in a detailed, unclassified report of over one thousand pages.

The Biological Sciences Experts Group (2006)

In November 2006, the National Counterproliferation Center within the Office of the Director of National Intelligence established the Biological Sciences Experts Group (BSEG) in order to improve the intelligence community's access to biological expertise.[45] The idea for the BSEG grew out of high-profile, public recommendations from the 2005 WMD Commission,[46] the National Academy of Sciences, and the U.S. House of Representatives Subcommittee on Prevention of Nuclear and Biological Attack of the Committee on Homeland Security.[47] In making their recommendations, each of these entities focused on the growing bioweapons threat from emerging biotechnologies.

In its report to President George W. Bush, the WMD Commission devoted a special section to the future threats posed by biological weapons, which the commission called "the greatest intelligence challenge."[48] The report warned that "in the near future, the biotechnology revolution will make even more potent and sophisticated weapons available to small or relatively unsophisticated groups."[49] The WMD Commission also cited the problem of "limited interaction between technical experts and political analysts," which leads to "a poor job of matching capabilities with intent to develop realistic biological attack scenarios for state and non-state actors alike."[50] Curiously, however, it failed to focus on this disconnect between technical and nontechnical forms of knowledge, centering its attention instead on the lack of technical expertise and technical outreach.[51] In its recommendations, the WMD Commission urged the White House to create "an elite, external biological science advisory group that would consist of America's leading life science experts. The group would be tasked to examine and advise the intelligence community on biological threats."[52] The WMD Commission chose to focus on the deficit of technical expertise in defining the bioweapons intelligence problem rather than consider how other expertise issues (lack of nontechnical, operational, and communal expertise) could also create blind spots and errors in assessments.

On Capitol Hill, Congress turned its attention to the science-related recommendations in the WMD Commission report. Representative John Linder, chairman of the Subcommittee on Prevention of Nuclear and Biological Attack of the Committee on Homeland Security, organized a set of congressional hearings to learn more about the bioweapons threats from the scientific community and the U.S. government's response to them. For the first hearing, which was aptly titled "Bioscience and the Intelligence Community" and was held in November 2005, the subcommittee asked reputable technical experts in the life science and biodefense communities to speak. After this hearing, Linder's staff summarized what it saw as the primary take-home messages: (1) the critical need for building a "robust, sustained and effective capability in the life sciences within the intelligence community"; and (2) the need for a "cadre of trained, motivated and educated personnel who can raise awareness and knowledge throughout the bioscience community of intelligence and the role it can play."[53] Linder's staff wrote a memo reiterating the need for more technical expertise in intelligence: "The intelligence community is only able to discern or anticipate a potential bioterrorist threat from seemingly innocuous research when intelligence analysts have a firm grasp of cutting edge bio-sciences and know what to look for. This knowledge base, unfortunately, does not lie in the intelligence community, but is based in the academic and research life science and engineering communities worldwide."[54] Linder and his staff emphasized the problem of emerging, cutting-edge biotechnologies and the lack of requisite scientific expertise to evaluate those technologies with respect to terrorist activities. No other types of expertise, methodologies, or other organizational problems were recognized as valid or important in addressing intelligence challenges with respect to bioweapons threats.

Then, in January 2006, the Committee on Advances in Technology and the Prevention of Their Application to Next Generation Bioterrorism and Biowarfare Threats, under the auspices of the U.S. National Research Council and the Institute of Medicine, published an influential report: *Globalization, Biosecurity, and the Future of the Life Sciences*. In this report, the committee examined future global scientific trends in biotechnology that could be developed into potential bioweapons threats. The committee warned, "It is clear that today's capabilities in the life sciences and related technologies have already changed the nature of the biothreat 'space.' The accelerating pace of discovery in the life sciences has fundamentally altered the threat spectrum."[55] One can see that the committee was drawing on the disruptive character of biotechnology as embodied in what I have called the biotech revolution frame. In the committee's report, the bioweapons problem was framed by technical experts—as it was in the Strategic Assessment Group's study.

Thus, it is not surprising that this committee emphasized the need for more technical knowledge to inform U.S. intelligence assessments. Moreover, it called for the establishment of an independent science and technology advisory group for the intelligence community to help it produce open and classified reports.[56]

In May 2006, Linder's staff organized a second, follow-up hearing on bioweapons issues that brought in high-level U.S. government officials with intelligence and counterterrorism responsibilities to discuss what the U.S. government was doing to address the shortcomings identified in the first hearing.[57] Ambassador Kenneth Brill, head of the National Counterproliferation Center, described what he saw as the most important issues facing the intelligence community regarding biological threats: "The key questions for the intelligence community are primarily *not* highly technical in nature. . . . We must determine if a state adversary has the intent to establish, maintain, or acquire a BW program, because a country of concern typically will also have dual-use capabilities in those areas. . . . Focusing on technology alone will not answer these key questions . . . it can lead to speculation, based on nightmare scenarios that are not necessarily grounded in reality."[58] Strangely, however, in talking about his center's new initiatives, Brill's testimony primarily focused on technically based responses to this bioweapons problem.[59] He described the creation of a new position—senior advisor for biological issues—within the National Counterproliferation Center; biologist Lawrence Kerr was appointed to the position in April 2006. To increase biological science expertise within the intelligence community, Kerr considered two different approaches: (1) improving internal competence and organization on bioscience issues within the intelligence community; and (2) creating an external science advisory group to bring in bioscience expertise. Opting to focus the bulk of his efforts on the latter, Kerr set up the BSEG as "the intelligence community's first broadly focused biological science advisory group."[60]

Throughout 2006, Kerr met with various members of the U.S. intelligence community to obtain suggestions for how to structure this new advisory group. The BSEG was modeled after another external science advisory group, Measurements of Earth Data for Environmental Analysis (MEDEA), which was established in 1993 to bring both academic and intelligence knowledge to bear on understanding the science behind global environmental concerns.[61] Approximately seventy scientists were recruited from academia, the private sector, and relevant government agencies, and they worked to compile a list of critical environmental issues and the technical data needed to address them. Because they had security clearances, these scientists were able to receive highly classified briefings to help them determine what archived classified data might be useful for environmental research. The briefings also helped inform the scientists about how existing classified satellites and other technological systems could be targeted to collect new environmental data.[62]

The BSEG's mission resembled that of MEDEA and the CIA's Strategic Assessment Group, but with some important differences in how it would produce knowledge. The BSEG consists of a cadre of external life science and bioweapons experts from universities, companies, and nongovernment organizations.[63] These experts serve as independent consultants to the National Counterproliferation Center; they are appointed through the National Intelligence Council (NIC) Associates Program.[64] Although contracts are renewed on an annual basis, BSEG consultants are expected to serve at least three years. An executive secretariat with a dedicated classified budget was designated within the Office of the Director of National Intelligence to support the BSEG's work. Thus, it is separate from any particular U.S. intelligence agency, although it was established to provide scientific advice on biological issues to all such agencies. An internal steering group for the BSEG, consisting of various representatives of the intelligence community, has been established to advise Kerr on specific issues the community would like the BSEG to review.

The BSEG consists of a core group of approximately thirty-four technical experts and a larger network of forty scientists.[65] Because there are a variety of subspecialties within the life sciences (and related technologies), the larger BSEG network is designed for future growth to allow the intelligence community access to a greater pool of technical expertise as the need arises. The BSEG was created as a dynamic entity that will change and grow as the needs of the intelligence community and developments in science and technology advance. To help recruit new members and raise awareness of the importance of bioscience expertise to the intelligence community, Kerr has given public talks to large scientific audiences and visited several universities across the United States.[66] The BSEG core members meet bimonthly, with network members drawn in for larger, annual BSEG meetings.

As with other NIC associates, BSEG members are offered confidentiality regarding their participation; individual member names are publicly released only with that member's permission. Unlike many intelligence activities, the name and existence of the BSEG is not classified. Yet, like Project Jefferson (see chapter 2), much of the BSEG's activities are conducted at highly classified levels (Top Secret, specific code word classification, and use of facilities that can work with Sensitive Compartmented Information). Although some of its products have been unclassified, they have not been made publicly available. Currently, BSEG members are not required to undergo a polygraph examination, but this could change, depending on the types of projects undertaken.

Any agency of the U.S. intelligence community may suggest to the National Counterproliferation Center specific topics or issues for exploration by the BSEG. From these submissions, Kerr prioritizes specific topics or issues and assigns them to specific BSEG members or to groups of members. The BSEG charter states that members may be assigned the following types of projects:

- Supporting intelligence customers in the design of scientific/technical experimental protocols, intelligence analyses, or collection methodologies against biological threat agents (BTA), biological warfare agents, and/or state and non-state actors which do or may pose a threat to the United States;
- Advising on strategies to improve the execution, or interpretation of results of experimental protocols, analysis, and collection against the aforementioned agents and/or actors;
- Undertaking technical assessments / performance review of the intelligence community's scientific/technical programs, analytical products, and collection methodologies against the aforementioned agents and/or actors;
- Address any other issues as requested by the National Counterproliferation Center or intelligence community departments or agencies.[67]

According to a government official familiar with the BSEG, for example, if the intelligence community were to capture a toxin recipe from al-Qaeda and would like to determine whether it posed a threat, BSEG members could be asked (1) to provide technical advice on how to design an experiment to replicate the toxin recipe; (2) to help the intelligence community interpret the results from the experiment; or (3) to serve as independent reviewers of the finished intelligence experiment.[68] Another official explained that the "BSEG has value in pointing analysts to open sources related to science and technology and what is going on in an open, vibrant and globalized S&T base."[69]

In comparing and contrasting the BSEG with the other two knowledge models discussed in this chapter, one can see several benefits and shortcomings of this approach. The establishment of the BSEG has made new, in-depth scientific expertise available to the U.S. intelligence community. This new structure has made it easier for CIA analysts to identify and call on specific outside technical experts to help assess the security implications of new biological developments. In part, the BSEG is attempting to play a role similar to that of the U.S. Army's Harry Diamond Lab, which served the CIA in the 1960s by providing in-depth expertise on technological, weapons-related issues. The difference, however, is that BSEG is not an established entity within the executive branch but merely a set of independent consultants (or contractors) who work only part time on discrete projects assigned to them by the National Counterproliferation Center. And, unlike at the Harry Diamond Lab, the CIA does not pull analysts out of the Agency to interact with technical experts for extended periods, nor are BSEG members assigned to work alongside intelligence analysts on specific intelligence projects. In practice, the BSEG's operation is similar to that of the SAG, in which outside technical experts are brought in on a part-time, peripheral basis.

With the Biological Sciences Experts Group, therefore, although scientific expertise may be applied to a given problem, it is not resident within specific intelligence agencies on a long-term basis. In the BSEG model, it remains in entities outside the CIA or other intelligence agencies and is used in specific, bounded briefings to the intelligence community. As a result, the BSEG does little to inculcate within the CIA and its management a culture that values experts resident within the Agency. Instead, the structure of the BSEG may continue to foster a preference for generalists and low-level technical experts for bioweapons assessments within the CIA. Also, because BSEG experts are not involved in specific intelligence assessments, it is unclear how their technical expertise is used in day-to-day, current intelligence work or assessments. It is likely that the BSEG has done little to change the current intelligence reporting culture that dominates the time and attention of bioweapons analysts throughout the intelligence community.

In focusing its efforts on security threats from the purely material and technical dimensions of new technologies, the BSEG works largely within a biotech revolution frame.[70] Also, it consists only of technical experts and conducts only technical reviews. In this way, it does not draw on social science methodologies or other information sources and tools to help shape its technical understandings about emerging biological threats. Although it does conduct its work using both individuals and groups, the teams are all comprised of technical experts; no other multidisciplinary, nontechnical types of expertise are brought to bear on the analyses. As a result, the BSEG's work privileges the authority of technical information over other kinds of information and expertise, in the same way that the SAG worked. Interestingly, BSEG members are hired through the NIC Associates Program, which was originally designed to bring multidisciplinary (typically social science) expertise to the CIA. But there is no indication that historians, social scientists, or relevant nontechnical experts have been incorporated into BSEG membership. Its leaders largely see the NIC Associates Program as a contracting mechanism to bring in technical experts, not as a source of valuable multidisciplinary expertise and different methodological approaches to study bioweapons threats.[71]

In its charter, the BSEG does have the mandate to conduct in-depth technical reviews, although as yet, it appears not to have done so. But it is not clear how such reviews would subsequently be used by CIA analysts. If the BSEG were to conduct in-depth research, for instance, then CIA analysts could continue to focus their time on current intelligence reporting rather than on conducting their own long-term strategic assessments. This result would be similar to the problem that the SAG encountered in its bioweapons assessments. Because each BSEG project is discrete and not part of a long-term research strategy, moreover, CIA analysts in this current intelligence reporting mode might simply incorporate the BSEG results as another "dot" in the analysis without trying to construct a longer-term, more contextualized perspective of the threat from emerging biotechnologies beyond the technical feedback that the BSEG provides.

Finally, with respect to secrecy, the BSEG's composition of external advisors has helped open up the intelligence community's expertise to outsiders. Nevertheless, secrecy continues to surround the BSEG and its work. Its membership has not been publicly released, and it works at highly classified levels. In addition, the Office of the Director of National Intelligence denied FOIA requests in 2010 seeking the release of the BSEG's annual report, even though the denial was not based on classification concerns but on what seem to be privacy issues.[72] The BSEG's conduct is quite different from that of the SAG, which conducted unclassified assessments with outside experts and discussed perspectives on bioweapons threats in unclassified settings. The BSEG does little to challenge the notion of the inherent value of "secrets" in intelligence assessment; in fact, it likely reinforces this idea. Instead of physically bringing intelligence analysts out of their classified world (as the SAG tried to do), the BSEG may actually work to keep analysts inside their classified domains.

In this way, the BSEG seems to fit what John Cloud has called a "shuttered box" model of knowledge production in intelligence. In Cloud's model, "shutters" serve as portals that enable the movement of people, ideas, and other resources between classified and unclassified domains. Cloud argues, however, that these shutters are limited in that they do not provide unfettered access or communication between those domains: "The Shuttered Box therefore preserves the security of the classified realm."[73] The BSEG serves as a type of shutter, allowing the movement of unclassified, academic expertise into the intelligence community. Yet the movement of expertise only travels so far. Because BSEG members are not working alongside WINPAC or other technical analysts in the intelligence community, they are kept at a distance from the final deliberations and analyses produced using BSEG input.

Cloud also writes that the shuttered box "transforms or disguises the identities of the elements passing through it."[74] The secrecy that structures the BSEG obscures the identities of its members. These identities, however, are important for understanding the kind of knowledge the BSEG produces. An intelligence analyst who attends BSEG meetings has noted that many of its members have overlapping membership with other technical advisory committees, such as the Defense Intelligence Agency's BioChem 20/20.[75] As a result, this analyst observes that instead of having alternative sets of outside expertise coming to bear on intelligence, there is instead a redundancy of perspectives about bioweapons threats—ones focused on the biotech revolution frame.[76] The risk, this analyst states, is that "the two groups are seen as corroborative by senior military and political leadership in their analysis, yet they are, in fact, the same body."[77]

As described in chapter 7, there can be a generative effect of secrecy on the knowledge produced in these classified spaces. This secrecy can create segregated intellectual geographies of knowledge that enable the construction of abstract, fanciful threats that overestimate an enemy's technological interests and capabilities. Because the BSEG largely draws on the popular biotech revolution frame, relies on largely technical and material factors in its assessments, and conducts its work in highly classified environments, it would not be surprising to find that the knowledge it produces has the same shortcomings as that of the other groups discussed here: a lack of connection between abstract technical speculation and

TABLE 8.3
Knowledge model for BSEG

FRAME
Biotech revolution: focus on codified knowledge and material aspects of biotechnology for its assessments
PRACTICES
Expertise:
Relies solely on technical experts and technical/quantitative approaches; does not draw on other types of expertise
Multidisciplinary expertise applies only to different forms of scientific and technical expertise
Expert is currently not involved in assessments but rather listens to intelligence briefings and provides scientific advice based on those briefings; experts provide updated information to intelligence analysts on new science and technology developments that are arising globally
Current reporting:
Experts currently do not do in-depth, strategic assessments; unclear how expertise is incorporated, if at all, into current intelligence reporting documents
Secrecy:
All work is highly classified
No dedicated effort to bring CIA analysts outside of classified domain
No effort to bring outside technical experts to work on assessments directly

on-the-ground reality. Table 8.3 summarizes the primary characteristics of the BSEG's production of knowledge.

Conclusion: A New Sociotechnical Approach for Bioweapons Assessments

Each of these three models for improving bioweapons assessment addresses important issues related to the production of knowledge about bioweapons threats, including the need for analysts to draw on outside expertise and unclassified information, to move away from current intelligence reporting, and to consider nontechnical analytic approaches. But none goes far enough to improve bioweapons assessments within the CIA in a genuine or permanent way; an alternate approach is needed.

Moving beyond the purely cognitive dimensions of intelligence analysis, I argue that analysis also includes important discursive, social, and material factors that shape and are shaped by individual, organizational, and governmental practices.[78] These practices can distort what the cognitive "eye" sees and understands. In looking at material factors, moreover, I argue that even the raw materials of intelligence work (data, databases, satellites, simulations, reports) are constituted by and reflect important social aspects. For example, as noted in chapter 5, the information included in a final intelligence report is not all that has been collected clandestinely. A reports officer (a special type of operations worker) is responsible for editing information received from the field to a form sent to analysts; as such, important contextual information can be added or left out. Social relationships between the analysts and the reports officer can identify hidden or lost information that could be beneficial to the analysis. In addition, the databases used by analysts and collectors have a social origin that shapes their design and implementation and thus their use for analysis. These considerations highlight the importance for analysts to reflect on the variety of social dimensions involved in the production of knowledge for intelligence assessments and how they can shape conclusions about threats.

In order to improve intelligence analysis on bioweapons issues, there are useful elements to pull out from the three models discussed in this chapter, but they must be supplemented with additional changes that get at the heart of how weapons knowledge is produced within its social context at the individual, organizational, and governmental levels. To do this, I suggest a new approach I call *strategic sociotechnical assessment*: "strategic" because the intelligence community needs its own long-term, in-depth research capabilities; "sociotechnical" because it must look carefully at the co-production of social and technical factors in weapons development and at the social practices that structure technical analyses of weapons issues. In this alternate model, assessments would have an in-depth focus rather than the short, journalistically styled, time-dependent focus of current intelligence reporting.

To test this model and then introduce it to the intelligence community, I would suggest the formation of an experimental research group, the Strategic Sociotechnical Assessment Group (SSAG), within the Central Intelligence Agency. The SSAG would analyze a critical problem in existing bioweapons threats using this new approach, conduct in-depth research, and create new knowledge that would result in a team-generated set of judgments. Of course, the SSAG would receive the necessary institutional resources and authorities to conduct its work.

At the macro level, the SSAG would conduct red team analyses, specifically challenging the dominant sociotechnical frames and analytic practices that have hindered existing bioweapons assessments. For example, it would not rely solely on the popular biotech revolution frame and its associated technological narratives to conceptualize biotechnology and bioweapons threats but would also use the biosocial frame proposed in chapters 3 and 4. The biosocial frame would place an importance on understanding in a qualitative, microlevel fashion the social dimensions of scientific and technological work, including tacit knowledge and organizational and management styles; the translation and adaption of techniques and technologies to a local context; and relevant training and laboratory practices. Instead of assuming a globalized, diffused, homogenized set of threats, the SSAG would work to study bioweapons threats associated with specific people, in specific places, with specific materials, in particular social contexts, and with localized practices and to analyze how these various elements interact. Thus, the microlevel analytic practices would acknowledge the tension between social and technical factors.

The SSAG would also consider broader organizational work practices. Various intelligence practitioners have highlighted the importance of creating knowledge teams for analysis.[79] Carl Ford has proposed a new and useful analytic paradigm for the creation of new knowledge teams for intelligence assessments—organizing analysts under the concept of "problem teams." Ford's model begins by defining an intelligence assessment as a team effort focused on a specific issue; these problem teams would have the following characteristics:

- A few "cat drivers" to ride herd over the motley crew of curmudgeons, misfits, prima donnas, and the other Star Wars–like cast of characters essential for any creative [knowledge-driven] exercise. Keep in mind an assembly line in action; then build just the opposite.

- A shift in the basic organizing principle from the analyst to the problem. [Analytic] units would vary in size from a handful to in the hundreds. Some would function essentially as permanent operations, while others would come and go as problems were solved or found to no longer be relevant.
- Analytic leaders, as opposed to cat drivers, to organize and size the problem teams based on the scope and complexity of the problem being addressed.
- Similar to a military formation, the team would largely be self-sufficient and have command authority over the full range of expertise and capabilities necessary to fulfill its mandate (e.g., all source analysts, special source analysts, processors—signals intelligence, human intelligence, open source intelligence).[80]

The SSAG could be formulated through these principles in order to promote a creative, flexible, multidisciplinary knowledge environment with sufficient resources and authorities to conduct in-depth analysis on a particular bioweapons intelligence problem. Without describing it in academic terms, Ford is essentially using a co-production framework that emphasizes the importance of considering the intertwining of the social and the material in the production of knowledge.

In February 2005, the Intelligence Science Board also emphasized the importance of analogous interdependent work teams for intelligence analysis. Like Ford, this board advocated that members of such work teams would be "collectively responsible for a significant piece of analytic work—work that . . . can be larger in size and potential significance than usually is possible for a task performed by any single individual. Members of work teams bring their own special expertise to the work, of course, and over time evolve specialized team roles—but it is the team as a whole that produces and is accountable for the analytic product."[81] The report also proposes teams composed of different expertise and specialties, which can "foster the kinds of cross-functional exchanges that . . . result in unanticipated insights and syntheses."[82] Ford and the Intelligence Science Board both implicitly recognize the connection between the production of knowledge and the production of social order, but a more explicit connection is needed. Analysts (and their managers) must be pushed to think carefully about the social, material, and discursive elements embedded in individual and organizational work practices and their potential biases on weapons assessments. As intelligence practitioner Matthew Herbert writes, "Intelligence analysis is about coping with epistemic complexity."[83]

My proposed Strategic Sociotechnical Assessment Group would work to include a wide range of expertise within a small group dedicated to a particular issue. For instance, it would consist of a core of dedicated CIA Operations and Analytic personnel representing different functional and regional areas related to the issue as well as individuals with expertise and on-the-ground, practical experience relevant to the work, such as linguists, former UN inspectors, or former bioweapons scientists. The SSAG would also be expected, encouraged, and enabled to draw on other internal and external experts for short- or long-term consultations and contractual work as needed.

The SSAG's full-time core staff would be dedicated to the project for a minimum of one year in order to promote in-depth research and analysis. During this time, its members would not be subject to current reporting requirements, although excerpts of its ongoing work could be included in current intelligence reporting if a significant finding were made. The SSAG would use both classified and unclassified information for its assessments and would set aside regular time, both individually and collectively, to reflect on how various analytic practices might be shaping the work. As an example, it could periodically discuss and evaluate the various secrecy practices underpinning the classified information it was

TABLE 8.4
Knowledge model for Strategic Sociotechnical Assessment Group

FRAME
Biosocial

PRACTICES
Expertise:
- Team effort
- Draws on multidisciplinary expertise (operations/analytic, inside/outside, technical/social/contextual)
- Uses both qualitative and quantitative methodologies
- Considers the social dimensions of scientific and technological work (know-how, disciplines, management, organization, and so on)
- Given authority to shape some collection efforts
- Stability in staffing: core personnel are assigned to the team

Current reporting:
- Assembles group to work on an issue for one to two years
- Team is not subject to current reporting demands
- Significant findings could be incorporated into current intelligence reports

Secrecy:
- Uses both classified and unclassified information
- Work within classified and unclassified spaces; opportunities to go outside of the classified domain (field research, expert consultations, site visits) to develop knowledge about a problem

using for its work and how such practices might be shaping what it received. The SSAG would also be encouraged and given generous resources to work outside of classified spaces to conduct unique field research as part of the project, to have expert consultations, and to conduct site visits as necessary. Specially cleared outside experts would also be brought in as sources of complementary and independent knowledge but also as objective outsiders who might interrogate approaches and assumptions.

In July 2008, the Office of the Director of National Intelligence issued "Intelligence Community Directive Number 205 (ICD 205): Analytic Outreach," which charges intelligence analysts to "leverage outside expertise as part of their work."[84] To do so, analysts are expected to know the leading experts in their areas of expertise and to seek opportunities to engage openly with them to "explore ideas and alternative perspectives, gain new insights, generate new knowledge, or obtain new information." The directive recognizes the importance of moving analysts out of their classified domains to tap into valuable outside knowledge and relevant expertise and to challenge the erroneous groupthink that can occur in the closed worlds of intelligence. Thus, an intelligence directive already exists supporting analysts' work with outside experts.

This new model for assessment would aim to create a new kind of sociotechnical work unit within the CIA that would inject new types of discourse, frames for thinking about biotechnology, and work practices for assessing bioweapons threats (table 8.4). Over time, this approach could lead to an evolution of both individual and institutional work practices and norms shaping the way the CIA conducts its bioweapons assessments. If it were to prove successful, this new approach could serve as a catalyst beyond the CIA, to change the way other intelligence, government, and nongovernment analysts assess bioweapons issues. Such new forms of knowledge making would better account for the messy and contingent aspects that characterize weapons development by state or nonstate actors and would provide a more holistic assessment of bioweapons threats.

Conclusion

Through its use of social understandings of science and technology, this volume has illustrated the combination of technological frames and analytic practices at the individual, organizational, and national levels that have shaped U.S. bioweapons assessments and policymaking since the 1990s. These frames and practices have produced and reinforced a popular technological narrative about bioweapons threats that has emphasized a hidden, diffuse, and growing set of abstracted, technologically advanced enemies. The power of these frames and practices to shape analysis and policy comes from their integrated discursive, social, and material elements, which work synergistically to reify, construct, and reinforce the technical logics underpinning U.S. bioweapons assessments and their associated policy responses. These outcomes, however, have fallen short of providing an understanding of the more complex and diverse character of bioweapons threats.

This technical focus has excluded from analytic and policy attention (1) a serious consideration of the social dimensions of biotechnology and its associated bioweapons implications; and (2) the social practices surrounding analytic work that can introduce biases into bioweapons assessments. In contrast, by drawing on the concept of co-production from the field of science and technology studies, this book demonstrates the critical importance of understanding how scientific and technical knowledge and social context are mutually constituted. Addressing the first point, in chapters 3 and 4 I described how existing bioweapons assessments have ignored the various forms of tacit knowledge and the scientific disciplines required for the successful development and replication of biotechnologies as well as organizational and management influences on biological work. When such considerations are included, bioweapons development and use become much more complex, difficult, and contingent, with multiple potential biological and bioweapons threat trajectories resulting. Therefore, even with the increasingly global character of science and technology, analysts need to probe the inherent local dimensions that constitute and characterize "global" technologies, as well as their diffusion and uptake, to produce more accurate threat assessments.

Second, the current analytic and policy focus on the need for technical expertise for bioweapons assessments has obscured the need for a deeper look at the social practices that underpin analytic work, particularly in the U.S. intelligence community. As my case study on Curveball illustrates, the CIA's intelligence failures regarding the Iraqi bioweapons program were not fundamentally or solely a "technical" problem. Rather, in tracing the CIA's collection and analytic practices at the grassroots level, it is possible to see the more serious and pervasive problems relating to issues of secrecy, expertise, and current intelligence reporting that have, over time, created taken-for-granted CIA organizational routines that led to fundamental misjudgments of Iraq's bioweapons capabilities. Consequently, various types of expertise, information, and alternative frameworks—inside and outside the CIA—were not considered in assessing Iraq's bioweapons capabilities, thus precluding a holistic understanding of the Iraqi mobile bioweapons threat.

In discussing the social context of analysis, Charles Perrow has argued that one should also consider the power of elites to push and reinforce certain organizational perspectives and practices.[1] It is clear that the George W. Bush administration privileged WMD issues in its analytic and policy priorities in the leadup to the 2003 Iraq War. In commenting on the politics surrounding the Curveball case, former National Intelligence Officer Paul Pillar reflects: "How the [intelligence] reporting is interpreted, including things like the Curveball reports, you can't separate out from the environment in which the analysts were operating. . . . When you've got fuzzy and incomplete [intelligence], as is always the case with these things, the political and policy environment in which you're operating is going to affect that. And [especially] when it's such an extremely strong, stultifying one, as was the case of this [Bush administration] policy environment."[2] Pillar has noted previously how policy officials can politicize assessments in subtle ways by constantly tasking analysts with questions and work on topics of interest to them, thus diverting attention from other important issues or perspectives.[3] During the period of the Curveball case, we know that Vice President Richard Cheney and his chief of staff Lewis "Scooter" Libby often tasked analysts with questions on biological weapons issues, and the Bush administration frequently requested intelligence briefings and information on these issues.

There are other ways, however, that policy officials can exert subtle, yet powerful, influences on what analysts and officials choose to work and report on. Former U.S. National Intelligence Council (NIC) officer Fulton Armstrong writes that one should not underestimate the power of an administration's flattery in shaping assessments. In reflecting on his experiences serving at the NIC, Armstrong relates a story about the great pleasure intelligence officers take at seeing their work please policy customers:

> The first congressional briefing I ever took part in as an NIO [National Intelligence Officer], along with my colleagues, included discussion of WMDs, and it started with fifteen minutes of paeans of praise by Jesse Helms, and other Republicans on the Senate Foreign Relations Committee, for our intelligence work. Several of the NIOs were praised for having embraced the findings of the Rumsfeld Commission, which pressed upon the Clinton Administration a hyped analysis of the missile threat (and rationale for an accelerated "missile defense strategy"). The NIOs clearly knew what was going on in that room. Intelligence officers are all trained to remind the recipients of their reports that they are never to take sides in a policy debate. These NIOs, however, said nothing and were clearly happy with the praise by the Republican committee members.[4]

Armstrong notes that he saw similar attitudes among his intelligence colleagues in the leadup to the Iraq War: "They were happy that challenges to their and the administration's assumptions about Iraq's chemical and biological weapons capabilities were minimal; after all, who's going to try to prove a negative?"[5] The CIA's desire to please its policy customers stems, in part, from events in the post–Cold War / post-9/11 security environments that have led some policymakers to question the relevance of traditional intelligence organizations and their functions.[6]

In the Curveball case, however, CIA's WINPAC analysts did not have to worry about their policy relevance. Nor did they have to worry about internal challenges to their assessments about the Iraqi mobile bioweapons threat until the fall of 2002, nearly two years after Curveball first began his reporting. By that time, they had circulated a stream of analytic documents across the intelligence and policy communities purporting a consensus on the existence of an Iraqi mobile bioweapons capability. Before Colin Powell's March 2003 speech, the internal dissent regarding Curveball at the CIA that had emerged since the fall of 2002 was obscured by CIA management. So the CIA provided the Bush administration with a solid, seemingly uncontestable account of Saddam's growing bioweapons threat. In return, the Bush administration was clearly a pleased customer and affirmed the relevance of CIA weapons assessments in policy and public pronouncements.

To acknowledge this role of power and politics, however, does not diminish the culpability of analysts and managers within the U.S. intelligence community for the poor production of knowledge on Iraq's WMD programs. As noted previously, the intelligence assessments on the Iraqi mobile bioweapons threat began circulating at the end of the Clinton administration, long before the Bush administration had identified Iraq as a war target. This indicates inherent problems in how CIA analysts produced knowledge about Iraq's bioweapons capabilities and its later use to promote policy priorities. As Carl Ford argues, "If the intelligence community had done a better job, it would have made a huge difference in the way that everything turned out. Maybe not completely, but I guarantee you if the intelligence community had said, 'You know, we think Iraq might be developing weapons but we don't know whether or not their program has started back up,' that it would have been extremely difficult for policymakers to say, 'Let's go beat up on Saddam'—certainly, in the timeframe that it occurred. Those [weapons assessments] were a driving issue that allowed them to say, 'Well, if we don't go in [to Iraq], they're going to blow up the world.' "[7]

Yet a discussion of the role of power in shaping assessments should not be limited to the Bush administration; policy initiatives on bioweapons threats were launched during the Clinton administration, under a president who had prioritized bioweapons issues in analysis and policymaking. This high-level government attention produced findings, experts, and organizational entities that drew on and promoted the biotech revolution frame's understanding of biotechnology and bioweapons threats. In the process, policy and intelligence analysts have ignored other ways of understanding bioweapons threats. To date, the exercise of power across administrations and across expert communities to frame and organize knowledge on narrow technical definitions of bioweapons threats has led to many flawed assessments inside and outside of government. In outlining these broader exercises of power, science studies scholar Sheila Jasanoff argues, "Power is constituted as much through the elision of marginalized alternatives as through the positive adoption of dominant viewpoints."[8] It is by pointing out what is missing in analyses that taken-for-granted assumptions can be exposed and debated for the benefit of policymaking.

Simply to note a deficiency in analysis, however, is not enough. As one former U.S. policy official commented to me, "If you argue that the technical model is incomplete, there must be ways to extend it within a technical model to account for the slighted 'sociotechnical' features. Rather than being told, 'I need a social scientist to get the right answer on some particular threat question,' can we rephrase that as, 'What additional technical factors do you need to understand or project before you can figure out how likely someone will be to use this particular piece of biotechnology as a weapon?' "[9] In this individual's mind, the answer to improving bioweapons assessments involves "tweaking" the technical model with additional information and approaches that fit into the existing biotech revolution frame. This official went on to note, "Technical model people will be comfortable with expanding the technical model. They will not understand what it means to adopt sociotechnical factors."[10]

As Jasanoff and other scholars have noted, however, the analytic utility of an S&TS approach does not merely reside in a simple addition (or subtraction) process of pieces of information, where "the social" is merely grafted onto the existing technical, quantitative frame used for assessment. This book's central argument is that the assumptions used to guide bioweapons analysis and policymaking are problematic exactly because of the frames and practices that have been used to construct understanding. Therefore, an entirely different model and starting point is needed for analysis. As Wiebe Bijker has noted, a sociotechnical perspective on analysis, with its understanding of the intertwining of the cognitive, discursive, social, and material, produces something sui generis.[11] It should involve a complete rethinking, from the ground up, of how one conducts and approaches bioweapons assessments, involving new kinds of understandings of science and technology and using new styles of analytic structures and practices to produce new kinds of knowledge.

As I illustrate in this book, a sociotechnical approach to bioweapons assessments would involve asking and emphasizing different kinds of analytical questions—the "how" type of questions, not just the "what" type. It would involve thick, qualitative descriptions of localized scientific and technological work in a laboratory and in an analytic cadre. A use of interview material and ethnographies of laboratory and analytic practices provides not simply factual or anecdotal data but also a rich, contextual understanding of how scientific and technological knowledge is produced and given authority. This volume illustrates the importance of taking into account the novel process and conclusions that result from using a co-production perspective to understand how weapons knowledge is produced, by both the enemy and the analyst. Through in-depth case studies, I have argued that privileging resources (monetary, organizational, manpower) into technological fixes, as has been the typical policy response, will not substantially improve bioweapons assessments and may actually lead to more intelligence failures.

Although this book has focused on bioweapons assessments, my arguments about the need to consider how the social and technical are co-produced in weapons development and analysis provide new ways to think about the analysis of other WMD or conventional weapons threats. My analysis of the Curveball case has revealed particular CIA organizational practices that are problematic not only for bioweapons assessments but also for other CIA analyses, as a brief examination of the agency's intelligence assessments on the development of Iraq's nuclear weapons program makes evident. Contemporaneous with the Curveball assessments, the CIA's nuclear weapons analysts in WINPAC also concluded that Iraq's nuclear weapons program was advancing, based on intelligence reports suggesting that Iraq had acquired aluminum tubes and uranium.[12] These assessments were also wrong; issues of current reporting, expertise, and secrecy also plagued those assessments and powerfully influenced how WINPAC nuclear analysts constructed their knowledge about Iraq's nuclear weapons program. In the nuclear case, however, the U.S. Departments of Energy and State had their own nuclear experts and information sources to counter the CIA's analytic judgments, both much earlier and repeatedly. The nuclear case reveals that an in-depth examination of the Curveball case is important for what it says more broadly about the analytic practices shaping the assessments on technical weapons issues—that the analytic problems that shaped Curveball were not an isolated event but indicate fundamental problems in how weapons analyses are conducted (and thus how knowledge is produced) within the CIA.[13]

This sociotechnical description of the problems underpinning weapons assessments leads to new and different policy prescriptions for improving analysis of weapons threats. For example, understanding the important role of know-how in weapons development suggests that future weapons assessments should focus attention and resources on explicating the role of know-how with respect to different kinds of technologies; in chapters 3 and 4, I provided some insights into how this could be done. In addition, understanding the problems with expertise, secrecy, and current intelligence reporting within U.S. intelligence suggests the need to go beyond merely improving analytic techniques.[14] Rather, new initiatives should focus on the creation and long-term support of new experimental analytic groups to explore the varied ways in which different kinds of expertise and knowledge environments could be ordered to produce better weapons assessments. In chapter 8, I offered one new model for how this could be done: the Strategic Sociotechnical Assessment Group.

By understanding how frames and analytic practices have shaped bioweapons assessments, one can consider a much larger category of points for possible intervention to improve analysis, as compared to mere technical fixes or the futility of changing cognitive processes. As an example of a focus on interventions related to work practices, analysts can be arranged to work in different kinds of organizational units and be given incentives, resources, promotion pathways, and rewards for participating in long-term, in-depth collaborative research projects exploring the complex social and technical character of weapons threats. As I noted in chapter 5, during the Cold War period, the CIA had a small percentage of analysts who conducted current intelligence reporting; the remainder conducted applied or basic research. Such historical examples illustrate that different analytic priorities and practices are possible—as long as managers and policy officials affirm the value of creating and sustaining more types of basic and applied research as a means to improve understandings of weapons threats.

In the academic and intelligence worlds, moreover, new funding streams and conferences could be organized to support new research practices on the sociotechnical dimensions of bioweapons issues. Graduate students could be encouraged to consider and incorporate sociotechnical frameworks in their dissertation research. Intelligence (or other government) analysts could be given short- or long-term sabbaticals from their agencies to conduct unclassified research projects in academic settings; similarly, S&TS scholars could be encouraged to work in the intelligence community and other policy units as "scholars-in-residence." These are just a few examples of different kinds of interventions that could be pursued to improve analysis of bioweapons threats at the micro and macro levels. Such prescriptions are in accordance with the 2009 National Intelligence Strategy, which emphasizes that the U.S. intelligence community must broaden its expertise, deepen understanding, enhance outreach, and improve collaboration.[15]

Inevitably, however, my attempt to construct an alternative conceptual framework for bioweapons assessments will be challenging. Therefore, I am realistic about the time and effort required to change them substantively—no less than a cultural change at the individual, institutional, and governmental levels. Such a cultural change, however, could be made through the use of specific analytic and managerial interventions at the grassroots level of analysis. This book illustrates the improvement in analysis and benefit to policymaking that can come from an alternative approach. As I illustrated in my proposal in chapter 8 to create a new experimental knowledge team within the CIA, I recommend starting with a targeted effort aimed at changing individual and institutional work practices that, over time, could lead to larger cultural changes. As I also described, there have been historical precedents for creating new analytic initiatives to improve intelligence assessments.

As is evident, analyzing weapons proliferation and terrorism from a science and technology studies perspective opens up new and fruitful ways for the policy community to think about these vexing problems in a post-9/11 world. S&TS researchers *can* be important sources of expertise for policymakers. Yet more work remains for those of us in the academic community to make our research directly applicable to policymakers' difficult task of protecting citizens from WMD threats in a responsible way. There is a need for more policy scholar-practitioners who can be engaged citizens in both the academic and the policy communities to introduce new lines of inquiry and new ways of thinking about and responding to security problems and thereby serve to transform the thinking of both communities. This book provides one way forward.

NOTES

Chapter 1 • Bioweapons and National Security

1. In 1992, the U.S. biodefense program annual spending was $75 million. For a description of these funding changes, see Leitenberg, "Studies of Military R&D"; Wright, "Prospects for Biological Disarmament in the 1990s," 458; Schuler, "Billions for Biodefense," 87.

2. Pearson, "Federal Funding for Biological Weapons Prevention and Defense, Fiscal Years 2001 to 2009." According to researchers from the University of Pittsburgh Medical Center, the Fiscal Year 2010 budget for civilian biodefense totaled $6.05 billion, the Fiscal Year 2011 budget totaled $6.48 billion, and the Fiscal Year 2012 budget totaled $6.42 billion. See Franco, "Billions for Biodefense," 291; Franco and Kirk Sell, "Federal Agency Biodefense Funding, FY2010–FY2011," 129; Franco and Kirk Sell, "Federal Agency Biodefense Funding, FY2011–FY2012," 117.

3. A focus on material aspects of weapons in U.S. security analyses and policymaking has also been critiqued by scholars studying other weapons technologies. For examples, see Biddle, *Military Power*; Levi, *On Nuclear Terrorism*.

4. In using the term *sociotechnical assemblage,* I am in conversation with scholars who have used this concept to discuss technology in context. For a few recent examples, see Ong and Collier, *Global Assemblages*; Rappert, "Prohibitions, Weapons, and Controversy." Also, much recent work that uses the concept of "assemblage" is based on Deleuze and Guattari, *A Thousand Plateaus.*

5. Other S&TS scholars have also noted this disconnect. See Rappert, Balmer, and Stone, "Science, Technology, and the Military," 732.

6. For a discussion of co-production and illustration of particular case studies, see Jasanoff, *States of Knowledge.*

7. Ibid., 6.

8. For some literature that discusses the importance of social conventions and routines in producing scientific knowledge within institutions, see Eden, *Whole World on Fire*; Vaughan, *The Challenger Launch Decision.*

9. Anonymous U.S. security policy expert, e-mail message to author, 22 October 2008.

10. For a brief overview of the utility of qualitative data and methods, see Guba and Lincoln, "Competing Paradigms in Qualitative Research," 17–21.

Chapter 2 • Technological Frames and Narratives in U.S. Bioweapons Assessments and Policymaking

1. Cohen, "Iraq Situation."
2. Powell, "U.S. Secretary of State Colin Powell Addresses the U.N. Security Council."
3. Powell, "U.S. Secretary of State."
4. Intelligence practitioner Jack Davis has defined an analytic mindset as "the distillation of the intelligence analyst's cumulative factual and conceptual knowledge into a framework for making estimative judgments on a complex subject." See Davis, "Combatting Mind-Set," 33. In contrast, *groupthink,* a term coined by social psychologist Irving Janis, is described in intelligence and policy analysis as "bad or irrational decisions as each member of the group attempts to conform his or her opinions to what they believe to be the consensus of the group." U.S. Senate, Select Committee on Intelligence, "Report on the U.S. Intelligence Community's Prewar Intelligence Assessments on Iraq," 18.
5. See Heuer, "Limits of Intelligence Analysis," 76, 80.
6. For an additional discussion of mindsets, see ibid., 79, 85; Heuer, *Psychology of Intelligence Analysis,* 10; Cooper, *Curing Analytic Pathologies,* 26; Klein, "A Data/Frame Theory of Sensemaking," 118.
7. Heuer, "Limits of Intelligence Analysis," 84. These discussions of mental models, mindsets, and groupthink, however, exhibit a cognitive bias that tends to overlook or ignore the practical work practices shaping how analysts see and interpret information.
8. For an exception, see Vogel, "Framing Biosecurity."
9. See Clark, "Scientific and Technical Intelligence Analysis," 293–297.
10. See Cutcliffe and Post, eds., *In Context*; MacKenzie and Wajcman, eds., *Social Shaping of Technology*; Bijker, Hughes, and Pinch, eds., *Social Construction of Technological Systems.*
11. Bijker, "Social Construction of Bakelite," 168.
12. Bijker, *Democratization of Technology.*
13. I use the term *biotech revolution* because it is often used by bioweapons-related analysts and policy officials to describe the impact of biotechnology on bioweapons threats. This use of the term has roots with the advent of molecular biology, where a variety of advocates claimed that biotechnology would completely transform the fields of medicine and food production and create entirely new industries. See Hilgartner, "Biotechnology," 1235–1236. An early linking of a biotech revolution to biological weapons threats is attributed to Douglas Feith, then the deputy assistant secretary of defense for negotiations policy in President Ronald Reagan's Department of Defense, in his testimony to the House Subcommittee on Oversight and Evaluation of the Permanent Select Committee on Intelligence on 8 August 1986. See Hilts, "Biological Weapons Reweighed."
14. For an overview of technological determinism, see Roe Smith and Marx, *Does Technology Drive History?*

15. The revolution language is analogous to other popular "revolutionary" phrases that have been used to articulate the impact of scientific and technological developments on society, such as the "revolution in military affairs," the "green revolution," or the "information revolution."

16. Roe Smith, "Technological Determinism in American Culture."

17. Donald MacKenzie and Judy Wajcman write that this way of thinking about weapons was strengthened during World War II and the postwar period, when large U.S. government budgets for research and development were planned and organized in order to structure a more ordered process of technological improvements to weaponry than had been used previously. By focusing primarily on the ordered processes, the popular historical and policy accounts of weapons development during this period and thereafter assumed a linear innovation and development process, rather than documenting the more complex and convoluted ways in which technologies were actually developed. Mackenzie and Wajcman, *Social Shaping of Technology,* 225. See also Leitenberg, "Studies of Military R&D and Weapons Development."

18. Shea, "Balancing Scientific Publication and National Security Concerns"; National Research Council, *Seeking Security*; National Research Council, "Scientific Openness and National Security Workshop, 2003"; *Nature,* "Editorial"; SRS Technologies, "Quantification of Open Source Research Publications."

19. Kobinger, Weiner, Yu, and Wilson, "Filovirus-Pseudotyped Lentiviral Vector."

20. Petro, "Intelligence Support."

21. Parkhill et al., "Genome Sequence of *Yersinia pestis*"; Whitfield, "Black Death's DNA."

22. National Research Council, "Better Plan Needed"; Mervis and Stokstad, "NAS Censors Report on Agriculture Threats."

23. Petro and Relman, "Understanding Threats."

24. See Center for Strategic and International Studies, *Security Controls,* 1.

25. See Collins, *Changing Order,* 57.

26. Nouri and Chyba, "Proliferation-Resistant Biotechnology," 235.

27. Carlson, "Pace and Proliferation," 209.

28. Behlke and Devor, "Chemical Synthesis of Oligonucleotides."

29. Ibid.

30. Institute of Medicine and National Research Council, *International Perspective on Advancing Technologies.*

31. ETC Group, "Extreme Genetic Engineering."

32. How these financial estimates were generated is not specified. See U.S. Congress, Office of Technology Assessment, *Technologies Underlying Weapons of Mass Destruction,* 86; Falkenrath, Newman, and Thayer, *America's Achilles Heel*; Miller, "Next to Old Rec Hall."

33. Blair, "Annual Threat Assessment," 21.

34. Endy, "Synthetic Biology and National Security"; Mulligan, "Commercial Gene Synthesis Technology"; Relman, "Working Group on Synthetic Genomics"; O'Toole, "Biotechnology Revolution."

35. Kuhn, "Defining the Terrorist Risk."

36. Institute of Medicine and National Research Council, *International Perspective on Advancing Technologies,* 36.

37. Daschle and Inglesby, "Foreword: Necessary Progress in Biosecurity," 263.

38. Clapper, "Statement for the Record on the Worldwide Threat Assessment," 5. See also Blair, "Annual Threat Assessment," 18; McConnell, "Annual Threat Assessment," 8.

39. See Nightingale and Martin, "Myth of the Biotech Revolution."

40. U.S. Central Intelligence Agency, "Darker Bioweapons Future."

41. U.S. National Intelligence Council, *Mapping the Global Future,* 100–101.

42. O'Toole, "Challenge of Bioterrorism."

43. Brent, "In the Valley of the Shadow of Death," 2.

44. Ibid., 5.

45. National Research Council, *Biotechnology Research in an Age of Terrorism,* 18.

46. Endy, "Synthetic Biology and National Security"; Mulligan, "Commercial Gene Synthesis Technology"; Relman, "Working Group on Synthetic Genomics"; O'Toole, "Biotechnology Revolution."

47. Chyba, "Biotechnology Proliferation."

48. Institute of Medicine and National Research Council, *Globalization, Biosecurity, and the Life Sciences,* viii.

49. Wheelis, "Will the New Biology Lead to New Weapons?" 6.

50. See Schmidt, "Diffusion of Synthetic Biology."

51. Schmidt et al., "SYNBIOSAFE e-Conference: Online Community Discussion on the Societal Aspects of Synthetic Biology," 12.

52. See DIYbio, http://diybio.org.

53. National Security Council, "National Strategy for Countering Biological Threats," 2.

54. Morgan, *Inventing the People,* 14.

55. See York, *Race to Oblivion.* As York and others have described, however, there existed contemporary disputants of these narratives inside and outside the U.S. government. See also Lind, "Doubtful Revolution"; Leitenberg, "Dynamics of Military Technology Today"; Gusterson, "Narrating Abolition," 13–18.

56. See Rumsfeld, "Transforming the Military"; Krepinevich, "Cavalry to Computer." Other technological threat narratives are described in Gormley, *Missile Contagion.*

57. See Hacking, *Social Construction of What?* 34.

58. The term *rogue state* was used by the Clinton administration to characterize states that were hostile to the United States and choosing to act outside of international norms; often this referred to concerns about these states developing ballistic missile and WMD programs as well as being state sponsors of terrorism. Jim Woolsey, then director of the CIA, described this growing set of intelligence targets as a "jungle filled with a bewildering variety of poisonous snakes." See Jehl, "C.I.A. Nominee Wary of Budget Cuts."

59. An important 1997 Department of Defense strategy document reflected these concerns by highlighting that these new adversaries "are likely to seek advantage over the United States by using unconventional approaches to circumvent or undermine our strengths while exploiting our vulnerabilities." U.S. Department of Defense, *Quadrennial Defense Review.*

60. Oehler, "Continuing Threat from Weapons of Mass Destruction."

61. See U.S. Congress, Office of Technology Assessment, *Proliferation of Weapons of Mass Destruction*; Bailey, *Doomsday Weapons in the Hands of Many*; U.S. Department of Defense, *Biotechnology and Genetic Engineering*; Tucker, "Future of Biological Warfare."

62. A well-known 1993 U.S. Office of Technology Assessment report calculated that 130,000 to 3,000,000 people could die in the Washington, D.C., area from a single airplane release of bioweapons agent; U.S. Congress, Office of Technology Assessment, *Proliferation of Weapons of Mass Destruction,* 54. The report indicates, however, that the figures represent "rough estimates . . . based on somewhat arbitrary assumptions . . . [that] suggest the following generalizations . . . in principle, biological weapons efficiently delivered under the right conditions against unprotected populations would, pound for pound of weapon, exceed the killing power of nuclear weapons." U.S. Congress, Office of Technology Assessment, *Proliferation of Weapons of Mass Destruction,* 52; see also Bailey, *Director's Series on Proliferation.*

63. Carus, *Poor Man's Atomic Bomb?*; Livingstone and Douglass Jr., *CBW: The Poor Man's Atomic Bomb*; Buchanan, "Poor Man's A-Bomb?"; Venter, "Biological Warfare."

64. See Ben Ouagrham-Gormley and Vogel, "Social Context Shaping Bioweapons (Non)Proliferation"; Moon, "U.S. Biological Weapons Program."

65. Alibek with Handelman, *Biohazard*; Leitenberg, "Biological Weapons Arms Control."

66. See Leitenberg, "Biological Weapons Arms Control," 3–16.

67. See Hart, "Soviet Biological Weapons Program."

68. Throughout the 1990s, there were varying accounts of the number of Soviet bioweaponeers, with numbers ranging from 10,000 to 60,000. The larger numbers (30,000–60,000) were often used in policy discussions, although they included personnel such as janitors and other support staff that were not directly involved in weapons activities. In 2000, the U.S. General Accounting Office estimated that there were approximately 15,000 Soviet bioweaponeers who posed significant proliferation risks. See U.S. General Accounting Office, *Biological Weapons,* 10.

69. See Ben Ouagrham-Gormley and Vogel, "Social Context Shaping Bioweapons (Non)Proliferation."

70. See chapter 4; see also Domaradskij and Orent, *Biowarrior.*

71. See Ben Ouagrham-Gormley and Vogel, "Social Context Shaping Bioweapons (Non)Proliferation." See also chapter 7.

72. See Tucker, "Bioweapons from Russia"; Davis, "Nuclear Blindness."

73. Project Clear Vision was so named because it was "an attempt to see into the future of biological warfare by understanding its past." Initially, CIA agents had tried to identify and buy a Soviet biological munition on the international black market; the inability in finding a seller led CIA analysts to try and create this technology in its own laboratories. Miller, Engelberg, and Broad, *Germs,* 290–291.

74. Ibid., 293.

75. See ibid., 176, 206, 210, 228; U.S. Central Intelligence Agency, "Unclassified Report."

76. Smith, "Russians Admit Firms Met Iraqis"; Miller, "Standoff with Iraq."

77. Broad and Miller, "Government Report Says Three Nations Hide Stocks of Smallpox"; U.S. Department of Defense, "Russian Biological Warfare Technology."

78. Commission on the Intelligence Capabilities of the United States, *Report to the President,* 81.

79. For a good overview of UNSCOM, see Koblentz, *Living Weapons,* 74–101.

80. Dual-use equipment is equipment that could be used for both legitimate biological work and weapons purposes. For example, a fermentor would be considered a dual-use piece of equipment. These concerns were first documented in an April 1995 Security Council report, S/1995/284, www.fas.org/news/un/iraq/s/s1995-0284.htm. See also an October 1995 report, www.fas.org/news/un/iraq/s/s1995-0864.htm; Trevan, *Saddam's Secrets.*

81. See October 1995 UNSCOM report www.fas.org/news/un/iraq/s/s1995-0864.htm.

82. Commission on the Intelligence Capabilities of the United States, *Report to the President,* 82.

83. Porter, "Quantification and the Accounting Ideal in Science," 645.

84. See Porter, *Trust in Numbers.*

85. One member of the group, Seiichi Endo, had a master's degree in biology from Kyoto University. See Leitenberg, *Assessing the Biological Weapons and Bioterrorism Threat,* 38; Leitenberg, "Aum Shinrikyo's Efforts to Produce Biological Weapons."

86. U.S. Senate, Permanent Subcommittee on Investigations, "Global Proliferation of Weapons of Mass Destruction."

87. See Roberts, *Hype or Reality.*

88. Leitenberg, "Experience of the Japanese Aum Shinrikyo Group and Biological Agents."

89. Leitenberg, *Assessing the Biological Weapons and Bioterrorism Threat*; Danzig et al., *Aum Shinrikyo.*

90. Ibid.

91. See Osterholm, "Bioterrorism."

92. See Hoffman, *Inside Terrorism.*

93. Danzig and Berkowsky, "Why Should We Be Concerned about Biological Warfare?"; Drell, Sofaer, and Wilson, *New Terror,* 71; Falkenrath, Newman, and Thayer, *America's Achilles Heel.*

94. Defense Science Board, *Defense Science Board 1997 Summer Study Task Force,* 47.

95. Block, "Living Nightmares."

96. Wright, "Terrorists and Biological Weapons"; see also Miller, Engelberg, and Broad, *Germs,* 142; Venter, *Life Decoded*; Marshall, "Public Health." The President's Foreign Intelligence Advisory Board through most of the 1990s served an instrumental role within the U.S. intelligence community to increase intelligence collection and analysis on biological weapons issues.

97. Institute of Medicine and National Research Council, *Globalization, Biosecurity, and the Life Sciences,* 237.

98. Project Jefferson was named after Thomas Jefferson because of his words, "Eternal vigilance is the price of liberty." Miller, Engelberg, and Broad, *Germs,* 309.

99. Anonymous former U.S. intelligence analyst, interview with author, Falls Church, Virginia, 31 July 2007.

100. See Pomerantsev et al., "Expression of Cereolysine AB Genes."

101. Ruppe, "Terrorism—Threat Mongering," 1220.

102. Leitenberg, *Assessing the Biological Weapons and Bioterrorism Threat,* 54–55. Leitenberg estimates that the Bachus team involved a rough total of over two hundred man-years of specialized experience. Leitenberg, personal communication with author, 7 October 2009.

103. The U.S. bioweapons program was launched during World War II and continued until President Richard M. Nixon abolished the program in 1969.

104. Benjamin and Simon, *Sacred Age of Terror,* 252; Wright, "Terrorism and Biological Weapons"; Miller, Engelberg, and Broad, *Germs.*

105. United Nations, *Unresolved Disarmament Issues.*

106. The use of airplanes, box-cutters, and knives as weapons was a trend that terrorist groups like al-Qaeda had been developing since the 1980s. See Hoffman, "Terrorism and Counterterrorism after September 11th"; Nesser, "Chronology of Jihadism in Western Europe 1994–2007"; Stenersen, *Al-Qaida's Quest for Weapons of Mass Destruction.*

107. Lemonic, "Bioterrorism: The Next Threat?"; O'Toole, "Six Years after Anthrax."

108. In 2008, the U.S. Federal Bureau of Investigations (FBI) identified a former scientist, Bruce Ivins, who worked at a U.S. biodefense facility, as the perpetrator. Ivins subsequently committed suicide before a trial could be held.

109. Danzig, *Catastrophic Bioterrorism,* 1–2.

110. See U.S. Homeland Security Council, "Planning Scenarios: Executive Summaries"; Epstein, "Security Is More than Public Health," 355; Falkenrath, "Testimony," 6; Davis, "Twentieth-Century Legacy," 124.

111. Petro and Relman, "Understanding Threats to Scientific Openness."

112. Leitenberg, *Assessing the Biological Weapons and Bioterrorism Threat,* 28–38.

113. Schmidt and Nakashima, "Moussaoui Said Not to Be Part of 9/11 Plot"; Leitenberg, *Assessing the Biological Weapons and Bioterrorism Threat,* 33.

114. Leitenberg, *Assessing the Biological Weapons and Bioterrorism Threat,* 38.

115. Commission on the Intelligence Capabilities of the United States, *Report to the President,* 269; however, some nongovernmental scholars have critiqued the WMD commission assessments on al-Qaeda. See Leitenberg, *Assessing the Biological Weapons and Bioterrorism Threat,* 38.

116. Jackson et al., "Expression of Mouse Interleukin-4"; Rosengaard et al., "Variola Virus Immune Evasion Design"; Cello, Paul, and Wimmer, "Chemical Synthesis of Poliovirus cDNA."

117. Smith et al., "Generating a Synthetic Genome by Whole Genome Assembly"; Tumpey et al., "Characterization of the Reconstructed 1918 Spanish Influenza Virus."

118. Tucker and Zilinskas, "Promise and Perils of Synthetic Biology," 42.

119. In 2000, the Defense Science Board created a task force on bioweapons issues. From this task force, the board published a set of studies on bioterrorism and biodefense-related issues. These studies emphasized the widespread availability and low cost of biological weapons technology. Defense Science Board, *The Defense Science Board 2000 Summer Study,* 5.

120. Office of Homeland Security, *National Strategy for Homeland Security,* 39.

121. Shea, "National Biodefense Analysis," 5; Padrón Carney, "Department of Homeland Security," 100.

122. U.S. Department of Homeland Security, "DHS Fact Sheet"; U.S. Department of Homeland Security, "DHS Issues Record"; Shea, "National Biodefense Analysis and Countermeasures Center."

123. Korch, "Leading Edge of Biodefense," slide 9.

124. Gottron and Shea, "Oversight of High Containment Biological Laboratories."

125. Fitch, "Science-Based Biodefense Analysis in an Uncertain World," slide 13.

126. Danzig, "Prevention of Biothreats."

127. U.S. Department of Homeland Security, "Homeland Security Presidential Directive 10."

128. Ibid.

129. Fitch, "Science-Based Biodefense Analysis in an Uncertain World," slide 16.

130. Applebaum, "Only a Game"; *Washington Post,* "Editorial: Not Science Fiction."

131. Meltzer et al., "Modeling Potential Responses."

132. Orent, "Bioterror Bugaboo."

133. See Lakoff, "Generic Biothreat." For early predecessors, see Fee and Brown, "Preemptive Biopreparedness."

134. Hamilton and Smith, "Atlantic Storm."

135. Ghamari-Tabrizi, *Worlds of Herman Kahn,* 132.

136. Ibid., 126.

137. Bakhtin, "Forms of Time," 84. I am grateful to Stefan Senders for introducing me to Bakhtin's notion of chronotope.

138. Ibid., 87–89.

139. Brooks, *Reading for the Plot,* 4.

140. For discussions of how science is displayed theatrically in public venues, see Hilgartner, *Science on Stage*; Goffman, *Presentation of Self in Everyday Life.*

141. Agre, *Computation and Human Experience,* 38.

142. MacKenzie, *Inventing Accuracy,* 384.

Overview · *The Biosocial Frame*

Epigraphs. Ken Alibek, interview with author, Manassas, Virginia, 23 July 2002; Aniko Paul, interview with author, Stony Brook, New York, 27 June 2006; Wynne, "Unruly Technology," 152.

1. In using the term *biosocial frame* here, I distinguish it from Paul Rabinow's term *biosociality,* which he uses to discuss how new social identities and politics are created when people come to align themselves in terms of genetic narratives and practices. See Rabinow, "Artificiality and Enlightenment."

2. Lynch, *Art and Artifact in Laboratory Science*; Knorr-Cetina, *Manufacture of Knowledge*; Latour, "Is it Possible to Reconstruct the Research Process?"; Latour and Woolgar, *Laboratory Life*; Star, "Simplification in Scientific Work"; Star, "Scientific Work and Uncer-

tainty"; Gooding, "Mapping Experiment"; Gooding, *Experiment and the Making of Meaning.*

3. Knorr-Cetina, *The Manufacture of Knowledge*, 94.

4. Lynch, *Art and Artifact*; Knorr-Cetina, *Manufacture of Knowledge*; Latour, "Is It Possible to Reconstruct the Research Process?"; Latour and Woolgar, *Laboratory Life*; Star, "Simplification in Scientific Work"; Star, "Scientific Work and Uncertainty"; Gooding, "Mapping Experiment"; Gooding, *Experiment and the Making of Meaning.*

5. Lynch, *Art and Artifact,* 152.

6. David Gooding also discusses how scientific texts reconstruct the world ordered as success rather than the world as explored. Gooding, "Mapping Experiment."

7. Star, "Scientific Work and Uncertainty," 393; see also Latour, "Is It Possible to Reconstruct the Research Process?" 72; Lynch, *Art and Artifact,* 145; Latour and Woolgar, *Laboratory Life,* 36–37.

8. Latour and Woolgar, *Laboratory Life,* 176.

9. Star, "Simplification in Scientific Work," 208.

10. Knorr-Cetina, *Manufacture of Knowledge,* 128.

11. Collins, "Tacit Knowledge," 72–83; Collins, *Changing Order.*

12. Lynch, *Art and Artifact,* 65.

13. Ibid., 154.

14. Lynch, "Protocols."

15. Wynne, "Unruly Technology," 152.

16. Gooding, "Mapping Experiment," 171–176.

17. Star, "Simplification," 206–207.

18. Gooding, "Mapping Experiment," 170.

19. Lynch, *Art and Artifact,* 4.

20. See Hopkins et al., "Myth of the Biotech Revolution"; Nightingale and Martin, "Myth of the Biotech Revolution."

21. Anonymous biopharmaceutical executive, interview with author, King of Prussia, Pennsylvania, 28 March 2008.

22. Anonymous biopharmaceutical executive, interview.

23. Anonymous biopharmaceutical executive, interview.

24. For a few examples, see Moon, "U.S. Biological Weapons Program"; Leitenberg, *Assessing the Biological Weapons and Bioterrorism Threat.*

25. Anonymous biopharmaceutical executive, interview.

26. See Edgerton, *Shock of the Old*; David, "Dynamo and the Computer."

27. Nightingale, "Technological Capabilities."

28. Pinch and Bijker, "Social Construction of Facts and Artefacts."

29. McLeish and Nightingale, "Biosecurity, Bioterrorism and the Governance of Science."

30. Anonymous U.S. government official, interview with author, Washington, D.C., 21 March 2007; see also National Research Council, *Interim Report on Methodological Improvements.*

Chapter 3 • Synthetic Genomics, the Biotech Revolution, and Bioterrorism

1. Schmidt et al., "Synbiosafe e-Conference"; Schmidt et al., *Synthetic Biology*; Samuel, Selgelid, and Kerridge, "Managing the Unimaginable"; Garfinkel et al., "Synthetic Genomics"; ETC Group, "Extreme Genetic Engineering"; Tucker and Zilinskas, "Promise and Perils of Synthetic Biology."

2. See *Economist,* "Biofuels from Algae"; Hamm, "Cheaper Artemisinin to Fight Malaria."

3. Cello, Paul, and Wimmer, "Chemical Synthesis of Poliovirus cDNA."

4. U.S. Congress, "Expressing Serious Concern." H.R. 514 did not ultimately garner enough political consensus to pass.

5. Smith et al., "Generating a Synthetic Genome by Whole Genome Assembly."

6. Warrick, "Custom-Built Pathogens."

7. National Science Advisory Board for Biosecurity, "Addressing Biosecurity Concerns Related to Synthetic Biology"; Presidential Commission for the Study of Bioethics, "Synthetic Biology: Meeting One," "Synthetic Biology: Meeting Two," "Synthetic Biology: Meeting Three"; U.S. Department of Health and Human Services, "Screening Framework Guidance."

8. Gilbert and Mulkay, *Opening Pandora's Box.*

9. See Molla, Paul, and Wimmer, "Cell-Free, De Novo Synthesis of Poliovirus"; Semler and Wimmer, *Molecular Biology of Picornaviruses.*

10. In contrast to the negative media attention from the 2002 synthesis experiment, the 1991 experiment was positively reported in the media. See Colata, "Polio Synthesized in the Test Tube."

11. The poliovirus data I discuss are based on interviews conducted with Wimmer, Paul, and Cello on two site visits to the Wimmer lab in Stony Brook, New York; two additional follow-up telephone interviews with the Wimmer lab researchers; and one additional in-person interview with Wimmer. I also conducted six telephone interviews in 2006 with Professor Wimmer's virology collaborators and competitors: Dr. Ellie Ehrenfeld, National Institutes of Health; Professor J. Bert Flanegan, University of Florida, Gainesville; and Professor David Barton, University of Colorado at Denver.

12. For example, see Pelham and Jackson, "Efficient mRNA-Dependent Translation System."

13. Molla, Paul, and Wimmer, "Cell-Free, De Novo Synthesis of Poliovirus."

14. As will be described below, it was not purely the mechanical preparation of HeLa cell–free cytoplasmic extracts that was problematic (although that did pose some challenges) but how poliovirus synthesis was catalyzed and sustained through the proper preparation of these extracts.

15. Aniko Paul, interview with author, Stony Brook, New York, 24 February 2006.

16. Cello et al., "Chemical Synthesis of Poliovirus"; see Data Supplement: Supporting Online Material.

17. Molla et al., "Cell Free, De Novo Synthesis of Poliovirus," 1650–1651.

18. Ibid., 1650.

19. Paul interview, 25 June 2006.

20. However, if a good batch is made, it can be frozen in aliquots and will last in the lab anywhere from one to two years, depending on the amount of lab work requiring the use of HeLa cell–free extracts. Paul interview, 27 June 2006.

21. Ibid.

22. Ellie Ehrenfeld, telephone interview with author, 27 July 2006.

23. Ibid.

24. Cell passaging is a cell growing technique whereby cells are split into multiple flasks at certain time points and diluted with fresh media to facilitate new growth over an extended period of time. If, however, cells are not split at the right time and become saturated, nutrients and toxic by-products accumulate, leading to cell death.

25. Instead of fetal bovine serum, the Wimmer lab has also used calf serum to grow HeLa cells. However, Paul states that using calf serum leads to very low and unreliable viral yields. Other commercially available cell extracts, such as rabbit reticulocyte lysate or wheat germ, do not work for poliovirus synthesis. Paul, e-mail communication with author, 20 November 2006.

26. Paul, interview with author, Stony Brook, New York, 26 June 2006.

27. Ibid.

28. Ehrenfeld interview, 27 July 2006.

29. Paul interview, 26 June 2006.

30. David Barton, telephone interview with author, 4 August 2006.

31. J. Bert Flanegan, telephone interview with author, 16 September 2006.

32. There are different sizes, styles, and materials for Dounce homogenizers. Although there are alternative ways of breaking cells, such as the use of detergents, the poliovirus researchers argue that these methods would denature important proteins, preventing poliovirus translation, an important precursor step to viral synthesis.

33. Paul interview, 26 June 2006.

34. Flanegan telephone interview.

35. Ibid.

36. Ehrenfeld interview, 27 July 2006.

37. Ehrenfeld states that she uses a set of stainless steel Dounces that she has had for decades. She prefers stainless steel over glass Dounces because she finds that since glass is a fluid material, it can show variations over time, which can affect the functioning of the dounce and quality of the extract. Ibid.

38. Ibid. The Wimmer lab has adopted a procedure of always keeping the extract sample on ice, even while checking the cells under the microscope. Paul, telephone interview, 8 November 2006.

39. Paul interview, 26 June 2006. Also, RNAase-treated / autoclaved water can affect the outcome because of changes in pH. I am grateful for this insight by an anonymous U.S. government official, e-mail communication with author, 24 January 2007.

40. Ehrenfeld, telephone interview with author, 8 August 2006.

41. In consultation with Flanegan, Ehrenfeld describes how her lab then changed their method of water preparation (to degrade nucleases) from using a chemical method to autoclaving their water samples. However, Ehrenfeld still wondered if the earlier method of preparation was the real cause of the problem. As an example, she wondered if the lab's

difficulty in making good extract might have something to do with a batch of plastic tubes that they used for the experiment—perhaps the tubes were manufactured with some kind of coating that caused problems? Or perhaps the manufacturer changed the process of making the tubes and something was leaching out? At the end of all of her lab's investigations into the problem, Ehrenfeld still wasn't sure what the exact problem was; interviews, 27 July and 8 August 2006.

42. Ibid.; Flanegan interview; and Barton, telephone interview with author, 15 September 2006.

43. Flanegan interview.

44. Ibid.

45. Barton interview, 4 August 2006. However, Barton argues that when he tried this dialysis step, it actually worsened his experimental results.

46. Paul interview, 8 November 2006.

47. Landecker, *Culturing Life*, 24.

48. These kinds of ritualistic practices in scientific work have been documented by science and technology studies researchers. For two examples, see Jordan and Lynch, "Sociology of a Genetic Engineering Technique"; Cambrosio and Keating, "Going Monoclonal."

49. Flanegan interview.

50. Ibid.

51. Barton interview, 15 September 2006.

52. Ibid.

53. Paul interview, 8 November 2006.

54. Barton interview, 15 September 2006.

55. Paul interview, 27 June 2006.

56. Barton interview, 15 September 2006.

57. Ibid.

58. "Molecular/Cellular biology labs are like modern-day 'guilds' where apprentices acquire the art through discipline from the mentor." U.S. government official, e-mail communication with author, 24 January 2007. Examples that show that such cell-free viral synthesis can be adopted to different viruses within *particular* communities of expertise are Svitkin and Sonenberg, "Cell-Free Synthesis"; Kobayashi et al., "Improved Cell-Free System."

59. The only reason why HeLa cell–free extract was used in the 2002 poliovirus experiment was to show that virus synthesis is possible in a cell-free biochemical environment, and that polio was a chemical that did not need a living host cell to be produced. The experiment was not designed to be a highly efficient or facile means for synthesizing the poliovirus. Paul interview, 26 June 2006.

60. Flanegan interview. Transfection techniques for making poliovirus have been available within the poliovirus community since the 1980s; see van der Werf et al., "Synthesis of Infectious Poliovirus RNA."

61. For a recent article describing continuing problems in HeLa cell contamination, see Chatterjee, "Cases of Mistaken Identity."

62. Racaniello and Baltimore, "Cloned Poliovirus Complementary DNA"; Paul interview, 27 June 2006.

63. Paul interview, 27 June 2006.

64. Paul interview, 25 June 2006.

65. Viruses range in size from about 3,000 to over a million nucleotides. For example, see www.lehigh.edu/~jas0/viralgenomes.html.

66. Sinsheimer, "Single-Stranded Deoxyribonucleic Acid from Bacteriophage."

67. Goulian, Kornberg, and Sinsheimer, "Enzymatic Synthesis of DNA, XXIV."

68. *Time,* "Molecular Biology."

69. Sanger et al., "Nucleotide Sequence of Bacteriophage phiX174."

70. Hutchison III et al., "Global Transposon Mutagenesis."

71. I conducted one site visit to the Venter Institute in December 2006 for an extended interview with J. Craig Venter, Clyde Hutchison, Hamilton Smith, and Cynthia Pfannkoch; this information was supplemented with a follow-up extended telephone interview with the researchers in January 2007.

72. Clyde Hutchison comments, however, that some early thoughts about phiX bacteriophage synthesis date back to the mid-1970s, when he initially sequenced the phiX genome, the first DNA molecule ever sequenced, while on sabbatical in Fred Sanger's lab. Clyde Hutchison, interview with author, Rockville, Maryland, 5 December 2006.

73. J. Craig Venter, interview with author, Rockville, Maryland, 5 December 2006.

74. Hutchison interview, 5 December 2006. This paper was Cho et al., "Ethical Considerations in Synthesizing a Minimal Genome."

75. Hutchison interview, 5 December 2006.

76. Stemmer et al., "Single-Step Assembly."

77. Cloning involves the transfer of a piece of DNA from one organism into the genetic material of a carrier, or "vector." Examples of vectors include bacteria, yeast cells, viruses, and plasmids. After the DNA is inserted, the vector is placed in laboratory conditions that prompt it to multiply, resulting in the DNA being copied many times.

78. Hutchison, telephone interview with author, 18 January 2007.

79. Baker, "Synthetic Genomes," 407.

80. Venter interview.

81. Hutchison interview, 18 January 2007.

82. Hutchison interview, 5 December 2006.

83. Ibid.

84. Smith et al., "Generating a Synthetic Genome," 15442.

85. Czar et al., "Gene Synthesis Demystified," 63–72.

86. Venter interview.

87. Ibid.

88. Hutchison interview, 5 December 2006.

89. Ibid.

90. Hamilton Smith, telephone interview with author, 18 January 2007.

91. Venter interview.

92. Hutchison interview, 5 December 2006.

93. Cynthia Pfannkoch, telephone interview with author, 18 January 2007.

94. Hutchison interview, 5 December 2006.

95. Ibid.

96. Smith interview, 18 January 2007.

97. Smith had developed computational models for biology in his previous education and research.

98. Hutchison interview, 18 January 2007.

99. Smith interview, 5 December 2006.

100. Smith et al., "Generating a Synthetic Genome," 15442.

101. Smith interview, 18 January 2007.

102. Hutchison interview, 18 January 2007.

103. PCA is similar to PCR but does not include a pair of primers in excess; instead, oligos are assembled in equimolar amounts and annealed. The annealed oligos are extended only from the 5' end of the DNA to the 3' end of the DNA. The resulting double-stranded DNA is melted and reannealed with extensions, again only once in the 5' end to 3' direction. Each extension reaction creates a progressively longer strand.

104. Hutchison interview, 5 December 2006.

105. Hutchison interview, 18 January 2007.

106. Smith et al., "Generating a Synthetic Genome," 15445.

107. The need for a visual plaque assay for the phiX protocol has been recognized as a limitation of this technique in subsequent scientific publications. For examples, see Kodumal et al., "Total Synthesis of Long DNA Sequences"; Carr et al., "Protein-Mediated Error Correction"; Binkowski et al., "Correcting Errors in Synthetic DNA"; Xiong et al., "A Simple, Rapid, High-Fidelity, and Cost-Effective PCR-Based Two-Step DNA Synthesis Method"; Young and Dong, "Two-Step Total Gene Synthesis Method."

108. Smith interview, 18 January 2007.

109. Hutchison interview, 5 December 2006.

110. Venter interview.

111. Hutchison interview, 18 January 2007.

112. Venter interview.

113. Anonymous U.S. government official, interview with author, McLean, Virginia, 29 June 2006.

114. Gibson et al., "Complete Chemical Synthesis."

115. A 2010 follow-up experiment shows the need for twenty-four researchers and continued complexity in the genome synthesis. See Gibson et al., "Creation of a Bacterial Cell."

116. Ball, "Genome Stitched Together by Hand."

117. Gibson et al., "Complete Chemical Synthesis," 1219.

118. Baker, "Synthetic Genomes," 403, 405–408.

119. The other cassettes were also synthesized by DNA2.0 and GeneArt.

120. Blue Heron Biotechnology, "Blue Heron the Primary Supplier of Genetic Material."

121. John Mulligan, telephone interview with author, 18 July 2006.

122. Ibid.

123. Czar et al., "Gene Synthesis Demystified," 63.

124. Ibid., 64.

125. Ibid., 70.

126. *GenomeWeb Daily News*, "Origene Buys Blue Heron."

127. Lynch, *Art and Artifact*; Knorr-Cetina, *Manufacture of Knowledge*; Latour and Woolgar, *Laboratory Life.*

128. David Barton noted that the 1991 experiment involved a dialysis step, which he believes causes proteins within the cells to precipitate out of solution. This is the same protocol used in the 2002 synthesis experiment. However, in contrast, Aniko Paul mentions that they have not had problems in their lab making virus and extract using the dialysis step, and she believes that the dialysis step helps reduce some of the contingencies related to variations in salt concentrations during the subsequent translation and viral synthesis steps. She speculates that some problems with the dialysis step may be due to differences in how different labs dounce the HeLa cells. Barton interviews, 4 August and 15 September 2006; Paul, telephone interviews, 8 and 9 November 2006.

129. Barton interview, 15 September 2006. Ellie Ehrenfeld also described how her lab did not spend time trying to work out the various factors associated with variability in making HeLa cell–free extracts. Ehrenfeld, telephone interview with author, 20 November 2006.

130. Barton interview, 4 August 2006.

131. Ehrenfeld interview, 20 November 2006.

132. Garfinkel et al., "Synthetic Genomics," 15.

133. For a few examples, see Garfinkel et al., "Synthetic Genomics"; National Science Advisory Board for Biosecurity, "Addressing Biosecurity Concerns"; Mukunda, Oye, and Mohr, "What Rough Beast?"

Chapter 4 • Soviet Bioweapons Know-How and Proliferation Threats

Epigraph. Lugar, "Statement of Richard Lugar."

1. U.S. Senate, "Global Proliferation of Weapons of Mass Destruction"; Potter, "Before the Deluge?"; Tucker and Vogel, "Preventing the Proliferation."

2. In 1991, Congress passed, through a strong bipartisan effort, the Soviet Nuclear Threat Reduction Act to address Russia's proliferation and offensive threats to U.S. national security. Under this act, a collection of U.S. agency programs are frequently referred to as the "Nunn-Lugar" programs, after Senators Sam Nunn and Richard Lugar, who cosponsored the original bill. Since its inception, these programs have expanded to include several of the former Soviet republics.

3. See Stem Cook and Woolf, "Preventing Proliferation of Biological Weapons"; Vogel, "Pathogen Proliferation."

4. See Hoffman, *Dead Hand*; National Research Council, *Biological Threat Reduction Program*; Alibek, *Biohazard*; Bozheyeva, Kunakbayev, and Yeleukenov, "Former Soviet Biological Weapons Facilities in Kazakhstan"; Leitenberg, "Conversion of Biological Warfare Research and Development Facilities"; Leitenberg, "Possibilities and Limitations of Biological Weapons Conversion"; Domaradskij and Orent, *Biowarrior.*

5. See Miller, Engelberg, and Broad, *Germs,* 206. Considering that many former Soviet scientists received only approximately $100-$300 per month, such an offer represented an enormous increase in their salaries.

6. For example, in 1991, Gennady Lepeshkin, the former director of a biological weapons facility in Stepnogorsk, Kazakhstan, said that he had been approached by Iranian

middlemen who disguised themselves as private businessmen looking for joint biotech commercial ventures. Although rebuffed in Kazakhstan, a scientific advisor for President of Iran Mohammad Khatami and delegations of Iranian clerics had traveled to several former Soviet biological weapons facilities in Russia seeking research collaborations involving a variety of pathogens as well as exchanges for broader scientific training in genetic engineering techniques. Russian scientists have acknowledged that at least five of their colleagues have since gone to work in Iran for either consultancy or teaching contracts. In 1997, Iranian officials visited the All-Russian Institute of Phytopathology in Golitsino, Russia, to explore possibilities for scientific exchanges on plant pathogen projects. It is known that four scientists from this facility have visited Tehran on business trips. That same year, the Russian Ministry of Science and Technology sponsored a biotechnology trade fair in Tehran. More than 100 leading biologists from former Soviet biological weapons institutes attended the meeting. Milton Leitenberg has documented, however, that only about 10 to 12 Russian biological scientists moved to Tehran—none were from bioweapons institutes. See Miller, Engelberg, and Broad, *Germs,* 176, 206, 210; M. Leitenberg, personal communication with author; Leitenberg, *Assessing the Biological Weapons and Bioterrorism Threat,* 19–20.

7. Marchesano and Della Ratta, "Preliminary Funding Analysis of the FY11 Budget Request"; U.S. Department of Defense, "Cooperative Threat Reduction: . . . Fiscal Year 2011"; U.S. Department of Defense, ". . . Fiscal Year 2009"; Pearson, "Federal Funding for Biological Weapons Prevention." Canada, the European Union, Japan, South Korea, Sweden, and the United Kingdom have also provided nonproliferation funding to the former Soviet biological weapons establishment. Typically, the cost is approximately $150,000–$500,000 for a three-year project, the cost varying with the number of bioweaponeers involved and the equipment and supplies needed for the project.

8. Leitenberg, *Assessing the Biological Weapons and Bioterrorism Threats,* 20.

9. U.S. Government Accountability Office, *Weapons of Mass Destruction,* 32.

10. Hymans, "Beautiful Stranger," 2.

11. U.S. Government Accountability Office, *DOE's Program to Assist Weapons Scientists in Russia,* 11–13.

12. See the comments of Senator Malcolm Wallop, *Congressional Record,* 25 November 1991, S18008.

13. Two studies have started to probe brain drain threats of the Soviet weapons establishment, but these are not in-depth, qualitative case studies: Ball and Gerber, "Russian Scientists and Rogue States"; Parachini et al., "Diversion of Nuclear, Biological, and Chemical Weapons Expertise." However, Jacques E. C. Hymans's forthcoming book, *Achieving Nuclear Ambitions,* discusses intriguing historical cases in the nuclear arena, in which brain drain technology transfer has shown to be difficult and costly for potential proliferators.

14. Part of this chapter draws on Vogel, "Bioweapons Proliferation."

15. This edict was given after the USSR had signed and ratified the Biological and Toxin Weapons Convention, which came into force in 1975. The Stepnogorsk facility was established in blatant violation of this treaty.

16. In 1979 an accidental release of anthrax bacteria occurred at a Soviet Ministry of Defense biological weapons facility in Sverdlovsk, Russia. In order to cover up this accident, Stepnogorsk was called on to take over Sverdlovsk's anthrax biological weapons tasks in 1982. Ken Alibek, interview with author, Manassas, Virginia, 22 August 2001.

17. In contrast, information on Soviet biological weapons development in Russian facilities is still considered extremely sensitive and difficult to acquire, since Russia does not officially acknowledge that it had an offensive biological weapons program during the Soviet period. Ken Alibek was deputy director, then director, of the Stepnogorsk facility when it became operational in 1983. Over the next four years he was directly involved in overseeing the development of Soviet anthrax biological weapons and other biological agents.

18. Unless otherwise noted, information on the Stepnogorsk facility and Anthrax 836 work in the following sections is based on interviews with K. Alibek by the author (Manassas, Virginia, 22 August 2001, 23 and 27 July 2002). The Soviets' Anthrax 836 weapon was based on a highly virulent Russian strain of the *Bacillus anthracis* bacterium isolated by Soviet Ministry of Defense scientists. The high virulence of this strain was based on several factors, including a thick protective capsule and an ability to produce large amounts of toxins. Initial research, development, and production of Anthrax 836 were conducted at a military microbiological facility in Sverdlovsk, Russia. Later, the Stepnogorsk facility also developed the production protocols for glanders, plague, and tularemia biological weapons. See Alibek, *Biohazard,* 87; Tucker, "Biological Weapons in the Former Soviet Union," 2.

19. Anonymous U.S. government official, interview with author, Washington, D.C., 22 November 2002.

20. PVC is a polymer compound that resists fire and water and so is frequently used in making raincoats and shower curtains. It is also resistant to acids and bases, chemical agents, and sunlight and is chargeable with negative static electricity—all useful properties for weaponization of biological agents.

21. See Alibek, *Biohazard*; Tucker, "Biological Weapons in the Former Soviet Union," 4.

22. This trouble was in spite of the fact that the existing Ministry of Defense anthrax weapon formulation had been developed at the Sverdlovsk facility, which possessed 100,000-liter fermenters. Anonymous U.S. government official, interview with author, Albuquerque, New Mexico, 7 November 2002.

23. Alibek interview, 27 July 2002.

24. Ibid. The former U.S. offensive bioweapons program also faced challenges in developing bacteria for large-scale bioweapons production. See Leitenberg, "Botulinum Toxin," 159.

25. Hoffman, *Dead Hand,* 300.

26. Alibek, *Biohazard,* 88–106.

27. The Stepnogorsk facility was constructed by Soviet prisoners who did not have any biological weapons or engineering background.

28. Alibek, *Biohazard,* 88–106.

29. Alibek interview, 23 July 2002.

30. Alibek, *Biohazard,* 97.

31. Ibid., 99.

32. Plant Progress produced *B. thuringiensis* as a biopesticide for Soviet agricultural use.

33. Alibek, *Biohazard,* 105; Bozheyeva et al., "Former Soviet Biological Weapons Facilities," 11.

34. Alibek, *Biohazard,* 105.

35. Alibek interview, 27 July 2002.

36. Anonymous U.S. government official, interview with author, Washington, D.C., 22 November 2002.

37. Alibek interview, 27 July 2002. This same opinion was held by Robert Oppenheimer, who opposed compartmentalization of scientific staff within Los Alamos National Laboratory during the Manhattan Project. See Rhodes, *Making of the Atomic Bomb,* 454–455.

38. Alibek interview, 27 July 2002.

39. Galison, *Image and Logic,* 308.

40. Anonymous U.S. government official, interview with author, Albuquerque, New Mexico, 7 November 2002.

41. Anonymous U.S. government official, interview with author, Washington, D.C., 22 November 2002.

42. Anonymous U.S. government official, interview with author, Albuquerque, New Mexico, 7 November 2002.

43. Anonymous U.S. government official, interview with author, Washington, D.C., 22 November 2002.

44. For example, Alibek states that in 1990 a group of Stepnogorsk technical staff went to a Russian biological weapons facility, known as VECTOR, to assist in the development of a new biological weapon. Alibek interview, 22 August 2001; anonymous U.S. government official, interview with author, Washington, D.C., 22 November 2002.

45. For an early articulation of tacit knowledge, see Polanyi, *Personal Knowledge.*

46. Collins, "Tacit Knowledge," 72–73. Collins has also described another set of tacit knowledge categories that include unrecognized knowledge, such as when researcher A performs aspects of an experiment in a certain way without realizing their importance, and researcher B will pick up the same habit during a visit, with neither party realizing that anything important has been passed on. He also describes uncognized/uncognizable knowledge, such as when people speak with acceptably formed phrases in their native language without knowing how they do it. Such abilities can be passed on only through apprenticeship and unconscious emulation. Collins states that aspects of experimental practice are similar.

47. Polyani, *Personal Knowledge.*

48. Cambrosio and Keating, "Going Monoclonal."

49. MacKenzie and Spinardi, "Tacit Knowledge, Weapons Design." See also Carrigan, "Learning to Build the Bomb"; Younger, *The Bomb: A New History.*

50. McNamara, "Ways of Knowing about Weapons," 147–180.

51. The original Soviet nuclear bomb took less time—approximately four years—to create. In contrast to the Anthrax 836 biological weapon, the Soviet nuclear weapon was based on an entirely new technology in a new industry.

52. Sims, "Revisiting the Uninvention Hypothesis."

53. Ibid. Hymans, in *Achieving Nuclear Ambitions,* also draws attention to the challenges of managing scientific workers in weapons programs. See also Galison, *Image and Logic,* 239–312.

54. See Ben Ouagrham-Gormley and Vogel, "Social Context Shaping Bioweapons (Non)Proliferation," 17.

55. See also Hoffman, *Dead Hand,* 299–300.

56. Trevor Pinch uses three distinct terms to describe different types of technological testing throughout the lifetime of a technology: prospective, current, and retrospective. Prospective testing is used to describe testing carried out on a new technology before its official release, to work out design and use issues. Current testing is carried out once a technology is formally put into use, to measure how well it is functioning and whether any particular operational issues have arisen since its use in a particular setting. Finally, retrospective testing is done following an accident or malfunction, to find out what went wrong with the technology. Pinch, "Testing," 27–28.

57. This example is also analogous to what Edward Constant finds in the development of testing practices for water turbines of the nineteenth century: such testing practices would unite, transform, and embody important scientific and technologically relevant information. Constant, "Scientific Theory and Technological Testability."

58. It is important to note, however, that some offensive work—on biological weapons agents such as plague, glanders, and tularemia—continued at the Stepnogorsk facility after 1987. Alibek interview, 22 August 2001.

59. In 1989, Vladimir Pasechnik was the first high-level Soviet bioweaponeer to defect to the West. From information that he provided to British intelligence, U.S. and British officials began putting diplomatic and political pressure on the Soviet Union, later Russia, to open up all of its military and nonmilitary biodefense facilities. One year later, in response to that pressure, President Gorbachev invited U.S. and British representatives to visit Pasechnik's facility as well as three other Soviet biological facilities. Problems in these early visits led to a formalization of future "visits" by the 1992 U.S.-U.K.-Soviet trilateral agreement. Under the agreement, Russia agreed to accept visits to any nonmilitary biological site in order to remove ambiguities about its offensive biological weapons program. Since the Stepnogorsk facility was not officially a Ministry of Defense facility, it could be subject to such inspections. See Kelly, "Trilateral Agreement."

60. Hayes, "Protection of Biological Weapons Proliferation through Cooperative Threat Reduction Programs"; Alibek interview, 22 August 2001; Alibek, *Biohazard,* 190.

61. Anonymous U.S. government official, interview with author, Washington, D.C., 22 November 2002.

62. For example, U.S. nonproliferation grants have funded bench-level laboratory research work at Stepnogorsk, not large-scale fermentation or aerosolization work.

63. See Ben Ouagrham and Vogel, "Conversion at Stepnogorsk," 59.

64. U.S. Department of Defense, *Report on Activities and Programs for Countering Proliferation,* 10.

65. Spinardi, "Defence Technology Enterprises."

66. Polyani, *Personal Knowledge*; MacKenzie and Spinardi, "Tacit Knowledge, Weapons Design." However, Hugh Gusterson has noted that science studies scholars have not

devoted enough attention to the issue of decay of knowledge. See Gusterson, "Pedagogy of Diminishing Returns," 75.

67. Sims and Henke, "Repairing Nuclear Weapons."

68. One of the first Stockpile Stewardship Program projects, the Los Alamos Nuclear Weapons Archiving Project, consisted of detailed interviews with former nuclear weapons scientists. This was an effort to document formally explicit and tacit knowledge about how to produce nuclear weapons. Los Alamos has created training programs that offer multiyear sets of courses with senior weapons scientists, along with individual mentoring, to learn about the "tricks" of nuclear weapons development. See McNamara, *Ways of Knowing about Weapons*; Masco, "Nuclear Technoaesthetics"; Gusterson, "Nuclear Futures"; Ratliff, "This Is Not a Test."

69. As Joseph Masco notes, the Stockpile Stewardship Program has been significantly more expensive, on a yearly basis, than the design, development, and testing of nuclear weapons throughout the Cold War. For example, during the Cold War, the U.S. national laboratories averaged about $4 billion per year for the nuclear design and testing program. See Masco, "Nuclear Technoaesthetics," 358, 363, 369.

70. Ferguson, *Engineering and the Mind's Eye*; Ferguson, "How Engineers Lose Touch"; Cambrosio and Keating, "Going Monoclonal."

71. Some critics believe that U.S. government officials have not pressed these bioweaponeers for answers in order to safeguard U.S. nonproliferation programs against attack by Congress or the executive branch. This reticence can be explained in terms of bureaucratic politics: the greater the number of weapons scientists on the U.S. government payroll, the more funding and attention these programs receive from Congress and the president. Therefore, it may be in the interests of certain U.S. officials to expand the list of "bioweaponeers" funded in their programs. Recently, some of these U.S. government programs have begun to fund nonproliferation activities not only with scientists involved in the former Soviet biological weapons program but also with those possessing "weapons-relevant" skills, a term yet to be defined.

72. MacKenzie and Spinardi, "Tacit Knowledge, Weapons Design"; Balmer, *Britain and Biological Warfare*; Lawrence, "Incommunicable Knowledge," 503–520.

73. For some examples, see Montgomery, "Ringing in Proliferation"; Gormley, *Missile Contagion*.

74. In addition, the CIA, the main U.S. civilian intelligence agency responsible for collecting information and assessing foreign threats, does not typically respond to tasks by the executive branch unless assigned by the president or vice president, who are seen as the CIA's primary customers. Therefore, policymakers working on nonproliferation issues are often at the mercy of what the intelligence community chooses to study (and share) with policymakers to inform their decision making.

75. I am currently working with Sonia Ben Ouagrham-Gormley at George Mason University on an in-depth, comparative case study of former U.S. and Soviet bioweaponeers. However, additional country case studies (for instance, Iraq, South Africa, France, Germany, Japan) would be extremely useful for comparison.

76. Pinch and Bijker, "Social Construction of Facts and Artifacts."

77. See also Ben Ouagrham-Gormley and Vogel, "Social Context Shaping Bioweapons (Non)Proliferation," 17–20.

78. For example, see Wright and Wallace, "Varieties of Secrets and Secret Varieties."

79. Gottemoeller, "Cooperative Inducements"; Kaser, "Prospects for Cooperative Threat Reduction."

80. National Academy of Sciences, *Global Security Engagement,* 32.

81. Ibid., 50.

82. Mitman, "ISN/CTR and the Global Threat Reduction (GTR) Programs"; Rao, "Biosecurity Engagement Program." However, some early bio-engagements to non-Soviet states began in 2004, when the State Department expanded its brain drain prevention program to former weapons scientists in Iraq and Libya. See Stone, "Nonproliferation"; U.S. Government Accountability Office, *Weapons of Mass Destruction,* 1. This program spawned new initiatives to Iraq and Libya. Starting in FY 2004, Congress passed the Defense Authorization Act (P.L. 108-136, Sec. 1308), which allowed the administration to use up to $50 million in unobligated funds from the Defense Department's Cooperative Threat Reduction Program in nations outside the former Soviet Union. A similar provision permitted the Bush administration to use up to $50 million in unobligated funds from the Department of Energy's program. Initially, these monies and effort were directed to Iraq and Libya.

83. U.S. Department of State's National Security Council paper, personal communication, May 2006.

84. Mitman, "ISN/CTR and the Global Threat Reduction (GTR) Programs."

85. Marchesano and Della Ratta, "Preliminary Funding Analysis of the FY11 Budget Request"; Marchesano, "Congressional Committee Action on FY09."

86. Longa and Giles, "Reported Accomplishments of Selected Threat Reduction," 13; Mitman, "ISN/CTR and the Global Threat Reduction (GTR) Program."

87. Marchesano and Della Ratta, "Preliminary Funding Analysis of the FY11 Budget Request"; Lacey, "Analysis of the State Department's FY2009 Nonproliferation Budget Request," 2.

88. Mitman, "ISN/CTR and the Global Threat Reduction (GTR) Program"; Stratford, "'Science Centers Program' Testimony," 4.

89. Also, the State Department no longer has a former Soviet bio-chem engagement program, having replaced it with "Global Biosecurity" and "Global Chemical Security" programs. Marchesano and Della Ratta, "Preliminary Funding Analysis of the FY11 Budget Request"; Lacey, "Analysis of the State Department's FY2009 Nonproliferation Budget Request," 2.

90. Lacey, "Analysis of the State Department's FY2009 Nonproliferation Budget Request," 2.

91. National Research Council, *Biological Threat Reduction Program,* 46.

92. Marchesano, "Congressional Committee Action on FY09 International WMD Security Programs," 9. However, in 2010 Russia declared its intention to withdraw its support from the ISTC. ISTC officials are negotiating to close the Moscow headquarters of the organization. Brumfiel, "Curtain Falls on Collaborative Work."

93. U.S. Department of Defense, "Cooperative Threat Reduction Annual Report to Congress Fiscal Year 2007."

94. National Research Council, *Biological Threat Reduction Program,* 67.

95. Ibid., 44–51.

96. Ibid., 6. Others have also noted the fading support for former Soviet weapons scientist engagement programs and activities. See Averre, "Enabling Biotechnology in a Regional Perspective"; Lacey, "Analysis of the U.S. State Department's Fiscal Year 2009 Budget Request."

97. National Research Council, *Biological Threat Reduction Program,* 60.

98. Ibid., 61.

99. Woolf, "Nonproliferation and Threat Reduction Assistance."

100. Ibid., 63.

101. U.S. Department of Defense, "Fiscal Year 2011 Budget Estimate."

Overview • "Curveball" and the Iraqi Mobile Bioweapons Threat

1. U.S. Senate, "Report on the U.S. Intelligence Community's Prewar Intelligence"; Commission on the Intelligence Capabilities, *Report to the President*; Drogin, *Curveball*; Duelfer, *Comprehensive Report*; Drumheller, *On the Brink.*

2. Mihailovich, "Faulty Intel Source 'Curve Ball' Revealed."

3. See also U.S. Senate, *Report on the Use . . . of Information Provided by the Iraqi National Congress,* 106–107.

4. Kurdish forces in late April 2003 took into custody a specialized tractor-trailer near Mosul and subsequently turned it over to U.S. military control. U.S. forces in late April also discovered a mobile laboratory truck in Baghdad. The U.S. military discovered a third mobile facility suspected to produce bioweapons agent in early May at the al-Kindi Research, Testing, Development, and Engineering facility in Mosul. See U.S. Central Intelligence Agency and U.S. Defense Intelligence Agency, "Iraqi Mobile Biological Warfare Agent Production Plants."

5. White House, "Interview of the President by TVP, Poland."

6. Duelfer, *Comprehensive Report,* vol. 3, 1. This report states that there was no direct evidence that Iraq, after 1996, had plans for a new bioweapons program or was conducting bioweapons-specific work for military purposes. The report finds that since the mid-1990s, despite evidence of continuing interest in nuclear and chemical weapons, there appears to have been a complete absence of discussion or even interest in biological weapons at the presidential level. The report noted that Iraq would have faced great difficulty in reestablishing an effective bioweapons agent production capability.

7. Gormley, "The Limits of Intelligence," 7.

8. Kerr et al., "Collection and Analysis on Iraq," 50.

9. Commission on the Intelligence Capabilities, *Report to the President,* 3.

10. For a few examples, see Drogin, *Curveball*; Jervis, "Politics and Psychology of Intelligence Reform"; Jervis, "Reports, Politics, and Intelligence Failures"; Pillar, "Intelligence, Policy, and the War in Iraq"; Pollack, "Spies, Lies, and Weapons"; U.S. Senate, "Report on the U.S. Intelligence Community's Prewar Intelligence"; Commission on the

Intelligence Capabilities, *Report to the President*; Drumheller, *On the Brink*; Gusterson, "Auditors."

11. U.S. Senate, "Report on the U.S. Intelligence Community's Prewar Intelligence"; Commission on the Intelligence Capabilities, *Report to the President*; Office of the Director of National Intelligence, "National Intelligence Strategy"; Miscik, "DDI's State of Analysis Speech."

12. Commission on the Intelligence Capabilities, *Report to the President.*

13. Carl Ford, telephone interview with author, 22 September 2008.

14. Eden, *Whole World on Fire,* 56.

15. Commission on the Intelligence Capabilities, *Report to the President,* 81.

16. These concerns were first documented in an April 1995 Security Council report, S/1995/284 of 10 April 1995, seventh report under resolution 715, www.fas.org/news/un/iraq/s/s1995-0284.htm.

17. U.S. Senate, "Report on the U.S. Intelligence Community's Prewar Intelligence," 150–151; U.S. Central Intelligence Agency, "Iraq's Weapons of Mass Destruction Programs," 17.

18. Previously, Al-Saadi was also Hussein Kamal's deputy in Iraq's Military Industrialization Commission, the commission responsible for Iraq's proscribed weapons programs. Unless otherwise noted, the information about the UN discussion with Al-Saadi comes from Richard Spertzel, telephone interview with author, 17 March 2008.

19. Ibid.; Gabriele Kraatz-Wadsack, interview with author, New York, 19 July 2007; Duelfer, *Comprehensive Report,* 79.

20. Kraatz-Wadsack interview.

21. Tyler Drumheller, interview with author, McLean, Virginia, 7 February 2008.

22. Ibid.

23. These reports were from the July 1999 National Intelligence Council memorandum "Iraq: Post–Desert Fox Activities and Estimated Status of WMD Programs" and August 1999 National Intelligence Estimate, "Worldwide BW program: Trends and Prospects (NIE 2000-12HCX)." Although these documents remain classified, the report findings on Iraqi bioweapons assessments are briefly summarized in U.S. Senate, "Report on the U.S. Intelligence Community's Prewar Intelligence," 143–144.

24. Anonymous former U.S. intelligence analyst, interview with author, Arlington, Virginia, 19 March 2007.

25. Anonymous former U.S. intelligence analyst, interview with author, Washington, D.C., 15 January 2007.

26. Commission on the Intelligence Capabilities, *Report to the President,* 83, 218.

27. Drogin, *Curveball,* 26.

28. U.S. Senate, "Report on the U.S. Intelligence Community's Prewar Intelligence," 149.

29. Anonymous former U.S. intelligence analyst, interview with author, Arlington, Virginia, 24 March 2007; Drogin, *Curveball,* 61–62; Commission on the Intelligence Capabilities, *Report to the President,* 90; Drogin and Goetz, "How U.S. Fell under the Spell of Curveball."

30. Anonymous former U.S. intelligence analyst, interview with author, Arlington, Virginia, 24 March 2007.

31. Drogin, *Curveball,* 51, 59.

32. The CIA and DIA were never given direct access to German transcripts of questions asked of and responses given by Curveball. It was not until the spring of 2004, a year after the U.S. invasion of Iraq, that the CIA was finally granted in-person access to Curveball. When a CIA operations officer finally spoke with him, the officer questioned him in detail about the mobile labs with evidence that countered his claims. It was during this discussion that the operations officer determined that Curveball had lied. U.S. Senate, "Report on the U.S. Intelligence Community's Prewar Intelligence," 26.

33. Drogin, *Curveball,* 72; U.S. Senate, "Report on the U.S. Intelligence Community's Prewar Intelligence," 163.

34. U.S. Senate, "Report on the U.S. Intelligence Community's Prewar Intelligence," 150.

35. Ibid., 150.

36. Ibid., 149.

37. Ibid., 164.

38. Ibid., 163.

39. Commission on the Intelligence Capabilities, *Report to the President,* 90.

40. Ibid.

41. U.S. Senate, "Report on the U.S. Intelligence Community's Prewar Intelligence," 152.

42. Commission on the Intelligence Capabilities, *Report to the President,* 92.

43. U.S. Senate, "Report on the U.S. Intelligence Community's Prewar Intelligence," 151.

44. Commission on the Intelligence Capabilities, *Report to the President,* 85, 225.

45. Ekeus, "Iraq Briefing."

46. Kay Mereish, Ewen Buchanan, and Peter Prosser, interview with author, New York City, 18 July 2007.

47. Borger and Norton-Taylor, "MI6 'Still Using' Disputed Informer on WMD."

48. U.S. Senate, "Report on the U.S. Intelligence Community's Prewar Intelligence," 246; Commission on the Intelligence Capabilities, *Report to the President,* 85.

49. Drogin, *Curveball,* 123. For more background on the British source, see Return to an Address of the Honourable the House of Commons, "Review of Intelligence on Weapons of Mass Destruction," 128.

50. U.S. Senate, "Report on the U.S. Intelligence Community's Prewar Intelligence," 149.

51. This conclusion was drawn as the George W. Bush administration had just entered office and several months before 11 September 2001. See Commission on the Intelligence Capabilities, *Report to the President,* 91, 92, 97–98, 219; Drogin, *Curveball,* 62, 85–88, 136, 139.

52. Anonymous former U.S. intelligence analyst, interview with author, Arlington, Virginia, 24 March 2007.

53. U.S. Senate, "Report on the U.S. Intelligence Community's Prewar Intelligence," 149.

54. Ibid.

55. Commission on the Intelligence Capabilities, *Report to the President,* 96–97.

56. U.S. Senate, "Report on the U.S. Intelligence Community's Prewar Intelligence," 162.

57. Commission on the Intelligence Capabilities, *Report to the President*, 91; Margaret Henoch, interview with author, Chevy Chase, Maryland, 1 October 2008.

58. Commission on the Intelligence Capabilities, *Report to the President,* 221.

59. Ibid., 91; Drogin, *Curveball,* 131.

60. Commission on the Intelligence Capabilities, *Report to the President,* 92; Drogin, *Curveball,* 131.

61. Commission on the Intelligence Capabilities, *Report to the President,* 219.

62. Ibid., 108–109.

63. Drogin, *Curveball,* 130.

64. Commission on the Intelligence Capabilities, *Report to the President,* 97.

65. Drogin, *Curveball,* 136.

66. Commission on the Intelligence Capabilities, *Report to the President,* 97, 102–103; Drumheller, *On the Brink,* 79–80.

67. Commission on the Intelligence Capabilities, *Report to the President,* 97.

68. Ibid., 96.

69. Drumheller interview, 7 February 2008.

70. Commission on the Intelligence Capabilities, *Report to the President,* 97.

71. Henoch interview, 1 October 2008.

72. Drogin, *Curveball,* 137.

73. Drumheller interview, 7 February 2008.

74. Commission on the Intelligence Capabilities, *Report to the President,* 97.

75. Drumheller interview, 7 February 2008.

76. Commission on the Intelligence Capabilities, *Report to the President,* 98.

77. Sims, "Things Fall Apart," 94; Bowker, *Science on the Run,* 10–14.

Chapter 5 • Expertise and Analytic Practice

Epigraph. David Kay, interview with author, Arlington, Virginia, 23 March 2007.

1. Intelligence scholar Stephen Marrin has noted that the "interplay between analyst and institution within the Intelligence Community remains poorly studied." Marrin, "Improving CIA Analysis," 41.

2. Murphy, *Sick Building Syndrome,* 10.

3. I thank S&TS scholar Rachel Maines for suggesting this query.

4. Anonymous former U.S. intelligence analyst, interview with author, Arlington, Virginia, 5 February 2008.

5. Commission on the Intelligence Capabilities, *Report to the President,* 97.

6. Henoch interview, 1 October 2008.

7. Richard Kerr, telephone interview with author, 1 April 2008.

8. Ibid.

9. Gentry, "Framework for Reform of the U.S. Intelligence Community."

10. Ibid.

11. Hulnick, "Managing Intelligence Analysis," 323.

12. Kerr interview.

13. Ibid.

14. Ibid. Intelligence expert Stephen Marrin has also noted the problems that come with the breakup of centralized knowledge in the CIA; see Marrin, "Improving CIA Analysis," 54–55.

15. The Nonproliferation Center was one of seven new "centers" established in the 1990s to centralize technical expertise as a way to better analyze transnational WMD threats. Richelson, *U.S. Intelligence Community,* 29.

16. Director of Central Intelligence, "Director of Central Intelligence Directive 7/2."

17. Between the disbanding of the Office of Scientific and Weapons Research and the creation of the Nonproliferation Center, a new temporary office, the Office of Weapons, Technology, and Proliferation, was created. Anonymous former U.S. intelligence analyst, interview with author, Arlington, Virginia, 5 February 2008.

18. Richelson, *U.S. Intelligence Community,* 29.

19. Ibid.

20. In 1996, the Directorate of Operations personnel who had been moved into the Nonproliferation Center were transferred to a new CIA unit created within the Directorate of Operations, the Counterproliferation Division.

21. Plame Wilson, *Fair Game,* 99; John Lauder, interview with author, Arlington, Virginia, 30 September 2008.

22. Kerr interview.

23. Ibid.

24. Ibid.

25. Anonymous former CIA analyst, telephone interview with author, 9 September 2008.

26. Kerr interview.

27. Ibid.

28. Commission on the Intelligence Capabilities. *Report to the President,* 244.

29. Drumheller, interview with author, McLean, Virginia, 19 March 2008.

30. Richelson, *U.S. Intelligence Community,* 22–23.

31. Henoch interview, 1 October 2008.

32. Ibid.

33. Drumheller interview, 19 March 2008.

34. Anonymous former U.S. intelligence analyst, interview with author, Arlington, Virginia, 24 March 2007.

35. Kerr et al., "Collection and Analysis on Iraq," 47.

36. Ibid., 50.

37. "Raw" or "unfinished" intelligence is information that has not been subjected to the formal process of analysis.

38. Drumheller interview, 7 February 2008.

39. Ibid.

40. Drogin, *Curveball,* 60, 196.

41. Henoch interview with author, Chevy Chase, Maryland, 30 January 2009.

42. Ibid.

43. Drumheller interview, 19 March 2008.

44. Commission on the Intelligence Capabilities. *Report to the President,* 106–107, 223.
45. Drumheller interview, 19 March 2008.
46. Ibid.
47. Ibid.
48. Henoch interview, 1 October 2008.
49. Ibid.
50. Henoch interview, 30 January 2009.
51. Ibid.
52. Commission on the Intelligence Capabilities, *Report to the President,* 223; Duelfer, *Comprehensive Report,* vol. 3, 73; Follath et al., "How German Intelligence Helped Justify the U.S. Invasion of Iraq."
53. Commission on the Intelligence Capabilities. *Report to the President,* 241.
54. Ibid., 88.
55. Drumheller interview, 19 March 2008.
56. Henoch interview, 30 January 2009.
57. Ibid.
58. Drumheller interview, 19 March 2008.
59. From the mid-1960s to the late 1980s, Carl Ford spent several years working as an Asian military analyst within the U.S. Defense Intelligence Agency and the CIA. He ultimately served as the National Intelligence Officer for East Asia in the CIA. Ford interview, 22 September 2008.
60. Ford, interview with author, Arlington, Virginia, 8 February 2008.
61. Kerr interview.
62. Ibid.
63. Ford interview, 8 February 2008.
64. In their determination of priority intelligence targets, collection managers are described as a way to connect policymakers, intelligence analysts, and collectors.
65. Ford interview, 22 September 2008.
66. Henoch interview, 30 January 2009.
67. Ford interview, 22 September 2008.
68. Operations officials typically call these individuals reports officers; analysts often call them processors.
69. The CIA does not have dedicated reports officers devoted to help analysts sort through open-source information. Rather, analysts are largely expected to act as their own collectors and processors of such information. The creation of the Open Source Center in 2005 by the Director of National Intelligence was aimed at rectifying these shortcomings, although it remains to be seen how deeply this center will affect the CIA's analytic work.
70. Henoch interview, 30 January 2009.
71. Ibid.
72. Ford interview, 8 February 2008.
73. Lowenthal, *Intelligence: From Secrets to Policy,* 45.
74. U.S. Senate, "Report on the U.S. Intelligence Community's Prewar Intelligence Assessments," 26; Commission on the Intelligence Capabilities, *Report to the President,* 90.

75. Anonymous former intelligence analyst, interview with author, Arlington, Virginia, 24 March 2007.

76. Kerr interview.

77. Shapin, "Invisible Technician"; see also Star, "Sociology of the Invisible."

78. For example, see U.S. Central Intelligence Agency, *Consumer's Guide to Intelligence,* cover.

79. Henoch interview, 30 January 2009.

80. Marrin, "Improving CIA Analysis," 45; Ford interview, 8 February 2008.

81. Ford interview, 8 February 2008.

82. Ford interview, 22 September 2008.

83. Ford interview, 8 February 2008.

84. Johnston, *Analytic Culture,* 70.

85. Anonymous former U.S. intelligence practitioner, personal communication with author, 2 February 2010.

86. Johnston, *Analytic Culture,* 73.

87. Ford, "Improving Analysis," 2.

88. Ibid., 4.

89. Weber, *Essays in Sociology,* 233–234.

90. Kerr et al., "Holistic Vision for the Analytic Unit."

91. Ford interview, 8 February 2008.

92. Gentry, *Lost Promise,* 100.

93. Marrin, "Improving CIA Analysis," 45.

94. Bruce, "Making Analysis More Reliable," 185.

95. Ford, "Improving Analysis," 5.

96. Ford interview, 8 February 2008.

97. Ibid.

98. Some intelligence practitioners are working to change this deficiency; see Rieber and Thomason, "Creation of a National Institute."

99. Kent, *Strategic Intelligence,* 74.

100. Russell, *Sharpening Strategic Intelligence,* 119.

101. Ford interview, 22 September 2008. Henoch, however, notes that in recruiting a technical human source, the case officer need not be technical, as the case officer needs to evaluate the whole person, not just the technical information, to determine if he or she is a credible source. Henoch, personal communication with author, 14 July 2011.

102. Dennis Gormley, telephone interview with author, 21 September 2008.

103. Ibid.

104. Russell, *Sharpening Strategic Intelligence,* 125.

105. Ford interview, 22 September 2008.

106. Henoch interview, 1 October 2008.

107. Ford interview, 22 September 2008.

108. Anonymous former CIA analyst, telephone interview with author, 9 September 2008.

109. Drumheller interview, 19 March 2008. See also Russell, *Sharpening Strategic Intelligence,* 107.

110. Russell, *Sharpening Strategic Intelligence,* 123.

111. Ibid.

112. Hitz, "Editorial."

113. Marrin, "CIA's Kent School," 628.

114. Drogin, *Curveball,* 65. Drogin writes that the vast majority of WINPAC analysts worked on supporting strategic arms control agreements and tracking illicit trade in nuclear technology and ballistic missiles.

115. Drumheller, *On the Brink,* 81.

116. Anonymous former U.S. intelligence analyst, interview with author, Arlington, Virginia, 24 March 2007.

117. Ibid.

118. Drumheller interview, 7 February 2008.

119. Drogin, *Curveball,* 221–222.

120. Drumheller interview, 19 March 2008.

121. Peter Prosser, interview with author, New York City, 18 July 2007.

122. Kay Mereish, interview with author, New York City, 18 July 2007.

123. Anonymous former intelligence analyst, interview with author, 24 March 2007.

124. See also Russell, *Sharpening Strategic Intelligence,* 121.

125. Anonymous former intelligence analyst, interview with author, 5 February 2008.

126. Henoch interview, 1 October 2008.

127. Shapin and Schaffer, *Leviathan and the Air Pump,* 332.

128. For another relevant historical example of how different regimes of perceptibility shape bioweapons assessments, see Barton, *Weapons Detective,* 18–42.

Chapter 6 • Current Intelligence Reporting and CIA Analytic Practice

Epigraph. Johnston, *Analytic Culture,* 27.

1. Bush, "2003 State of the Union Address."
2. Lawrence Wilkerson, interview with author, Vienna, Virginia, 31 July 2007.
3. Simon, "Faulty Intel Source 'Curveball' Revealed."
4. Woodward, *Plan of Attack.*
5. Wilkerson interview.
6. Ibid.
7. *Washington Post,* "Irrefutable."
8. Gordon, "Powell's Case against Iraq."
9. See Richelson, *U.S. Intelligence Community,* 369–374.
10. U.S. Central Intelligence Agency, *Consumer's Guide to Intelligence,* 43.
11. For examples, see Johnson, *Analytic Culture*; Gormley, "Transforming Intelligence"; Zegart, "'CNN with Secrets,'"; Treverton, *Next Steps in Reshaping Intelligence*; Commission on the Intelligence Capabilities, *Report to the President.*
12. Johnson, "Glimpses into the Gems of American Intelligence," 355. See also Ford, cited in Gormley, *Transforming Intelligence,* 18; Gentry, "Framework for Reform of the U.S. Intelligence Community."
13. Johnson, "Glimpses into the Gems of American Intelligence," 355.

14. Ford interview, 5 February 2008. See also Gentry, "Framework for Reform."

15. See Marrin, "CIA's Kent School," 627.

16. Johnston, *Analytic Culture,* 15.

17. Ford interview, 5 February 2008.

18. Johnston, *Analytic Culture,* 27.

19. Ibid., 101.

20. Ibid., 27.

21. Gormley, *Transforming Intelligence*; Commission on the Intelligence Capabilities, *Report to the President,* 174–175; Zegart, "'CNN with Secrets.'"

22. Gans, *Deciding What's News.*

23. Gans, *Deciding What's News,* 82.

24. Ibid., 67, 208.

25. Ibid., 282–283.

26. Boyle Mahle, *Denial and Deception,* 94.

27. Marrin, "Homeland Security," 10.

28. Quoted in Goldstein, "Modeling Terrorists."

29. Anonymous former U.S. intelligence analyst, interview with author, Arlington, Virginia, 24 March 2007.

30. Marrin, "Homeland Security," 10.

31. Johnston, *Analytic Culture,* 22.

32. Ibid., 18.

33. Anonymous former U.S. intelligence analyst, interview with author, 5 February 2008.

34. Johnston, *Analytic Culture,* 24.

35. Ibid., 25.

36. Ibid.

37. George and Bruce, *Analyzing Intelligence,* 7.

38. Anonymous former U.S. intelligence analyst, interview with author, 24 March 2007.

39. Ford interview, 5 February 2008.

40. Johnston, *Analytic Culture,* 15.

41. Anonymous former U.S. intelligence analyst, interview with author, 5 February 2008.

42. Heuer Jr., *Psychology of Intelligence Analysis,* 60.

43. Gormley, *Transforming Intelligence,* 11.

44. Anonymous former U.S. intelligence analyst, interview with author, 24 March 2007.

45. Ibid.

46. Ibid.

47. Johnston, *Analytic Culture,* 25.

48. Ibid.

49. Gans, *Deciding What's News,* 90.

50. Ibid.

51. For more background on PDBs, see Johnson, "Glimpses into Gems of American Intelligence."

52. Bumiller, "White House Letter."

53. Commission on the Intelligence Capabilities, *Report to the President,* 402–403.

54. Lieberthal, *U.S. Intelligence Community,* 11. See also Pincus, "Under Bush."

55. On occasion, for a technically complex issue, a CIA technical expert will accompany the PDB briefers to help answer questions from the president. Anonymous former U.S. intelligence analyst, interview with author, Arlington, Virginia, 24 March 2007.

56. Ibid.

57. Lieberthal, *U.S. Intelligence Community,* 10; see also Johnson, "Glimpses," 336–338. For an interesting historical description of the PDB process, see Marshall, "Memorandum."

58. Anonymous former U.S. intelligence analyst, interview with author, Arlington, Virginia, 24 March 2007.

59. Note that the coordination process depends on the coordinator and the other participants in the coordination process. The process itself does not prohibit extended interrogation of the claims made in the current intelligence report. In practice, however, the time demands of producing a current intelligence report typically inhibit extended interrogation of the assumptions and methodologies used in the report.

60. Anonymous former U.S. intelligence analyst, interview with author, 5 February 2008.

61. Johnston, *Analytic Culture,* 15.

62. Anonymous former U.S. intelligence analyst, interview with author, 24 March 2007. Interestingly, the Directorate of Operations is not required to share—and, due to classification issues, is sometimes prohibited from sharing—this newly inserted clarifying intelligence information with the analyst but sends it directly to the PDB editorial staff.

63. Gans, *Deciding What's News,* 84.

64. Gentry, "Intelligence Analyst/Manager Relations," 137–138; Gentry, *Lost Promise,* 29–30.

65. U.S. Senate, "Report on the U.S. Intelligence Community's Prewar Intelligence Assessments," 8.

66. Gans, *Deciding What's News,* 101.

67. Anonymous former U.S. intelligence analyst, interview with author, Arlington, Virginia, 24 March 2007.

68. Ibid.

69. Commission on the Intelligence Capabilities, *Report to the President,* 420.

70. Johnston, *Analytic Culture,* 27.

71. Anonymous former U.S. intelligence analyst, interview with author, Arlington, Virginia, 24 March 2007.

72. Ibid. See also Gentry, "Intelligence Analyst/Manager Relations."

73. George, "Beyond Analytic Tradecraft," 300.

74. Gans, *Deciding What's News,* 98.

75. Steiner, "Challenging the Red Line," 6.

76. Anonymous former U.S. intelligence analyst, interview with author, Arlington, Virginia, 24 March 2007.

77. Ibid. See also Russell, *Sharpening Strategic Intelligence,* 133; Johnson, "Glimpses," 338.

78. Marrin, "Homeland Security," 13.

79. Anonymous former U.S. intelligence analyst, interview with author, Arlington, Virginia, 24 March 2007.

80. Pillar, "Intelligence, Policy, and the War in Iraq."

81. Commission on the Intelligence Capabilities, *Report to the President,* 50, 420. In other instances, intelligence suggesting the existence of weapons programs was included in a PDB, but subsequent information casting doubt on the validity of that intelligence was not.

82. Gans, *Deciding What's News,* 109.

83. Lieberthal, *U.S. Intelligence Community,* 37.

84. Johnston, *Analytic Culture,* 13.

85. Because analysts do not stay long, this also contributes to the internal reliance on "generalist" expertise (see chapter 5). In contrast, intelligence analysts at the State Department's Office of Intelligence and Research (INR) typically have an average of fourteen years of analytic experience working on a specific issue area. Ford interview, 8 February 2008; Wilkerson interview.

86. Anonymous former U.S. intelligence analyst, interview with author, 5 February 2008.

87. Ibid. See also Priest and Arkin, "National Security, Inc."

88. Gormley, "Transforming Intelligence," 10; Johnston, *Analytic Culture,* xii.

89. Ford, "Improving Analysis," personal communication from Ford to author, 4.

90. Johnston, *Analytic Culture,* 16; Commission on the Intelligence Capabilities, *Report to the President,* 402.

91. Anonymous former U.S. intelligence analyst, interview with author, 24 March 2007. As this former analyst notes, "Your supervisors will come and ask you, 'I need your rag sheet.'" The term *rag sheet* is commonly used to denote a kind of daily or weekly tabloid.

92. Anonymous former U.S. intelligence analyst, interview with author, 24 March 2007.

93. Anonymous former U.S. intelligence analyst, interview with author, 5 February 2008.

94. Anonymous former U.S. intelligence analyst, interview with author, 24 March 2007.

95. Anonymous former U.S. intelligence analyst, interview with author, 5 February 2008.

96. Intelligence expert Mark Lowenthal has referred to oral briefings as "probably the most important analytical service provided by the intelligence community" because of the interaction it permits between consumers and producers of intelligence. Lowenthal, "Intelligence Analysis," 227.

97. Paul Pillar, "Interview from 'The Dark Side.' "; see also Johnston, *Analytic Culture,* 107.

98. Anonymous former U.S. intelligence analyst, interview with author, 24 March 2007.

99. Russell, *Sharpening Strategic Intelligence,* 124–125.

100. Anonymous former U.S. intelligence analyst, interview with author, Arlington, Virginia, 24 March 2007.

101. Director of the CIA Office of Training and Education, quoted in Gentry, *Lost Promise,* 45.

102. Commission on the Roles and Capabilities of the U.S. Intelligence Community, *Preparing for the 21st Century*; Warner and McDonald, *U.S. Intelligence Community,* 34.

103. Anonymous U.S. intelligence analyst, interview with author, Washington, D.C., 6 February 2008.

104. Drogin, *Curveball,* 139.

105. Commission on the Intelligence Capabilities, *Report to the President,* 83; anonymous former U.S. intelligence analyst, interview with author, Arlington, Virginia, 19 March 2007.

106. U.S. Senate, "Report on Whether Public Statements regarding Iraq," 23.

107. Drogin, *Curveball,* 73.

108. Commission on the Intelligence Capabilities, *Report to the President,* 83, 215.

109. Anonymous former U.S. intelligence analyst, interview with author, Arlington, Virginia, 24 March 2007; Commission on the Intelligence Capabilities, *Report to the President,* 83, 215.

110. Commission on the Intelligence Capabilities, *Report to the President,* 83, 215.

111. U.S. Senate, "Report on Whether Public Statements regarding Iraq," 24.

112. NIEs are intelligence assessments that express the coordinated judgments of all of the members of the U.S. intelligence community. Commission on the Intelligence Capabilities, *Report to the President,* 83, 215; U.S. Senate, "Report on the U.S. Intelligence," 144.

113. Commission on the Intelligence Capabilities, *Report to the President,* 83.

114. U.S. Senate, "Report on the U.S. Intelligence," 147.

115. Ibid., 144–145, 298.

116. Ibid., 144–145.

117. Commission on the Intelligence Capabilities. *Report to the President,* 83, 215.

118. Ibid., 215–216.

119. Ibid., 93, 219.

120. Ibid., 83, 215. Additional CIA current reports on Iraq biological weapons threats produced during 2001 include *Developing Biological Weapons as a Strategic Deterrent* and *The Iraqi Threat*; see U.S. Senate, "Report on Whether Public Statements regarding Iraq," 20.

121. U.S. Senate, "Report on the U.S. Intelligence," 145.

122. Anonymous former U.S. intelligence analyst, interview with author, Arlington, Virginia, 24 March 2007.

123. Ibid.

124. U.S. Senate, "Report on the U.S. Intelligence," 248; U.S. Senate, "Report on Whether Public Statements regarding Iraq," 24. For the original news articles, see Kennedy, "Defector"; Rose, "Iraq's Arsenal of Terror."

125. Commission on the Intelligence Capabilities, *Report to the President,* 93.

126. Anonymous former U.S. intelligence analyst, interview with author, Arlington, Virginia, 24 March 2007.

127. U.S. Senate, "Report on Whether Public Statements regarding Iraq," 21.

128. Isikoff and Corn, *Hubris,* 130.

129. Commission on the Intelligence Capabilities, *Report to the President,* 84, 216.

130. Ibid., 216.

131. U.S. Senate, "Report on the U.S. Intelligence," 186.

132. Commission on the Intelligence Capabilities, *Report to the President,* 84.

133. U.S. Senate, "Report on the U.S. Intelligence," 298–299.

134. Ford interview, 5 February 2008.

135. U.S. Senate, "Report on the U.S. Intelligence," 146.

136. Emphasis added. Director of Central Intelligence, "National Intelligence Estimate: Iraq's Continuing Programs," 1.

137. Ibid., 6; Commission on the Intelligence Capabilities, *Report to the President,* 80.

138. U.S. Senate, "Report on the U.S. Intelligence," 149.

139. Director of Central Intelligence, "National Intelligence Estimate: Iraq's Continuing Programs," 7.

140. Commission on the Intelligence Capabilities, *Report to the President,* 85, 217.

141. Drogin, *Curveball,* 134, 138.

142. Anonymous former U.S. intelligence analyst, interview with author, Arlington, Virginia, 24 March 2007. A CIA-funded contractor, Battelle-Memorial, was also involved in creating some portion of the graphics used in Powell's speech. See Leitenberg, "Unresolved Questions," part 1 of 3, "Further Information," part 2 of 3, "Further Information," part 3 of 3.

143. Commission on the Intelligence Capabilities, *Report to the President,* 85, 217.

144. For a discussion of PDD-35, see "PDD-35 Intelligence Requirements," 2 March 1995. www.fas.org/irp/offdocs/pdd35.htm.

145. Anonymous former U.S. intelligence analyst, interview with author, Arlington, Virginia, 24 March 2007.

146. Lauder interview.

147. Anonymous former CIA analyst, telephone interview with author, 9 September 2008.

148. Commission on the Intelligence Capabilities, *Report to the President,* 217.

149. Anonymous former U.S. intelligence analyst, interview with author, 24 March 2007.

150. U.S. Central Intelligence Agency and U.S. Defense Intelligence Agency, "Iraqi Mobile Biological Warfare Agent Production Plants."

151. Broad, "U.S., in Assessment."

152. Miller and Broad, "Some Analysts of Iraq Trailers."

153. Anonymous former U.S. intelligence analyst, interview with author, Washington, D.C., 15 January 2007.

154. Warrick, "Lacking Biolabs."

155. Anonymous former U.S. intelligence analyst, interview with author, Washington, D.C., 15 January 2007.

156. Warrick, "Lacking Biolabs." Three weeks later, a more comprehensive 122-page final report was issued by the team.

157. The Iraq Survey Group (ISG) was an international team organized by the Pentagon and CIA in the spring of 2003 to hunt for suspected Iraqi WMD stockpiles, expertise, and other related infrastructure. The ISG issued a formal report in September 2004; see Duelfer, *Comprehensive Report.*

158. Although the ISG report carefully states that these conclusions cannot disprove the existence of Iraqi mobile bio-facilities, it also states that it was unable to uncover any evidence of such systems; see Duelfer, *Comprehensive Report,* vol. 3, 44.

159. Ford interview, 5 February 2008.

160. Ibid.

161. Ibid.

162. Feder, "Forecasting for Policy Making," 119.

163. Ford interview, 22 September 2008.

164. Anonymous former U.S. intelligence analyst, interview with author, 5 February 2008.

165. Commission on the Intelligence Capabilities, *Report to the President,* 83–84; U.S. Senate, "Report on the U.S. Intelligence," 149.

166. Kerr interview.

167. Ibid.

168. Ford interview, 22 September 2008.

Chapter 7 • Secrecy and the Production of the Iraqi Mobile Bioweapons Threat

Epigraph. Simmel, "Secrecy," 330.

1. Shulsky and Schmitt, *Silent Warfare,* 171.

2. Stephen Hilgartner's concept of "technologies of privacy" usefully describes the variety of artifacts, physical and material spaces, and social practices that constitute the classification practices described below. See Hilgartner, *Science on Stage,* 17.

3. U.S. Central Intelligence Agency, *Consumer's Guide to Intelligence,* 48.

4. For some background on the use of codewords, see U.S. Central Intelligence Agency, "Critique."

5. Johnston, *Analytic Culture,* 103.

6. CIA analysts also work with other classified databases and information systems; for a discussion of these, see Marrin, "Homeland Security and the Analysis of Foreign Intelligence," 7.

7. For more information on the CIA's IT system, see Berkowitz, "Failing to Keep Up."

8. Commission on the Intelligence Capabilities, *Report to the President,* 439.

9. Johnston, *Analytic Culture,* 100.

10. Galison, "Removing Knowledge," 237; see also Bellman, "Paradox of Secrecy."

11. This generative or productive effect draws from Michel Foucault's notion that the exercise of power can produce or enable certain kinds of discourses, practices, and institutions for the production of knowledge. Foucault, *Discipline and Punish.* See also Masco, "Lie Detectors"; Wright and Wallace, "Secrecy in the Biotechnology Industry"; Balmer, "Secret Formula"; Rappert, "Making Silence Matter."

12. Shapin, "Placing the View from Nowhere," 6.

13. Anonymous former U.S. intelligence analyst, interview with author, Arlington, Virginia, 24 March 2007.

14. U.S. Senate, "Report on the U.S. Intelligence," 184.

15. Director of Central Intelligence, "National Intelligence Estimate: Iraq's Continuing Programs,"5.

16. Anonymous former U.S. intelligence analyst, interview with author, Arlington, Virginia, 19 March 2007.

17. Ibid.

18. Kay Mereish, interview with author, New York City, 18 July 2007.

19. Ibid.

20. Ibid.

21. Ibid.

22. Drogin, *Curveball,* 171.

23. Ibid., 172.

24. Ibid., 172–173; Commission on the Intelligence Capabilities, *Report to the President,* 219.

25. U.S. Senate, "Report on the U.S. Intelligence," 20.

26. Dimitri Perricos was deputy executive chairman of UNMOVIC at this time. According to Mereish, this conversation was particularly striking, because it was the first time that Iraq did not require "minders" to attend discussions between Iraqi scientists and UN inspectors; previously, these minders would interrupt or prevent certain lines of UN questioning of Iraqi officials and scientists. Mereish interview.

27. Ibid.

28. Ibid.

29. Ibid.

30. Johnston, *Analytic Culture,* 24.

31. Drumheller interview, 7 February 2008.

32. Mereish interview.

33. Peter Prosser, interview with author, New York City, 18 July 2007.

34. Ewen Buchanan, interview with author, New York City, 18 July 2007.

35. Buchanan interview.

36. See also Jones, "Intelligence, Verification, and Iraq's WMD," 202.

37. Henoch interview, 1 October 2008.

38. Henoch, personal communication, 14 July 2011.

39. "You have to assume that there is something there, because you cannot believe that analysts—who are your grade and senior—and their bosses and your bosses are going to let something that is clearly so flawed go forward." Henoch, personal communication.

40. Anonymous former U.S. government official, telephone interview with author, 18 February 2008.

41. U.S. Senate, "Report on the U.S. Intelligence," 26.

42. Anonymous former U.S. intelligence analyst, interview with author, 5 February 2008.

43. See Johnston, *Analytic Culture,* 25.

44. Jervis, "Reports, Politics, and Intelligence Failures," 30.

45. Anonymous former U.S. intelligence analyst, interview with author, 24 March 2007.

46. Geoffrey Walford has argued that such kinds of generalization invoked in the name of protecting an actor's identity can be used to make particular arguments resistant to challenge. See Walford, "Why Don't Researchers Name Their Research Sites?" For a discussion of the power that resides in the use of such graphical representations, see Latour, "Drawing Things Together"; Latour and Woolgar, *Laboratory Life*; Goodwin, "Seeing in Depth"; Tufte, *Cognitive Style of PowerPoint.*

47. Drumheller interview, 19 March 2008.

48. Drogin, *Curveball,* 67.

49. Drumheller interview, 19 March 2008.

50. Ibid.

51. As noted in chapter 5, the Counterproliferation Division is responsible for intelligence collection on WMDs; Henoch interview.

52. Ibid.

53. Ibid.

54. Ibid.

55. Ibid.

56. Riles, *Documents.*

57. Drumheller interview, 19 March 2008.

58. Commission on the Intelligence Capabilities. *Report to the President,* 109.

59. Ibid., 84, 85, 225.

60. Ibid., 109–110; U.S. Senate, "Report on the U.S. Intelligence," 160–161.

61. Commission on the Intelligence Capabilities. *Report to the President,* 225.

62. Ibid., 93.

63. Ibid., 109.

64. Ibid.

65. Ford interview, 8 February 2008.

66. Ibid.

67. See Alexander, "Intelligence Role for the Footnote"; Evans, "Against Footnotes."

68. Commission on the Intelligence Capabilities. *Report to the President,* 108–110.

69. Drumheller interview, 19 March 2008.

70. Dennis, "Science and Secrecy Revisited," 6–7.

71. Ibid.

72. Ibid; also, see Dennis, "Our First Line of Defense," 430–440.

73. Commission on the Intelligence Capabilities. *Report to the President,* 431.

74. Commission on the Intelligence Capabilities. *Report to the President,* 88.

75. Drumheller interview, 19 March 2008.

76. Commission on the Intelligence Capabilities. *Report to the President,* 89.

77. Drumheller interview, 19 March 2008.

78. Henoch interview.

79. Ibid.

80. Weber, *Essays in Sociology,* 233–234.

81. Commission on the Intelligence Capabilities. *Report to the President,* 91; U.S. Senate, "Report on the U.S. Intelligence," 190; U.S. Senate, "Report on the Use by the Intelligence Community," 106.

82. U.S. Senate, "Report on the Use by the Intelligence Community," 105.

83. U.S. Senate, "Report on the U.S. Intelligence," 149.

84. Anonymous former U.S. intelligence analyst, interview with author, Vienna, Virginia, 31 July 2007.

85. Warrick, "Lacking Biolabs, Trailers Carried Case for War"; anonymous former U.S. intelligence analyst, interview with author, Vienna, Virginia, 31 July 2007.

86. Anonymous former U.S. intelligence analyst, interview with author, Washington, D.C., 15 January 2007.

87. U.S. Central Intelligence Agency and U.S. Defense Intelligence Agency, "Iraqi Mobile Biological Warfare Agent Production Plants."

88. Ford interview, 8 February 2008.

89. However, Tenet and McLaughlin have publicly stated that they were unaware of the problems with Curveball's reporting at the time. See Tenet, "Statement"; McLaughlin, "Statement."

90. Anonymous former U.S. intelligence analyst, interview with author, Washington, D.C., 15 January 2007.

91. U.S. Senate, "Report on Postwar Findings," 35.

92. Warrick, "Lacking Biolabs, Trailers Carried Case for War."

93. Anonymous former U.S. intelligence analyst, interview with author, Washington, D.C., 15 January 2007.

94. Ibid.

95. Wright and Wallace, "Secrecy in the Biotechnology Industry," 369.

96. Drumheller interview, 7 February 2008.

97. For a discussion of this topic, see Drogin, *Curveball,* 14–19.

98. Drumheller interview, 19 March 2008.

99. Commission on the Intelligence Capabilities. *Report to the President,* 91.

100. Henoch interview.

101. Wright and Wallace, "Secrecy in the Biotechnology Industry," 369.

102. For other examples, see Gusterson, *Nuclear Rites*; Rappert and Balmer, "Rethinking 'Secrecy' and 'Disclosure' "; Masco, "Lie Detectors."

103. Simmel, "Secrecy," 332.

104. Ibid., 333.

105. Henoch interview.

106. Ford interview, 22 September 2008.

107. Anonymous former U.S. intelligence analyst, interview with author, 15 January 2007.

108. Kerr interview.

109. Anonymous former U.S. intelligence analyst, interview with author, 24 March 2007.

110. Dennis, "Secrecy and Science Revisited," 14; see also Agar and Balmer, "British Scientists."

111. Commission on the Intelligence Capabilities. *Report to the President,* 444.

112. Henoch interview.

113. Henoch personal communication.

114. Rappert, "Making Silence Matter," 247.

115. Balmer, "Secret Formula," 692.

116. U.S. Senate, "Report on the U.S. Intelligence," 149.

117. Lynch and Bogen's study of the Iran-Contra hearings examines how documents can be used to create an "official" account of events, but one that differs from the messy and disparate sources of perspective and information that are actually available; Lynch and Bogen, *Spectacle of History.*

118. Balmer, "Secret Formula," 695.

119. For an interesting commentary on this contextual approach to analysis, see Jones, "Intelligence Reform."

Chapter 8 • A New Knowledge Model for Bioweapons Intelligence Assessments

1. Fingar, "Reducing Uncertainty."

2. The Office of Transnational Issues (OTI) was created to produce analytic assessments on critical intelligence-related issues that transcended regional and national boundaries. The OTI focused on four core program areas: weapons, foreign technologies, economic security, and societal conflicts. Parts of OTI were formed from the merger of the Office of Weapons, Technology, and Proliferation and the Office of Scientific and Weapons Research, which had both been responsible for various kinds of technical weapons assessments. The OTI was distinct from other regional or geographical analytic units within the CIA's Directorate of Intelligence. Richelson, *U.S. Intelligence Community,* 28.

3. Anonymous former CIA analyst, telephone interview with author, 9 September 2008.

4. For example, for some of their studies, SAG analysts worked with famous futurist Peter Schwartz. Ibid.

5. Ibid.

6. Ibid.

7. Ibid.

8. Ibid.

9. Ibid.

10. Ibid.

11. See Hopkins et al., "Myth of the Biotech Revolution." Another example comes from the Soviet bioweapons program. When the Soviets tried to develop a multi-antibiotic–resistant

strain of plague bacteria, the novel pathogen became so environmentally unstable from these genetic manipulations that it could not be grown outside of very controlled laboratory conditions, making it a poor candidate for development into a biological weapon. See Domaradskij and Orent, *Biowarrior.*

12. Anonymous former CIA analyst, telephone interview with author.

13. Ibid.

14. Ibid.

15. Ibid.

16. Ibid.

17. Ibid.

18. Aftergood, "Overcoming Secrecy in a Day."

19. Ibid.

20. Ibid.

21. Ibid.

22. Ibid.

23. Barton, *Weapons Detective,* 229.

24. See Gellman, "Odyssey of Frustration"; Gellman, "Covert Unit Hunted for Iraqi Arms."

25. Duelfer, *Comprehensive Report, vol. 1.*

26. See Shuster, "Iraq Survey Group."

27. David Kay, interview with author, Arlington, Virginia, 23 March 2007.

28. Ibid.

29. However, the ISG did have the previously published technical reports and other classified information on the trailers and Curveball at its disposal. Ibid.

30. Ibid. See also Shuster, "Iraq Survey Group," 240–241.

31. Kay interview.

32. Ibid.

33. Ibid.

34. Ibid.

35. Ibid.

36. Commission on the Intelligence Capabilities, *Report to the President,* 106, 223.

37. Kay interview.

38. Rod Barton states that the ISG found "a folder of documentation about the trailers that included the original contract for their construction, acceptance trials and operating 'manual,' all indicating that the trailers were for hydrogen production for artillery balloons"; Barton, "Oversight Hearing," 2.

39. Kay interview.

40. See Duelfer, *Comprehensive Report,* vol. 3, 79–98.

41. See also Shuster, "Iraq Survey Group," 231–233.

42. Barton, *Weapons Detective,* 243.

43. Kay interview.

44. Barton, *Weapons Detective,* 240, 242.

45. Biological Sciences Experts Group, "Charter." The Office of the Director of National Intelligence was a new entity created in 2005 to oversee U.S. intelligence agencies

and to establish objectives and priorities for intelligence collection, analysis, and dissemination.

46. The WMD Commission was organized to investigate the Iraqi intelligence failures and identify future intelligence gaps; see Commission on the Intelligence Capabilities, *Report to the President,* 510–516.

47. Institute of Medicine and National Research Council, *Globalization, Biosecurity, and the Life Sciences*; Brill, "Statement for the Record," 4 May 2006.

48. Commission on the Intelligence Capabilities, *Report to the President,* 503.

49. Ibid., 504.

50. Ibid., 507.

51. Curiously, in the report, the recommendation for the creation of the BSEG is separated, physically and intellectually, from the discussion of the Iraq intelligence failures—there appears to be only a cursory reference to the Iraq intelligence failures in the discussion of the challenges assessing future bioweapons threats. See Commission on the Intelligence Capabilities, *Report to the President,* 501–516.

52. Ibid., 511.

53. Anonymous former Linder staff member, telephone interview with author, 24 August 2007.

54. Pre-circulated email announcement of 4 May 2006 Bioscience Hearings by Linder staff member, Anonymous former Linder staff member, email communication with author, 24 August 2007.

55. Institute of Medicine and National Research Council, *Globalization, Biosecurity, and the Life Sciences,* 5.

56. Ibid., 216.

57. Anonymous former Linder staff member, telephone interview with author; Brill, "Statement for the Record."

58. Brill, "Statement for the Record," 2, emphasis in original.

59. To date, the BSEG continues to maintain a technical focus in its activities; anonymous U.S. policy official, e-mail communication with author, 9 October 2010.

60. Brill, "Statement for the Record.

61. See Belt and Gore, "Arctic Breakthrough," 36; U.S. Department of Defense, "Transcript: DoD News Briefing."

62. Through negotiations with MEDEA, the intelligence community agreed to image selected sites of environmental significance periodically. Interestingly, MEDEA has served as an advocacy group in favor of further declassification of intelligence data for scientific research. For example, MEDEA scientists successfully lobbied to declassify over 800,000 images produced by the Corona, Argon, and Lanyard photoreconnaissance satellites; see Richelson, "Scientists in Black," 48.

63. In addition, the BSEG Charter explicitly states that the following technical areas are of current interest to the group: microbiology, molecular biology, synthetic biology, forensic sciences (microbial forensics), biochemistry, medicine, pharmacology, pathology (plant/human/animal), immunology, public health, epidemiology, veterinary medicine, food safety/security/production, agricultural sciences, pharmaceutical, biosecurity/biosafety, counterproliferation/counterterrorism issues, former or current state bioweapons programs,

former or current biological terrorist programs; see Biological Sciences Experts Group, "Charter."

64. The National Intelligence Council (NIC) Associates Program was designed to enhance cooperation among academia, think tanks, the corporate world, and the intelligence community. In the past, NIC associates have followed a particular region or transnational topic for at least ten years and are U.S. citizens. As the NIC Associates website states, "NIC associates make their expertise and knowledge available strictly to help U.S. leaders better understand the context and complexities of foreign trends and events." See U.S. National Intelligence Council, "IC Associates Program."

65. Bhattacharjee, "Panel Provides Peer Review."

66. Brill, Elder, and Kerr, "Intelligence Reform"; Kerr, "Integrating Science and Security."

67. Biological Sciences Experts Group, "Charter."

68. Anonymous U.S. government official, interview with author, Arlington, Virginia, 22 March 2007.

69. Anonymous U.S. policy official, personal written communication with author, 10 October 2009.

70. Anonymous U.S. policy official, e-mail communication with author, 9 October 2010.

71. Anonymous U.S. policy official, e-mail communication with author, 9 October 2010.

72. See Hackett, "Letter from the Office of the Director of National Intelligence."

73. Cloud, "Imaging the World in a Barrel," 240.

74. Ibid.

75. Anonymous U.S. intelligence analyst, personal communication with author, Washington, D.C., 11 March 2010. BioChem 20/20's mission was to "lead and focus the defense intelligence community's assessments of emerging technologies that nation-states or terrorists could use for biological or chemical warfare and to mitigate technological surprise from foreign biological warfare programs." The group would be responsible for preparing a variety of classified, technical intelligence studies for the DIA on biological and chemical weapons issues focused on the warrior. Although its composition has changed from time to time, BioChem 20/20 has typically consisted of about 15 to 20 prominent technical experts in the life sciences and related biochemical technologies from government, academia, and private industry. See Institute of Medicine and National Research Council, *Globalization, Biosecurity, and the Life Sciences,* 237.

76. Anonymous U.S. intelligence analyst, personal communication with author, Washington, D.C., 11 March 2010.

77. Anonymous U.S. intelligence analyst, personal communication with author, Washington, D.C., 11 March 2010.

78. The classical work using a cognitive approach often referenced is Heuer, Jr., *The Psychology of Intelligence Analysis.* A 2011 National Academy of Sciences report outlines some alternative social science approaches for intelligence analysis; see National Research Council, *Intelligence Analysis for Tomorrow,* 33–48.

79. For examples, see Johnston, "Integrating Methodologists"; Marrin, "Improving CIA Analysis"; Clark, *Intelligence Analysis*; Kerr et al., "Holistic Vision for the Analytic Unit."

80. Carl Ford, "Analytic Office for the 21st Century: The Problem Teams" (personal written communication to author), 9 April 2009.

81. Hackman and O'Connor, "What Makes for a Great Analytic Team?" 3–4.

82. Ibid., 11.

83. Herbert, "Intelligence Analyst as Epistemologist," 667.

84. Office of the Director of National Intelligence, "Intelligence Community Directive 205."

Conclusion

1. Perrow, *Normal Accidents,* 379–380.

2. Paul Pillar, interview with author, Washington, D.C., 20 July 2007.

3. Pillar, "Intelligence, Policy, and the War in Iraq."

4. Armstrong, "CIA and WMDs: The Damning Evidence."

5. Ibid.

6. In the immediate post–Cold War period, policy officials openly discussed the peace dividend that would result from a downsizing of the national security apparatus. Later, the CIA's well-publicized intelligence failures on issues such as detecting Saddam Hussein's nuclear program and assessing India's nuclear test in 1998—as well as broader intelligence problems leading to the 9/11 attacks—drew public attention to the shortcomings in U.S. intelligence assessments. Moreover, the creation of rival, ad hoc intelligence units within the U.S. government has further challenged the privilege and authority given to traditional intelligence organizations such as the CIA. For example, during the George W. Bush administration, Undersecretary for Policy Douglas Faith established a new intelligence unit, the Office of Special Plans, within the Pentagon to provide alternative intelligence assessments and current intelligence reporting to senior White House officials.

7. Ford interview, 22 September 2008.

8. Jasanoff, *States of Knowledge,* 280.

9. Anonymous U.S. policy official, private e-mail communication with author, 22 October 2007.

10. Ibid.

11. Bijker, "Do Not Despair," 125.

12. For examples, see U.S. Senate, "Report on the U.S. Intelligence," 20–21, 28–29, 49, 52–53, 60, 62, 88–119.

13. For some additional critiques on weapons-related assessments, see Russell, "Weak Pillar"; Levi, *On Nuclear Terrorism*; Macfarlane, "Underlying Yucca Mountain"; Biddle, *Military Power.*

14. Although the intelligence community has introduced a renewed focus on analytic tradecraft and techniques, Roger George notes that these are merely "processes for reviewing assumptions, data, and hypotheses. They do nothing to guarantee that the

CIA has the right expertise or knowledge from which to reach judgments." See U.S. Central Intelligence Agency, "Continuous Learning in the DI"; George, "Beyond Analytic Tradecraft."

15. Office of the Director of National Intelligence, "National Intelligence Strategy," August 2009, 8.

Aftergood, Steven. "Overcoming Secrecy in a Day." *Secrecy News*, no. 28 (2 April 2003). www.fas.org/sgp/news/secrecy/2003/04/040203.html.

Agar, Jon, and Brian Balmer. "British Scientists and the Cold War: The Defence Research Policy Committee and Information Networks, 1947–1963." *Historical Studies in the Physical Sciences* 28, no. 2 (1998): 209–252.

Agre, Philip E. *Computation and Human Experience.* Cambridge, U.K.: Cambridge University Press, 1997.

Alexander, John. "An Intelligence Role for the Footnote." *Studies in Intelligence* 8, no. 3 (1964): 59–67.

Alibek, Ken, with Stephen Handelman. *Biohazard: The Chilling True Story of the Largest Covert Biological Weapons Program in the World.* New York: Random House, 1999.

Applebaum, Anne. "Only a Game." *Washington Post*, 19 January 2005, A19.

Armstrong, Fulton. "The CIA and WMDs: The Damning Evidence." *New York Review of Books*, 19 August 2010. www.nybooks.com/articles/archives/2010/aug/19/cia-and-wmds-damning-evidence/.

Averre, Derek. "Enabling Biotechnology in a Regional Perspective: Experiences and Opportunities in Russia/NIS." Fourth IWG-LNCV and PGS Workshop: Strengthening Global Biosecurity/Biosafety Framework and Coping with the Biotechnology Revolution. Como, Italy, October 2007. www.partnershipforglobalsecurity.org/documents/averre.pdf.

Bailey, Kathleen, ed. *Director's Series on Proliferation.* Livermore, CA: Lawrence Livermore National Laboratory, 23 May 1994.

Bailey, Kathleen C. *Doomsday Weapons in the Hands of Many: The Arms Control Challenge of the 1990s.* Champagne: University of Illinois Press, 1991.

Baker, Monya. "Synthetic Genomes: The Next Step for the Synthetic Genome." *Nature* 473 (19 May 2011): 403–408.

Bakhtin, M. M. "Forms of Time and of the Chronotrope in the Novel." In *The Dialogic Imagination: Four Essays*, edited by Michael Holquist, 84–258. Austin: University of Texas Press, 1981.

Ball, Deborah Yarsike, and Theodore P. Gerber. "Russian Scientists and Rogue States: Does Western Assistance Reduce the Proliferation Threat?" *International Security* 29, no. 4 (Spring 2005): 50–77.

Ball, Philip. "Genome Stitched Together by Hand." *Nature News* 15 (24 January 2008). www.nature.com/news/2008/080124/full/news.2008.522.html.

Balmer, Brian. *Britain and Biological Warfare: Expert Advice and Science Policy, 1930–65.* Houndmills, U.K.: Palgrave, 2001.

———. "A Secret Formula, a Rogue Patent, and Public Knowledge about Nerve Gas: Secrecy as a Spatial-Epistemic Tool." *Social Studies of Science* 36, no. 5 (October 2006): 691–722.

Barton, Rod. "An Oversight Hearing on Pre-War Intelligence Relating to Iraq." Senate Democratic Policy Committee Hearing, 26 June 2006. http://dpc.senate.gov/hearings/hearing33/barton.pdf.

———. *The Weapons Detective.* Melbourne, Australia: Blank, 2006.

Behlke, Mark A., and Eric J. Devor. "Chemical Synthesis of Oligonucleotides." Integrated DNA Technologies, 2005. www.crchul.ulaval.ca/ronyweb/DOWNLOADS/Chemical_Synthesis_of_Oligonucleotides.pdf.

Bellman, Beryl L. "The Paradox of Secrecy." *Human Studies* 4, no. 1 (1981): 1–24.

Belt, Don, and Al Gore. "An Arctic Breakthrough." *National Geographic* 191, no. 2 (February 1997): 36–57.

Benjamin, Daniel, and Steven Simon. *Sacred Age of Terror.* New York: Random House, 2002.

Ben Ouagrham, Sonia, and Kathleen M. Vogel. "Conversion at Stepnogorsk: What the Future Holds for Former Bioweapons Facilities." Occasional Paper no. 28. Ithaca, NY: Cornell University Peace Studies Program, 2003.

Ben Ouagrham-Gormley, Sonia, and Kathleen M. Vogel. "The Social Context Shaping Bioweapons (Non)Proliferation." *Biosecurity and Bioterrorism: Biodefense Strategy, Practice, and Science* 8, no. 1 (March 2010): 9–24.

Berkowitz, Bruce. "Failing to Keep Up with the Information Revolution: The DI and 'IT.'" *Studies in Intelligence* 47, no. 1 (2003): 67–74.

Bhattacharjee, Yudhijit. "Panel Provides Peer Review of Intelligence Research." *Science* 318, no. 5856 (7 December 2007): 1538.

Biddle, Stephen. *Military Power: Explaining Victory and Defeat in Modern Battle.* Princeton, NJ: Princeton University Press, 2004.

Bijker, Wiebe E. "Democratization of Technology: Who are the Experts?" World Series on Culture and Technology. www.angelfire.com/la/esst/bijker.html.

———. "Do Not Despair: There's Life after Constructivism." *Science, Technology, and Human Values* 18, no. 1 (January 1993): 113–138.

———. "The Social Construction of Bakelite: Toward a Theory of Invention." In *The Social Construction of Technological Systems,* edited by Wiebe E. Bijker, Thomas P. Hughes, and Trevor Pinch, 159–187. Cambridge, MA: MIT Press, 1989.

Bijker, Wiebe E., Thomas P. Hughes, and Trevor Pinch. *The Social Construction of Technological Systems.* Cambridge, MA: MIT Press, 1989.

Binkowski, Brock F., Kathryn E. Richmond, James Kaysen, Michael R. Sussman, and Peter J. Belshaw. "Correcting Errors in Synthetic DNA through Consensus Shuffling." *Nucleic Acids Research* 33, no. 6 (March 2005): 1–8.

Biological Sciences Experts Group. "Charter." Unclassified document. www.fas.org/irp/eprint/bseg-concept.pdf.

Blair, Dennis C. "Annual Threat Assessment of the Intelligence Community for the House Permanent Select Committee on Intelligence." 25 February 2009. www.dni.gov/testimonies/20090225_testimony.pdf.

———. "Annual Threat Assessment of the Intelligence Community for the Senate Armed Services Committee." 10 March 2009. www.dni.gov/testimonies/20090310_testimony.pdf.

Block, Steven M. "Living Nightmares: Biological Threats Enabled by Molecular Biology." In *The New Terror: Facing the Threat of Biological and Chemical Weapons,* edited by Sidney D. Drell, Abraham D. Sofaer, and George D. Wilson, 39–75. Stanford, CA: Hoover Institution Press, 1999.

Blue Heron Biotechnology. "Blue Heron the Primary Supplier of Genetic Material for First Synthetic Bacterial Genome." 24 January 2008. www.blueheronbio.com/company/press/jan24-08.html.

Borger, Julian, and Richard Norton-Taylor. "MI6 'Still Using' Disputed Informer on WMD." *Guardian,* 13 July 2004. www.guardian.co.uk/world/2004/jul/14/iraq.uk.

Bowker, Geoffrey C. *Science on the Run: Information Management and Industrial Geophysics at Schlumberger, 1920–1940.* Cambridge, MA: MIT Press, 1994.

Boyle Mahle, Melissa. *Denial and Deception: An Insider's View of the CIA from Iran-Contra to 9/11.* New York: Nation Books, 2004.

Bozheyeva, G., Y. Kunakbayev, and D. Yeleukenov. "Former Soviet Biological Weapons Facilities in Kazakhstan: Past, Present, and Future." Occasional Paper no. 1. Monterey, CA: Monterey Institute of International Studies, June 1999.

Brent, Roger. "In the Valley of the Shadow of Death." 1 November 2005. http://dspace.mit.edu/bitstream/1721.1/34914/1/Valley2006.pdf.

Brill, Kenneth. "Statement for the Record: Hearing on Bioscience and the Intelligence Community (Part II): Closing the Gap." Subcommittee on Prevention of Nuclear and Biological Attack of the U.S. House of Representatives Committee on Homeland Security, 4 May 2006. www.gpo.gov/fdsys/pkg/CHRG-109hhrg35695/html/CHRG-109hhrg35695.htm.

Brill, Kenneth, Melanie Elder, and Lawrence Kerr. "Intelligence Reform: Science and Technology and the Counterproliferation Challenge." Presentation at AAAS Center for Science, Technology, and Security Policy, Washington, D.C., 5 June 2007. http://cstsp.aaas.org/content.html?contentid=927.

Broad, William J. "U.S. in Assessment, Terms Trailers Germ Laboratories." *New York Times,* 29 May 2003, A12.

Broad, William J., and Judith Miller. "Government Report Says 3 Nations Hide Stocks of Smallpox." *New York Times,* 13 June 1999, A1.

Brooks, Peter. *Reading for the Plot: Design and Intention in Narrative.* New York: Knopf, 1984.

Bruce, James B. "Making Analysis More Reliable: Why Epistemology Matters to Intelligence." In *Analyzing Intelligence: Origins, Obstacles, and Innovations,* edited by Roger Z.

George and James B. Bruce, 172–190. Washington, DC: Georgetown University Press, 2008.

Brumfiel, Geoff. "Curtain Falls on Collaborative Work." *Nature* 468, no. 16 (2010). www.nature.com/news/2010/101101/full/468016a.html?s=news_rss.

Buchanan, H. Lee. "Poor Man's A-Bomb?" *U.S. Naval Institute Proceedings* 123, no. 4 (April 1997): 83–86.

Bumiller, Elisabeth. "White House Letter: Black and White and Read by Precious Few." *New York Times,* 10 November 2003, 19.

Bush, George W. "Text of President Bush's 2003 State of the Union Address." *Washington Post,* 28 January 2003. www.washingtonpost.com/wp-srv/onpolitics/transcripts/bushtext_012803.html and http://usgovinfo.about.com/library/weekly/aasou2003_text.htm.

Cambrosio, Alberto, and Peter Keating. "Going Monoclonal: Art, Science, and Magic in Day-to-Day Use of Hybridoma Technology." *Social Problems* 35, no. 3 (June 1988): 244–260.

Carlson, Robert. "The Pace and Proliferation of Biological Technologies." *Biosecurity and Bioterrorism: Biodefense Strategy, Practice, and Science* 1, no. 3 (September 2003): 203–214.

———. "Written Comments of Dr. Robert Carlson. Prepared for the Presidential Commission on Bioethical Issues." Washington, D.C., 8 July 2010.

Carr, Peter A., Jason S. Park, Yoon-Jae Lee, Tiffany Yu, Shuguang Zhang, and Joseph M. Jacobson. "Protein-Mediated Error Correction for De Novo DNA Synthesis." *Nucleic Acids Research* 32, no. 20 (November 2004): 1–9.

Carrigan, Alisa L. "Learning to Build the Bomb." *Physics Today* 60, no. 12 (December 2007): 54–55.

Carus, W. Seth. *The Poor Man's Atomic Bomb? Biological Weapons in the Middle East.* Policy Paper no. 23. Washington, DC: Washington Institute for Near East Policy, 1991.

Cello, Jeronimo, Aniko V. Paul, and Eckard Wimmer. "Chemical Synthesis of Poliovirus cDNA: Generation of Infectious Virus in the Absence of Natural Template." *Science* 297, no. 5583 (August 2002): 1016–1018. Published online 11 July 2002, Science Express Reports. 10.1126/science.1072266.

Center for Strategic and International Studies. "Security Controls on Scientific Information and the Conduct of Scientific Research: A White Paper of the Commission on Scientific Communication and National Security." (June 2005). http://thefdp.org/CSIS_0506_cscans.pdf.

Chatterjee, Rhitu. "Cases of Mistaken Identity." *Science* 315, no. 5814 (16 February 2007): 928–931.

Cho, Mildred K., David Magnus, Arthur L. Caplan, Daniel McGee, and Ethics of Genomics Group. "Ethical Considerations in Synthesizing a Minimal Genome." *Science* 286, no. 5447 (10 December 1999): 2087–2090.

Chyba, Christopher. "Biotechnology Proliferation: Benefits, Dangers, and Management." Paper presented at Carnegie International Nonproliferation Conference, Washington, D.C., 25 June 2007. www.carnegieendowment.org/files/biotechnology_proliferation1.pdf.

Clapper, James R. "Statement for the Record on the Worldwide Threat Assessment of the U.S. Intelligence Community for the House Permanent Select Committee on Intelligence." 10 February 2011. http://dni.gov/testimonies/20110210_testimony_clapper.pdf.

Clark, Robert M. *Intelligence Analysis: A Target-Centric Approach,* 2d ed. Washington, DC: CQ Press, 2007.

———. "Scientific and Technical Intelligence Analysis." In *Inside CIA's Private World,* edited by H. Bradford Westerfield, 293–304. New Haven, CT: Yale University Press, 1995.

Cloud, John. "Imaging the World in a Barrel: CORONA and the Clandestine Convergence of the Earth Sciences." *Social Studies of Science* 31, no. 2 (April 2001): 231–251.

Cohen, William S. "The Iraq Situation." *This Week.* ABC Television, 16 November 1997. http://homepage.ntlworld.com/jksonc/docs/abc-cohen-19971116.html.

Colata, Gina. "Polio Synthesized in the Test Tube." *New York Times,* 13 December 1991, A37.

Collins, H. M. *Changing Order: Replication and Induction in Scientific Practice.* Chicago: University of Chicago Press, 1985.

———. "Tacit Knowledge, Trust, and the Q of Sapphire." *Social Studies of Science* 31, no. 1 (February 2001): 71–85.

Commission on the Intelligence Capabilities of the United States Regarding Weapons of Mass Destruction. *Report to the President of the United States.* 31 March 2005. www.ise.gov/sites/default/files/wmd_report_0.pdf.

Commission on the Roles and Capabilities of the U.S. Intelligence Community. *Preparing for the 21st Century: An Appraisal of U.S. Intelligence.* 1 March 1996. www.gpoaccess.gov/int/report.html.

Constant, Edward W. "Scientific Theory and Technological Testability: Science, Dynamometers, and Water Turbines in the Nineteenth Century." *Technology and Culture* 24, no. 2 (1983): 183–198.

Cooper, Jeffrey R. *Curing Analytic Pathologies: Pathways to Improved Intelligence Analysis.* Washington, DC: Center for the Study of Intelligence, U.S. Central Intelligence Agency, December 2005.

Cutcliffe, Stephen H., and Robert C. Post, eds. *In Context: History and the History of Technology—Essays in Honor of Melvin Kranzberg.* Bethlehem, PA: Lehigh University Press, 1989.

Czar, Michael J., J. Christopher Anderson, Joel S. Bader, and Jean Peccoud. "Gene Synthesis Demystified." *Trends in Biotechnology* 27, no. 2 (February 2009): 63–72.

Danzig, Richard. *Catastrophic Bioterrorism—What Is to Be Done?* Washington, DC: Center for Technology and National Security Policy, National Defense University, August 2003.

———. "Prevention of Biothreats: A Look Ahead." Center for Biosecurity of UPMC, Washington, D.C., 6 October 2009. http://216.251.248.90/video/prevention_2009/vid7-richard_danzig.html.

Danzig, Richard, and Pamela B. Berkowsky. "Why Should We Be Concerned about Biological Warfare?" In *Biological Weapons: Limiting the Threat,* edited by Joshua Lederberg, 9–14. Cambridge, MA: MIT Press, 1999.

Danzig, Richard, Marc Sageman, Terrance Leighton, Lloyd Hough, Hidemi Yuki, Rui Kotani, and Zachary M. Hosford. *Aum Shinrikyo: Insights into How Terrorists Develop Biological and Chemical Weapons.* Washington, DC: Center for New American Security, July 2011. www.cnas.org/files/documents/publications/CNAS_AumShinrikyo_Danzig_1.pdf.

Daschle, Tom, and Tom Inglesby. "Foreword: Necessary Progress in Biosecurity." *Harvard Law and Policy Review* 4, no. 2 (2010): 263–270.

David, Paul A. "The Dynamo and the Computer: An Historical Perspective on the Modern Productivity Paradox." *American Economic Review* 80, no. 2 (May 1990): 355–361.

Davis, Christopher J. "Nuclear Blindness: An Overview of the Biological Weapons Programs of the Former Soviet Union and Iraq." *Emerging Infectious Diseases* 5, no. 4 (July/August 1999): 509–512.

———. "Twentieth-Century Legacy: The Challenge of Biological Threats to Twenty-First Century Bio-Medical Science and Society." In *U.S. National Academy of Sciences, Science and Technology to Counter Terrorism: Proceedings of an Indo-U.S. Workshop,* 121–132. Washington, DC: National Academies Press, 2007.

Davis, Jack. "Combatting Mind-Set." *Studies in Intelligence* 36, no. 5 (1992): 33–38.

Defense Science Board. *The Defense Science Board 1997 Summer Study Task Force on DoD Responses to Transnational Threats, Vol. I, Final Report.* October 1997. www.dtic.mil/docs/citations/ADA333273.

———. *The Defense Science Board 2000 Summer Study Task Force on Protecting the Homeland, Volume I.* February 2001. www.au.af.mil/au/awc/awcgate/dod/dsb_protecting.pdf.

Deleuze, Gilles, and Felix Guattari. *A Thousand Plateaus: Capitalism and Schizophrenia,* translated by B. Massumi. Minneapolis: University of Minnesota Press, 1987.

Dennis, Michael. "Our First Line of Defense: Two University Laboratories in the Postwar American State." *Isis* 85, no. 3 (September 1994): 427–455.

———. "Science and Secrecy Revisited: From Politics to Historical Practice and Back." In *Secrecy and Knowledge Production,* Occasional Paper no. 28. edited by Judith Reppy, 1–16. Ithaca, NY: Cornell University Peace Studies Program, 1999.

Director of Central Intelligence. "Director of Central Intelligence Directive 7/2: Oversight of the U.S. Intelligence Community's Efforts to Combat the Proliferation of Weapons of Mass Destruction and Their Means of Delivery." 7 May 1999. www.fas.org/irp/offdocs/dcid7-2.htm.

———. "National Intelligence Estimate: Iraq's Continuing Programs for Weapons of Mass Destruction." October 2002, declassified April 2004. Accessed 11 April 2007. www.fas.org/irp/cia/product/iraq-wmd-nie.pdf.

Domaradskij, Igor V., and Wendy Orent. *Biowarrior: Inside the Soviet/Russian Biological War Machine.* New York: Prometheus Books, 2003.

Drell, Sidney D., Abraham D. Sofaer, and George D. Wilson, eds. *The New Terror: Facing the Threat of Biological and Chemical Weapons.* Stanford, CA: Hoover Institution Press, 1999.

Drogin, Bob. *Curveball: Spies, Lies, and the Con Man Who Caused a War.* New York: Random House, 2007.

Drogin, Bob, and John Goetz. "How U.S. Fell under the Spell of Curveball." *Los Angeles Times,* 20 November 2005, A1.

Drumheller, Tyler, with Elaine Monaghan. *On the Brink: An Insider's Account of How the White House Compromised American Intelligence.* New York: Carroll and Graf, 2006.

Duelfer, Charles. *Comprehensive Report of the Special Advisor to the DCI on Iraq's WMD,* 30 September 2004. www.gpoaccess.gov/duelfer/index.html.

The Economist. "Biofuels from Algae: Craig's Twist." 15 July 2009. www.economist.com/sciencetechnology/displaystory.cfm?story_id=14029874.

Eden, Lynn. *Whole World on Fire: Organizations, Knowledge, and Nuclear Weapons Devastation.* Ithaca, NY: Cornell University Press, 2004.

Edgerton, David. *Shock of the Old: Technology and Global History since 1900.* Oxford, U.K.: Oxford University Press, 2006.

Ekeus, Rolf. "Iraq Briefing." Remarks given at Carnegie Endowment for International Peace, Washington, D.C., 3 February 2003. www.carnegieendowment.org/events/index.cfm?fa=eventDetail&id=574&.

Endy, Drew. "Synthetic Biology and National Security." 2007. http://mit.edu/endy/www/scraps/talks/090307.Princeton/Endy.Princeton.pdf.

Epstein, Gerald L. "Biodefense: Building a Medical Countermeasure Capability." Testimony before the Bioterrorism and Public Health Preparedness Subcommittee, Health, Education, Labor, and Pensions Committee, United States Senate, 8 February 2005.

———. "Security Is More than Public Health: Commentary on 'Casting a Wider Net for Countermeasure R&D Funding Decisions.'" *Biosecurity and Bioterrorism: Biodefense Strategy, Practice, and Science* 5, no. 4 (December 2007): 353–357.

ETC Group. "Extreme Genetic Engineering: An Introduction to Synthetic Biology." January 2007. www.etcgroup.org/en/issues/synthetic_biology.html.

Evans, Allan. "Against Footnotes." *Studies in Intelligence* 8, no. 4 (1964): 67–69.

Falkenrath, Richard. "Testimony before the United States Senate Committee on Health, Education, Labor, and Pensions." 16 March 2006. http://help.senate.gov/Hearings/2006_03_16/Falkenrath.pdf.

Falkenrath, Richard A., Robert D. Newman, and Bradley A. Thayer. *America's Achilles Heel: Nuclear, Biological, and Chemical Terrorism and Covert Attack.* Cambridge, MA: MIT Press, 1998.

Feder, Stanley A. "Forecasting for Policy Making in the Post–Cold War Period." *Annual Review of Political Science* 5 (June 2002): 111–125.

Fee, Elizabeth, and Theodore M. Brown. "Preemptive Biopreparedness: Can We Learn Anything from History?" *American Journal of Public Health* 91, no. 5 (May 2001): 721–726.

Ferguson, Eugene S. *Engineering and the Mind's Eye.* Cambridge, MA: MIT Press, 1992.

———. "How Engineers Lose Touch." *American Heritage of Invention and Technology* 8, no. 3 (Winter 1993): 16–24.

Fingar, Thomas. "Reducing Uncertainty: Intelligence and National Security Myths, Fears, and Expectations." Payne Lecture no. 1, Spogli Institute for International Studies, Stanford University, Stanford, California, 11 March 2009. http://fsi.stanford.edu/events

/payne_distinguished_lecture_series_2009__reducing_uncertainty_intelligence_and_national_security_lecture_1_myths_fears_and_expectations.

Fitch, J. Patrick. "Science-Based Biodefense Analysis in an Uncertain World." Science and Security Seminar Series, Center for Strategic and International Studies, Washington, D.C., 12 May 2008. http://csis.org/event/science-based-biodefense-analysis-uncertain-world.

Follath, Eric, John Goetz, Marcel Rosenbach, and Holger Stark. "How German Intelligence Helped Justify the U.S. Invasion of Iraq." *Spiegel Online,* 22 March 2008. www.spiegel.de/international/world/0,1518,542840,00.html.

Ford, Carl. "Improving Analysis: The Hard Part of Intelligence Reform." Unpublished memorandum.

Foucault, Michel. *Discipline and Punish: The Birth of the Prison,* translated by Alan Sheridan. New York: Random House, 1977.

Franco, Crystal. "Billions for Biodefense: Federal Agency Biodefense Funding, FY2009–FY2010." *Biosecurity and Bioterrorism: Biodefense Strategy, Practice, and Science* 7, no. 3 (September 2009): 291–149.

Franco, Crystal, and Tara Kirk Sell. "Federal Agency Biodefense Funding, FY2010–FY2011." *Biosecurity and Bioterrorism: Biodefense Strategy, Practice, and Science* 8, no. 2 (June 2010): 129–130.

———. "Federal Agency Biodefense Funding, FY2011–FY2012." *Biosecurity and Bioterrorism: Biodefense Strategy, Practice, and Science* 9, no. 2 (June 2011): 117–137.

Galison, Peter. *Image and Logic: A Material Culture of Microphysics.* Chicago: University of Chicago Press, 1997.

———. "Removing Knowledge." *Critical Inquiry* 31 (Autumn 2004): 229–243.

Gans, Herbert J. *Deciding What's News: A Study of CBS Evening News, NBC Nightly News, Newsweek, and Time.* New York: Pantheon, 1979.

Garfinkel, Michele S., Drew Endy, Gerald L. Epstein, and Robert S. Friedman. "Synthetic Genomics: Options for Governance." October 2007. www.jcvi.org/cms/fileadmin/site/research/projects/synthetic-genomics-report/synthetic-genomics-report.pdf.

Gellman, Barton. "Covert Unit Hunted for Iraqi Arms: Amid Raids and Rescue, Task Force 20 Failed to Pinpoint Weapons." *Washington Post,* 13 June 2003, A1.

———. "Odyssey of Frustration: In Search for Weapons, Army Team Finds Vacuum Cleaners." *Washington Post,* 18 May 2003, A1.

GenomeWeb Daily News. "Origene Buys Blue Heron." 13 August 2010. www.genomeweb.com/origene-buys-blue-heron.

Gentry, John A. "A Framework for Reform of the U.S. Intelligence Community." 6 June 1995. www.fas.org/irp/gentry/.

———. "Intelligence Analyst/Manager Relations at the CIA." In *Intelligence Analysis and Assessment,* edited by David A. Charters, Anthony Stuart Farson, and Glenn P. Hastedt, 133–148. London: Frank Cass, 1996.

———. *Lost Promise: How CIA Analysis Misserves the Nation.* Lanham, MD: University Press of America, 1993.

George, Roger Z. "Beyond Analytic Tradecraft." *International Journal of Intelligence and CounterIntelligence* 23, no. 2 (2010): 296–306.

George, Roger Z., and James B. Bruce, eds. *Analyzing Intelligence: Origins, Obstacles, Innovations.* Washington, DC: Georgetown University Press, 2008.

Ghamari-Tabrizi, Sharon. *The Worlds of Herman Kahn: The Intuitive Science of Thermonuclear War.* Cambridge, MA: Harvard University Press, 2005.

Gibson, Daniel G., Gwynedd A. Benders, Cynthia Andrews-Pfannkoch, Evgeniya A. Denisova, Holly Baden-Tillson, Jayshree Zaveri, et al. "Complete Chemical Synthesis, Assembly, and Cloning of a Mycoplasma genitalium Genome." *Science* 319, no. 5867 (29 February 2008): 1215–1220.

Gibson, Daniel G., John I. Glass, Carole Lartigue, Vladimir N. Noskov, Ray-Yuan Chuang, Mikkel A. Algire et al. "Creation of a Bacterial Cell Controlled by a Chemically Synthesized Genome." *Science* 329, no. 5987 (2 July 2010): 52–56.

Gilbert, G. Nigel, and Michael Mulkay. *Opening Pandora's Box: A Sociological Analysis of Scientists' Discourse.* New York: Cambridge University Press, 1984.

Goffman, Erving. *The Presentation of Self in Everyday Life.* Garden City, NY: Doubleday/Anchor, 1959.

Goldstein, Harry. "Modeling Terrorists." *IEEE Spectrum* (September 2006). http://spectrum.ieee.org/sep06/4424.

Gooding, David. *Experiment and the Making of Meaning: Human Agency in Scientific Observation and Experiment.* Dordrecht, the Netherlands: Kluwer, 1990.

———. "Mapping Experiment as a Learning Process: How the First Electromagnetic Motor Was Invented." *Science, Technology, and Human Values* 15, no. 2 (Spring 1990): 165–201.

Goodwin, Charles. "Seeing in Depth." *Social Studies of Science* 25, no. 2 (May 1995): 237–274.

Gordon, Michael R. "Powell's Case against Iraq: Piling Up the Evidence." *New York Times,* 6 February 2003. www.nytimes.com/2003/02/06/international/middleeast/06ASSE.html?pagewanted=1.

Gormley, Dennis M. "The Limits of Intelligence: Iraq's Lessons." *Survival* 46, no. 3 (Autumn 2004): 7–28.

———. *Missile Contagion: Cruise Missile Proliferation and the Threat to International Security.* Westport, CT: Praeger, 2008.

———. *Transforming Intelligence through New Institutional Arrangements.* Ridgway Center Working Papers. Pittsburgh, PA: Matthew B. Ridgway Center for International Security Studies, 2007. www.isn.ethz.ch/isn/Digital-Library/Publications/Detail/?ots591=0C54E3B3-1E9C-BE1E-2C24-A6A8C7060233&lng=en&id=45992f.

Gottemoeller, Rose. "Cooperative Inducements: Crafting New Tools for Nonproliferation." In *Ultimate Security: Combating Weapons of Mass Destruction,* edited by Janne E. Nolan, Bernard I. Finel, and Brian D. Findlay, 127–154. New York: Century Foundation Press, 2003.

Gottron, Frank and Dana Shea. "Oversight of High-Containment Biological Laboratories: Issues for Congress." 4 May 2009. www.fas.org/sgp/crs/terror/R40418.pdf.

Goulian, M., A. Kornberg, and R. L. Sinsheimer. "Enzymatic synthesis of DNA, XXIV: Synthesis of Infectious Phage phi-X174 DNA." *Proceedings of the National Academy of Sciences U.S.A.* 58, no. 6 (December 1967): 2321–2328.

Guba, Egon G., and Yvonna S. Lincoln. "Competing Paradigms in Qualitative Research: Theories and Issues." In *Approaches to Qualitative Research: A Reader on Theory and Practice,* edited by Sharlene Nagy Hesse-Biber and Patricia Leavy, 17–38. New York: Oxford University Press, 2004.

Gusterson, Hugh. "The Auditors: Bad Intelligence and the Loss of Public Trust." *Boston Review* (November/December 2005). http://bostonreview.net/BR30.6/gusterson.html.

———. "Narrating Abolition." *Bulletin of the Atomic Scientists* 65, no. 3 (May 2009): 13–18.

———. "Nuclear Futures: Anticipatory Knowledge, Expert Judgment, and the Lack That Cannot Be Filled." *Science and Public Policy* 35, no. 8 (October 2008): 551–560.

———. *Nuclear Rites.* Berkeley: University of California Press, 1996.

———. "A Pedagogy of Diminishing Returns: Scientific Involution across Three Generations of Nuclear Weapons Science." In *Pedagogy and the Practice of Science,* edited by David Kaiser, 75–109. Cambridge: MIT Press, 2005.

Hackett, John F. Letter from Office of the Director of National Intelligence to Steven Aftergood. 20 September 2010. www.fas.org/irp/dni/icd/icd-701.pdf.

Hacking, Ian. *The Social Construction of What?* Cambridge, MA: Harvard University Press, 2000.

Hackman, J. Richard, and Michael O'Connor. "What Makes for a Great Analytic Team? Individual versus Team Approaches to Intelligence Analysis." Intelligence Science Board Task Force Report, February 2005. www.fas.org/irp/dni/isb/analytic.pdf.

Hamilton, Daniel S., and Bradley T. Smith. "Atlantic Storm." *EMBO Reports* 7, no. 1 (January 2006): 4–9. www.nature.com/embor/journal/v7/n1/pdf/7400606.pdf.

Hamm, Steve. "Cheaper Artemisinin to Fight Malaria." *Business Week,* 15 January 2009. www.businessweek.com/magazine/content/09_04/b4117083623738.htm.

Hart, John. "The Soviet Biological Weapons Program." In *Deadly Cultures: Biological Weapons since 1945,* edited by Mark Wheelis, Lajos Rozsa, and Malcolm Dando, 132–156. Cambridge, MA: Harvard University Press, 2006.

Hayes, Brian. "Protection of Biological Weapons Proliferation through Cooperative Threat Reduction Programs." Presentation at conference on Former Biological Weapons Facilities: Dismantlement and Prospects for Conversion, Stepnogorsk, Kazakhstan, 24 July 2000.

Herbert, Matthew. "The Intelligence Analyst as Epistemologist." *International Journal of Intelligence and Counterintelligence* 19, no. 4 (2006): 666–684.

Heuer, Richards J., Jr. "Limits of Intelligence Analysis." *Orbis* 49, no. 1 (Winter 2005): 75–94.

———. *Psychology of Intelligence Analysis.* Washington, DC: Center for the Study of Intelligence, U.S. Central Intelligence Agency, 1999.

Hilgartner, Stephen. "Biotechnology." In *International Encyclopedia of the Social and Behavior Sciences,* vol. 2, edited by Neil J. Smelser and Paul B. Baltes, 1235–1240. Amsterdam: Elsevier, 2001.

———. *Science on Stage: Expert Advice as Public Drama.* Palo Alto, CA: Stanford University Press, 2000.

Hilts, Philip J. "Biological Weapons Reweighed." *Washington Post,* 17 August 1986, A17.

Hitz, Frederick P. "Editorial: Not Just a Lack of Intelligence, a Lack of Skills." The *Washington Post,* 21 October 2001, B3.

Hoffman, Bruce. *Inside Terrorism.* New York: Columbia University Press, 1999.

———. "Terrorism and Counterterrorism after September 11th." U.S. Foreign Policy Agenda, November 2001. www.iwar.org.uk/cyberterror/resources/threat-assessment/pj63hoffman.htm.

Hoffman, David E. *The Dead Hand: The Untold Story of the Cold War Arms Race and Its Dangerous Legacy.* New York: Doubleday, 2009.

Hopkins, Michael M., Paul A. Martin, Paul Nightingale, Alison Kraft, and Surya Mahdi. 2007. "The Myth of the Biotech Revolution: An Assessment of Technological, Clinical and Organisational Change." *Research Policy* 36, no. 4 (May 2007): 566–589.

Hulnick, Arthur S. "Managing Intelligence Analysis: Strategies for Playing the End Game." *International Journal of Intelligence and Counterintelligence* 2, no. 3 (1988): 321–343.

Hutchison, C. A., III, S. N. Peterson, S. R. Gill, R. T. Cline, O. White, C. M. Fraser et al. "Global Transposon Mutagenesis and a Minimal Mycoplasma Genome." *Science* 286, no. 5447 (10 December 1999): 2165–2169.

Hymans, Jacques E. C. "Beautiful Stranger: The Proliferation Implications of Footloose Nuclear Scientists," draft paper provided to author.

———. *Achieving Nuclear Ambitions: Scientists, Politicians, and Proliferation.* Cambridge, U.K.: Cambridge University Press, 2012.

Institute of Medicine and National Research Council. *Globalization, Biosecurity, and the Life Sciences.* Washington, DC: National Academies Press, 2006.

———. *An International Perspective on Advancing Technologies and Strategies for Managing Dual-Use Risks: Report of a Workshop.* Washington, DC: National Academies Press, 2005.

Isikoff, Michael, and David Corn. *Hubris: The Inside Story of Spin, Scandal, and the Selling of the Iraq War.* New York: Three Rivers Press, 2006.

Jackson, Ronald J., Alistair J. Ramsay, Carina D. Christensen, Sandra Beaton, Diana F. Hall, and Ian A. Ramshaw. "Expression of Mouse Interleukin-4 by a Recombinant Ectromelia Virus Suppresses Cytolytic Lymphocyte Responses and Overcomes Genetic Resistance to Mousepox." *Journal of Virology* 75, no. 3 (February 2001): 1205–1210.

Jasanoff, Sheila, ed., *States of Knowledge: The Co-Production of Science and the Social Order.* London: Routledge, 2004.

Jehl, Douglas. "C.I.A. Nominee Wary of Budget Cuts." *New York Times,* 3 February 1993, A18.

Jervis, Robert. "The Politics and Psychology of Intelligence Reform." *Forum* 4, no. 1 (May 2006): 1–9.

———. "Reports, Politics, and Intelligence Failures: The Case of Iraq." *Journal of Strategic Studies* 29, no. 1 (February 2006): 3–52.

Johnson, Loch K. "Glimpses into Gems of American Intelligence: The President's Daily Brief and the National Intelligence Estimate." *Intelligence and National Security* 23, no. 3 (June 2008): 333–370.

Johnston, Rob. *Analytic Culture in the U.S. Intelligence Community: An Ethnographic Study.* Washington, DC: Center for the Study of Intelligence, 2005.

———. "Integrating Methodologists into Teams of Substantive Experts: Reducing Analytic Error." *Studies in Intelligence* 47, no. 1 (2003). www.cia.gov/library/center-for-the-study-of-intelligence/csi-publications/csi-studies/studies/vol47no1/article06.html.

Jones, Brian. "Intelligence, Verification, and Iraq's WMD." In *Verification Yearbook 2004,* edited by Trevor Findlay. London: VERTIC, 2004. www.vertic.org/media/Archived_Publications/Yearbooks/2004/VY04_Jones.pdf.

Jones, Calvert. "Intelligence Reform: The Logic of Information Sharing." *Intelligence and National Security* 22, no. 3 (June 2007): 384–401.

Jordan, Kathleen, and Michael Lynch. "The Sociology of a Genetic Engineering Technique: Ritual and Rationality in the Performance of the Plasmid Prep." In *The Right Tools for the Job: At Work in Twentieth-Century Life Sciences,* edited by Adele E. Clarke and Joan H. Fujimura, 77–114. Princeton, NJ: Princeton University Press, 1992.

Kaser, Greg. "Prospects for Cooperative Threat Reduction beyond the FSU." In *Prevention, Detection, and Response to Nuclear and Radiological Threats,* edited by S. Apikyan, D. Diamond, and R. Way, 19–45. London: Springer Verlag, 2007.

Kelly, David C. "The Trilateral Agreement: Lessons for Biological Weapons Verification." In *Verification Yearbook 2002,* edited by Trevor Findlay and Oliver Meier, 93–109. London: VERTIC, 2002.

Kennedy, Helen. "Defector: I Bought Iraq Nukes." *New York Daily News,* 3 April 2002. http://articles.nydailynews.com/2002-04-03/news/18193949_1_iraqi-defector-reactor-fuel-rods-iraqi-national-congress.

Kent, Sherman. *Strategic Intelligence for American World Policy.* Princeton, NJ: Princeton University Press, 1951.

Kerr, Lawrence. "Integrating Science and Security: Making Intelligent Decisions." National Institutes of Health, 28 September 2006. http://videocast.nih.gov/PastEvents.asp?c=58.

Kerr, Richard, Thomas Wolfe, Rebecca Donegan, and Aris Pappas. "Collection and Analysis on Iraq: Issues for the U.S. Intelligence Community." *Studies in Intelligence* 49, no. 3 (2005): 47–54.

———. "A Holistic Vision for the Analytic Unit." *Studies in Intelligence* 50, no. 2 (2006): 47–56.

Klein, Gary, Jennifer K. Phillips, Erica L. Rall, and Deborah A. Peluso. "A Data/Frame Theory of Sensemaking." In *Expertise out of Context: Proceedings of the Sixth International Conference on Naturalistic Decision Making,* edited by Robert R. Hoffman, 113–155. New York: Taylor and Francis, 2007.

Knorr-Cetina, Karin. *The Manufacture of Knowledge: An Essay on the Constructivist and Contextual Nature of Science.* Oxford: Pergamon Press, 1981.

Kobayashi, Tominari, Satoshi Mikami, Shigeyuki Yokoyama, and Hiroaki Imataka. "An Improved Cell-Free System for Picornavirus Synthesis." *Journal of Virological Methods* 142, nos. 1-2 (June 2007): 182–188.

Kobinger, Gary P., Daniel J. Weiner, Qian-Chun Yu, and James M. Wilson. "Filovirus-Pseudotyped Lentiviral Vector Can Efficiently and Stably Transduce Airway Epithelia In Vivo." *Nature Biotechnology* 19, no. 3 (March 2001): 225–230.

Koblentz, Gregory. *Living Weapons: Biological Warfare and International Security.* Ithaca, NY: Cornell University Press, 2009.

Kodumal, Sarah J., Kedar G. Patel, Ralph Reid, Hugo G. Menzella, Mark Welch, and Daniel V. Santi. "Total Synthesis of Long DNA Sequences: Synthesis of a Contiguous 32-kb Polyketide Synthase Gene Cluster." *Proceedings of the National Academy of Sciences U.S.A.* 101, no. 44 (2 November 2004): 15573–15578.

Korch, George W., Jr. "Leading Edge of Biodefense: The National Biodefense Analysis and Countermeasures Center." Presentation at the Department of Defense Pest Management Workshop, Jacksonville Naval Air Station, Florida, 9 February 2004.

Krepinevich, Andrew F. "Cavalry to Computer: The Pattern of Military Revolutions." *National Interest* 37 (Fall 1994): 30–42.

Kuhn, Jens H. "Defining the Terrorist Risk." From the discussion forum "Is the Availability of Genetic Information Dangerous?" *Bulletin of the Atomic Scientists* website, 18 December 2007. www.thebulletin.org/web-edition/roundtables/is-the-availability-genetic-information-dangerous.

Lacey, Jennifer. "Analysis of the State Department's FY2009 Nonproliferation Budget Request." Partnership for Global Security, 2 April 2008. www.partnershipforglobalsecurity.org/Publications/Congress%20and%20Budget/index.asp.

Lakoff, Andrew. "The Generic Biothreat, or, How We Became Unprepared." *Cultural Anthropology* 23, no. 3 (August 2008): 399–428.

Landecker, Hannach. *Culturing Life: How Cells Became Technologies.* Cambridge, MA: Harvard University Press, 2007.

Latour, Bruno. "Drawing Things Together." In *Representation in Scientific Practice,* edited by Michael Lynch and Steve Woolgar, 19–68. Cambridge, MA: MIT Press, 1990.

———. "Is It Possible to Reconstruct the Research Process? Sociology of a Brain Peptide." In *The Social Process of Scientific Investigation,* edited by Karin D. Knorr, Roger Krohn, and Richard Whitley, 53–73. Dordrecht, the Netherlands: D. Reidel, 1980.

Latour, Bruno, and Steve Woolgar. *Laboratory Life: The Construction of Scientific Facts.* Princeton, NJ: Princeton University Press, 1986.

Lawrence, Christopher. "Incommunicable Knowledge: Science, Technology and the Clinical Art in Britain, 1850–1914." *Journal of Contemporary History* 20 (1985): 503–520.

Ledford, Heidi. "Garage biotech: Life hackers." *Nature* 467, no. 7316 (7 October 2010): 650–652.

Leitenberg, Milton. *Assessing the Biological Weapons and Bioterrorism Threats.* Carlisle, PA: U.S. Army War College, 2005.

———. "Aum Shinrikyo's Efforts to Produce Biological Weapons: A Case Study in the Serial Propagation of Misinformation." *Terrorism and Political Violence* 11, no. 4 (Winter 1999): 149–158.

———. "Biological Weapons Arms Control." Project on Rethinking Arms Control, Paper no. 16. College Park, MD: Center for International and Security Studies, May 1996. www.cissm.umd.edu/papers/files/prac.pdf.

———. "Botulinum Toxin: The Linkage with Bioterrorism." In Institute of Medicine, *Addressing Foodborne Threats to Health: Policies, Practices, and Global Coordination,* Workshop Summary, 150–168. Washington, DC: National Academies Press, 2006.

———. "The Conversion of Biological Warfare Research and Development Facilities to Peaceful Uses." In *Control of Dual-Threat Agents: The Vaccines for Peace Programme,* edited by Erhard Geissler and John P. Woodall, 77–105. Stockholm International Peace Research Institute, *Chemical and Biological Warfare Studies* no. 15. London: Oxford University Press, 1994.

———. "The Dynamics of Military Technology Today." *International Social Science Journal* 25, no. 3 (1973): 336–357.

———. "The Experience of the Japanese Aum Shinrikyo Group and Biological Agents." In *Hype or Reality: The "New Terrorism" and Mass Casualty Attacks,* edited by Brad Roberts, 159–172. Alexandria, VA: Chemical and Biological Arms Control Institute, 2000.

———. "Further Information regarding U.S. Government Attribution of a Mobile Biological Production Capacity in Iraq." Part 2 of 3 (13 August 2006), accessed 14 April 2007. www.fas.org/irp/eprint/leitenberg.html.

———. "Further Information regarding U.S. Government Attribution of a Mobile Biological Production Capacity in Iraq." Part 3 of 3 (August 2006), accessed 14 April 2007. www.fas.org/irp/eprint/leitenberg3.html.

———. "The Possibilities and Limitations of Biological Weapons Conversion." In *Conversion of Former BTW Facilities,* edited by Erhard Geissler, 119–133. Dordrecht, the Netherlands: Kluwer, 1998.

———. "Studies of Military R&D and Weapons Development." 1984. www.fas.org/man/eprint/leitenberg/.

———. "Unresolved Questions regarding U.S. Government Attribution of a Mobile Biological Production Capacity by Iraq." Part 1 of 3 (29 June 2006), accessed 14 April 2007, 4 April 2012. www.fas.org/irp/eprint/unresolved.pdf.

Lemonic, Michael D. "Bioterrorism: The Next Threat?" *Time,* 24 September 2001. www.time.com/time/printout/0,8816,176066,00.html.

Levi, Michael A. *On Nuclear Terrorism.* Cambridge, MA: Harvard University Press, 2007.

Lieberthal, Kenneth G. *The U.S. Intelligence Community and Foreign Policy: Getting Analysis Right.* Foreign Policy Paper Series no. 18. Washington, DC: Brookings Institution, September 2009. www.brookings.edu/papers/2009/09_intelligence_community_lieberthal.aspx#.

Lind, William S. "A Doubtful Revolution." *Issues in Science and Technology* 1, no. 3 (Spring 1985): 26–30.

Livingstone, Neil C., and Joseph D. Douglass Jr. *CBW: The Poor Man's Atomic Bomb.* Cambridge, MA: Institute for Foreign Policy Analysis, 1984.

Longa, Joseph, and Matthew Giles. "Reported Accomplishments of Selected Threat Reduction and Nonproliferation Programs, By Agency, for Fiscal Year 2007." PGS Policy Update (September 2008). www.partnershipforglobalsecurity.org.

Lowenthal, Mark. "Intelligence Analysis: Management and Transformation Issues." In *Transforming U.S. Intelligence,* edited by Jennifer E. Sims and Burton Gerber, 220–238. Washington, DC: Georgetown University Press, 2005.

———. *Intelligence: From Secrets to Policy.* Washington, DC: CQ Press, 2003.

Lugar, Richard. "Statement of Richard Lugar: Press Conference on His Trip to Russia." Office of Senator Richard Lugar, Washington, D.C., 24 November 1998.

Lynch, Michael. *Art and Artifact in Laboratory Science: A Study of Shop Work and Shop Talk in a Research Laboratory.* London: Routledge and Kegan Paul, 1985.

———. "Protocols, Practices, and the Reproduction of Technique in Molecular Biology." *British Journal of Sociology* 53, no. 2 (June 2002): 203–220.

Lynch, Michael, and David Bogen. *The Spectacle of History: Speech, Text, and Memory at the Iran-Contra Hearings.* Durham, NC: Duke University Press, 1996.

Macfarlane, Allison. "Underlying Yucca Mountain: The Interplay of Geology and Policy in Nuclear Waste Disposal." *Social Studies of Science* 33, no. 5 (October 2003): 783–807.

MacKenzie, Donald. *Inventing Accuracy: A Historical Sociology of Nuclear Missile Guidance.* Cambridge, MA: MIT Press, 1993.

MacKenzie, Donald, and Graham Spinardi. "Tacit Knowledge, Weapons Design, and the Uninvention of Nuclear Weapons." *American Journal of Sociology* 101, no. 1 (1995): 44–99.

MacKenzie, Donald, and Judy Wajcman, eds. *The Social Shaping of Technology,* 1st ed. Milton Keynes, U.K.: Open University Press, 1985.

———. *The Social Shaping of Technology,* 2d ed. Buckingham, U.K.: Open University, 1999.

Marchesano, Michelle. "Congressional Committee Action on FY09 International WMD Security Programs." Partnership for Global Security, April 2009. www.partnershipfor globalsecurity.org.

Marchesano, Michelle, and Raphael Della Ratta, with Kenneth N. Luongo. "Preliminary Funding Analysis of the FY11 Budget Request for International WMD Security Programs." Updated 23 March 2010. www.partnershipforglobalsecurity.org/PDFFrameset .asp?PDF=fy11_wmd_budget_request_analysis.pdf.

Marrin, Stephen. "CIA's Kent School: Improving Training for New Analysts." *International Journal of Intelligence and Counterintelligence* 16, no. 4 (2003): 609–637.

———. "Homeland Security and the Analysis of Foreign Intelligence." Markle Foundation Task Force on National Security In the Information Age. 15 July 2002. http://web zoom.freewebs.com/swnmia/7-15-2002--Marrin--Homeland%20Security%20and %20the%20Analysis%20of%20Foreign%20Intelligence.pdf.

———. "Improving CIA Analysis by Overcoming Institutional Obstacles." In *Bringing Intelligence About: Practitioners Reflect on Best Practices,* edited by Russell G. Swenson, 41–60. Joint Military Intelligence College, Center for Strategic Intelligence Research, May 2003. www.dia.mil/college/engagement/pdf/Intel%20Strategy%202007.pdf.

Marshall, A. W. "Memorandum for Henry A. Kissinger: Evaluation of the Process Leading to the President's Morning Intelligence Reading Package." 18 March 1970. www.nixon library.gov/virtuallibrary/documents/mandatoryreview.php.

Marshall, Eliot. "Public Health: Bioterror Defense Initiative Injects Shot of Cash." *Science* 283, no. 5406 (26 February 1999): 1234.

Masco, Joseph. "Lie Detectors: On Secrets and Hypersecurity in Los Alamos." *Public Culture* 14, no. 3 (2002): 441–467.

———. "Nuclear Technoaesthetics: Sensory Politics from Trinity to the Virtual Bomb in Los Alamos." *American Ethnologist* 31, no. 3 (August 2004): 349–373.

McConnell, J. Michael. "Annual Threat Assessment of the Director of National Intelligence for the Senate Armed Services Committee." 27 February 2007. www.dni.gov/testimonies/20070227_testimony.pdf.

McLaughlin, John E. "Statement of John E. McLaughlin, Former Deputy Director of Central Intelligence." 1 April 2005. www.gwu.edu/~nsarchiv/NSAEBB/NSAEBB234/McLaughlin_Statement.pdf.

McLeish, Caitriona, and Paul Nightingale. "Biosecurity, Bioterrorism, and the Governance of Science: The Increasing Convergence of Science and Security Policy." *Research Policy* 26, no. 10 (December 2007): 1635–1654.

McNamara, Laura. "Ways of Knowing about Weapons: The Cold War's End at the Los Alamos National Laboratory." Ph.D. diss., University of New Mexico, 2001.

Meltzer, Martin I., Inger Damon, James W. LeDuc, and J. Donald Millar. "Modeling Potential Responses to Smallpox as a Bioterrorist Weapon." *Emerging Infectious Diseases* 7, iss 6(November–December 2001): 959–969.

Mervis, Jeffrey, and Erik Stokstad. "NAS Censors Report on Agriculture Threats." *Science* 297, no. 5589 (20 September 2002): 1973–1975.

Mihailovich, Draggin. "Faulty Intel Source 'Curve Ball' Revealed." *60 Minutes,* 11 February 2009. www.cbsnews.com/stories/2007/11/01/60minutes/main3440577.shtml.

Miller, Judith. "Next to Old Rec Hall, a 'Germ-Making Plant.'" *New York Times,* 4 September 2001. www.nytimes.com/2001/09/04/international/04BIOW.html.

———. "Standoff with Iraq: The Dealings; Officials Confirm Russia-Iraq Deal on Plant." *New York Times,* 18 February 1998, A8.

Miller, Judith, and William J. Broad. "Some Analysts of Iraq Trailers Reject Germ Use." *New York Times,* 7 June 2003, A1.

Miller, Judith, Stephen Engelberg, and William Broad. *Germs: Biological Weapons and America's Secret War.* New York: Simon and Schuster, 2001.

Miscik, Jami. "DDI's State of Analysis Speech." 11 February 2004. www.fas.org/irp/cia/product/021104miscik.pdf.

Mitman, Matthias. "ISN/CTR and the Global Threat Reduction (GTR) Programs." www.state.gov/documents/organization/110582.pdf.

Molla, A., A. V. Paul, and E. Wimmer. "Cell-Free, De Novo Synthesis of Poliovirus." *Science* 254, no. 5038 (13 December 1991): 1647–1651.

Montgomery, Alex H. "Ringing in Proliferation: How to Dismantle an Atomic Bomb Network." *International Security* 30, no. 2 (Fall 2005): 153–187.

Moon, John Ellis van Courtland. "The U.S. Biological Weapons Program." In *Deadly Cultures: Biological Weapons since 1945,* edited by Mark Wheelis, Lajos Rozsa, and Malcolm Dando, 9–46. Cambridge, MA: Harvard University Press, 2006.

Morgan, Edmund S. *Inventing the People: The Rise of Popular Sovereignty in England and America.* New York: Norton, 1988.

Mukunda, Gautam, Kenneth A. Oye, and Scott C. Mohr. "What Rough Beast? Synthetic Biology, Uncertainty, and the Future of Biosecurity." *Politics and the Life Sciences* 28, no. 2 (September 2009): 2–26.

Mulligan, John. "Commercial Gene Synthesis Technology." 2006. http://openwetware.org/images/c/c9/Mulligan.ppt.

Murphy, Michelle. *Sick Building Syndrome and the Problem of Uncertainty: Environmental Politics, Technoscience, and Women Workers.* Durham, NC: Duke University Press, 2006.

National Academy of Sciences. *Global Security Engagement: A New Model for Cooperative Threat Reduction.* Washington, DC: U.S. National Academies Press, 2009.

National Research Council. "Better Plan Needed to Protect U.S. Agriculture from Bioterror Attack." 19 September 2002. www8.nationalacademies.org/onpinews/newsitem.aspx?RecordID=10505.

———. *The Biological Threat Reduction Program of the Department of Defense: From Foreign Assistance to Sustainable Partnerships.* Washington, DC: National Academies Press, 2007.

———. *Biotechnology Research in an Age of Terrorism.* Washington, DC: National Academies Press, 2004.

———. *Intelligence Analysis for Tomorrow: Advances from the Behavioral and Social Sciences.* Washington, DC: National Academies Press, 2011.

———. *Interim Report on Methodological Improvements to the Department of Homeland Security's Biological Agent Risk Analysis.* Washington, DC: National Academies Press, 2007.

———. "Scientific Openness and National Security Workshop." 9 January 2003. http://csis.org/files/attachments/030109_agenda.pdf.

———. *Seeking Security: Pathogens, Open Access, and Genome Databases.* Washington, DC: National Academies Press, 2004.

National Science Advisory Board for Biosecurity. "Addressing Biosecurity Concerns Related to Synthetic Biology." April 2010. http://oba.od.nih.gov/biosecurity/pdf/NSABB%20SynBio%20DRAFT%20Report-FINAL%20(2)_6-7-10.pdf.

———. "Addressing Biosecurity Concerns Related to the Synthesis of Select Agents." December 2006. http://oba.od.nih.gov/biosecurity/pdf/Final_NSABB_Report_on_Synthetic_Genomics.pdf.

National Security Council. "National Strategy for Countering Biological Threats." November 2009. www.whitehouse.gov/sites/default/files/National_Strategy_for_Countering_BioThreats.pdf.

Nature. "Editorial: Statement on the Consideration of Biodefence and Biosecurity." *Nature* 421 (20 February 2003): 771.

Nesser, Peter. "Chronology of Jihadism in Western Europe 1994–2007: Planned, Prepared, and Executed Terrorist Attacks." *Studies in Conflict and Terrorism* 31, no. 10 (2008): 924–946.

Nightingale, Paul. "Technological Capabilities, Invisible Infrastructure, and the Un-Social Construction of Predictability: The Overlooked Fixed Costs of Useful Research." *Research Policy* 33, no. 9 (November 2004): 1259–1284.

Nightingale, Paul, and Paul Martin. "The Myth of the Biotech Revolution." *Trends in Biotechnology* 22, no. 11 (November 2004): 564–569.

Nouri, Ali, and Christopher F. Chyba. "Proliferation-Resistant Biotechnology: An Approach to Improve Biological Security." *Nature Biotechnology* 27, no. 3 (March 2009): 234–236.

Oehler, Gordon C. "The Continuing Threat from Weapons of Mass Destruction." Testimony to the Senate Armed Services Committee, 27 March 1996. www.cia.gov/news-information/speeches-testimony/1996/go_toc_032796.html.

Office of Homeland Security. *National Strategy for Homeland Security.* July 2002. www.ncs.gov/library/policy_docs/nat_strat_hls.pdf.

Office of the Director of National Intelligence. "Intelligence Community Directive 205: Analytic Outreach." 16 July 2008. www.dni.gov/electronic_reading_room/ICD_205.pdf.

———. "The National Intelligence Strategy of the United States of America." August 2009. www.dni.gov/reports/2009_NIS.pdf.

Ong, Aihwa, and Stephen J. Collier. *Global Assemblages: Technology, Politics, and Ethics as Anthropological Problems.* Oxford, U.K.: Blackwell, 2005.

Orent, Wendy. "The Bioterror Bugaboo." *Los Angeles Times,* 17 July 2009. http://articles.latimes.com/2009/jul/17/opinion/oe-orent17.

Osterholm, Michael T. "Bioterrorism: Media Hype or Real Potential Nightmare?"*American Journal of Infection Control* 27 (December 1999): 461–462.

O'Toole, Tara. "The Biotechnology Revolution and the Bioweapons Threat." 1 February 2004. www.biosecurity.sandia.gov/subpages/pastConf/20032005/securing/05Biotechnology-Revolution-Tara-OToole.pdf.

———. "The Challenge of Bioterrorism: Present and Future." Remarks delivered at the Commissioned Training of Major Infectious Disease Emergencies and Bioterrorism Preparedness at Princess Margaret's Hospital, Hong Kong, November 2008. www.upmc-biosecurity.org/website/resources/multimedia/2009-hongkonglectures/2008-11-20-hongkong/Biothreat.swf.

———. "Six Years after Anthrax: Are We Better Prepared to Respond to Bioterrorism?" Testimony to U.S. Senate, Committee on Homeland Security and Governmental Affairs. 23 October 2007. http://hsgac.senate.gov/public/_files/102307OToole1.pdf.

Padrón Carney, Joanne. "Department of Homeland Security." In *AAAS Report XXXIV: Research and Development FY 2010,* 99–102. Washington, DC: AAAS, 2009. www.aaas.org/spp/rd/rdreport2010/ch11.pdf.

Parachini, John V., David E. Mosher, John Baker, Keith Crane, Michael Chase, and Michael Daugherty. "Diversion of Nuclear, Biological, and Chemical Weapons Expertise from the Former Soviet Union: Understanding an Evolving Problem." Santa Monica, CA: RAND National Security and Research Division, 2005. www.rand.org/pubs/documented_briefings/2005/RAND_DB457.pdf.

Parkhill, J., B. W. Wren, N. R. Thomson, R. W. Titball, M. T. Holden, M. B. Prentice et al. "Genome Sequence of *Yersinia pestis*: The Causative Agent of Plague." *Nature* 413, no. 6855 (4 October 2001): 523–527.

Pearson, Alan. "Federal Funding for Biological Weapons Prevention and Defense, Fiscal Years 2001 to 2009." Center for Arms Control and Non-Proliferation, 15 April 2008. http://armscontrolcenter.org/policy/biochem/articles/fy09_biodefense_funding/.

Pelham, Hugh R. B., and Richard J. Jackson. "An Efficient mRNA-Dependent Translation System from Reticulocyte Lysates." *European Journal of Biochemistry* 67, no. 1 (August 1976): 247–256.

Perrow, Charles. *Normal Accidents: Living with High-Risk Technologies.* Princeton, NJ: Princeton University Press, 1999.

Petro, James B. "Intelligence Support to the Life Science Community: Mitigating Threats from Bioterrorism." *Studies in Intelligence* 48, no. 3 (2004): 57–68. www.cia.gov/library/center-for-the-study-of-intelligence/kent-csi/pdf/v48i3a06p.pdf.

Petro, James B., Theodore R. Plasse, and Jack A. McNulty. "Biotechnology: Impact on Biological Warfare and Biodefense." *Biosecurity and Bioterrorism: Biodefense Strategy, Practice, and Science* (1 September 2003).

Petro, James B., and David A. Relman. "Understanding Threats to Scientific Openness." *Science* 302, no. 5652 (12 December 2003): 1898.

Pillar, Paul R. "Intelligence, Policy, and the War in Iraq." *Foreign Affairs* 85, no. 2 (March/April 2006): 15–28.

———. "Interview from 'The Dark Side.'" *Frontline.* PBS video. 20 June 2006. www.pbs.org/wgbh/pages/frontline/darkside/interviews/pillar.html.

Pinch, Trevor. "Testing—One, Two, Three . . . Testing! Towards a Sociology of Testing." *Science, Technology, and Human Values* 18, no. 1 (Winter 1993): 25–41.

Pinch, Trevor J., and Wiebe E. Bijker. "The Social Construction of Facts and Artefacts: Or How the Sociology of Science and the Sociology of Technology Might Benefit Each Other." *Social Studies of Science* 14, no. 3 (August 1984): 399–441.

Pincus, Walter. "Under Bush, the Briefing Gets Briefer." The *Washington Post,* 24 May 2002, A33.

Polanyi, Michael. *Personal Knowledge.* London: Routledge and Kegan Paul, 1958.

Pollack, Kenneth M. "Spies, Lies, and Weapons: What Went Wrong." *Atlantic Monthly* 293, no. 1 (January/February 2004): 78–92.

Pomerantsev, A. P., N. A. Staritsin, Y. V. Mockov, and L. I. Marinin. "Expression of Cereolysine AB Genes in Bacillus Anthracis Vaccine Strain Ensures Protection against Experimental Hemolytic Anthrax Infection." *Vaccine* 15, no. 17-18 (December 1997): 1846–1850.

Porter, Theodore M. "Quantification and the Accounting Ideal in Science." *Social Studies of Science* 22 (November 1992): 633–652.

———. *Trust in Numbers: The Pursuit of Objectivity in Science and Public Life.* Princeton, NJ: Princeton University Press, 1996.

Potter, William C. "Before the Deluge? Assessing the Threat of Nuclear Leakage from the Post-Soviet States." *Arms Control Today* 25, no. 8 (October 1995): 9–16.

Powell, Colin. "U.S. Secretary of State Colin Powell Addresses the U.N. Security Council." 5 February 2003. www.cnn.com/2003/US/02/05/sprj.irq.powell.transcript.05/index.html.

Presidential Commission for the Study of Bioethics. "Synthetic Biology: Meeting One." Washington, D.C., 8–9 July 2010, http://bioethics.gov/cms/meeting-one.

———. "Synthetic Biology: Meeting Two." Philadelphia, Pennsylvania, 13–14 September 2010. http://bioethics.gov/cms/meeting-two.

———. "Synthetic Biology: Meeting Three." Atlanta, Georgia, 16–17 November 2010. http://bioethics.gov/cms/meeting-three.

Priest, Dana, and William Arkin. "National Security, Inc." *Washington Post,* 20 July 2010, A1.

Rabinow, Paul. "Artificiality and Enlightenment: From Sociobiology to Biosociality." In *The Science Studies Reader,* edited by Mario Biagioli, 407–416. New York: Routledge, 1999.

Racaniello, Vincent, and David Baltimore. "Cloned Poliovirus Complementary DNA Is Infectious in Mammalian Cells." *Science* 214, no. 4523 (20 November 1981): 916–919.

Rao, Jason. "Biosecurity Engagement Program." http://ironside.sandia.gov/AsiaConference/JasonRao-BEP.pdf.

Rappert, Brian. "Making Silence Matter: The Place of the Absences in Ethnography." EPIC 2010 Proceedings, 2010, no. 1 (August/September 2010): 260–273.

———. "Prohibitions, Weapons, and Controversy: Managing the Problems of Ordering." *Social Studies of Science* 35, no. 2 (April 2005): 211–240.

Rappert, Brian, and Brian Balmer. "Rethinking 'Secrecy' and 'Disclosure': What Science and Technology Studies Can Offer Attempts to Governing WMD Threats." In *Technology and Security,* edited by B. Rappert, 45–65. London: Palgrave, 2007.

Rappert, Brian, Brian Balmer, and John Stone. "Science, Technology, and the Military: Priorities, Preoccupations, and Possibilities." In *The Handbook of Science and Technology Studies,* 3rd ed., edited by E. J. Hackett, O. Amsterdamska, M. Lynch, and J. Wajcman, 719–739. Cambridge: MIT Press, 2008.

Ratliff, Evan. "This Is Not a Test." *Wired* 10, no. 3 (March 2002). www.wired.com/wired/archive/10.03/nukes.html.

Relman, David A. "Working Group on Synthetic Genomics: Progress Report." NSABB Meeting, 30 March 2006. http://oba.od.nih.gov/biosecurity/meetings/200603/FINAL%20SYNTHETIC%20Progress%20Report%20from%20033006%20Relman%20presentation.pdf.

Return to an Address of the Honourable the House of Commons. "Review of Intelligence on Weapons of Mass Destruction, Report of a Committee of Privy Counsellors, Chairman: The Rt Hon The Lord Butler of Brockwell KG GCB CVO, 14 July." London: The Stationary Office, 2004. www.archive2.official-documents.co.uk/document/deps/hc/hc898/898.pdf.

Rhodes, Richard. *The Making of the Atomic Bomb.* New York: Simon and Schuster, 1988.

Richelson, Jeffrey. "Scientists in Black." *Scientific American* 278, no. 2 (February 1998): 48–55.

———. *The U.S. Intelligence Community,* 4th ed. Boulder, CO: Westview Press, 1999.

Rieber, Steven, and Neil Thomason. "Creation of a National Institute for Analytic Methods: Toward Improving Intelligence Analysis." *Studies in Intelligence* 49, no. 4 (2005): 71–80.

Riles, Annelise, ed. *Documents: Artifacts of Modern Knowledge.* Ann Arbor: University of Michigan Press, 2006.

Roberts, Brad, ed. *Hype or Reality: The "New Terrorism" and Mass Casualty Attacks.* Alexandria, VA: Chemical and Biological Arms Control Institute, 2000.

Roe Smith, Merritt. "Technological Determinism in American Culture." In *Does Technology Drive History? The Dilemma of Technological Determinism,* edited by Merritt Roe Smith and Leo Marx, 1–35. Cambridge, MA: MIT Press, 1994.

Roe Smith, Merrit, and Leo Marx, eds. *Does Technology Drive History? The Dilemma of Technological Determinism.* Cambridge, MA: MIT Press, 1994.

Rose, David. "Iraq's Arsenal of Terror." *Vanity Fair* no. 501 (May 2002): 120–127.

Rosengard, Ariella M., Yu Liu, Zhiping Nie, and Robert Jimenez. "Variola Virus Immune Evasion Design: Expression of a Highly Efficient Inhibitor of Human Complement." *Proceedings of the National Academy of Sciences U.S.A.* 99, no. 13 (25 June 2002): 8808–8813.

Rumsfeld, Donald H. "Transforming the Military." *Foreign Affairs* 81, no. 3 (May/June 2002): 20–32.

Ruppe, David. "Terrorism—Threat Mongering." *National Journal* 37, no. 17 (23 April 2005): 1218–1225.

Russell, Richard L. *Sharpening Strategic Intelligence.* Cambridge, U.K.: Cambridge University Press, 2007.

———. "A Weak Pillar for American National Security: The CIA's Dismal Performance against WMD Threats." *Intelligence and National Security* 20, no. 3 (September 2005): 466–485.

Samuel, Gabrielle N., Michael J. Selgelid, and Ian Kerridge. "Managing the Unimaginable: Regulatory Responses to the Challenges Posed by Synthetic Biology and Synthetic Genomics." *EMBO Reports* 10, no. 1 (2009): 7–11.

Sanger, F., G. M. Air, B. G. Barrell, N. L. Brown, A. R. Coulson, C. A. Fiddes et al. "The Nucleotide Sequence of Bacteriophage phiX174." *Journal of Molecular Biology* 125, no. 2 (1978): 225–246.

Schmidt, Markus. "Diffusion of Synthetic Biology: A Challenge to Biosafety." *Systems and Synthetic Biology* 2, nos. 1-2 (2008): 1–6.

Schmidt, Markus, Alexander Kelle, A. Mitra-Ganguli, and H. de Vriend, eds. *Synthetic Biology: The Technoscience and Its Societal Consequences.* New York: Springer Academic Publishing, 2009.

Schmidt, Markus, Helge Torgersen, Agomoni Ganguli-Mitra, Alexander Kelle, Anna Deplazes, and Nikola Biller-Andorn. "SYNBIOSAFE e-Conference: Online Community Discussion on the Societal Aspects of Synthetic Biology." *Systems and Synthetic Biology* 2, nos. 1-2 (2008): 7–17.

Schmidt, Susan, and Ellen Nakashima. "Moussaoui Said Not to Be Part of 9/11 Plot." *Washington Post,* 28 March 2003, A4.

Schuler, Ari. "Billions for Biodefense: Federal Agency Biodefense Funding, FY 2001–FY 2005." *Biosecurity and Bioterrorism: Biodefense Strategy, Practice, and Science* 2, no. 2 (June 2004): 86–96.

Semler, Bert L., and Eckard Wimmer, eds. *Molecular Biology of Picornaviruses.* Washington, DC: ASM Press, 2002.

Shapin, Steven. "The Invisible Technician." *American Scientist* 77, no. 6 (1989): 554–563.

———. "Placing the View from Nowhere: Historical and Sociological Problems in the Location of Science." *Transactions of the Institute of British Geographers* 23, no. 1 (April 1998): 5–12.

Shapin, Steven, and Simon Schaffer. *Leviathan and the Air-Pump: Hobbes, Boyle, and the Experimental Life.* Princeton, NJ: Princeton University Press, 1985.

Shea, Dana A. "Balancing Scientific Publication and National Security Concerns: Issues for Congress." CRS Report for Congress, 2006. www.fas.org/sgp/crs/secrecy/RL31695.pdf.

———. "The National Biodefense Analysis and Countermeasures Center: Issues for Congress." CRS Report for Congress, 15 February 2007. www.fas.org/sgp/crs/homesec/RL32891.pdf.

Shulsky, Abram N., and Gary J. Schmitt. *Silent Warfare: Understanding the World of Intelligence.* Washington, DC: Potomac Books, 2002.

Shuster, Richard J. "The Iraq Survey Group: From Weapons of Mass Destruction to Counterinsurgency." *Journal of Strategic Studies* 31, no. 2 (April 2008): 229–256.

Simmel, Georg. "Secrecy." In *The Sociology of Georg Simmel,* translated and edited by Kurt H. Wolff, 330–344. Glencoe, IL: Free Press, 1950.

Simon, Bob. "Faulty Intel Source 'Curveball' Revealed." *60 Minutes.* CBS News, 11 February 2009. www.cbsnews.com/stories/2007/11/01/60minutes/main3440577.shtml.

Sims, Benjamin. "Revisiting the Uninvention Hypothesis: A Transactional View of Tacit Knowledge in Nuclear Weapons Design." Paper presented at Society for Social Studies of Science annual meeting, Montreal, Canada, October 2007.

———. "Things Fall Apart: Disaster, Infrastructure, and Risk." *Social Studies of Science* 37, no. 1 (February 2007): 93–95.

Sims, Benjamin, and Christopher Henke. "Repairing Nuclear Weapons: Maintenance and Transformation in U.S. Nuclear Weapons since the Cold War." Paper presented at the American Sociological Association annual meeting, New York City, 11 August 2007. www.allacademic.com//meta/p_mla_apa_research_citation/1/8/2/9/5/pages182950/p182950-1.php.

Sinsheimer, Robert L. "A Single-Stranded Deoxyribonucleic Acid from Bacteriophage." *Journal of Molecular Biology* 1, iss. 1 (April 1959): 43–53.

Smith, Hamilton O., Clyde A. Hutchinson III, Cynthia Pfannkoch, and Craig J. Venter. "Generating a Synthetic Genome by Whole Genome Assembly: pX174 Bacteriophage from Synthetic Oligonucleotides." *Proceedings of the National Academy of Sciences* 100, no. 26 (3 November 2003): 15440–15445.

Smith, R. Jeffrey. "Russians Admit Firms Met Iraqis: Plant That Could Make Germ Weapons at Issue." *Washington Post,* 18 February 1998, A16.

Spinardi, Graham. "Defence Technology Enterprises: A Case Study in Technology Transfer." *Science and Public Policy* 19, no. 4 (1992): 198–206.

SRS Technologies. "Quantification of Open Source Research Publications in Biological Sciences for Biological Weapons Development Utility." 16 June 2003. www.fas.org/irp/agency/dod/dtra/bw-open.pdf.

Star, Susan Leigh. "Scientific Work and Uncertainty." *Social Studies of Science* 15, no. 3 (August 1985): 391–427.

———. "Simplification in Scientific Work: An Example from Neuroscience Research." *Social Studies of Science* 13, no. 2 (May 1983): 205–228.

———. "The Sociology of the Invisible: The Primacy of Work in the Writings of Anselm Strauss." In *Social Organization and Social Process: Essays in Honor of Anselm Strauss,* edited by David R. Maines, 265–283. New York: Aldine De Gruyter, 1991.

Steiner, James E. "Challenging the Red Line between Intelligence and Policy." Institute for the Study of Diplomacy, Edmund A. Walsh School of Foreign Service, Georgetown University, 6. www.guisd.org/redline.pdf.

Stem Cook, Michelle, and Amy F. Woolf. "Preventing Proliferation of Biological Weapons: U.S. Assistance to the Former Soviet States." CRS Report for Congress, 10 April 2002. www.fas.org/spp/starwars/crs/RL31368.pdf.

Stemmer, W. P., A. Crameri, K. D. Ha, T. M. Brennan, and H. L. Heyneker. "Single-Step Assembly of a Gene and Entire Plasmid from Large Numbers of Oliogodeoxyribonucleotides." *Gene* 164, no. 1 (16 October 1995): 49–53.

Stenersen, Anne. *Al-Qaida's Quest for Weapons of Mass Destruction: The History behind the Hype.* Saarbrücken, Germany: VDM Verlag, 2008.

Stone, Richard. "Nonproliferation: New Initiatives Reach Out to Iraq's Scientific Elite." *Science* 303, no. 5664 (12 March 2004): 1594.

Stratford, Richard J. K. "'Science Centers Program' Testimony before the House Committee on Energy and Commerce, Subcommittee on Oversight and Investigations." 23 January 2008. http://democrats.energycommerce.house.gov/images/stories/Documents /Hearings/PDF/110-oi-hrg.012308.Stratford-testimony.pdf.

Svitkin, Yuri V., and Nahum Sonenberg. "Cell-Free Synthesis of Encephalomyocarditis Virus." *Journal of Virology* 77, no. 11 (June 2003): 6551–6555.

Tenet, George J. "Statement of George J. Tenet, Former Director of Central Intelligence." 1 April 2005. www.gwu.edu/~nsarchiv/NSAEBB/NSAEBB234/20050104_Tenet_Statement.pdf.

Time. "Molecular Biology: Closer to Synthetic Life." 90, no. 25 (22 December 1967). www.time.com/time/magazine/article/0,9171,899940-1,00.html.

Trevan, Tim. *Saddam's Secrets: The Hunt for Iraq's Hidden Weapons.* London: Harper Collins, 1999.

Treverton, Gregory F. *The Next Steps in Reshaping Intelligence.* Santa Monica, CA: RAND, 2005.

Tucker, Jonathan B. "Biological Weapons in the Former Soviet Union: An Interview with Dr. Kenneth Alibek." *Nonproliferation Review* 6, no. 3 (Spring–Summer 1999): 1–10.

———. "Bioweapons from Russia: Stemming the Flow." *Issues in Science and Technology* 15, no. 3 (Spring 1999): 34–38.

———. "The Future of Biological Warfare." In *The Proliferation of Advanced Weaponry,* edited by W. Thomas Wander and Eric H. Arnett, 61–71. Washington, DC: American Association for the Advancement of Science, 1992.

Tucker, Jonathan B., and Kathleen M. Vogel. "Preventing the Proliferation of Chemical and Biological Materials and Know-How." *Nonproliferation Review* 7, no. 1 (Spring 2000): 88–96.

Tucker, Jonathan B., and Raymond A. Zilinskas. "The Promise and Perils of Synthetic Biology." *New Atlantis* 12 (Spring 2006): 25–45.

Tufte, Edward R. *The Cognitive Style of PowerPoint.* Cheshire, U.K.: Graphics Press, 2003.

Tumpey, Terrence M., Christopher F. Basler, Patricia V. Aguilar et al. "Characterization of the Reconstructed 1918 Spanish Influenza Virus." *Science* 310, no. 5745 (7 October 2005): 77–80.

United Nations. *Unresolved Disarmament Issues: Iraq's Proscribed Weapons Programmes.* 6 March 2003. www.un.org/Depts/unmovic/new/documents/cluster_document.pdf.

U.S. Central Intelligence Agency. *A Consumer's Guide to Intelligence.* Washington, DC: U.S. Central Intelligence Agency, Office of Public Affairs, 1999.

———. "Continuous Learning in the DI: The May 2004 Review of Analytic Tradecraft Fundamentals." *Tradecraft Review* 1, no. 1 (August 2004): 1–10.

———. "Critique of the Codeword Compartment in the CIA." Center for the Study of Intelligence, March 1977. www.fas.org/sgp/othergov/codeword.html.

———. "The Darker Bioweapons Future." 3 November 2003. www.fas.org/irp/cia/product/bw1103.pdf.

———. "Iraq's Weapons of Mass Destruction Programs." October 2002. www.fas.org/irp/cia/product/Iraq_Oct_2002.pdf.

———. "Unclassified Report to Congress on the Acquisition of Technology Relating to Weapons of Mass Destruction and Advanced Conventional Munitions, 1 July through 30 December 1999." www.cia.gov/library/reports/archived-reports-1/july_dec1999.htm.

———. "The Work of the CIA." www.cia.gov/library/publications/additional-publications/the-work-of-a-nation/86402%20Factbook-low.pdf.

U.S. Central Intelligence Agency and U.S. Defense Intelligence Agency. "Iraqi Mobile Biological Warfare Agent Production Plants." 28 May 2003, accessed 11 April 2007. www.cia.gov/library/reports/general-reports-1/iraqi_mobile_plants/index.html.

U.S. Congress. "Expressing Serious Concern regarding the Publication of Instructions on How to Create a Synthetic Human Polio Virus, and for Other Purposes." 107th Congress, 2d session, H.R. 514, 26 July 2002, accessed 6 November 2006. http://thomas.loc.gov/cgi-bin/query/z?c107:H.RES.514.

U.S. Congress, Office of Technology Assessment. *Proliferation of Weapons of Mass Destruction: Assessing the Risks.* OTA-ISC-559. Washington, DC: U.S. Government Printing Office, August 1993.

———. *Technologies Underlying Weapons of Mass Destruction.* OTA-BP-ISC-115. Washington, DC: U.S. Government Printing Office, December 1993.

U.S. Department of Defense. *Biotechnology and Genetic Engineering: Implications for the Development of New Warfare Agents.* Washington, DC: U.S. Government Printing Office, 1996.

———. "Cooperative Threat Reduction: Annual Report to Congress Fiscal Year 2007." www.nti.org/e_research/official_docs/dod/2006/040705.pdf.

———. "Cooperative Threat Reduction: Annual Report to Congress Fiscal Year 2009." www.dtra.mil/documents/oe/ctr/FY09%20CTR%20Annual%20Report%20to%20Congress.pdf.

———. "Cooperative Threat Reduction: Annual Report to Congress Fiscal Year 2011." February 2010. http://comptroller.defense.gov/defbudget/fy2011/budget_justification/pdfs/01_Operation_and_Maintenance/O_M_VOL_1_PARTS/CTR_FY11.pdf.

———. "Fiscal Year 2011 Budget Estimate Cooperative Threat Reduction Program." February 2010. http://comptroller.defense.gov/defbudget/fy2011/budget_justification/pdfs/01_Operation_and_Maintenance/O_M_VOL_1_PARTS/CTR_FY11.pdf.

———. *Quadrennial Defense Review.* Washington, DC: U.S. Department of Defense, May 1997. www.dod.mil/pubs/qdr/.

———. *Report on Activities and Programs for Countering Proliferation and NBC Terrorism.* Vol. 1. July 2009. www.acq.osd.mil/cp/cpreports/cprc09xsm.pdf.

———. "Russian Biological Warfare Technology." May 1994. www.gulflink.osd.mil/declassdocs/dia/19950719/950719_22010910_94a.html.

———. "Transcript: DoD News Briefing: Dr. Ashton Carter, ASD (International Security Policy)." 31 January 1996. www.defense.gov/transcripts/transcript.aspx?transcriptid=275.

U.S. Department of Health and Human Services. "Screening Framework Guidance for Providers of Synthetic Double-Stranded DNA." 13 October 2010. www.phe.gov/Preparedness/legal/guidance/syndna/Pages/default.aspx.

U.S. Department of Homeland Security. "DHS Fact Sheet: National Biodefense Analysis and Countermeasures Center." 24 February 2005. www.dhs.gov/xnews/releases/press_release_0627.shtm.

———. "DHS Issues Record of Decision on Proposed National Bio- and Agro-Defense Facility." 16 January 2009. www.dhs.gov/xnews/releases/pr_1232132671186.shtm.

———. "Homeland Security Presidential Directive 10: Biodefense for the Twenty-First Century." 28 April 2004. www.fas.org/irp/offdocs/nspd/hspd-10.html.

U.S. General Accounting Office. "Biological Weapons: Effort to Reduce Former Soviet Threat Offers Benefits, Poses New Risks." GAO-NSIAD-00-138. Washington, DC: U.S. General Accounting Office, April 2000.

U.S. Government Accountability Office. *DOE's Program to Assist Weapons Scientists in the Russia and Other Countries needs to be Reassessed.* GAO-08-189. Washington, DC: U.S. General Accountability Office, 2007.

———. *Weapons of Mass Destruction: Nonproliferation Programs Need Better Integration.* GAO-05-157. Washington, DC: U.S. General Accountability Office, 2005.

U.S. Homeland Security Council. "Planning Scenarios: Executive Summaries Created for Use in National, Federal, State, and Local Homeland Security Preparedness Activities." July 2004. www.globalsecurity.org/security/library/report/2004/hsc-planning-scenarios-jul04.htm.

U.S. National Intelligence Council. "IC Associates Program." www.dni.gov/nic/IC_associates.html.

———. *Mapping the Global Future: Report of the National Intelligence Council's Project, NIC-2004-13.* December 2004. www.foia.cia.gov/2020/2020.pdf.

U.S. Senate, Permanent Subcommittee on Investigations, Committee on Government Affairs. "Staff Statement: Global Proliferation of Weapons of Mass Destruction: A Case Study on Aum Shinrikyo." *Global Proliferation of Weapons of Mass Destruction, Part I.* 31 October 1995. Washington, DC: U.S. Government Printing Office, 1996.

U.S. Senate, Select Committee on Intelligence. "Report on the Use by the Intelligence Community of Information Provided by the Iraqi National Congress." 109th Congress, 2d session, 8 September 2006. http://intelligence.senate.gov/phaseiiinc.pdf.

———. "Report on Postwar Findings about Iraq's WMD Programs and Links to Terrorism and How They Compare with Prewar Assessments." 109th Congress, 2d session, 8 September 2006. http://intelligence.senate.gov/pub109thcongress.html.

———. "Report on the U.S. Intelligence Community's Prewar Intelligence Assessments on Iraq." 108th Congress, 2d session, S report 108–301, 9 July 2004. http://intelligence.senate.gov/108301.pdf.

———."Report on Whether Public Statements regarding Iraq by U.S. Government Officials Were Substantiated by Intelligence Information." Senate Report 110–335, 110th Congress, 2d session, 5 June 2008. http://intelligence.senate.gov/pdfs/110345.pdf.

van der Werf, S., J. Bradley, E. Wimmer, F. W. Studier, and J. J. Dunn. "Synthesis of Infectious Poliovirus RNA by Purified T7 RNA Polymerase." *Proceedings of the National Academy of Sciences U.S.A.* 83, no. 8 (April 1986): 2330–2334.

Vaughan, Diane. *The Challenger Launch Decision: Risky Technology, Culture, and Deviance at NASA.* Chicago: University of Chicago Press, 1997.

Venter, Al J. "Biological Warfare: The Poor Man's Atomic Bomb." *Jane's Intelligence Review* 11, no. 3 (March 1999): 42–47.

Venter, J. Craig. *A Life Decoded: My Genome, My Life.* New York: Viking, 2007.

Vogel, Kathleen M. "Bioweapons Proliferation: Where Science Studies and Public Policy Collide." *Social Studies of Science* 36 (October 2006): 659–690.

———. "Framing Biosecurity: An Alternative to the Biotech Revolution Model?" *Science and Public Policy* 35, no. 1 (February 2008): 45–54.

———. "Pathogen Proliferation: Threats from the Former Soviet BW Complex." *Politics and the Life Sciences* 19, no. 1 (March 2000): 3–16.

Walford, Geoffrey. "Why Don't Researchers Name Their Research Sites?" In *Debates and Developments in Ethnographic Methodology, vol 6,* edited by G. Walford, 95–105. Amsterdam, New York, Oxford: JAI, 2002.

Warner, Michael, and J. Kenneth McDonald. *U.S. Intelligence Community Reform Studies since 1947.* Washington, DC: Center for the Study of Intelligence, April 2005.

Warrick, Joby. "Custom-Built Pathogens Raise Fears of Bioterror." *Washington Post,* 31 July 2006, A1.

———. "Lacking Biolabs, Trailers Carried Case for War: Administration Pushed Notion of Banned Iraqi Weapons Despite Evidence to Contrary." *Washington Post,* 12 April 2006. www.washingtonpost.com/wp-dyn/content/article/2006/04/11/AR2006041101888.html.

Washington Post. "Editorial: Irrefutable." 6 February 2003. www.washingtonpost.com/ac2/wp-dyn/A32515-2003Feb5?language=printer.

———. "Editorial: Not Science Fiction." 27 January 2005, A18.

Weber, Max. *Essays in Sociology,* translated and edited by H. H. Gerth and C. Wright Mills. New York: Oxford University Press, 1946.

Whalen, Jeanne. "In Attics and Closets, 'Biohackers' Discover Their Inner Frankenstein." *Wall Street Journal,* 12 May 2009.

Wheelis, Mark. "Will the New Biology Lead to New Weapons?" *Arms Control Today* 34, no. 6 (July/August 2004): 6–13.

White House. "Interview of the President by TVP, Poland." 29 May 2003. www.whitehouse.gov/g8/interview5.html.

Whitfield, John. "Black Death's DNA." *Nature Science Update,* 4 October 2001. www.nature.com/news/2001/011004/full/news011004-12.html.

Wilson, Valerie Plame. *Fair Game.* New York: Simon and Schuster, 2007.

Wimmer, Eckard. "The Test-Tube Synthesis of a Chemical Called Poliovirus." *EMBO Reports* 7, no. S1 (July 2006): S3-S9.

Woodward, Bob. *Plan of Attack: The Definitive Account of the Decision to Invade Iraq.* New York: Simon and Schuster, 2004.

Woolf, Amy F. "Nonproliferation and Threat Reduction Assistance: U.S. Programs in the Former Soviet Union." CRS Report to Congress, 26 March 2008. http://assets.opencrs.com/rpts/RL31957_20080326.pdf.

Wright, Susan. "Prospects for Biological Disarmament in the 1990s." *Transnational Law and Contemporary Problems* 2 (Fall 1992): 453–492.

———. "Terrorists and Biological Weapons: Forging the Linkage in the Clinton Administration." *Politics and the Life Sciences* 25, nos. 1-2 (15 February 2007): 57–115.

Wright, Susan, and David A. Wallace. "Secrecy in the Biotechnology Industry: Implications for the Biological Weapons Convention." In *Biological Warfare and Disarmament: New Problems/New Perspectives,* edited by Susan Wright, 369–390. Lanham, MD: Rowman and Littlefield, 2002.

———. "Varieties of Secrets and Secret Varieties: The Case of Biotechnology." *Politics and the Life Sciences* 19, no. 1 (March 2000): 45–57.

Wynne, Brian. "Unruly Technology: Practical Rules, Impractical Discourses and Public Understanding." *Social Studies of Science* 18, no. 1 (February 1988): 147–167.

Xiong, Ai-Sheng, Quan-Hong Yao, Ri-He Pent, Xian Li, Hui-Qin Fan, Zong-Ming Chen, and Yi Li. "A Simple, Rapid, High-Fidelity and Cost-Effective PCR-Based Two-Step DNA Synthesis Method for Long Gene Sequences." *Nucleic Acids Research* 32, no. 12, (July 2004): 1–10.

York, Herbert F. *Race to Oblivion: A Participant's View of the Arms Race.* New York: Simon and Schuster, 1970.

Young, Lei, and Qihan Dong. "Two-Step Total Gene Synthesis Method." *Nucleic Acids Research* 32, no. 7 (April 2004): 1–6.

Younger, Stephen M. *The Bomb: A New History.* New York: Harper Collins, 2009.

Yu, Edward H. "Looking Ahead." FBI Weapons of Mass Destruction Directorate, 11 March 2010. www.synbioproject.org/process/assets/files/6409/_draft/you_presentation.pdf.

Zegart, Amy B. "'CNN with Secrets': 9/11, the CIA, and the Organizational Roots of Failure." *International Journal of Intelligence and Counterintelligence* 20, no. 1 (Spring 2007): 18–49.

INDEX